I0822586

The Collected Works of Charlotte Perkins Gilman:

The Yellow Wallpaper
Why I Wrote 'The Yellow Wallpaper'
Women and Economics
Herland
Suffrage Songs and Verses

ISBN: 978-1-78943-268-8

Contents

THE YELLOW WALLPAPER

THE YELLOW WALLPAPER

It is very seldom that mere ordinary people like John and myself secure ancestral halls for the summer.

A colonial mansion, a hereditary estate, I would say a haunted house, and reach the height of romantic felicity—but that would be asking too much of fate!

Still I will proudly declare that there is something queer about it.

Else, why should it be let so cheaply? And why have stood so long untenanted?

John laughs at me, of course, but one expects that in marriage.

John is practical in the extreme. He has no patience with faith, an intense horror of superstition, and he scoffs openly at any talk of things not to be felt and seen and put down in figures.

John is a physician, and PERHAPS—(I would not say it to a living soul, of course, but this is dead paper and a great relief to my mind)—PERHAPS that is one reason I do not get well faster.

You see he does not believe I am sick!

And what can one do?

If a physician of high standing, and one's own husband, assures friends and relatives that there is really nothing the matter with one but temporary nervous depression—a slight hysterical tendency—what is one to do?

My brother is also a physician, and also of high standing, and he says the same thing.

So I take phosphates or phosphites—whichever it is, and tonics, and journeys, and air, and exercise, and am absolutely forbidden to "work" until I am well again.

Personally, I disagree with their ideas.

Personally, I believe that congenial work, with excitement and change, would do me good.

But what is one to do?

I did write for a while in spite of them; but it DOES exhaust me a good deal—having to be so sly about it, or else meet with heavy opposition.

I sometimes fancy that in my condition if I had less opposition and more society and stimulus—but John says the very worst thing I can do is to think about my condition, and I confess it always makes me feel bad.

So I will let it alone and talk about the house.

The most beautiful place! It is quite alone, standing well back from the road, quite three miles from the village. It makes me think of English places that you read about, for there are hedges and walls and gates that lock, and lots of separate little houses for the gardeners and people.

There is a DELICIOUS garden! I never saw such a garden—large and shady, full of box-bordered paths, and lined with long grape-covered arbors with seats under them.

There were greenhouses, too, but they are all broken now.

There was some legal trouble, I believe, something about the heirs and coheirs; anyhow, the place has been empty for years.

That spoils my ghostliness, I am afraid, but I don't care—there is something strange about the house—I can feel it.

I even said so to John one moonlight evening, but he said what I felt was a DRAUGHT, and shut the window.

I get unreasonably angry with John sometimes. I'm sure I never used to be so sensitive. I think it is due to this nervous condition.

But John says if I feel so, I shall neglect proper self-control; so I take pains to control myself—before him, at least, and that makes me very tired.

I don't like our room a bit. I wanted one downstairs that opened on the piazza and had roses all over the window, and such pretty old-fashioned chintz hangings! but John would not hear of it.

He said there was only one window and not room for two beds, and no near room for him if he took another.

He is very careful and loving, and hardly lets me stir without special direction.

I have a schedule prescription for each hour in the day; he takes all care from me, and so I feel basely ungrateful not to value it more.

He said we came here solely on my account, that I was to have perfect rest and all the air I could get. "Your exercise depends on your strength, my dear," said he, "and your food somewhat on your appetite; but air you can absorb all the time." So we took the nursery at the top of the house.

It is a big, airy room, the whole floor nearly, with windows that look all ways, and air and sunshine galore. It was nursery first and then playroom and gymnasium, I should judge; for the windows are barred for little children, and there are rings and things in the walls.

The paint and paper look as if a boys' school had used it. It is stripped off—the paper—in great patches all around the head of my bed, about as far as I can reach, and in a great place on the other side of the room low down. I never saw a worse paper in my life.

One of those sprawling flamboyant patterns committing every artistic sin.

It is dull enough to confuse the eye in following, pronounced enough to constantly irritate and provoke study, and when you follow the lame uncertain curves for a little distance they suddenly commit suicide—plunge off at outrageous angles, destroy themselves in unheard of contradictions.

The color is repellent, almost revolting; a smouldering unclean yellow, strangely faded by the slow-turning sunlight.

It is a dull yet lurid orange in some places, a sickly sulphur tint in others.

No wonder the children hated it! I should hate it myself if I had to live in this room long.

There comes John, and I must put this away,—he hates to have me write a word.

We have been here two weeks, and I haven't felt like writing before, since that first day.

I am sitting by the window now, up in this atrocious nursery, and there is nothing to hinder my writing as much as I please, save lack of strength.

John is away all day, and even some nights when his cases are serious.

I am glad my case is not serious!

But these nervous troubles are dreadfully depressing.

John does not know how much I really suffer. He knows there is no REASON to suffer, and that satisfies him.

Of course it is only nervousness. It does weigh on me so not to do my duty in any way!

I meant to be such a help to John, such a real rest and comfort, and here I am a comparative burden already!

Nobody would believe what an effort it is to do what little I am able,—to dress and entertain, and order things.

It is fortunate Mary is so good with the baby. Such a dear baby!

And yet I CANNOT be with him, it makes me so nervous.

I suppose John never was nervous in his life. He laughs at me so about this wall-paper!

At first he meant to repaper the room, but afterwards he said that I was letting it get the better of me, and that nothing was worse for a nervous patient than to give way to such fancies.

He said that after the wall-paper was changed it would be the heavy bedstead, and then the barred windows, and then that gate at the head of the stairs, and so on.

"You know the place is doing you good," he said, "and really, dear, I don't care to renovate the house just for a three months' rental."

"Then do let us go downstairs," I said, "there are such pretty rooms there."

Then he took me in his arms and called me a blessed little goose, and said he would go down to the cellar, if I wished, and have it whitewashed into the bargain.

But he is right enough about the beds and windows and things.

It is an airy and comfortable room as any one need wish, and, of course, I would not be so silly as to make him uncomfortable just for a whim.

I'm really getting quite fond of the big room, all but that horrid paper.

Out of one window I can see the garden, those mysterious deepshaded arbors, the riotous old-fashioned flowers, and bushes and gnarly trees.

Out of another I get a lovely view of the bay and a little private wharf belonging to the estate. There is a beautiful shaded lane that runs down there from the house. I always fancy I see people walking in these numerous paths and arbors, but John has cautioned me not to give way to fancy in the least. He says that with my imaginative power and habit of story-making, a nervous weakness like mine is sure to lead to all manner of excited fancies, and that I ought to use my will and good sense to check the tendency. So I try.

I think sometimes that if I were only well enough to write a little it would relieve the press of ideas and rest me.

But I find I get pretty tired when I try.

It is so discouraging not to have any advice and companionship about my work. When I get really well, John says we will ask Cousin Henry and Julia down for a long visit; but he says he would as soon put fireworks in my pillow-case as to let me have those stimulating people about now.

I wish I could get well faster.

But I must not think about that. This paper looks to me as if it KNEW what a vicious influence it had!

There is a recurrent spot where the pattern lolls like a broken neck and two bulbous eyes stare at you upside down.

I get positively angry with the impertinence of it and the everlastingness. Up and down and sideways they crawl, and those absurd, unblinking eyes are everywhere. There is one place where two breadths didn't match, and the eyes go all up and down the line, one a little higher than the other.

I never saw so much expression in an inanimate thing before, and we all know how much expression they have! I used to lie awake as a child and get more entertainment and terror out of blank walls and plain furniture than most children could find in a toy store.

I remember what a kindly wink the knobs of our big, old bureau used to have, and there was one chair that always seemed like a strong friend.

I used to feel that if any of the other things looked too fierce I could always hop into that chair and be safe.

The furniture in this room is no worse than inharmonious, however, for we had to bring it all from downstairs. I suppose when this was used as a playroom they had to take the nursery things out, and no wonder! I never saw such ravages as the children have made here.

The wall-paper, as I said before, is torn off in spots, and it sticketh closer than a brother—they must have had perseverance as well as hatred.

Then the floor is scratched and gouged and splintered, the plaster itself is dug out here and there, and this great heavy bed which is all we found in the room, looks as if it had been through the wars.

But I don't mind it a bit—only the paper.

There comes John's sister. Such a dear girl as she is, and so careful of me! I must not let her find me writing.

She is a perfect and enthusiastic housekeeper, and hopes for no better profession. I verily believe she thinks it is the writing which made me sick!

But I can write when she is out, and see her a long way off from these windows.

There is one that commands the road, a lovely shaded winding road, and one that just looks off over the country. A lovely country, too, full of great elms and velvet meadows.

This wall-paper has a kind of sub-pattern in a different shade, a particularly irritating one, for you can only see it in certain lights, and not clearly then.

But in the places where it isn't faded and where the sun is just so—I can see a strange, provoking, formless sort of figure, that seems to skulk about behind that silly and conspicuous front design.

There's sister on the stairs!

Well, the Fourth of July is over! The people are gone and I am tired out. John thought it might do me good to see a little company, so we just had mother and Nellie and the children down for a week.

Of course I didn't do a thing. Jennie sees to everything now.

But it tired me all the same.

John says if I don't pick up faster he shall send me to Weir Mitchell in the fall.

But I don't want to go there at all. I had a friend who was in his hands once, and she says he is just like John and my brother, only more so!

Besides, it is such an undertaking to go so far.

I don't feel as if it was worth while to turn my hand over for anything, and I'm getting dreadfully fretful and querulous.

I cry at nothing, and cry most of the time.

Of course I don't when John is here, or anybody else, but when I am alone.

And I am alone a good deal just now. John is kept in town very often by serious cases, and Jennie is good and lets me alone when I want her to.

So I walk a little in the garden or down that lovely lane, sit on the porch under the roses, and lie down up here a good deal.

I'm getting really fond of the room in spite of the wall-paper. Perhaps BECAUSE of the wall-paper.

It dwells in my mind so!

I lie here on this great immovable bed—it is nailed down, I believe—and follow that pattern about by the hour. It is as good as gymnastics, I assure you. I start, we'll say, at the bottom, down in the corner over there where it has not been touched, and

I determine for the thousandth time that I WILL follow that pointless pattern to some sort of a conclusion.

I know a little of the principle of design, and I know this thing was not arranged on any laws of radiation, or alternation, or repetition, or symmetry, or anything else that I ever heard of.

It is repeated, of course, by the breadths, but not otherwise.

Looked at in one way each breadth stands alone, the bloated curves and flourishes—a kind of "debased Romanesque" with delirium tremens—go waddling up and down in isolated columns of fatuity.

But, on the other hand, they connect diagonally, and the sprawling outlines run off in great slanting waves of optic horror, like a lot of wallowing seaweeds in full chase.

The whole thing goes horizontally, too, at least it seems so, and I exhaust myself in trying to distinguish the order of its going in that direction.

They have used a horizontal breadth for a frieze, and that adds wonderfully to the confusion.

There is one end of the room where it is almost intact, and there, when the crosslights fade and the low sun shines directly upon it, I can almost fancy radiation after all,—the interminable grotesques seem to form around a common centre and rush off in headlong plunges of equal distraction.

It makes me tired to follow it. I will take a nap I guess.

I don't know why I should write this.

I don't want to.

I don't feel able.

And I know John would think it absurd. But I MUST say what I feel and think in some way—it is such a relief!

But the effort is getting to be greater than the relief.

Half the time now I am awfully lazy, and lie down ever so much.

John says I musn't lose my strength, and has me take cod liver oil and lots of tonics and things, to say nothing of ale and wine and rare meat.

Dear John! He loves me very dearly, and hates to have me sick. I tried to have a real earnest reasonable talk with him the other day, and tell him how I wish he would let me go and make a visit to Cousin Henry and Julia.

But he said I wasn't able to go, nor able to stand it after I got there; and I did not make out a very good case for myself, for I was crying before I had finished.

It is getting to be a great effort for me to think straight. Just this nervous weakness I suppose.

And dear John gathered me up in his arms, and just carried me upstairs and laid me on the bed, and sat by me and read to me till it tired my head.

He said I was his darling and his comfort and all he had, and that I must take care of myself for his sake, and keep well.

He says no one but myself can help me out of it, that I must use my will and self-control and not let any silly fancies run away with me.

There's one comfort, the baby is well and happy, and does not have to occupy this nursery with the horrid wall-paper.

If we had not used it, that blessed child would have! What a fortunate escape! Why, I wouldn't have a child of mine, an impressionable little thing, live in such a room for worlds.

I never thought of it before, but it is lucky that John kept me here after all, I can stand it so much easier than a baby, you see.

Of course I never mention it to them any more—I am too wise,—but I keep watch of it all the same.

There are things in that paper that nobody knows but me, or ever will.

Behind that outside pattern the dim shapes get clearer every day.

It is always the same shape, only very numerous.

And it is like a woman stooping down and creeping about behind that pattern. I don't like it a bit. I wonder—I begin to think—I wish John would take me away from here!

It is so hard to talk with John about my case, because he is so wise, and because he loves me so.

But I tried it last night.

It was moonlight. The moon shines in all around just as the sun does.

I hate to see it sometimes, it creeps so slowly, and always comes in by one window or another.

John was asleep and I hated to waken him, so I kept still and watched the moonlight on that undulating wall-paper till I felt creepy.

The faint figure behind seemed to shake the pattern, just as if she wanted to get out.

I got up softly and went to feel and see if the paper DID move, and when I came back John was awake.

"What is it, little girl?" he said. "Don't go walking about like that—you'll get cold."

I though it was a good time to talk, so I told him that I really was not gaining here, and that I wished he would take me away.

"Why darling!" said he, "our lease will be up in three weeks, and I can't see how to leave before.

"The repairs are not done at home, and I cannot possibly leave town just now. Of course if you were in any danger, I could and would, but you really are better, dear, whether you can see it or not. I am a doctor, dear, and I know. You are gaining flesh and color, your appetite is better, I feel really much easier about you."

"I don't weigh a bit more," said I, "nor as much; and my appetite may be better in the evening when you are here, but it is worse in the morning when you are away!"

"Bless her little heart!" said he with a big hug, "she shall be as sick as she pleases! But now let's improve the shining hours by going to sleep, and talk about it in the morning!"

"And you won't go away?" I asked gloomily.

"Why, how can I, dear? It is only three weeks more and then we will take a nice little trip of a few days while Jennie is getting the house ready. Really dear you are better!"

"Better in body perhaps—" I began, and stopped short, for he sat up straight and looked at me with such a stern, reproachful look that I could not say another word.

"My darling," said he, "I beg of you, for my sake and for our child's sake, as well as for your own, that you will never for one instant let that idea enter your mind! There is nothing so dangerous, so fascinating, to a temperament like yours. It is a false and foolish fancy. Can you not trust me as a physician when I tell you so?"

So of course I said no more on that score, and we went to sleep before long. He thought I was asleep first, but I wasn't, and lay there for hours trying to decide whether that front pattern and the back pattern really did move together or separately.

On a pattern like this, by daylight, there is a lack of sequence, a defiance of law, that is a constant irritant to a normal mind.

The color is hideous enough, and unreliable enough, and infuriating enough, but the pattern is torturing.

You think you have mastered it, but just as you get well underway in following, it turns a back-somersault and there you are. It slaps you in the face, knocks you down, and tramples upon you. It is like a bad dream.

The outside pattern is a florid arabesque, reminding one of a fungus. If you can imagine a toadstool in joints, an interminable string of toadstools, budding and sprouting in endless convolutions—why, that is something like it.

That is, sometimes!

There is one marked peculiarity about this paper, a thing nobody seems to notice but myself, and that is that it changes as the light changes.

When the sun shoots in through the east window—I always watch for that first long, straight ray—it changes so quickly that I never can quite believe it.

That is why I watch it always.

By moonlight—the moon shines in all night when there is a moon—I wouldn't know it was the same paper.

At night in any kind of light, in twilight, candle light, lamplight, and worst of all by moonlight, it becomes bars! The outside pattern I mean, and the woman behind it is as plain as can be.

I didn't realize for a long time what the thing was that showed behind, that dim sub-pattern, but now I am quite sure it is a woman.

By daylight she is subdued, quiet. I fancy it is the pattern that keeps her so still. It is so puzzling. It keeps me quiet by the hour.

I lie down ever so much now. John says it is good for me, and to sleep all I can.

Indeed he started the habit by making me lie down for an hour after each meal.

It is a very bad habit I am convinced, for you see I don't sleep.

And that cultivates deceit, for I don't tell them I'm awake—O no!

The fact is I am getting a little afraid of John.

He seems very queer sometimes, and even Jennie has an inexplicable look.

It strikes me occasionally, just as a scientific hypothesis,—that perhaps it is the paper!

I have watched John when he did not know I was looking, and come into the room suddenly on the most innocent excuses, and I've caught him several times LOOKING AT THE PAPER! And Jennie too. I caught Jennie with her hand on it once.

She didn't know I was in the room, and when I asked her in a quiet, a very quiet voice, with the most restrained manner possible, what she was doing with the paper—she turned around as if she had been caught stealing, and looked quite angry—asked me why I should frighten her so!

Then she said that the paper stained everything it touched, that she had found yellow smooches on all my clothes and John's, and she wished we would be more careful!

Did not that sound innocent? But I know she was studying that pattern, and I am determined that nobody shall find it out but myself!

Life is very much more exciting now than it used to be. You see I have something more to expect, to look forward to, to watch. I really do eat better, and am more quiet than I was.

John is so pleased to see me improve! He laughed a little the other day, and said I seemed to be flourishing in spite of my wall-paper.

I turned it off with a laugh. I had no intention of telling him it was BECAUSE of the wall-paper—he would make fun of me. He might even want to take me away.

I don't want to leave now until I have found it out. There is a week more, and I think that will be enough.

I'm feeling ever so much better! I don't sleep much at night, for it is so interesting to watch developments; but I sleep a good deal in the daytime.

In the daytime it is tiresome and perplexing.

There are always new shoots on the fungus, and new shades of yellow all over it. I cannot keep count of them, though I have tried conscientiously.

It is the strangest yellow, that wall-paper! It makes me think of all the yellow things I ever saw—not beautiful ones like buttercups, but old foul, bad yellow things.

But there is something else about that paper—the smell! I noticed it the moment we came into the room, but with so much air and sun it was not bad. Now we have had a week of fog and rain, and whether the windows are open or not, the smell is here.

It creeps all over the house.

I find it hovering in the dining-room, skulking in the parlor, hiding in the hall, lying in wait for me on the stairs.

It gets into my hair.

Even when I go to ride, if I turn my head suddenly and surprise it—there is that smell!

Such a peculiar odor, too! I have spent hours in trying to analyze it, to find what it smelled like.

It is not bad—at first, and very gentle, but quite the subtlest, most enduring odor I ever met.

In this damp weather it is awful, I wake up in the night and find it hanging over me.

It used to disturb me at first. I thought seriously of burning the house—to reach the smell.

But now I am used to it. The only thing I can think of that it is like is the COLOR of the paper! A yellow smell.

There is a very funny mark on this wall, low down, near the mopboard. A streak that runs round the room. It goes behind every piece of furniture, except the bed, a long, straight, even SMOOCH, as if it had been rubbed over and over.

I wonder how it was done and who did it, and what they did it for. Round and round and round—round and round and round—it makes me dizzy!

I really have discovered something at last.

Through watching so much at night, when it changes so, I have finally found out.

The front pattern DOES move—and no wonder! The woman behind shakes it!

Sometimes I think there are a great many women behind, and sometimes only one, and she crawls around fast, and her crawling shakes it all over.

Then in the very bright spots she keeps still, and in the very shady spots she just takes hold of the bars and shakes them hard.

And she is all the time trying to climb through. But nobody could climb through that pattern—it strangles so; I think that is why it has so many heads.

They get through, and then the pattern strangles them off and turns them upside down, and makes their eyes white!

If those heads were covered or taken off it would not be half so bad.

I think that woman gets out in the daytime!

And I'll tell you why—privately—I've seen her!

I can see her out of every one of my windows!

It is the same woman, I know, for she is always creeping, and most women do not creep by daylight.

I see her on that long road under the trees, creeping along, and when a carriage comes she hides under the blackberry vines.

I don't blame her a bit. It must be very humiliating to be caught creeping by daylight!

I always lock the door when I creep by daylight. I can't do it at night, for I know John would suspect something at once.

And John is so queer now, that I don't want to irritate him. I wish he would take another room! Besides, I don't want anybody to get that woman out at night but myself.

I often wonder if I could see her out of all the windows at once.

But, turn as fast as I can, I can only see out of one at one time.

And though I always see her, she MAY be able to creep faster than I can turn!

I have watched her sometimes away off in the open country, creeping as fast as a cloud shadow in a high wind.

If only that top pattern could be gotten off from the under one! I mean to try it, little by little.

I have found out another funny thing, but I shan't tell it this time! It does not do to trust people too much.

There are only two more days to get this paper off, and I believe John is beginning to notice. I don't like the look in his eyes.

And I heard him ask Jennie a lot of professional questions about me. She had a very good report to give.

She said I slept a good deal in the daytime.

John knows I don't sleep very well at night, for all I'm so quiet!

He asked me all sorts of questions, too, and pretended to be very loving and kind.

As if I couldn't see through him!

Still, I don't wonder he acts so, sleeping under this paper for three months.

It only interests me, but I feel sure John and Jennie are secretly affected by it.

Hurrah! This is the last day, but it is enough. John is to stay in town over night, and won't be out until this evening.

Jennie wanted to sleep with me—the sly thing! but I told her I should undoubtedly rest better for a night all alone.

That was clever, for really I wasn't alone a bit! As soon as it was moonlight and that poor thing began to crawl and shake the pattern, I got up and ran to help her.

I pulled and she shook, I shook and she pulled, and before morning we had peeled off yards of that paper.

A strip about as high as my head and half around the room.

And then when the sun came and that awful pattern began to laugh at me, I declared I would finish it to-day!

We go away to-morrow, and they are moving all my furniture down again to leave things as they were before.

Jennie looked at the wall in amazement, but I told her merrily that I did it out of pure spite at the vicious thing.

She laughed and said she wouldn't mind doing it herself, but I must not get tired.

How she betrayed herself that time!

But I am here, and no person touches this paper but me—not ALIVE!

She tried to get me out of the room—it was too patent! But I said it was so quiet and empty and clean now that I believed I would lie down again and sleep all I could; and not to wake me even for dinner—I would call when I woke.

So now she is gone, and the servants are gone, and the things are gone, and there is nothing left but that great bedstead nailed down, with the canvas mattress we found on it.

We shall sleep downstairs to-night, and take the boat home to-morrow.

I quite enjoy the room, now it is bare again.

How those children did tear about here!

This bedstead is fairly gnawed!

But I must get to work.

I have locked the door and thrown the key down into the front path.

I don't want to go out, and I don't want to have anybody come in, till John comes.

I want to astonish him.

I've got a rope up here that even Jennie did not find. If that woman does get out, and tries to get away, I can tie her!

But I forgot I could not reach far without anything to stand on!

This bed will NOT move!

I tried to lift and push it until I was lame, and then I got so angry I bit off a little piece at one corner—but it hurt my teeth.

Then I peeled off all the paper I could reach standing on the floor. It sticks horribly and the pattern just enjoys it! All those strangled heads and bulbous eyes and waddling fungus growths just shriek with derision!

I am getting angry enough to do something desperate. To jump out of the window would be admirable exercise, but the bars are too strong even to try.

Besides I wouldn't do it. Of course not. I know well enough that a step like that is improper and might be misconstrued.

I don't like to LOOK out of the windows even—there are so many of those creeping women, and they creep so fast.

I wonder if they all come out of that wall-paper as I did?

But I am securely fastened now by my well-hidden rope—you don't get ME out in the road there!

I suppose I shall have to get back behind the pattern when it comes night, and that is hard!

It is so pleasant to be out in this great room and creep around as I please!

I don't want to go outside. I won't, even if Jennie asks me to.

For outside you have to creep on the ground, and everything is green instead of yellow.

But here I can creep smoothly on the floor, and my shoulder just fits in that long smooch around the wall, so I cannot lose my way.

Why there's John at the door!

It is no use, young man, you can't open it!

How he does call and pound!

Now he's crying for an axe.

It would be a shame to break down that beautiful door!

"John dear!" said I in the gentlest voice, "the key is down by the front steps, under a plantain leaf!"

That silenced him for a few moments.

Then he said—very quietly indeed, "Open the door, my darling!"

"I can't," said I. "The key is down by the front door under a plantain leaf!"

And then I said it again, several times, very gently and slowly, and said it so often that he had to go and see, and he got it of course, and came in. He stopped short by the door.

"What is the matter?" he cried. "For God's sake, what are you doing!"

I kept on creeping just the same, but I looked at him over my shoulder.

"I've got out at last," said I, "in spite of you and Jane. And I've pulled off most of the paper, so you can't put me back!"

Now why should that man have fainted? But he did, and right across my path by the wall, so that I had to creep over him every time!

WHY I WROTE *THE YELLOW WALLPAPER*

Many and many a reader has asked that. When the story first came out, in the *New England Magazine* about 1891, a Boston physician made protest in *The Transcript*. Such a story ought not to be written, he said; it was enough to drive anyone mad to read it.

Another physician, in Kansas I think, wrote to say that it was the best description of incipient insanity he had ever seen, and--begging my pardon--had I been there?

Now the story of the story is this:

For many years I suffered from a severe and continuous nervous breakdown tending to melancholia--and beyond. During about the third year of this trouble I went, in devout faith and some faint stir of hope, to a noted specialist in nervous diseases, the best known in the country. This wise man put me to bed and applied the rest cure, to which a still-good physique responded so promptly that he concluded there was nothing much the matter with me, and sent me home with solemn advice to "live as domestic a life as far as possible," to "have but two hours' intellectual life a day," and "never to touch pen, brush, or pencil again" as long as I lived. This was in 1887.

I went home and obeyed those directions for some three months, and came so near the borderline of utter mental ruin that I could see over.

Then, using the remnants of intelligence that remained, and helped by a wise friend, I cast the noted specialist's advice to the winds and went to work again--work, the normal life of every human being; work, in which is joy and growth and service, without which one is a pauper and a parasite--ultimately recovering some measure of power.

Being naturally moved to rejoicing by this narrow escape, I wrote *The Yellow Wallpaper*, with its embellishments and additions, to carry out the ideal (I never had hallucinations or objections to my mural decorations) and sent a copy to the physician who so nearly drove me mad. He never acknowledged it.

The little book is valued by alienists and as a good specimen of one kind of literature. It has, to my knowledge, saved one woman from a similar fate--so terrifying her family that they let her out into normal activity and she recovered.

But the best result is this. Many years later I was told that the great specialist had admitted to friends of his that he had altered his treatment of neurasthenia since reading *The Yellow Wallpaper.*

It was not intended to drive people crazy, but to save people from being driven crazy, and it worked.

WOMEN AND ECONOMICS

A Study of the Economic Relation Between Men and Women as a Factor in Social Evolution

PROEM

In dark and early ages, through the primal forests faring,
Ere the soul came shining into prehistoric night,
Twofold man was equal; they were comrades dear and daring,
Living wild and free together in unreasoning delight.

Ere the soul was born and consciousness came slowly,
Ere the soul was born, to man and woman, too,
Ere he found the Tree of Knowledge, that awful tree and holy,
Ere he knew he felt, and knew he knew.

Then said he to Pain, "I am wise now, and I know you!
No more will I suffer while power and wisdom last!"
Then said he to Pleasure, "I am strong, and I will show you
That the will of man can seize you,–aye, and hold you fast!"

Food he ate for pleasure, and wine he drank for gladness.
And woman? Ah, the woman! the crown of all delight!
His now,–he knew it! He was strong to madness
In that early dawning after prehistoric night.

His,–his forever! That glory sweet and tender!
Ah, but he would love her! And she should love but him!
He would work and struggle for her, he would shelter and defend her,–
She should never leave him, never, till their eyes in death were dim.

Close, close he bound her, that she should leave him never;

Weak still he kept her, lest she be strong to flee;
And the fainting flame of passion he kept alive forever
With all the arts and forces of earth and sky and sea.

And, ah, the long journey! The slow and awful ages
They have labored up together, blind and crippled, all astray!
Through what a mighty volume, with a million shameful pages,
From the freedom of the forests to the prisons of to-day!

Food he ate for pleasure, and it slew him with diseases!
Wine he drank for gladness, and it led the way to crime!
And woman? He will hold her,–he will have her when he pleases–
And he never once hath seen her since the prehistoric time!

Gone the friend and comrade of the day when life was younger,
She who rests and comforts, she who helps and saves.
Still he seeks her vainly, with a never-dying hunger;
Alone beneath his tyrants, alone above his slaves!

Toiler, bent and weary with the load of thine own making!
Thou who art sad and lonely, though lonely all in vain!
Who hast sought to conquer Pleasure and have her for the taking,
And found that Pleasure only was another name for Pain–

Nature hath reclaimed thee, forgiving dispossession!
God hath not forgotten, though man doth still forget!
The woman-soul is rising, in despite of thy transgression–
Loose her now, and trust her! She will love thee yet!

Love thee? She will love thee as only freedom knoweth!
Love thee? She will love thee while Love itself doth live!
Fear not the heart of woman! No bitterness it showeth!
The ages of her sorrow have but taught her to forgive!

PREFACE

This book is written to offer a simple and natural explanation of one of the most common and most perplexing problems of human life,–a problem which presents itself to almost every individual for practical solution, and which demands the most serious attention of the moralist, the physician, and the sociologist–

To show how some of the worst evils under which we suffer, evils long supposed to be inherent and ineradicable in our natures, are but the result of certain arbitrary conditions of our own adoption, and how, by removing those conditions, we may remove the evil resultant–

To point out how far we have already gone in the path of improvement, and how irresistibly the social forces of to-day are compelling us further, even without our knowledge and against our violent opposition,–an advance which may be greatly quickened by our recognition and assistance–

To reach in especial the thinking women of to-day, and urge upon them a new sense, not only of their social responsibility as individuals, but of their measureless racial importance as makers of men.

It is hoped also that the theory advanced will prove sufficiently suggestive to give rise to such further study and discussion as shall prove its error or establish its truth.

Charlotte Perkins Stetson

I.

SINCE we have learned to study the development of human life as we study the evolution of species throughout the animal kingdom, some peculiar phenomena which have puzzled the philosopher and moralist for so long, begin to show themselves in a new light. We begin to see that, so far from being inscrutable problems, requiring another life to explain, these sorrows and perplexities of our lives are but the natural results of natural causes, and that, as soon as we ascertain the causes, we can do much to remove them.

In spite of the power of the individual will to struggle against conditions, to resist them for a while, and sometimes to overcome them, it remains true that the human creature is affected by his environment, as is every other living thing. The power of the individual will to resist natural law is well proven by the life and death of the ascetic. In any one of those suicidal martyrs may be seen the will, misdirected by the ill-informed intelligence, forcing the body to defy every natural impulse,–even to the door of death, and through it.

But, while these exceptions show what the human will can do, the general course of life shows the inexorable effect of conditions upon humanity. Of these conditions we share with other living things the environment of the material universe. We are affected by climate and locality, by physical, chemical, electrical forces, as are all animals and plants. With the animals, we farther share the effect of our own activity, the reactionary force of exercise. What we do, as well as what is done to us, makes us what we are. But, beyond these forces, we come under the effect of a third set of conditions peculiar to our human status; namely, social conditions. In the organic interchanges which constitute social life, we are affected by each other to a degree beyond what is found even among the most gregarious of animals. This third factor, the social environment, is of enormous force as a modifier of human life. Throughout all these environing conditions, those which affect us through our economic necessities are most marked in their influence.

Without touching yet upon the influence of the social factors, treating the human being merely as an individual animal, we see that he is modified most by his economic conditions, as is every other animal. Differ as they may in color and size, in strength and speed, in minor adaptation to minor conditions, all animals that live on grass have distinctive traits in common, and all animals that eat flesh have distinctive traits in common,–so distinctive and so common that it is by teeth, by nutritive apparatus in general, that they are classified, rather than by means of defence or locomotion. The food supply of the animal is the largest passive factor in his development; the processes by which he obtains his food supply, the largest active factor in his development. It is these activities, the incessant repetition of the exertions by which he is fed, which most modify his structure and develope his functions. The sheep, the cow, the deer, differ in their adaptation to the weather, their locomotive ability, their means of defence; but they agree in main characteristics, because of their common method of nutrition.

The human animal is no exception to this rule. Climate affects him, weather affects him, enemies affect him; but most of all he is affected, like every other living creature, by what he does for his living. Under all the influence of his later and wider life, all the reactive effect of social institutions, the individual is still inexorably modified by his means of livelihood: "the hand of the dyer is subdued to what he works in." As one clear, world-known instance of the effect of economic conditions upon the human creature, note the marked race-modification of the Hebrew people under the enforced restrictions of the last two thousand years. Here is a people rising to national prominence, first as a pastoral, and then as an agricultural nation; only partially commercial through race affinity with the Phoenicians, the pioneer traders of the world. Under the social power of a united Christendom–united at least in this most unchristian deed–the Jew was forced to get his livelihood by commercial methods solely. Many effects can be traced in him to the fierce pressure of the social conditions to which he was subjected: the intense family devotion of a people who had no country, no king, no room for joy and pride except the family; the reduced size and tremendous vitality and endurance of the pitilessly selected survivors of the Ghetto; the repeated bursts of erratic genius from the human spirit so inhumanly restrained. But more patent still is the effect of the economic conditions,–the artificial development of a race of traders and dealers in money, from the lowest pawnbroker to the house of Rothschild; a special kind of people, bred of the economic environment in which they were compelled to live.

One rough but familiar instance of the same effect, from the same cause, we can all see in the marked distinction between the pastoral, the agricultural, and the manufacturing classes in any nation, though their other conditions be the same. On the clear line of argument that functions and organs are developed by use, that what we use most is developed most, and that the daily processes of supplying economic needs are the processes that we most use, it follows that, when we find special economic conditions affecting any special class of people, we may look for special results, and find them.

In view of these facts, attention is now called to a certain marked and peculiar economic condition affecting the human race, and unparalleled in the organic world. We are the only animal species in which the female depends on the male for food, the only animal species in which the sex-relation is also an economic relation. With us an entire sex lives in a relation of economic dependence upon the other sex, and the economic relation is combined with the sex-relation. The economic status of the human female is relative to the sex-relation.

It is commonly assumed that this condition also obtains among other animals, but such is not the case. There are many birds among which, during the nesting season, the male helps the female feed the young, and partially feeds her; and, with certain of the higher carnivora, the male helps the female feed the young, and partially feeds her. In no case does she depend on him absolutely, even during this season, save in that of the hornbill, where the female, sitting on her nest in a hollow tree, is walled in with clay by the male, so that only her beak projects; and then he feeds her while the eggs are developing. But even the female hornbill does not expect to be fed at any other time. The female bee and ant are economically dependent, but not on the male. The workers are females, too, specialized to economic functions solely. And with the carnivora, if the young are to lose one parent, it might far better be the father: the mother is quite competent to take care of them herself. With many species, as in the case of the common cat, she not only feeds herself and her young, but has to defend the young against the male as well. In no case is the female throughout her life supported by the male.

In the human species the condition is permanent and general, though there are exceptions, and though the present century is witnessing the beginnings of a great change in this respect. We have not been accustomed to face this fact beyond our loose generalization that it was "natural," and that other animals did so, too.

To many this view will not seem clear at first; and the case of working peasant women or females of savage tribes, and the general household industry of women, will be instanced against it. Some careful and honest discrimination is needed to make plain to ourselves the essential facts of the relation, even in these cases. The horse, in his free natural condition, is economically independent. He gets his living by his own exertions, irrespective of any other creature. The horse, in his present condition of slavery, is economically dependent. He gets his living at the hands of his master; and his exertions, though strenuous, bear no direct relation to his living. In fact, the horses who are the best fed and cared for and the horses who are the hardest worked are quite different animals. The horse works, it is true; but what he gets to eat depends on the power and will of his master. His living comes through another. He is economically dependent. So with the hard-worked savage or peasant women. Their labor is the property of another: they work under another will; and what they receive depends not on their labor, but on the power and will of another. They are economically dependent. This is true of the human female both individually and collectively.

In studying the economic position of the sexes collectively, the difference is most marked. As a social animal, the economic status of man rests on the combined and exchanged services of vast numbers of progressively specialized individuals. The economic progress of the race, its maintenance at any period, its continued advance, involve the collective activities of all the trades, crafts, arts, manufactures, inventions, discoveries, and all the civil and military institutions that go to maintain them. The economic status of any race at any time, with its involved effect on all the constituent individuals, depends on their world-wide labors and their free exchange. Economic progress, however, is almost exclusively masculine. Such economic processes as women have been allowed to exercise are of the earliest and most primitive kind. Were men to perform no economic services save such as are still performed by women, our racial status in economics would be reduced to most painful limitations.

To take from any community its male workers would paralyze it economically to a far greater degree than to remove its female workers. The labor now performed by the women could be performed by the men, requiring only the setting back of many advanced workers into earlier forms of industry; but the labor now performed by the men could not be performed by the women without generations of effort and adaptation. Men can cook, clean, and sew as well as women; but the making and managing of the great engines of modern industry, the threading of earth and sea in our vast systems of transportation, the handling of our elaborate machinery of trade, commerce, government,–these things could not be done so well by women in their present degree of economic development.

This is not owing to lack of the essential human faculties necessary to such achievements, nor to any inherent disability of sex, but to the present condition of woman, forbidding the development of this degree of economic ability. The male human being is thousands of years in advance of the female in economic status. Speaking collectively, men produce and distribute wealth; and women receive it at their hands. As men hunt, fish, keep cattle, or raise corn, so do women eat game, fish, beef, or corn. As men go down to the sea in ships, and bring coffee and spices and silks and gems from far away, so do women partake of the coffee and spices and silks and gems the men bring.

The economic status of the human race in any nation, at any time, is governed mainly by the activities of the male: the female obtains her share in the racial advance only through him.

Studied individually, the facts are even more plainly visible, more open and familiar. From the day laborer to the millionnaire, the wife's worn dress or flashing jewels, her low roof or her lordly one, her weary feet or her rich equipage,–these speak of the economic ability of the husband. The comfort, the luxury, the necessities of life itself, which the woman receives, are obtained by the husband, and given her by him. And, when the woman, left alone with no man to "support" her, tries to meet her own economic necessities, the difficulties which confront her prove conclusively what the general economic status of the woman is. None can deny these patent facts,–that the economic status of women generally depends upon that of men generally, and that the economic status of women individually depends upon that of men individually, those men to whom they are related. But we are instantly confronted by the commonly received opinion that, although it must be admitted that men make and distribute the wealth of the world, yet women earn their share of it as wives. This assumes either that the husband is in the position of employer and the wife as employee, or that marriage is a "partnership," and the wife an equal factor with the husband in producing wealth.

Economic independence is a relative condition at best. In the broadest sense, all living things are economically dependent upon others,–the animals upon the vegetables, and man upon both. In a narrower sense, all social life is economically interdependent, man producing collectively what he could by no possibility produce separately. But, in the closest interpretation, individual economic independence among human beings means that the individual pays for what he gets, works for what he gets, gives to the other an equivalent for what the other gives him. I depend on the shoemaker for shoes, and the tailor for coats; but, if I give the shoemaker and the tailor enough of my own labor as a house-builder to pay for the shoes and coats they give me, I retain my personal independence. I have not taken of their product, and given nothing of mine. As long as what I get is obtained by what I give, I am economically independent.

Women consume economic goods. What economic product do they give in exchange for what they consume? The claim that marriage is a partnership, in which the two persons married produce wealth which neither of them, separately, could produce, will not bear examination. A man happy and comfortable can produce more than one unhappy and uncomfortable, but this is as true of a father or son as of a husband. To take from a man any of the conditions which make him happy and strong is to cripple his industry, generally speaking. But those relatives who make him happy are not therefore his business partners, and entitled to share his income.

Grateful return for happiness conferred is not the method of exchange in a partnership. The comfort a man takes with his wife is not in the nature of a business partnership, nor are her frugality and industry. A housekeeper, in her place, might be as frugal, as industrious, but would not therefore be a partner. Man and wife are partners truly in their mutual obligation to their children,–their common love, duty, and service. But a manufacturer who marries, or a doctor, or a lawyer, does not take a partner in his business, when he takes a partner in parenthood, unless his wife is also a manufacturer, a doctor, or a lawyer. In his business, she cannot even advise wisely without training and experience. To love her husband, the composer, does not enable her to compose; and the loss of a man's wife, though it may break his heart, does not cripple his business, unless his mind is affected by grief. She is in no sense a business partner, unless she contributes capital or experience or labor, as a man would in like relation. Most men would hesitate very seriously before entering a business partnership with any woman, wife or not.

If the wife is not, then, truly a business partner, in what way does she earn from her husband the food, clothing, and shelter she receives at his hands? By house service, it will be instantly replied. This is the general misty idea upon the subject,– that women earn all they get, and more, by house service. Here we come to a very practical and definite economic ground. Although not producers of wealth, women serve in the final processes of preparation and distribution. Their labor in the household has a genuine economic value.

For a certain percentage of persons to serve other persons, in order that the ones so served may produce more, is a contribution not to be overlooked. The labor of women in the house, certainly, enables men to produce more wealth than they otherwise could; and in this way women are economic factors in society. But so are horses. The labor of horses enables men to produce more wealth than they otherwise could. The horse is an economic factor in society. But the horse is not economically independent, nor is the woman. If a man plus a valet can perform more useful service than he could minus a valet, then the valet is performing useful service. But, if the valet is the property of the man, is obliged to perform this service, and is not paid for it, he is not economically independent.

The labor which the wife performs in the household is given as part of her functional duty, not as employment. The wife of the poor man, who works hard in a small house, doing all the work for the family, or the wife of the rich man, who wisely and gracefully manages a large house and administers its functions, each is entitled to fair pay for services rendered.

To take this ground and hold it honestly, wives, as earners through domestic service, are entitled to the wages of cooks, housemaids, nursemaids, seamstresses, or housekeepers, and to no more. This would of course reduce the spending money of the wives of the rich, and put it out of the power of the poor man to "support" a wife at all, unless, indeed, the poor man faced the situation fully, paid his wife her wages as house servant, and then she and he combined their funds in the support of their children. He would be keeping a servant: she would be helping keep the family. But nowhere on earth would there be "a rich woman" by these means. Even the highest class of private housekeeper, useful as her services are, does not accumulate a fortune. She does not buy diamonds and sables and keep a carriage. Things like these are not earned by house service.

But the salient fact in this discussion is that, whatever the economic value of the domestic industry of women is, they do not get it. The women who do the most work get the least money, and the women who have the most money do the least work. Their labor is neither given nor taken as a factor in economic exchange. It is held to be their duty as women to do this work; and their economic status bears no relation to their domestic labors, unless an inverse one. Moreover, if they were thus fairly paid,–given what they earned, and no more,–all women working in this way would be reduced to the economic status of the house servant. Few women–or men either–care to face this condition. The ground that women earn their living by domestic labor is instantly forsaken, and we are told that they obtain their livelihood as mothers. This is a peculiar position. We speak of it commonly enough, and often with deep feeling, but without due analysis.

In treating of an economic exchange, asking what return in goods or labor women make for the goods and labor given them,–either to the race collectively or to their husbands individually,–what payment women make for their clothes and shoes and furniture and food and shelter, we are told that the duties and services of the mother entitle her to support.

If this is so, if motherhood is an exchangeable commodity given by women in payment for clothes and food, then we must of course find some relation between the quantity or quality of the motherhood and the quantity and quality of the pay. This being true, then the women who are not mothers have no economic status at all; and the economic status of those who are must be shown to be relative to their motherhood. This is obviously absurd. The childless wife has as much money as the mother of many,–more; for the children of the latter consume what would otherwise be hers; and the inefficient mother is no less provided for than the efficient one. Visibly, and upon the face of it, women are not maintained in economic prosperity proportioned to their motherhood. Motherhood bears no relation to their economic status. Among primitive races, it is true,–in the patriarchal period, for instance,–there was some truth in this position. Women being of no value whatever save as bearers of children, their favor and indulgence did bear direct relation to maternity; and they had reason to exult on more grounds than one when they could boast a son. To-day, however, the maintenance of the woman is not conditioned upon this. A man is not allowed to discard his wife because she is barren. The claim of motherhood as a factor in economic exchange is false to-day. But suppose it were true. Are we willing to hold this ground, even in theory? Are we willing to consider motherhood as a business, a form of commercial exchange? Are the cares and duties of the mother, her travail and her love, commodities to be exchanged for bread?

It is revolting so to consider them; and, if we dare face our own thoughts, and force them to their logical conclusion, we shall see that nothing could be more repugnant to human feeling, or more socially and individually injurious, than to make motherhood a trade. Driven off these alleged grounds of women's economic independence; shown that women, as a class, neither produce nor distribute wealth; that women, as individuals, labor mainly as house servants, are not paid as such, and would not be satisfied with such an economic status if they were so paid; that wives are not business partners or co-producers of wealth with their husbands, unless they actually practise the same profession; that they are not salaried as mothers, and that it would be unspeakably degrading if they were,–what remains to those who deny that women are supported by men? This (and a most amusing position it is),–that the function of maternity unfits a woman for economic production, and, therefore, it is right that she should be supported by her husband.

The ground is taken that the human female is not economically independent, that she is fed by the male of her species. In denial of this, it is first alleged that she is economically independent,–that she does support herself by her own industry in the house. It being shown that there is no relation between the economic status of woman and the labor she performs in the home, it is then alleged that not as house servant, but as mother, does woman earn her living. It being shown that the economic status of woman bears no relation to her motherhood, either in quantity or quality, it is then alleged that motherhood renders a woman unfit for economic production, and that, therefore, it is right that she be supported by her husband. Before going farther, let us seize upon this admission,–that she is supported by her husband.

Without going into either the ethics or the necessities of the case, we have reached so much common ground: the female of genus homo is supported by the male. Whereas, in other species of animals, male and female alike graze and browse, hunt and kill, climb, swim, dig, run, and fly for their livings, in our species the female does not seek her own living in the specific activities of our race, but is fed by the male.

Now as to the alleged necessity. Because of her maternal duties, the human female is said to be unable to get her own living. As the maternal duties of other females do not unfit them for getting their own living and also the livings of their young, it would seem that the human maternal duties require the segregation of the entire energies of the mother to the service of the child during her entire adult life, or so large a proportion of them that not enough remains to devote to the individual interests of the mother.

Such a condition, did it exist, would of course excuse and justify the pitiful dependence of the human female, and her support by the male. As the queen bee, modified entirely to maternity, is supported, not by the male, to be sure, but by her co-workers, the "old maids," the barren working bees, who labor so patiently and lovingly in their branch of the maternal duties of the hive, so would the human female, modified entirely to maternity, become unfit for any other exertion, and a helpless dependant.

Is this the condition of human motherhood? Does the human mother, by her motherhood, thereby lose control of brain and body, lose power and skill and desire for any other work? Do we see before us the human race, with all its females segregated entirely to the uses of motherhood, consecrated, set apart, specially developed, spending every power of their nature on the service of their children?

We do not. We see the human mother worked far harder than a mare, laboring her life long in the service, not of her children only, but of men; husbands, brothers, fathers, whatever male relatives she has; for mother and sister also; for the church a little, if she is allowed; for society, if she is able; for charity and education and reform,–working in many ways that are not the ways of motherhood.

It is not motherhood that keeps the housewife on her feet from dawn till dark; it is house service, not child service. Women work longer and harder than most men, and not solely in maternal duties. The savage mother carries the burdens, and does all menial service for the tribe. The peasant mother toils in the fields, and the working-man's wife in the home. Many mothers, even now, are wage-earners for the family, as well as bearers and rearers of it. And the women who are not so occupied, the women who belong to rich men,–here perhaps is the exhaustive devotion to maternity which is supposed to justify an admitted economic dependence. But we do not find it even among these. Women of ease and wealth provide for their children better care than the poor woman can; but they do not spend more time upon it themselves, nor more care and effort. They have other occupation.

In spite of her supposed segregation to maternal duties, the human female, the world over, works at extra-maternal duties for hours enough to provide her with an independent living, and then is denied independence on the ground that motherhood prevents her working!

If this ground were tenable, we should find a world full of women who never lifted a finger save in the service of their children, and of men who did all the work besides, and waited on the women whom motherhood prevented from waiting on themselves. The ground is not tenable. A human female, healthy, sound, has twenty-five years of life before she is a mother, and should have twenty-five years more after the period of such maternal service as is expected of her has been given. The duties of grandmotherhood are surely not alleged as preventing economic independence.

The working power of the mother has always been a prominent factor in human life. She is the worker par excellence, but her work is not such as to affect her economic status. Her living, all that she gets,–food, clothing, ornaments, amusements, luxuries,–these bear no relation to her power to produce wealth, to her services in the house, or to her motherhood. These things bear relation only to the man she marries, the man she depends on,–to how much he has and how much he is willing to give her. The women whose splendid extravagance dazzles the world, whose economic goods are the greatest, are often neither houseworkers nor mothers, but simply the women who hold most power over the men who have the most money. The female of genus homo is economically dependent on the male. He is her food supply.

II.

KNOWING how important a factor in the evolution of species is the economic relation, and finding in the human species an economic relation so peculiar, we may naturally look to find effects peculiar to our race. We may expect to find phenomena in the sex-relation and in the economic relation of humanity of a unique character,–phenomena not traceable to human superiority, but singularly derogatory to that superiority; phenomena so marked, so morbid, as to give rise to much speculation as to their cause. Are these natural inferences fulfilled? Are these peculiarities in the sex-relation and in the economic relation manifested in human life? Indisputably these are,–so plain, so prominent, so imperiously demanding attention, that human thought has been occupied from its first consciousness in trying some way to account for them. To explain and relate these phenomena, separating what is due to normal race-development from what is due to this abnormal sexuo-economic relation, is the purpose of the line of study here suggested.

As the racial distinction of humanity lies in its social relation, so we find the distinctive gains and losses of humanity to lie also in its social relation. We are more affected by our relation to each other than by our physical environment.

Disadvantages of climate, deficiencies in food supply, competition from other species,–all these conditions society, in its organic strength, is easily able to overcome or to adjust. But in our inter-human relations we are not so successful. The serious dangers and troubles of human life arise from difficulties of adjustment with our social environment, and not with our physical environment. These difficulties, so far, have acted as a continual check to social progress. The more absolutely a nation has triumphed over physical conditions, the more successful it has become in its conquest of physical enemies and obstacles, the more it has given rein to the action of social forces which have ultimately destroyed the nation, and left the long ascent to be begun again by others.

There is the moral of all human tales:
'Tis but the same rehearsal of the past,–
First Freedom, and then Glory; when that fails,
Wealth, Vice, Corruption,–barbarism at last.
And History, with all her volumes vast,
Hath but one page.*

*Childe Harold's Pilgrimage, Canto IV., cviii.

The path of history is strewn with fossils and faint relics of extinct races,–races which died of what the sociologist would call internal diseases rather than natural causes. This, too, has been clear to the observer in all ages. It has been easily seen that there was something in our own behavior which did us more harm than any external difficulty; but what we have not seen is the natural cause of our unnatural conduct, and how most easily to alter it.

Rudely classifying the principal fields of human difficulty, we find one large proportion lies in the sex-relation, and another in the economic relation, between the individual constituents of society. To speak broadly, the troubles of life as we find them are mainly traceable to the heart or the purse. The other horror of our lives–disease–comes back often to these causes,–to something wrong either in economic relation or in sex-relation. To be ill-fed or ill-bred, or both, is largely what makes us the sickly race we are. In this wrong breeding, this maladjustment of the sex-relation in humanity, what are the principal features? We see in social evolution two main lines of action in this department of life. One is a gradual orderly development of monogamous marriage, as the form of sex-union best calculated to advance the interests of the individual and of society. It should be clearly understood that this is a natural development, inevitable in the course of social progress; not an artificial condition, enforced by laws of our making. Monogamy is found among birds and mammals: it is just as natural a condition as polygamy or promiscuity or any other form of sex-union; and its permanence and integrity are introduced and increased by the needs of the young and the advantage to the race, just as any other form of reproduction was introduced. Our moral concepts rest primarily on facts. The moral quality of monogamous marriage depends on its true advantage to the individual and to society. If it were not the best form of marriage for our racial good, it would not be right. All the way up, from the promiscuous horde of savages, with their miscellaneous matings, to the lifelong devotion of romantic love, social life has been evolving a type of sex-union best suited to develope and improve the individual and the race. This is an orderly process, and a pleasant one, involving only such comparative pain and difficulty as always attend the assumption of new processes and the extinction of the old; but accompanied by far more joy than pain.

But with the natural process of social advancement has gone an unnatural process,–an erratic and morbid action, making the sex-relation of humanity a frightful source of evil. So prominent have been these morbid actions and evil results that hasty thinkers of all ages have assumed that the whole thing was wrong, and that celibacy was the highest virtue. Without the power of complete analysis, without knowledge of the sociological data essential to such analysis, we have sweepingly condemned as a whole what we could easily see was so allied with pain and loss. But, like all natural phenomena, the phenomena of sex may be studied, both the normal and the abnormal, the physiological and the pathological; and we are quite capable of understanding why we are in such evil case, and how we may attain more healthful conditions.

So far, the study of this subject has rested on the assumption that man must be just as we find him, that man behaves just as he chooses, and that, if he does not choose to behave as he does, he can stop. Therefore, when we discovered that human behavior in the sex-relation was productive of evil, we exhorted the human creature to stop so behaving, and have continued so to exhort for many centuries. By law and religion, by education and custom, we have sought to enforce upon the human individual the kind of behavior which our social sense so clearly showed was right.

But always there has remained the morbid action. Whatever the external form of sex-union to which we have given social sanction, however Bible and Koran and Vedas have offered instruction, some hidden cause has operated continuously against the true course of social evolution, to pervert the natural trend toward a higher and more advantageous sex-relation; and to maintain lower forms, and erratic phases, of a most disadvantageous character.

Every other animal works out the kind of sex-union best adapted to the reproduction of his species, and peacefully practises it. We have worked out the kind that is best for us,–best for the individuals concerned, for the young resultant, and for society as a whole; but we do not peacefully practise it. So palpable is this fact that we have commonly accepted it, and taken it for granted that this relation must be a continuous source of trouble to humanity. "Marriage is a lottery," is a common saying among us. "The course of true love never did run smooth." And we quote with unction Punch's advice to those about to marry,–"Don't!" That peculiar sub-relation which has dragged along with us all the time that monogamous marriage has been growing to be the accepted form of sex-union–prostitution–we have accepted, and called a "social necessity." We also call it "the social evil." We have tacitly admitted that this relation in the human race must be more or less uncomfortable and wrong, that it is part of our nature to have it so.

Now let us examine the case fairly and calmly, and see whether it is as inscrutable and immutable as hitherto believed. What are the conditions? What are the natural and what the unnatural features of the case? To distinguish these involves a little study of the evolution of the processes of reproduction.

Very early in the development of species it was ascertained by nature's slow but sure experiments that the establishment of two sexes in separate organisms, and their differentiation, was to the advantage of the species. Therefore, out of the mere protoplasmic masses, the floating cells, the amorphous early forms of life, grew into use the distinction of the sexes,–the gradual development of masculine and feminine organs and functions in two distinct organisms. Developed and increased by use, the distinction of sex increased in the evolution of species. As the distinction increased, the attraction increased, until we have in all the higher races two markedly different sexes, strongly drawn together by the attraction of sex, and fulfilling their use in the reproduction of species. These are the natural features of sex-distinction and sex-union, and they are found in the human species as in others. The unnatural feature by which our race holds an unenviable distinction consists mainly in this,–a morbid excess in the exercise of this function.

It is this excess, whether in marriage or out, which makes the health and happiness of humanity in this relation so precarious. It is this excess, always easily seen, which law and religion have mainly striven to check. Excessive sex-indulgence is the distinctive feature of humanity in this relation.

To define "excess" in this connection is not difficult. All natural functions that require our conscious co-operation for their fulfilment are urged upon our notice by an imperative desire. We do not have to desire to breathe or to digest or to circulate the blood, because that is done without our volition; but we do have to desire to eat and drink, because the stomach cannot obtain its supplies without in some way spurring the whole organism to secure them. So hunger is given us as an essential factor in our process of nutrition. In the same manner sex-attraction is an essential factor in the fulfilment of our processes of reproduction. In a normal condition the amount of hunger we feel is exactly proportioned to the amount of food we need. It tells us when to eat and when to stop. In some diseased conditions "an unnatural appetite" sets in; and we are impelled to eat far beyond the capacity of the stomach to digest, of the body to assimilate. This is an excessive hunger.

We, as a race, manifest an excessive sex-attraction, followed by its excessive indulgence, and the inevitable evil consequence. It urges us to a degree of indulgence which bears no relation to the original needs of the organism, and which is even so absurdly exaggerated as to react unfavorably on the incidental gratification involved; an excess which tends to pervert and exhaust desire as well as to injure reproduction.

The human animal manifests an excess in sex-attraction which not only injures the race through its morbid action on the natural processes of reproduction, but which injures the happiness of the individual through its morbid reaction on his own desires.

What is the cause of this excessive sex-attraction in the human species? The immediately acting cause of sex-attraction is sex-distinction. The more widely the sexes are differentiated, the more forcibly they are attracted to each other. The more highly developed becomes the distinction of sex in either organism, the more intense is its attraction for the other. In the human species we find sex-distinction carried to an excessive degree. Sex-distinction in humanity is so marked as to retard and confuse race-distinction, to check individual distinction, seriously to injure the race. Accustomed as we are simply to accept the facts of life as we find them, to consider people as permanent types instead of seeing them and the whole race in continual change according to the action of many forces, it seems strange at first to differentiate between familiar manifestations of sex distinction, and to say: "This is normal, and should not be disturbed. This is abnormal, and should be removed." But that is precisely what must be done.

Normal sex-distinction manifests itself in all species in what are called primary and secondary sex-characteristics. The primary are those organs and functions essential to reproduction; the secondary, those modifications of structure and function which subserve the uses of reproduction ultimately, but are not directly essential,–such as the horns of the stag, of use in sex-combat; the plumage of the peacock, of use in sex-competition. All the minor characteristics of beard or mane, comb, wattles, spurs, gorgeous color or superior size, which distinguish the male from the female,–these are distinctions of sex. These distinctions are of use to the species through reproduction only, the processes of race-preservation. They are not of use in self-preservation. The creature is not profited personally by his mane or crest or tail-feathers: they do not help him get his dinner or kill his enemies.

On the contrary, they react unfavorably upon his personal gains, if, through too great development, they interfere with his activity or render him a conspicuous mark for enemies. Such development would constitute excessive sex-distinction, and this is precisely the condition of the human race. Our distinctions of sex are carried to such a degree as to be disadvantageous to our progress as individuals and as a race. The sexes in our species are differentiated not only enough to perform their primal functions; not only enough to manifest all sufficient secondary sexual characteristics and fulfil their use in giving rise to sufficient sex-attraction; but so much as seriously to interfere with the processes of self-preservation on the one hand; and, more conspicuous still, so much as to react unfavorably upon the very processes of race-preservation which they are meant to serve. Our excessive sex-distinction, manifesting the characteristics of sex to an abnormal degree, has given rise to a degree of attraction which demands a degree of indulgence that directly injures motherhood and fatherhood. We are not better as parents, nor better as people, for our existing degree of sex-distinction, but visibly worse. To what conditions are we to look for the developing cause of these phenomena?

Let us first examine the balance of forces by which these two great processes, self-preservation and race-preservation, are conducted in the world. Self-preservation involves the expenditure of energy in those acts, and their ensuing modifications of structure and function, which tend to the maintenance of the individual life. Race-preservation involves the expenditure of energy in those acts, and their ensuing modifications of structure and function, which tend to the maintenance of the racial life, even to the complete sacrifice of the individual. This primal distinction should be clearly held in mind. Self-preservation and race-preservation are in no way identical processes, and are often directly opposed. In the line of self-preservation, natural selection, acting on the individual, developes those characteristics which enable it to succeed in "the struggle for existence," increasing by use those organs and functions by which it directly profits. In the line of race-preservation, sexual selection, acting on the individual, developes those characteristics which enable it to succeed in what Drummond has called "the struggle for the existence of others," increasing by use those organs and functions by which its young are to profit, directly or indirectly. The individual has been not only modified to its environment, under natural selection, but modified to its mate, under sexual selection, each sex developing the qualities desired by the other by the simple process of choice, those best sexed being first chosen, and transmitting their sex-development as well as their racial development.

The order mammalia is the resultant of a primary sex-distinction developed by natural selection; but the gorgeous plumage of the peacock's tail is a secondary sex-distinction developed by sexual selection. If the peacock's tail were to increase in size and splendor till it shone like the sun and covered an acre,–if it tended so to increase, we will say,–such excessive sex-distinction would be so inimical to the personal prosperity of that peacock that he would die, and his tail-tendency would perish with him. If the pea-hen, conversely, whose sex-distinction attracts in the opposite direction, not by being large and splendid, but small and dull,–if she should grow so small and dull as to fail to keep herself and her young fed and defended, then she would die; and there would be another check to excessive sex-distinction. In herds of deer and cattle the male is larger and stronger, the female smaller and weaker; but, unless the latter is large and strong enough to keep up with the male in the search for food or the flight from foes, one is taken and the other left, and there is no more of that kind of animal. Differ as they may in sex, they must remain alike in species, equal in race-development, else destruction overtakes them. The force of natural selection, demanding and producing identical race-qualities, acts as a check on sexual selection, with its production of different sex-qualities. As sexes, they perform different functions, and therefore tend to develope differently. As species, they perform the same functions, and therefore tend to develope equally.

And as sex-functions are only used occasionally, and race-functions are used all the time,–as they mate but yearly or tri-monthly, but eat daily and hourly,–the processes of obtaining food or of opposing constant enemies act more steadily than the processes of reproduction, and produce greater effect.

We find the order mammalia accordingly producing and suckling its young in the same manner through a wide variety of species which obtain their living in a different manner. The calf and colt and cub and kitten are produced by the same process; but the cow and horse, the bear and cat, are produced by different processes. And, though cow and bull, mare and stallion, differ as to sex, they are alike in species; and the likeness in species is greater than the difference in sex. Cow, mare, and cat are all females of the order mammalia, and so far alike; but how much more different they are than similar!

Natural selection develops race. Sexual selection develops sex. Sex-development is one throughout its varied forms, tending only to reproduce what is. But race-development rises ever in higher and higher manifestation of energy. As sexes, we share our distinction with the animal kingdom almost to the beginning of life, and with the vegetable world as well. As races, we differ in ascending degree; and the human race stands highest in the scale of life so far.

When, then, it can be shown that sex-distinction in the human race is so excessive as not only to affect injuriously its own purposes, but to check and pervert the progress of the race, it becomes a matter for most serious consideration. Nothing could be more inevitable, however, under our sexuo-economic relation. By the economic dependence of the human female upon the male, the balance of forces is altered. Natural selection no longer checks the action of sexual selection, but co-operates with it. Where both sexes obtain their food through the same exertions, from the same sources, under the same conditions, both sexes are acted upon alike, and developed alike by their environment. Where the two sexes obtain their food under different conditions, and where that difference consists in one of them being fed by the other, then the feeding sex becomes the environment of the fed. Man, in supporting woman, has become her economic environment. Under natural selection, every creature is modified to its environment, developing perforce the qualities needed to obtain its livelihood under that environment. Man, as the feeder of woman, becomes the strongest modifying force in her economic condition. Under sexual selection the human creature is of course modified to its mate, as with all creatures. When the mate becomes also the master, when economic necessity is added to sex-attraction, we have the two great evolutionary forces acting together to the same end; namely, to develope sex-distinction in the human female. For, in her position of economic dependence in the sex-relation, sex-distinction is with her not only a means of attracting a mate, as with all creatures, but a means of getting her livelihood, as is the case with no other creature under heaven. Because of the economic dependence of the human female on her mate, she is modified to sex to an excessive degree. This excessive modification she transmits to her children; and so is steadily implanted in the human constitution the morbid tendency to excess in this relation, which has acted so universally upon us in all ages, in spite of our best efforts to restrain it. It is not the normal sex-tendency, common to all creatures, but an abnormal sex-tendency, produced and maintained by the abnormal economic relation which makes one sex get its living from the other by the exercise of sex-functions. This is the immediate effect upon individuals of the peculiar sexuo-economic relation which obtains among us.

III.

IN establishing the claim of excessive sex-distinction in the human race, much needs to be said to make clear to the general reader what is meant by the term. To the popular mind, both the coarsely familiar and the over-refined, "sexual" is thought to mean "sensual"; and the charge of excessive sex-distinction seems to be a reproach. This should be at once dismissed, as merely showing ignorance of the terms used. A man does not object to being called "masculine," nor a woman to being called "feminine." Yet whatever is masculine or feminine is sexual. To be distinguished by femininity is to be distinguished by sex. To be over-feminine is to be over-sexed. To manifest in excess any of the distinctions of sex, primary or secondary, is to be over-sexed. Our hypothetical peacock, with his too large and splendid tail, would be over-sexed, and no offence to his moral character!

The primary sex-distinctions in our race as in others consist merely in the essential organs and functions of reproduction. The secondary distinctions, and this is where we are to look for our largest excess–consist in all those differences in organ and function, in look and action, in habit, manner, method, occupation, behavior, which distinguish men from women. In a troop of horses, seen at a distance, the sexes are indistinguishable. In a herd of deer the males are distinguishable because of their antlers. The male lion is distinguished by his mane, the male cat only by a somewhat heavier build. In certain species of insects the male and female differ so widely in appearance that even naturalists have supposed them to belong to separate species. Beyond these distinctions lies that of conduct. Certain psychic attributes are manifested by either sex. The intensity of the maternal passion is a sex-distinction as much as the lion's mane or the stag's horns. The belligerence and dominance of the male is a sex-distinction: the modesty and timidity of the female is a sex-distinction. The tendency to "sit" is a sex-distinction of the hen: the tendency to strut is a sex-distinction of the cock. The tendency to fight is a sex-distinction of males in general: the tendency to protect and provide for, is a sex-distinction of females in general.

With the human race, whose chief activities are social, the initial tendency to sex-distinction is carried out in many varied functions. We have differentiated our industries, our responsibilities, our very virtues, along sex lines. It will therefore be clear that the claim of excessive sex-distinction in humanity, and especially in woman, does not carry with it any specific "moral" reproach, though it does in the larger sense prove a decided evil in its effect on human progress.

In primary distinctions our excess is not so marked as in the farther and subtler development; yet, even here, we have plain proof of it. Sex-energy in its primal manifestation is exhibited in the male of the human species to a degree far greater than is necessary for the processes of reproduction,–enough, indeed, to subvert and injure those processes. The direct injury to reproduction from the excessive indulgence of the male, and the indirect injury through its debilitating effect upon the female, together with the enormous evil to society produced by extra-marital indulgence,–these are facts quite generally known. We have recognized them for centuries, and sought to check the evil action by law, civil, social, moral. But we have treated it always as a field of voluntary action, not as a condition of morbid development. We have held it as right that man should be so, but wrong that man should do so. Nature does not work in that way. What it is right to be, it is right to do. What it is wrong to do, it is wrong to be. This inordinate demand in the human male is an excessive sex-distinction. In this, in a certain over-coarseness and hardness, a too great belligerence and pride, a too great subservience to the power of sex-attraction, we find the main marks of excessive sex-distinction in men. It has been always checked and offset in them by the healthful activities of racial life. Their energies have been called out and their faculties developed along all the lines of human progress. In the growth of industry, commerce, science, manufacture, government, art, religion, the male of our species has become human, far more than male. Strong as this passion is in him, inordinate as is his indulgence, he is a far more normal animal than the female of his species,–far less over-sexed. To him this field of special activity is but part of life,–an incident. The whole world remains besides. To her it is the world. This has been well stated in the familiar epigram of Madame de Staël,–"Love with man is an episode, with woman a history." It is in woman that we find most fully expressed the excessive sex-distinction of the human species,–physical, psychical, social. See first the physical manifestation.

To make clear by an instance the difference between normal and abnormal sex-distinction, look at the relative condition of a wild cow and a "milch cow," such as we have made. The wild cow is a female. She has healthy calves, and milk enough for them; and that is all the femininity she needs. Otherwise than that she is bovine rather than feminine. She is a light, strong, swift, sinewy creature, able to run, jump, and fight, if necessary. We, for economic uses, have artificially developed the cow's capacity for producing milk. She has become a walking milk-machine, bred and tended to that express end, her value measured in quarts. The secretion of milk is a maternal function,–a sex-function. The cow is over-sexed. Turn her loose in natural conditions, and, if she survive the change, she would revert in a very few generations to the plain cow, with her energies used in the general activities of her race, and not all running to milk.

Physically, woman belongs to a tall, vigorous, beautiful animal species, capable of great and varied exertion. In every race and time when she has opportunity for racial activity, she developes accordingly, and is no less a woman for being a healthy human creature. In every race and time where she is denied this opportunity,–and few, indeed, have been her years of freedom,–she has developed in the lines of action to which she was confined; and those were always lines of sex-activity. In consequence the body of woman, speaking in the largest generalization, manifests sex-distinction predominantly.

Woman's femininity–and "the eternal feminine" means simply the eternal sexual–is more apparent in proportion to her humanity than the femininity of other animals in proportion to their caninity or felinity or equinity. "A feminine hand" or "a feminine foot" is distinguishable anywhere. We do not hear of "a feminine paw" or "a feminine hoof." A hand is an organ of prehension, a foot an organ of locomotion: they are not secondary sexual characteristics. The comparative smallness and feebleness of woman is a sex-distinction. We have carried it to such an excess that women are commonly known as "the weaker sex." There is no such glaring difference between male and female in other advanced species. In the long migrations of birds, in the ceaseless motion of the grazing herds that used to swing up and down over the continent each year, in the wild, steep journeys of the breeding salmon, nothing is heard of the weaker sex. And among the higher carnivora, where longer maintenance of the young brings their condition nearer ours, the hunter dreads the attack of the female more than that of the male. The disproportionate weakness is an excessive sex-distinction. Its injurious effect may be broadly shown in the Oriental nations, where the female in curtained harems is confined most exclusively to sex-functions and denied most fully the exercise of race-functions. In such peoples the weakness, the tendency to small bones and adipose tissue of the over-sexed female, is transmitted to the male, with a retarding effect on the development of the race. Conversely, in early Germanic tribes the comparatively free and humanly developed women–tall, strong, and brave–transmitted to their sons a greater proportion of human power and much less of morbid sex-tendency.

The degree of feebleness and clumsiness common to women, the comparative inability to stand, walk, run, jump, climb, and perform other race-functions common to both sexes, is an excessive sex-distinction; and the ensuing transmission of this relative feebleness to their children, boys and girls alike, retards human development. Strong, free, active women, the sturdy, field-working peasant, the burden-bearing savage, are no less good mothers for their human strength. But our civilized "feminine delicacy," which appears somewhat less delicate when recognized as an expression of sexuality in excess,–makes us no better mothers, but worse. The relative weakness of women is a sex-distinction. It is apparent in her to a degree that injures motherhood, that injures wifehood, that injures the individual. The sex-usefulness and the human usefulness of women, their general duty to their kind, are greatly injured by this degree of distinction. In every way the over-sexed condition of the human female reacts unfavorably upon herself, her husband, her children, and the race.

In its psychic manifestation this intense sex-distinction is equally apparent. The primal instinct of sex-attraction has developed under social forces into a conscious passion of enormous power, a deep and lifelong devotion, overwhelming in its force. This is excessive in both sexes, but more so in women than in men,–not so commonly in its simple physical form, but in the unreasoning intensity of emotion that refuses all guidance, and drives those possessed by it to risk every other good for this one end. It is not at first sight easy, and it may seem an irreverent and thankless task, to discriminate here between what is good in the "master passion" and what is evil, and especially to claim for one sex more of this feeling than for the other; but such discrimination can be made.

It is good for the individual and for the race to have developed such a degree of passionate and permanent love as shall best promote the happiness of individuals and the reproduction of species. It is not good for the race or for the individual that this feeling should have become so intense as to override all other human faculties, to make a mock of the accumulated wisdom of the ages, the stored power of the will; to drive the individual–against his own plain conviction–into a union sure to result in evil, or to hold the individual helpless in such an evil union, when made.

Such is the condition of humanity, involving most evil results to its offspring and to its own happiness. And, while in men the immediate dominating force of the passion may be more conspicuous, it is in women that it holds more universal sway. For the man has other powers and faculties in full use, whereby to break loose from the force of this; and the woman, specially modified to sex and denied racial activity, pours her whole life into her love, and, if injured here, she is injured irretrievably. With him it is frequently light and transient, and, when most intense, often most transient. With her it is a deep, all-absorbing force, under the action of which she will renounce all that life offers, take any risk, face any hardships, bear any pain. It is maintained in her in the face of a lifetime of neglect and abuse. The common instance of the police court trials–the woman cruelly abused who will not testify against her husband–shows this. This devotion, carried to such a degree as to lead to the mismating of individuals with its personal and social injury, is an excessive sex-distinction.

But it is in our common social relations that the predominance of sex-distinction in women is made most manifest. The fact that, speaking broadly, women have, from the very beginning, been spoken of expressively enough as "the sex," demonstrates clearly that this is the main impression which they have made upon observers and recorders. Here one need attempt no farther proof than to turn the mind of the reader to an unbroken record of facts and feelings perfectly patent to every one, but not hitherto looked at as other than perfectly natural and right. So utterly has the status of woman been accepted as a sexual one that it has remained for the woman's movement of the nineteenth century to devote much contention to the claim that women are persons! That women are persons as well as females,–an unheard of proposition!

In a "Handbook of Proverbs of All Nations," a collection comprising many thousands, these facts are to be observed: first, that the proverbs concerning women are an insignificant minority compared to those concerning men; second, that the proverbs concerning women almost invariably apply to them in general,–to the sex. Those concerning men qualify, limit, describe, specialize. It is "a lazy man," "a violent man," "a man in his cups." Qualities and actions are predicated of man individually, and not as a sex, unless he is flatly contrasted with woman, as in "A man of straw is worth a woman of gold," "Men are deeds, women are words," or "Man, woman, and the devil are the three degrees of comparison." But of woman it is always and only "a woman," meaning simply a female, and recognizing no personal distinction: "As much pity to see a woman weep as to see a goose go barefoot." "He that hath an eel by the tail and a woman by her word hath a slippery handle." "A woman, a spaniel, and a walnut-tree,–the more you beat 'em, the better they be." Occasionally a distinction is made between "a fair woman" and "a black woman"; and Solomon's "virtuous woman," who commanded such a high price, is familiar to us all. But in common thought it is simply "a woman" always. The boast of the profligate that he knows "the sex," so recently expressed by a new poet,–"The things you will learn from the Yellow and Brown, they'll 'elp you an' 'eap with the White"; the complaint of the angry rejected that "all women are just alike!"–the consensus of public opinion of all time goes to show that the characteristics common to the sex have predominated over the characteristics distinctive of the individual,–a marked excess in sex-distinction.

From the time our children are born, we use every means known to accentuate sex-distinction in both boy and girl; and the reason that the boy is not so hopelessly marked by it as the girl is that he has the whole field of human expression open to him besides. In our steady insistence on proclaiming sex-distinction we have grown to consider most human attributes as masculine attributes, for the simple reason that they were allowed to men and forbidden to women.

A clear and definite understanding of the difference between race-attributes and sex-attributes should be established. Life consists of action. The action of a living thing is along two main lines,–self-preservation and race-preservation. The processes that keep the individual alive, from the involuntary action of his internal organs to the voluntary action of his external organs,–every act, from breathing to hunting his food, which contributes to the maintenance of the individual life,–these are the processes of self-preservation. Whatever activities tend to keep the race alive, to reproduce the individual, from the involuntary action of the internal organs to the voluntary action of the external organs; every act from the development of germ-cells to the taking care of children, which contributes to the maintenance of the racial life,–these are the processes of race-preservation. In race-preservation, male and female have distinctive organs, distinctive functions, distinctive lines of action. In self-preservation, male and female have the same organs, the same functions, the same lines of action. In the human species our processes of race-preservation have reached a certain degree of elaboration; but our processes of self-preservation have gone farther, much farther.

All the varied activities of economic production and distribution, all our arts and industries, crafts and trades, all our growth in science, discovery, government, religion,–these are along the line of self-preservation: these are, or should be, common to both sexes. To teach, to rule, to make, to decorate, to distribute,–these are not sex-functions: they are race-functions. Yet so inordinate is the sex-distinction of the human race that the whole field of human progress has been considered a masculine prerogative. What could more absolutely prove the excessive sex-distinction of the human race? That this difference should surge over all its natural boundaries and blazon itself across every act of life, so that every step of the human creature is marked "male" or "female,"–surely, this is enough to show our over-sexed condition.

Little by little, very slowly, and with most unjust and cruel opposition, at cost of all life holds most dear, it is being gradually established by many martyrdoms that human work is woman's as well as man's. Harriet Martineau must conceal her writing under her sewing when callers came, because "to sew" was a feminine verb, and "to write" a masculine one. Mary Somerville must struggle to hide her work from even relatives, because mathematics was a "masculine" pursuit. Sex has been made to dominate the whole human world,–all the main avenues of life marked "male," and the female left to be a female, and nothing else.

But while with the male the things he fondly imagined to be "masculine" were merely human, and very good for him, with the female the few things marked "feminine" were feminine, indeed; and her ceaseless reiterance of one short song, however sweet, has given it a conspicuous monotony. In garments whose main purpose is unmistakably to announce her sex; with a tendency to ornament which marks exuberance of sex-energy, with a body so modified to sex as to be grievously deprived of its natural activities; with a manner and behavior wholly attuned to sex-advantage, and frequently most disadvantageous to any human gain; with a field of action most rigidly confined to sex-relations; with her overcharged sensibility, her prominent modesty, her "eternal femininity,"–the female of genus homo is undeniably oversexed.

This excessive distinction shows itself again in a marked precocity of development. Our little children, our very babies, show signs of it when the young of other creatures are serenely asexual in general appearance and habit. We eagerly note this precocity. We are proud of it. We carefully encourage it by precept and example, taking pains to develope the sex-instinct in little children, and think no harm. One of the first things we force upon the child's dawning consciousness is the fact that he is a boy or that she is a girl, and that, therefore, each must regard everything from a different point of view. They must be dressed differently, not on account of their personal needs, which are exactly similar at this period, but so that neither they, nor any one beholding them, may for a moment forget the distinction of sex.

Our peculiar inversion of the usual habit of species, in which the male carries ornament and the female is dark and plain, is not so much a proof of excess indeed, as a proof of the peculiar reversal of our position in the matter of sex-selection. With the other species the males compete in ornament, and the females select. With us the females compete in ornament, and the males select. If this theory of sex-ornament is disregarded, and we prefer rather to see in masculine decoration merely a form of exuberant sex-energy, expending itself in non-productive excess, then, indeed, the fact that with us the females manifest such a display of gorgeous adornment is another sign of excessive sex-distinction. In either case the forcing upon girl children of an elaborate ornamentation which interferes with their physical activity and unconscious freedom, and fosters a premature sex-consciousness, is as clear and menacing a proof of our condition as could be mentioned. That the girl-child should be so dressed as to require a difference in care and behavior, resting wholly on the fact that she is a girl,–a fact not otherwise present to her thought at that age,–is a precocious insistence upon sex-distinction, most unwholesome in its results. Boys and girls are expected, also, to behave differently to each other, and to people in general,–a behavior to be briefly described in two words. To the boy we say, "Do"; to the girl, "Don't." The little boy must "take care" of the little girl, even if she is larger than he is. "Why?" he asks. Because he is a boy. Because of sex. Surely, if she is the stronger, she ought to take care of him, especially as the protective instinct is purely feminine in a normal race. It is not long before the boy learns his lesson. He is a boy, going to be a man; and that means all. "I thank the Lord that I was not born a woman," runs the Hebrew prayer. She is a girl, "only a girl," "nothing but a girl," and going to be a woman,–only a woman. Boys are encouraged from the beginning to show the feelings supposed to be proper to their sex. When our infant son bangs about, roars, and smashes things, we say proudly that he is "a regular boy!" When our infant daughter coquettes with visitors, or wails in maternal agony because her brother has broken her doll, whose sawdust remains she nurses with piteous care, we say proudly that "she is a perfect little mother already!" What business has a little girl with the instincts of maternity? No more than the little boy should have with the instincts of paternity. They are sex-instincts, and should not appear till the period of adolescence. The most normal girl is the "tom-boy,"–whose numbers increase among us in these wiser days,–a healthy young creature, who is human through and through, not feminine till it is time to be. The most normal boy has calmness and gentleness as well as vigor and courage. He is a human creature as well as a male creature, and not aggressively masculine till it is time to be. Childhood is not the period for these marked manifestations of sex. That we exhibit them, that we admire and encourage them, shows our over-sexed condition.

IV.

HAVING seen the disproportionate degree of sex-distinction in humanity and its greater manifestation in the female than in the male, and having seen also the unique position of the human female as an economic dependant on the male of her species, it is not difficult to establish a relation between these two facts. The general law acting to produce this condition of exaggerated sex-development was briefly referred to in the second chapter. It is as follows: the natural tendency of any function to increase in power by use causes sex-activity to increase under the action of sexual selection. This tendency is checked in most species by the force of natural selection, which diverts the energies into other channels and developes race-activities. Where the female finds her economic environment in the male, and her economic advantage is directly conditioned upon the sex-relation, the force of natural selection is added to the force of sexual selection, and both together operate to develope sex-activity. In any animal species, free from any other condition, such a relation would have inevitably developed sex to an inordinate degree, as may be readily seen in the comparatively similar cases of those insects where the female, losing economic activity and modified entirely to sex, becomes a mere egg-sac, an organism with no powers of self-preservation, only those of race-preservation. With these insects the only race-problem is to maintain and reproduce the species, and such a condition is not necessarily evil; but with a race like ours, whose development as human creatures is but comparatively begun, it is evil because of its check to individual and racial progress. There are other purposes before us besides mere maintenance and reproduction.

It should be clear to any one accustomed to the working of biological laws that all the tendencies of a living organism are progressive in their development, and are held in check by the interaction of their several forces. Each living form, with its dominant characteristics, represents a balance of power, a sort of compromise. The size of earth's primeval monsters was limited by the tensile strength of their material. Sea monsters can be bigger, because the medium in which they move offers more support. Birds must be smaller for the opposite reason. The cow requires many stomachs of a liberal size, because her food is of low nutritive value; and she must eat large quantities to keep her machine going. The size of arboreal animals, such as monkeys or squirrels, is limited by the nature of their habitat: creatures that live in trees cannot be so big as creatures that live on the ground. Every quality of every creature is relative to its condition, and tends to increase or decrease accordingly; and each quality tends to increase in proportion to its use, and to decrease in proportion to its disuse. Primitive man and his female were animals, like other animals. They were strong, fierce, lively beasts; and she was as nimble and ferocious as he, save for the added belligerence of the males in their sex-competition. In this competition, he, like the other male creatures, fought savagely with his hairy rivals; and she, like the other female creatures, complacently viewed their struggles, and mated with the victor. At other times she ran about the forest, and helped herself to what there was to eat as freely as he did.

There seems to have come a time when it occurred to the dawning intelligence of this amiable savage that it was cheaper and easier to fight a little female, and have it done with, than to fight a big male every time. So he instituted the custom of enslaving the female; and she, losing freedom, could no longer get her own food or that of her young. The mother ape, with her maternal function well fulfilled, flees leaping through the forest,–plucks her fruit and nuts, keeps up with the movement of the tribe, her young one on her back or held in one strong arm. But the mother woman, enslaved, could not do this. Then man, the father, found that slavery had its obligations: he must care for what he forbade to care for itself, else it died on his hands. So he slowly and reluctantly shouldered the duties of his new position. He began to feed her, and not only that, but to express in his own person the thwarted uses of maternity: he had to feed the children, too. It seems a simple arrangement. When we have thought of it at all, we have thought of it with admiration. The naturalist defends it on the grounds of advantage to the species through the freeing of the mother from all other cares and confining her unreservedly to the duties of maternity. The poet and novelist, the painter and sculptor, the priest and teacher, have all extolled this lovely relation. It remains for the sociologist, from a biological point of view, to note its effects on the constitution of the human race, both in the individual and in society.

When man began to feed and defend woman, she ceased proportionately to feed and defend herself. When he stood between her and her physical environment, she ceased proportionately to feel the influence of that environment and respond to it. When he became her immediate and all-important environment, she began proportionately to respond to this new influence, and to be modified accordingly. In a free state, speed was of as great advantage to the female as to the male, both in enabling her to catch prey and in preventing her from being caught by enemies; but, in her new condition, speed was a disadvantage. She was not allowed to do the catching, and it profited her to be caught by her new master. Free creatures, getting their own food and maintaining their own lives, develope an active capacity for attaining their ends. Parasitic creatures, whose living is obtained by exertions of others, develope powers of absorption and of tenacity,–the powers by which they profit most. The human female was cut off from the direct action of natural selection, that mighty force which heretofore had acted on male and female alike with inexorable and beneficial effect, developing strength, developing skill, developing endurance, developing courage,–in a word, developing species. She now met the influence of natural selection acting indirectly through the male, and developing, of course, the faculties required to secure and obtain a hold on him. Needless to state that these faculties were those of sex-attraction, the one power that has made him cheerfully maintain, in what luxury he could, the being in whom he delighted. For many, many centuries she had no other hold, no other assurance of being fed. The young girl had a prospective value, and was maintained for what should follow; but the old woman, in more primitive times, had but a poor hold on life. She who could best please her lord was the favorite slave or favorite wife, and she obtained the best economic conditions.

With the growth of civilization, we have gradually crystallized into law the visible necessity for feeding the helpless female; and even old women are maintained by their male relatives with a comfortable assurance. But to this day,–save, indeed, for the increasing army of women wage-earners, who are changing the face of the world by their steady advance toward economic independence–the personal profit of women bears but too close a relation to their power to win and hold the other sex. From the odalisque with the most bracelets to the débutante with the most bouquets, the relation still holds good,–woman's economic profit comes through the power of sex-attraction.

When we confront this fact boldly and plainly in the open market of vice, we are sick with horror. When we see the same economic relation made permanent, established by law, sanctioned and sanctified by religion, covered with flowers and incense and all accumulated sentiment, we think it lovely, innocent, and right. The transient trade we think evil. The bargain for life we think good. But the biological effect remains the same. In both cases the female gets her food from the male by virtue of her sex-relationship to him. In both cases, perhaps even more in marriage because of its perfect acceptance of the situation, the female of genus homo, still living under natural law, is inexorably modified to sex in an increasing degree.

Followed in specific detail, the action of the changed environment upon women has been in given instances as follows: In the matter of mere passive surroundings she has been immediately restricted in her range. This one factor has an immense effect on man and animal alike. An absolutely uniform environment, one shape, one size, one color, one sound, would render life, if any life could be, one helpless, changeless thing. As the environment increases and varies, the development of the creature must increase and vary with it; for he acquires knowledge and power, as the material for knowledge and the need for power appear. In migratory species the female is free to acquire the same knowledge as the male by the same means, the same development by the same experiences. The human female has been restricted in range from the earliest beginning. Even among savages, she has a much more restricted knowledge of the land she lives in. She moves with the camp, of course, and follows her primitive industries in its vicinity; but the war-path and the hunt are the man's. He has a far larger habitat. The life of the female savage is freedom itself, however, compared with the increasing constriction of custom closing in upon the woman, as civilization advanced, like the iron torture chamber of romance. Its culmination is expressed in the proverb: "A woman should leave her home but three times,–when she is christened, when she is married, and when she is buried." Or this: "The woman, the cat, and the chimney should never leave the house." The absolutely stationary female and the wide-ranging male are distinctly human institutions, after we leave behind us such low forms of life as the gypsy moth, whose female seldom moves more than a few feet from the pupa moth. She has aborted wings, and cannot fly. She waits humbly for the winged male, lays her myriad eggs, and dies,–a fine instance of modification to sex.

To reduce so largely the mere area of environment is a great check to race-development; but it is not to be compared in its effects with the reduction in voluntary activity to which the human female has been subjected. Her restricted impression, her confinement to the four walls of the home, have done great execution, of course, in limiting her ideas, her information, her thought-processes, and power of judgment; and in giving a disproportionate prominence and intensity to the few things she knows about; but this is innocent in action compared with her restricted expression, the denial of freedom to act. A living organism is modified far less through the action of external circumstances upon it and its reaction thereto, than through the effect of its own exertions. Skin may be thickened gradually by exposure to the weather; but it is thickened far more quickly by being rubbed against something, as the handle of an oar or of a broom. To be surrounded by beautiful things has much influence upon the human creature; to make beautiful things has more. To live among beautiful surroundings and make ugly things is more directly lowering than to live among ugly surroundings and make beautiful things. What we do modifies us more than what is done to us. The freedom of expression has been more restricted in women than the freedom of impression, if that be possible. Something of the world she lived in she has seen from her barred windows. Some air has come through the purdah's folds, some knowledge has filtered to her eager ears from the talk of men. Desdemona learned somewhat of Othello. Had she known more, she might have lived longer. But in the ever-growing human impulse to create, the power and will to make, to do, to express one's spirit in new forms,–here she has been utterly debarred. She might work as she had worked from the beginning,–at the primitive labors of the household; but in the inevitable expansion of even those industries to professional levels we have striven to hold her back. To work with her own hands, for nothing, in direct body-service to her own family,–this has been permitted,–yes, compelled. But to be and do anything further from this she has been forbidden. Her labor has not only been limited in kind, but in degree. Whatever she has been allowed to do must be done in private and alone, the first-hand industries of savage times.

Our growth in industry has been not only in kind, but in class. The baker is not in the same industrial grade with the house-cook, though both make bread. To specialize any form of labor is a step up: to organize it is another step. Specialization and organization are the basis of human progress, the organic methods of social life. They have been forbidden to women almost absolutely. The greatest and most beneficent change of this century is the progress of women in these two lines of advance. The effect of this check in industrial development, accompanied as it was by the constant inheritance of increased racial power, has been to intensify the sensations and emotions of women, and to develope great activity in the lines allowed. The nervous energy that up to present memory his impelled women to labor incessantly at something, be it the veriest folly of fancy work, is one mark of this effect.

In religious development the same dead-line has held back the growth of women through all the races and ages. In dim early times she was sharer in the mysteries and rites; but, as religion developed, her place receded, until Paul commanded her to be silent in the churches. And she has been silent until to-day. Even now, with all the ground gained, we have but the beginnings–the slowly forced and disapproved beginnings–of religious equality for the sexes. In some nations, religion is held to be a masculine attribute exclusively, it being even questioned whether women have souls. An early Christian council settled that important decision by vote, fortunately deciding that they had. In a church whose main strength has always been derived from the adherence of women, it would have been an uncomfortable reflection not to have allowed them souls. Ancient family worship ran in the male line. It was the son who kept the sacred grandfathers in due respect, and poured libations to their shades. When the woman married, she changed her ancestors, and had to worship her husband's progenitors instead of her own. This is why the Hindu and the Chinaman and many others of like stamp must have a son to keep them in countenance,–a deep-seated sex-prejudice, coming to slow extinction as women rise in economic importance.

It is painfully interesting to trace the gradual cumulative effect of these conditions upon women: first, the action of large natural laws, acting on her as they would act on any other animal; then the evolution of social customs and laws (with her position as the active cause), following the direction of mere physical forces, and adding heavily to them; then, with increasing civilization, the unbroken accumulation of precedent, burnt into each generation by the growing force of education, made lovely by art, holy by religion, desirable by habit; and, steadily acting from beneath, the unswerving pressure of economic necessity upon which the whole structure rested. These are strong modifying conditions, indeed.

The process would have been even more effective and far less painful but for one important circumstance. Heredity has no Salic law. Each girl-child inherits from her father a certain increasing percentage of human development, human power, human tendency; and each boy as well inherits from his mother the increasing percentage of sex-development, sex-power, sex-tendency. The action of heredity has been to equalize what every tendency of environment and education made to differ. This has saved us from such a female as the gypsy moth. It has held up the woman, and held down the man. It has set iron bounds to our absurd effort to make a race with one sex a million years behind the other. But it has added terribly to the pain and difficulty of human life,–a difficulty and a pain that should have taught us long since that we were living on wrong lines. Each woman born, re-humanized by the current of race activity carried on by her father and re-womanized by her traditional position, has had to live over again in her own person the same process of restriction, repression, denial; the smothering "no" which crushed down all her human desires to create, to discover, to learn, to express, to advance. Each woman has had, on the other hand, the same single avenue of expression and attainment; the same one way in which alone she might do what she could, get what she might. All other doors were shut, and this one always open; and the whole pressure of advancing humanity was upon her. No wonder that young Daniel in the apocryphal tale proclaimed: "The king is strong! Wine is strong! But women are stronger!"

To the young man confronting life the world lies wide. Such powers as he has he may use, must use. If he chooses wrong at first, he may choose again, and yet again. Not effective or successful in one channel, he may do better in another. The growing, varied needs of all mankind call on him for the varied service in which he finds his growth. What he wants to be, he may strive to be. What he wants to get, he may strive to get. Wealth, power, social distinction, fame,–what he wants he can try for.

To the young woman confronting life there is the same world beyond, there are the same human energies and human desires and ambition within. But all that she may wish to have, all that she may wish to do, must come through a single channel and a single choice. Wealth, power, social distinction, fame,–not only these, but home and happiness, reputation, ease and pleasure, her bread and butter,–all must come to her through a small gold ring. This is a heavy pressure. It has accumulated behind her through heredity, and continued about her through environment. It has been subtly trained into her through education, till she herself has come to think it a right condition, and pours its influence upon her daughter with increasing impetus. Is it any wonder that women are over-sexed? But for the constant inheritance from the more human male, we should have been queen bees, indeed, long before this. But the daughter of the soldier and the sailor, of the artist, the inventor, the great merchant, has inherited in body and brain her share of his development in each generation, and so stayed somewhat human for all her femininity.

All morbid conditions tend to extinction. One check has always existed to our inordinate sex-development,–nature's ready relief, death. Carried to its furthest excess, the individual has died, the family has become extinct, the nation itself has perished, like Sodom and Gomorrah. Where one function is carried to unnatural excess, others are weakened, and the organism perishes. We are familiar with this in individual cases,–at least, the physician is. We can see it somewhat in the history of nations. From younger races, nearer savagery, nearer the healthful equality of pre-human creatures, has come each new start in history. Persia was older than Greece, and its highly differentiated sexuality has produced the inevitable result of enfeebling the racial qualities. The Greek commander stripped the rich robes and jewels from his Persian captives, and showed their unmanly feebleness to his men. "You have such bodies as these to fight for such plunder as this," he said. In the country, among peasant classes, there is much less sex-distinction than in cities, where wealth enables the women to live in absolute idleness; and even the men manifest the same characteristics. It is from the country and the lower classes that the fresh blood pours into the cities, to be weakened in its turn by the influence of this unnatural distinction until there is none left to replenish the nation.

The inevitable trend of human life is toward higher civilization; but, while that civilization is confined to one sex, it inevitably exaggerates sex-distinction, until the increasing evil of this condition is stronger than all the good of the civilization attained, and the nation falls. Civilization, be it understood, does not consist in the acquisition of luxuries. Social development is an organic development. A civilized State is one in which the citizens live in organic industrial relation. The more full, free, subtle, and easy that relation; the more perfect the differentiation of labor and exchange of product, with their correlative institutions,–the more perfect is that civilization. To eat, drink, sleep, and keep warm,–these are common to all animals, whether the animal couches in a bed of leaves or one of eiderdown, sleeps in the sun to avoid the wind or builds a furnace-heated house, lies in wait for game or orders a dinner at a hotel. These are but individual animal processes. Whether one lays an egg or a million eggs, whether one bears a cub, a kitten, or a baby, whether one broods its chickens, guards its litter, or tends a nursery full of children, these are but individual animal processes. But to serve each other more and more widely; to live only by such service; to develope special functions, so that we depend for our living on society's return for services that can be of no direct use to ourselves,–this is civilization, our human glory and race-distinction.

All this human progress has been accomplished by men. Women have been left behind, outside, below, having no social relation whatever, merely the sex-relation, whereby they lived. Let us bear in mind that all the tender ties of family are ties of blood, of sex-relationship. A friend, a comrade, a partner,–this is a human relative. Father, mother, son, daughter, sister, brother, husband, wife,–these are sex-relatives. Blood is thicker than water, we say. True. But ties of blood are not those that ring the world with the succeeding waves of progressive religion, art, science, commerce, education, all that makes us human. Man is the human creature. Woman has been checked, starved, aborted in human growth; and the swelling forces of race-development have been driven back in each generation to work in her through sex-functions alone.

This is the way in which the sexuo-economic relation has operated in our species, checking race-development in half of us, and stimulating sex-development in both.

V.

THE facts stated in the foregoing chapters are familiar and undeniable, the argument seems clear; yet the mind reacts violently from the conclusions it is forced to admit, and tries to find relief in the commonplace conditions of every-day life. From this looming phantom of the over-sexed female of genus homo we fly back in satisfaction to familiar acquaintances and relatives,–to Mrs. John Smith and Miss Imogene Jones, to mothers and sisters and daughters and sweethearts and wives. We feel that such a dreadful state of things cannot be true, or we should surely have noticed it. We may even perform that acrobatic feat so easy to most minds,–admit that the statement may be theoretically true, but practically false!

Two simple laws of brain action are responsible for the difficulty of convincing the human race of any large general truths concerning itself. One is common to all brains, to all nerve sensations indeed, and is cheerfully admitted to have nothing to do with the sexuo-economic relation. It is this simple fact, in popular phrase,–that what we are used to we do not notice. This rests on the law of adaptation, the steady, ceaseless pressure that tends to fit the organism to the environment. A nerve touched for the first time with a certain impression feels this first impression far more than the hundredth or thousandth, though the thousandth be far more violent than the first. If an impression be constant and regular, we become utterly insensitive to it, and only respond under some special condition, as the ticking of a clock, the noise of running water or waves on the beach, even the clatter of railroad trains, grows imperceptible to those who hear it constantly. It is perfectly possible for an individual to become accustomed to the most disadvantageous conditions, and fail to notice them.

It is equally possible for a race, a nation, a class, to become accustomed to most disadvantageous conditions, and fail to notice them. Take, as an individual instance, the wearing of corsets by women. Put a corset, even a loose one, on a vigorous man or woman who never wore one, and there is intense discomfort, and a vivid conciousness thereof. The healthy muscles of the trunk resent the pressure, the action of the whole body is checked in the middle, the stomach is choked, the process of digestion interfered with; and the victim says, "How can you bear such a thing?"

But the person habitually wearing a corset does not feel these evils. They exist, assuredly, the facts are there, the body is not deceived; but the nerves have become accustomed to these disagreeable sensations, and no longer respond to them. The person "does not feel it." In fact, the wearer becomes so used to the sensations that, when they are removed,–with the corset,–there is a distinct sensation of loss and discomfort. The heavy folds of the cravat, stock, and neckcloth of earlier men's fashions, the heavy horse-hair peruke, the stiff high collar of to-day, the kind of shoes we wear,–these are perfectly familiar instances of the force of habit in the individual.

This is equally true of racial habits. That a king should rule because he was born, passed unquestioned for thousands of years. That the eldest son should inherit the titles and estates was a similar phenomenon as little questioned. That a debtor should be imprisoned, and so entirely prevented from paying his debts, was common law. So glaring an evil as chattel slavery was an unchallenged social institution from earliest history to our own day among the most civilized nations of the earth. Christ himself let it pass unnoticed. The hideous injustice of Christianity to the Jew attracted no attention through many centuries. That the serf went with the soil, and was owned by the lord thereof, was one of the foundations of society in the Middle Ages.

Social conditions, like individual conditions, become familiar by use, and cease to be observed. This is the reason why it is so much easier to criticise the customs of other persons or other nations than our own. It is also the reason why we so naturally deny and resent the charges of the critic. It is not necessarily because of any injustice on the one side or dishonesty on the other, but because of a simple and useful law of nature. The Englishman coming to America is much struck by America's political corruption; and, in the earnest desire to serve his brother, he tells us all about it. That which he has at home he does not observe, because he is used to it. The American in England finds also something to object to, and omits to balance his criticism by memories of home.

When a condition exists among us which began in those unrecorded ages back of tradition even, which obtains in varying degree among every people on earth, and which begins to act upon the individual at birth, it would be a miracle past all belief if people should notice it. The sexuo-economic relation is such a condition. It began in primeval savagery. It exists in all nations. Each boy and girl is born into it, trained into it, and has to live in it. The world's progress in matters like these is attained by a slow and painful process, but one which works to good ends.

In the course of social evolution there are developed individuals so constituted as not to fit existing conditions, but to be organically adapted to more advanced conditions. These advanced individuals respond in sharp and painful consciousness to existing conditions, and cry out against them according to their lights. The history of religion, of political and social reform, is full of familiar instances of this. The heretic, the reformer, the agitator, these feel what their compeers do not, see what they do not, and, naturally, say what they do not. The mass of the people are invariably displeased by the outcry of these uneasy spirits. In simple primitive periods they were promptly put to death. Progress was slow and difficult in those days. But this severe process of elimination developed the kind of progressive person known as a martyr; and this remarkable sociological law was manifested: that the strength of a current of social force is increased by the sacrifice of individuals who are willing to die in the effort to promote it. "The blood of the martyrs is the seed of the church." This is so commonly known to-day, though not formulated, that power hesitates to persecute, lest it intensify the undesirable heresy. A policy of "free speech" is found to let pass most of the uneasy pushes and spurts of these stirring forces, and lead to more orderly action. Our great anti-slavery agitation, the heroic efforts of the "women's rights" supporters, are fresh and recent proofs of these plain facts: that the mass of the people do not notice existing conditions, and that they are not pleased with those who do. This is one strong reason why the sexuo-economic relation passes unobserved among us, and why any statement of it will be so offensive to many.

The other law of brain action which tends to prevent our perception of general truth is this: it is easier to personalize than to generalize. This is due primarily to the laws of mental development, but it is greatly added to by the very relation under discussion. As a common law of mental action, the power to observe and retain an individual impression marks a lower degree of development than the power to classify and collate impressions and make generalizations therefrom. There are savages who can say "hot fire," "hot stone," "hot water," but cannot say "heat," cannot think it. Similarly, they can say "good man," "good knife," "good meat," but they cannot say "goodness," they cannot think it. They have observed specific instances, but are unable to collate them, to generalize therefrom. So, in our common life, individual instances of injustice or cruelty are observed long before the popular mind is able to see that it is a condition which causes these things, and that the condition must be altered before the effects can be removed. A bad priest, a bad king, a bad master, were long observed and pointedly objected to before it began to be held that the condition of monarchy or the condition of slavery must needs bear fruit, and that, if we did not like the fruit, we might better change the tree. Any slaveholder would admit that there were instances of cruelty, laziness, pride, among masters, and of deceit, laziness, dishonesty, among slaves. What the slaveholder did not see was that, given the relation of chattel slavery, it inevitably tended to produce these evils, and did produce them, in spite of all the efforts of the individual to the contrary. To see the individual instance is easy. To see the general cause is harder, requires a further brain development. We, as a race, have long since reached the degree of general intelligence which ought to enable us to judge more largely and wisely of social questions; but here the deteriorating effect of the sexuo-economic relation is shown.

The sex relation is intensely personal. All the functions and relations ensuing are intensely personal. The spirit of "me and my wife, my son John and his wife, us four, and no more," is the natural spirit of this phase of life. By confining half the world to this one set of functions, we have confined it absolutely to the personal. And man that is born of woman is reared by her in this same atmosphere of concentrated personality, and afterward spends a large part of his life in it. This condition tends to magnify the personal and minimize the general in our minds, with results that are familiar to us all. The difficulty of enforcing sanitary laws, where personal convenience must be sacrificed to general safety, the size of the personal grievance as against the general, the need of "having it brought home to us," which hinders every step of public advancement, and our eager response when it is "brought home to us,"–these are truisms. So far as a comparison can be made, women are in this sense more personal than men, more personally sensitive, less willing to "stand in line" and "take turns," less able to see why a general restriction is just when it touches them or their children. This is natural enough, inevitable enough, and only mentioned here as partially explaining why people do not see the general facts as to our over-sexed condition. Yet they are patent everywhere, not only patent, but painful. Being used to them, we do not notice them, or, forced to notice them, we attribute the pain we feel to the evil behavior of some individual, and never think of it as being the result of a condition common to us all.

If we have among us such a condition as has been stated,–a state of morbid and excessive sex-development,–it must, of course, show itself in daily life in a thousand ways. The non-observer, not having seen any such manifestation, concludes that there is none, and so denies the alleged condition,–says it sounds all right, but he does not see any proof of it! Having clearly in mind that, if such proof exists, such commensurate evil in common life as would naturally result from an abnormal sex-distinction, these evils must be so common and habitual as to pass unobserved; and, farther, that, when forced upon our notice, we only see them as matters of personal behavior,–let us, in spite of these hindrances, see if the visible results among us are not such as must follow such a cause, and let us seek them merely in the phenomena of every-day life as we know it, not in the deeper sexual or social results.

A concrete instance, familiar as the day, and unbelievable in its ill effects, is the attitude of the mother toward her children in regard to the sex-relation. With very few exceptions, the mother gives her daughter no warning or prevision of what life holds for her, and so lets innocence and ignorance go on perpetuating sickness and sin and pain through ceaseless generations. A normal motherhood wisely and effectively guards its young from evil. An abnormal motherhood, over-anxious and under-wise, hovers the child to its harm, and turns it out defenceless to the wost of evils. This is known to millions and millions personally. Only very lately have we thought to consider it generally. And not yet do we see that it is not the fault of the individual mother, but of her economic status. Because of our abnormal sex-development, the whole field has become something of an offence,–a thing to be hidden and ignored, passed over without remark or explanation. Hence this amazing paradox of mothers ashamed of motherhood, unable to explain it, and–measure this well–lying to their children about the primal truths of life,–mothers lying to their own children about motherhood!

The pressure under which this is done is an economic one. The girl must marry: else how to live? The prospective husband prefers the girl to know nothing. He is the market, the demand. She is the supply. And with the best intentions the mother serves her child's economic advantage by preparing her for the market. This is an excellent instance. It is common. It is most evil. It is plainly traceable to our sexuo-economic relation.

Another instance of so grossly unjust, so palpable, so general an evil that it has occasionally aroused some protest even from our dull conciousness is this: the enforced attitude of the woman toward marriage. To the young girl, as has been previously stated, marriage is the one road to fortune, to life. She is born highly specialized as a female: she is carefully educated and trained to realize in all ways her sex-limitations and her sex-advantages. What she has to gain even as a child is largely gained by feminine tricks and charms. Her reading, both in history and fiction, treats of the same position for women; and romance and poetry give it absolute predominance. Pictorial art, music, the drama, society, everything, tells her that she is she, and that all depends on whom she marries. Where young boys will plan for what they will achieve and attain, young girls plan for whom they will achieve and attain. Little Ellie and her swan's nest among the reeds is a familiar illustration. It is the lover on the red roan steed she planned for. It is Lancelot riding through the sheaves that called the Lady from her loom at Shalott: "he" is the coming world.

With such a prospect as this before her; with an organization specially developed to this end; with an education adding every weight of precept and example, of wisdom and virtue, to the natural instincts; with a social environment the whole machinery of which is planned to give the girl a chance to see and be seen, to provide her with "opportunities"; and with all the pressure of personal advantage and self-interest added to the sex-instinct,–what one would logically expect is a society full of desperate and eager husband-hunters, regarded with popular approval.

Not at all! Marriage is the woman's proper sphere, her divinely ordered place, her natural end. It is what she is born for, what she is trained for, what she is exhibited for. It is, moreover, her means of honorable livelihood and advancement. But–she must not even look as if she wanted it! She must not turn her hand over to get it. She must sit passive as the seasons go by, and her "chances" lessen with each year. Think of the strain on a highly sensitive nervous organism to have so much hang on one thing, to see the possibility of attaining it grow less and less yearly, and to be forbidden to take any step toward securing it! This she must bear with dignity and grace to the end.

To what end? To the end that, if she does not succeed in being chosen, she becomes a thing of mild popular contempt, a human being with no further place in life save as an attachée, a dependant upon more fortunate relatives, an old maid. The open derision and scorn with which unmarried women used to be treated is lessening each year in proportion to their advance in economic independence. But it is not very long since the popular proverb, "Old maids lead apes in hell," was in common use; since unwelcome lovers urged their suit with the awful argument that they might be the last askers; since the hapless lady in the wood prayed for a husband, and, when the owl answered, "Who? who?" cried, "Anybody, good Lord!" There is still a pleasant ditty afloat as to the "Three Old Maids of Lynn," who did not marry when they could, and could not when they would.

The cruel and absurd injustice of blaming the girl for not getting what she is allowed no effort to obtain seems unaccountable; but it becomes clear when viewed in connection with the sexuo-economic relation. Although marriage is a means of livelihood, it is not honest employment where one can offer one's labor without shame, but a relation where the support is given outright, and enforced by law in return for the functional service of the woman, the "duties of wife and mother." Therefore no honorable woman can ask for it. It is not only that the natural feminine instinct is to retire, as that of the male is to advance, but that, because marriage means support, a woman must not ask a man to support her. It is economic beggary as well as a false attitude from a sex point of view.

Observe the ingenious cruelty of the arrangement. It is just as humanly natural for a woman as for a man to want wealth. But, when her wealth is made to come through the same channels as her love, she is forbidden to ask for it by her own sex-nature and by business honor. Hence the millions of mismade marriages with "anybody, good Lord!" Hence the million broken hearts which must let all life pass, unable to make any attempt to stop it. Hence the many "maiden aunts," elderly sisters and daughters, unattached women everywhere, who are a burden on their male relatives and society at large. This is changing for the better, to be sure, but changing only through the advance of economic independence for women. A "bachelor maid" is a very different thing from "an old maid."

This, then, is the reason for the Andromeda position of the possibly-to-be-married young woman, and for the ridicule and reproach meted out to her. Since women are viewed wholly as creatures of sex even by one another, and since everything is done to add to their young powers of sex-attraction; since they are marriageable solely on this ground, unless, indeed, "a fortune" has been added to their charms,–failure to marry is held a clear proof of failure to attract, a lack of sex-value. And, since they have no other value, save in a low order of domestic service, they are quite naturally despised. What else is the creature good for, failing in the functions for which it was created? The scorn of male and female alike falls on this sexless thing: she is a human failure.

It is not strange, therefore, though just as pitiful,–this long chapter of patient, voiceless, dreary misery in the lives of women; and it is not strange, either, to see the marked and steady change in opinion that follows the development of other faculties in woman besides those of sex. Now that she is a person as well as a female, filling economic relation to society, she is welcomed and accepted as a human creature, and need not marry the wrong man for her bread and butter. So sharp is the reaction from this unlovely yoke that there is a limited field of life to-day wherein women choose not to marry, preferring what they call "their independence,"–a new-born, hard-won, dear-bought independence. That any living woman should prefer it to home and husband, to love and motherhood, throws a fierce light on what women must have suffered for lack of freedom before.

This tendency need not be feared, however. It is merely a reaction, and a most natural one. It will pass as naturally, as more and more women become independent, when marriage is not the price of liberty. The fear exhibited that women generally, once fully independent, will not marry, is proof of how well it has been known that only dependence forced them to marriage as it was. There will be needed neither bribe nor punishment to force women to true marriage with independence.

Along this line it is most interesting to mark the constant struggle between natural instinct and natural law, and social habit and social law, through all our upward course. Beginning with the natural functions and instincts of sex, holding her great position as selecter of the best among competing males, woman's beautiful work is to improve the race by right marriage. The feeling by which this is accomplished, growing finer as we become more civilized, developes into that wide, deep, true, and lasting love which is the highest good to individual human beings. Following its current, we have always reverenced and admired "true love"; and our romances, from the earliest times, abound in praise of the princess who marries the page or prisoner, venerating the selective power in woman, choosing "the right man" for his own sake. Directly against this runs the counter-current, resulting in the marriage of convenience, a thing which the true inner heart of the world has always hated. Young Lochinvar is not an eternal hero for nothing. The personified type of a great social truth is sure of a long life. The poor young hero, handsome, brave, good, but beset with difficulties, stands ever against the wealth and power of the bad man. The woman is pulled hither and thither between them, and the poor hero wins in the end. That he is heaped with honor and riches, after all, merely signifies our recognition that he is the higher good. This is better than a sun-myth. It is a race-myth, and true as truth.

So we have it among us in life to-day, endlessly elaborated and weakened by profuse detail, as is the nature of that life, but there yet. The girl who marries the rich old man or the titled profligate is condemned by the popular voice; and the girl who marries the poor young man, and helps him live his best, is still approved by the same great arbiter. And yet why should we blame the woman for pursuing her vocation? Since marriage is her only way to get money, why should she not try to get money in that way? Why cast the weight of all self-interest on the "practical" plane so solidly against the sex-interest of the individual and of the race? The mercenary marriage is a perfectly natural consequence of the economic dependence of women.

On the other hand, note the effect of this dependence upon men. As the excessive sex-distinction and economic dependence of women increase, so do the risk and difficulty of marriage increase, so is marriage deferred and avoided, to the direct injury of both sexes and society at large. In simpler relations, in the country, wherever women have a personal value in economic relation as well as a feminine value in sex-relation, an early marriage is an advantage. The young farmer gets a profitable servant when he marries. The young business man gets nothing of the kind,–a pretty girl, a charming girl, ready for "wifehood and motherhood"–so far as her health holds out,–but having no economic value whatever. She is merely a consumer, and he must wait till he can "afford to marry." These are instances frequent everywhere, and familiar to us all, of the palpable effects in common life of our sexuo-economic relation.

If there is one unmixed evil in human life, it is that known to us in all ages, and popularly called "the social evil," consisting of promiscuous and temporary sex-relations. The inherent wrong in these relations is sociological before it is legal or moral. The recognition by the moral sense of a given thing as wrong requires that it be wrong, to begin with. A thing is not wrong merely because it is called so. The wrongness of this form of sex-relation in an advanced social state rests solidly on natural laws. In the evolution of better and better means of reproducing the species, a longer period of infancy was developed. This longer period of infancy required longer care, and it was accordingly developed that the best care during this time was given by both parents. This induced a more permanent mating. And the more permanent mating, bound together by the common interests and duties, developed higher psychic attributes in the parents by use, in the children by heredity. That is why society is right in demanding of its constituent individuals the virtue of chastity, the sanctity of marriage. Society is perfectly right, because social evolution is as natural a process as individual evolution; and the permanent parent is proven an advantageous social factor. But social evolution, deep, unconscious, slow, is one thing; and self-conscious, loud-voiced society is another.

The deepest forces of nature have tended to evolve pure, lasting, monogamous marriage in the human race. But our peculiar arrangement of feeding one sex by the other has tended to produce a very different thing, and has produced it. In no other animal species is the female economically dependent on the male. In no other animal species is the sex-relation for sale. A coincidence. Where, on the one hand, every condition of life tends to develope sex in women, to crush out the power and the desire for economic production and exchange, and to develope also the age-long habit of seeking all earthly good at a man's hands and of making but one return; where, on the other hand, man inherits the excess in sex-energy, and is never blamed for exercising it, and where he developes also the age-long habit of taking what he wants from women, for whose helpless acquiescence he makes an economic return,–what should naturally follow? Precisely what has followed. We live in a world of law, and humanity is no exception to it. We have produced a certain percentage of females with inordinate sex-tendencies and inordinate greed for material gain. We have produced a certain percentage of males with inordinate sex-tendencies and a cheerful willingness to pay for their gratification. And, as the percentage of such men is greater than the percentage of such women, we have worked out most evil methods of supplying the demand. But always in the healthy social heart we have known that it was wrong, a racial wrong, productive of all evil. Being a man's world, it was quite inevitable that he should blame woman for their mutual misdoing. There is reason in it, too. Bad as he is, he is only seeking gratification natural in kind, though abnormal in degree. She is not only in some cases doing this, but in most cases showing the falseness of the deed by doing it for hire,–physical falsehood,–a sin against nature.

It is a true instinct that revolts against obtaining bread by use of the sex-functions. Why, then, are we so content to do this in marriage? Legally and religiously, we say that it is right; but in its reactionary effect on the parties concerned and on society at large it is wrong. The physical and psychical effects are evil, though modified by our belief that it is right. The physical and psychical effects of prostitution were still evil when the young girls of Babylon earned their dowries thereby in the temple of Bela, and thought it right. What we think and feel alters the moral quality of an act in our consciousness as we do it, but does not alter its subsequent effect. We justify and approve the economic dependence of women upon the sex-relation in marriage. We condemn it unsparingly out of marriage. We follow it with our blame and scorn up to the very doors of marriage,–the mercenary bride,–but think no harm of the mercenary wife, filching her husband's pockets in the night. Love sanctifies it, we say: love must go with it.

Love never yet went with self-interest. The deepest antagonism lies between them: they are diametrically opposed forces. In the beautiful progress of evolution we find constant opposition between the instincts and processes of self-preservation and the instinct and processes of race-preservation. From those early forms where birth brought death, as in the flowering aloe, the ephemeral may-fly, up to the highest glory of self-effacing love; these two forces work in opposition. We have tied them together. We have made the woman, the mother,–the very source of sacrifice through love,–get gain through love,–a hideous paradox. No wonder that our daily lives are full of the flagrant evils produced by this unnatural state. No wonder that men turn with loathing from the kind of women they have made.

VI.

THE peculiar combination of functions which we are studying has not only an immediate effect on individuals through sex-action, and through the sex-affected individuals upon society, but also an effect upon society through economic action, and through the economically affected society upon the individual.

The economic aspect of the question brings it prominently forward to-day as influencing not only our private health and happiness and the processes of reproduction, but our public health and happiness and the processes of social economics as well. Society is confronted in this age with most pressing problems in economics, and we need the fullest understanding of the factors involved. These problems are almost wholly social rather than physical, and concern not the capacity of a given society to produce and distribute enough wealth for its maintenance, but some maladjustment of internal processes which checks that production and distribution, and developes such irregular and morbid processes of innutrition, malnutrition, and over-nutrition as continually to injure the health and activity of the social organism. Our difficulty about wealth is not in getting it out of the earth, but in getting it away from one another. We have phenomena before us in the development of social economic relations analogous to those accompanying our development in sex-relation.

In the original constituents of society, the human animal in its primitive state, economic processes were purely individual. The amount of food obtained by a given man bore direct relation to his own personal exertions. Other men were to him merely undesirable competitors for the same goods; and, the fewer these competitors were, the more goods remained for him. Therefore, he killed as many of his rivals as possible. Given a certain supply of needed food, as the edible beasts or fruits in a forest, and a certain number of individuals to get this food, each by his own exertions, it follows that, the more numerous the individuals, the less food to be obtained by each; and, conversely, the fewer the individuals, the more food to be obtained by each. Wherefore, the primitive savage slew his fellow-man at sight, on good economic grounds. This is the extreme of individual competition, perfectly logical, and, in its time, economically right. That time is forever past. The basic condition of human life is union; the organic social relation, the interchange of functional service, wherein the individual is most advantaged, not by his own exertions for his own goods, but by the exchange of his exertions with the exertions of others for goods produced by them together. We are not treating here of any communistic theory as to the equitable division of the wealth produced, but of a clear truth in social economics,–that wealth is a social product. Whatever one may believe as to what should be done with the wealth of the world, no one can deny that the production of this wealth requires the combined action of many individuals. From the simplest combination of strength that enables many men to overcome the mammoth or to lift the stone–an achievement impossible to one alone–to the subtle and complex interchange of highly specialized skilled labor which makes possible our modern house; the progress of society rests upon the increasing collectivity of human labor.

The evolution of organic life goes on in geometrical progression: cells combine, and form organs; organs combine, and form organisms; organisms combine, and form organizations. Society is an organization. Society is the fourth power of the cell. It is composed of individual animals of genus homo, living in organic relation. The course of social evolution is the gradual establishment of organic relation between individuals, and this organic relation rests on purely economic grounds. In the simplest combination of primordial cells the force that drew and held them together was that of economic necessity. It profited them to live in combination. Those that did so survived, and those that did not perished. So with the appearance of the most elaborate organisms: it profited them to become a complex bundle of members and organs in indivisible relation. A creature so constructed survived, where the same amount of living matter unorganized would have perished. And so it is, literally and exactly, in a complex society, with all its elaborate specialization of individuals in arts and crafts, trades and professions. A society so constructed survives, where the same number of living beings, unorganized, would perish. The specialization of labor and exchange of product in a social body is identical in its nature with the specialization and exchange of function in an individual body. This process, on orderly lines of evolution, involves the gradual subordination of individual effort for individual good to the collective effort for the collective good,–not from any so-called "altruism," but from the economic necessities of the case. It is as natural, as "selfish" for society so to live, the individual citizens working together for the social good, as for one's own body to live by the hands and feet, teeth and eyes, heart and lungs, working together for the individual good. Social evolution tends to an increasing specialization in structure and function, and to an increasing interdependence of the component parts, with a correlative decrease through disuse of the once valuable process of individual struggle for success; and this is based absolutely on the advantage to the individual as well as to the social body.

But, as we study this process of development, noting with admiration the progressive changes in human relation, the new functions, the extended structure, the increase of sensation in the socialized individuals with its enormous possibilities of joy and healthful sensitiveness to pain, we are struck by the visible presence of some counter-force, acting against the normal development and producing most disadvantageous effects. As in our orderly progress in social sex-development we are checked by the tenacious hold of rudimentary impulses artificially maintained by false conditions, so in our orderly progress in social economic development we see the same peculiar survival of rudimentary impulses, which should have been long since easily outgrown. It is no longer of advantage to the individual to struggle for his own gain at the expense of others: his gain now requires the co-ordinate efforts of these others; yet he continues so to struggle.

In this lack of adjustment between the individual and the social interest lies our economic trouble. An illustration of this may be seen in the manufacture of prepared foods. This is a process impossible to the individual singly, and of great advantage to the individual in collective relation,–a perfectly natural economic process, advantageous in proportion to the amount and quality of the food manufactured. This we constantly find accompanied by a morbid process of dilution and adulteration, by which society is injured, in order that the individual concerned in the manufacture may be benefited. This is as though one of the organs of the body–the liver, for instance–should deliberately weaken or poison its quota of secretion, in order that by giving less it might retain more, and become large and fat individually. An organ can do so, does do so; but such action is morbid action, and constitutes disease. The body is injured, weakened, destroyed, and so ultimately the organ perishes also. It is a false conception of gain, and the falsehood lies in not recognizing the true relation between individual and social interests. This failure to recognize or, at least, to act up to a recognition of social interests, owing to the disproportionate pressure of individual interests, is the underlying cause of our economic distress. As society is composed of individuals, we must look to them for the action causing these morbid social processes; and, as individuals act under the pressure of conditions, we must look to the conditions affecting the individuals for the causes of their action.

In general, under social law, men develope right action; but some hidden spring seems to force them continually into wrong action. We have our hand upon this hidden spring in the sexuo-economic relation. If we had remained on an individual economic basis, the evil influence would have had far less ill effect; but, as we grow into the social economic relation, it increases with our civilization. The sex-relation is primarily and finally individual. It is a physical relation between individual bodies; and, while it may also extend to a psychical relation between individual souls, it does not become a social relation, though it does change its personal development to suit social needs.

In all its processes, to all its results, the sex-relation is personal, working through individuals upon individuals, and developing individual traits and characteristics, to the great advantage of society. The qualities developed by social relation are built into the race through the sex-relation, but the sex-relation itself is wholly personal. Our economic relation, on the contrary, though originally individual, becomes through social evolution increasingly collective. By combining the human sex-relation with the human economic relation, we have combined a permanently individual process with a progressively collective one. This involves a strain on both, which increases in direct proportion to our socialization, and, so far, has resulted in the ultimate destruction of the social organism acted upon by such irreconcilable forces.

As has been shown, this combination has affected the sex-relation of individuals by bringing into it a tendency to collectivism with economic advantage, best exhibited in our distinctive racial phenomenon of prostitution. On the other hand, it has affected the economic relation of society by bringing into it a tendency to individualism with sex-advantage, best exhibited in the frequent practice of sacrificing public good to personal gain, that the individual may thereby "support his family." We are so used to considering it the first duty of a man to support his family that it takes a very glaring instance of bribery and corruption in their interests to shake our conviction; but, as a sociological law, every phase of the prostitution of public service to private gain, from the degradation of the artist to the exploitation of the helpless unskilled laborer, marks a diseased social action. Our social status rests upon our common consent, common action, common submission to the common will. No individual interests can stand for a moment against the interests of the common weal, either when war demands the last sacrifice of individual property and life or when peace requires the absolute submission of individual property and life to common law,–the fixed expression of the people's will. The maintenance of "law and order" involves the very spirit of socialism,–the sinking of personal interest in common interest. All this rests upon the evolution of the social spirit, the keen sense of social duty, the conscientious fulfilment of social service; and it is here that the excessive individualism maintained by our sexuo-economic relation enters as a strong and increasingly disadvantageous social factor. We have dimly recognized the irreconcilability of the sex-relation with economic relations on both sides,–in our sharp condemnation of making the sex-functions openly commercial, and in the drift toward celibacy in collective institutions. Bodies of men or women, actuated by the highest religious impulses, desiring to live nobly and to serve society, have always recognized something antagonistic in the sex-relation. They have thought it inherent in the relation itself, not seeing that it was the economic side which made it reactionary. Yet this action was practically admitted by the continued existence of communal societies where the sex-relation did exist, in an unacknowledged form, and without the element of economic exchange. It is admitted also by the noble and self-sacrificing devotion of married missionaries of the Protestant Church, who are supported by contributions. If the missionary were obliged to earn his wife's living and his own, he could do little mission work.

The highest human attributes are perfectly compatible with the sex-relation, but not with the sexuo-economic relation. We see this opposition again in the tendency to collectivity in bodies of single men,–their comradeship, equality, and mutual helpfulness as compared with the attitude of the same men toward one another, when married. This is why the quality of "organizability" is stronger in men than in women; their common economic interests force them into relation, while the isolated and even antagonistic economic interests of women keep them from it. The condition of individual economic dependence in which women live resembles that of the savage in the forest. They obtain their economic goods by securing a male through their individual exertions, all competing freely to this end. No combination is possible. The numerous girls at a summer resort, in their attitude toward the scant supply of young men, bear an unconscious resemblance to the emulous savages in a too closely hunted forest. And here may be given an economic reason for the oft-noted bitterness with which the virtuous women regard the vicious. The virtuous woman stands in close ranks with her sisters, refusing to part with herself–her only economic goods–until she is assured of legal marriage, with its lifelong guarantee of support. Under equal proportions of birth in the two sexes, every woman would be tolerably sure of obtaining her demands. But here enters the vicious woman, and offers the same goods–though of inferior quality, to be sure–for a far less price. Every one of such illegitimate competitors lowers the chances of the unmarried women and the income of the married. No wonder those who hold themselves highly should be moved to bitterness at being undersold in this way. It is the hatred of the trade-unionist for "scab labor."

On the woman's side we are steadily maintaining the force of primitive individual competition in the world as against the tendency of social progress to develope co-operation in its place, and this tendency of course is inherited by their sons. On the man's side the same effect is produced through another feature of the relation. The tendency to individualism with sex-advantage is developed in man by an opposite process to that operating on the woman. She gets her living by getting a husband. He gets his wife by getting a living. It is to her individual economic advantage to secure a mate. It is to his individual sex-advantage to secure economic gain. The sex-functions to her have become economic functions. Economic functions to him have become sex-functions. This has confounded our natural economic competition, inevitably growing into economic co-operation, with the element of sex-competition,–an entirely different force.

Competition among males, with selection by the female of the superior male, is the process of sexual selection, and works to racial improvement. So far as the human male competes freely with his peers in higher and higher activities, and the female chooses the winner, so far we are directly benefited. But there is a radical distinction between sex-competition and marriage by purchase. In the first the male succeeds by virtue of what he can do; in the second, by virtue of what he can get. The increased power to do, transmitted to the young, is of racial advantage. But mere possessions, with no question as to the method of their acquisition, are not necessarily of advantage to the individual as a father. To make the sexual gain of the male rest on his purchasing power puts the immense force of sex-competition into the field of social economics, not only as an incentive to labor and achievement, which is good, but as an incentive to individual gain, however obtained, which is bad; thus accounting for our multiplied and intensified desire to get,–the inordinate greed of our industrial world. The tournament of the Middle Ages was a brutal sport perhaps, with its human injury, pain, and death, under the cry of: "Fight on, brave knights! Fair eyes are looking on you!" but it represents a healthier process than our modern method of securing the wherewithal to maintain the sex-relation. As so beautifully phrased by Jean Ingelow:–

"I worked afar that I might rear
  A happy home on English soil;
I labored for the gold and gear,
        I loved my toil.

"Forever in my spirit spake
  The natural whisper, 'Well 'twill be
When loving wife and children break

Their bread with thee!'"

Or, put more broadly by Kipling:–

"But since our women must walk gay,
And money buys their gear,
The sealing vessels filch this way
At hazard, year by year."

The contest in every good man's heart to-day between the "ought to" and the "must," between his best work and the "potboiler," is his personal share of this incessant struggle between social interest and self-interest. For himself and by himself he would be glad to do his best work, to be true to his ideals, to be brave in meeting loss for that truth's sake. But as the compromising capitalist says in "Put Yourself in His Place," when his sturdy young friend–a bachelor–wonders at his giving in to unjust demands, "Marriage makes a mouse of a man." To the young business man who falls into evil courses in the sex-relation the open greed of his fair dependant is a menace to his honesty, to his business prospects. On the same man married the needs of his wife often operate in the same way. The sense of the dependence of the helpless creature whose food must come through him does not stimulate courage, but compels submission.

The foregoing distinction should be clearly held in mind. Legitimate sex-competition brings out all that is best in man. To please her, to win her, he strives to do his best. But the economic dependence of the female upon the male, with its ensuing purchasability, does not so affect a man: it puts upon him the necessity for getting things, not for doing them. In the lowest grades of labor, where there is no getting without doing and where the laborer always does more than he gets, this works less palpable evil than in the higher grades, the professions and arts, where the most valuable work is always ahead of the market, and where to work for the market involves a lowering of standards. The young artist or poet or scientific student works for his work's sake, for art, for science, and so for the best good of society. But the artist or student married must get gain, must work for those who will pay; and those who will pay are not those who lift and bear forward the standard of progress. Community of interest is quite possible with those who are working most disinterestedly for the social good; but bring in the sex-relation, and all such solidarity disintegrates,–resolves itself into the tiny groups of individuals united on a basis of sex-union, and briskly acting in their own immediate interests at anybody's or everybody's expense.

The social perception of the evil resultant from the intrusion of sex-influence upon racial action has found voice in the heartless proverb, "There is no evil without a woman at the bottom of it." When a man's work goes wrong, his hopes fail, his ambitions sink, cynical friends inquire, "Who is she?" It is not for nothing that a man's best friends sigh when he marries, especially if he is a man of genius. This judgment of the world has obtained side by side with its equal faith in the ennobling influence of woman. The world is quite right. It does not have to be consistent. Both judgments are correct. Woman affecting society through the sex-relation or through her individual economic relation is an ennobling influence. Woman affecting society through our perverse combination of the two becomes a strange influence, indeed.

One of the amusing minor results of these conditions is that, while we have observed the effect of marriage upon social economic relation and the effect of social economic relation upon marriage,–seeing that the devoted servant of the family was a poor servant of society and that the devoted servant of society was a poor servant of the family, seeing the successful collectivity of celibate institutions,– we have jumped to the conclusion that collective prosperity was conditioned upon celibacy, and that we did not want it. That is why the popular mind is so ready to associate socialistic theories with injury to marriage. Having seen that marriage makes us less collective, we infer conversely that collectivity will make us less married,–that it will "break up the home," "strike at the roots of the family."

When we make plain to ourselves that a pure, lasting, monogamous sex-union can exist without bribe or purchase, without the manacles of economic dependence, and that men and women so united in sex-relation will still be free to combine with others in economic relation, we shall not regard devotion to humanity as an unnatural sacrifice, nor collective prosperity as a thing to fear.

Besides this maintenance of primeval individualism in the growing collectivity of social economic process and the introduction of the element of sex-combat into the narrowing field of industrial competition, there is another side to the evil influence of the sexuo-economic relation upon social development. This is in the attitude of woman as a non-productive consumer.

In the industrial evolution of the human race, that marvellous and subtle drawing out and interlocking of special functions which constitute the organic life of society, we find that production and consumption go hand in hand; and production comes first. One cannot consume what has not been produced. Economic production is the natural expression of human energy,–not sex-energy at all, but race-energy,–the unconscious functioning of the social organism. Socially organized human beings tend to produce, as a gland to secrete: it is the essential nature of the relation. The creative impulse, the desire to make, to express the inner thought in outer form, "just for the work's sake, no use at all i' the work!"–this is the distinguishing character of humanity. "I want to mark!" cries the child, demanding the pencil. He does not want to eat. He wants to mark. He is not seeking to get something into himself, but to put something out of himself. He generally wants to do whatever he sees done,–to make pie-crust or to make shavings, as it happens. The pie he may eat, the shavings not; but he likes to make both. This is the natural process of production, and is followed by the natural process of consumption, where practicable. But consumption is not the main end, the governing force. Under this organic social law, working naturally, we have the evolution of those arts and crafts in the exercise of which consists our human living, and on the product of which we live. So does society evolve within itself–secrete as it were–the social structure with all its complex machinery; and we function therein as naturally as so many glands, other things being equal.

But other things are not equal. Half the human race is denied free productive expression, is forced to confine its productive human energies to the same channels as its reproductive sex-energies. Its creative skill is confined to the level of immediate personal bodily service, to the making of clothes and preparing of food for individuals. No social service is possible. While its power of production is checked, its power of consumption is inordinately increased by the showering upon it of the "unearned increment" of masculine gifts. For the woman there is, first, no free production allowed; and, second, no relation maintained between what she does produce and what she consumes. She is forbidden to make, but encouraged to take. Her industry is not the natural output of creative energy, not the work she does because she has the inner power and strength to do it; nor is her industry even the measure of her gain. She has, of course, the natural desire to consume; and to that is set no bar save the capacity or the will of her husband.

Thus we have painfully and laboriously evolved and carefully maintain among us an enormous class of non-productive consumers,–a class which is half the world, and mother of the other half. We have built into the constitution of the human race the habit and desire of taking, as divorced from its natural precursor and concomitant of making. We have made for ourselves this endless array of "horse-leech's daughters, crying. Give! give!" To consume food, to consume clothes, to consume houses and furniture and decorations and ornaments and amusements, to take and take and take forever,–from one man if they are virtuous, from many if they are vicious, but always to take and never to think of giving anything in return except their womanhood,–this is the enforced condition of the mothers of the race. What wonder that their sons go into business "for what there is in it"! What wonder that the world is full of the desire to get as much as possible and to give as little as possible! What wonder, either, that the glory and sweetness of love are but a name among us, with here and there a strange and beautiful exception, of which our admiration proves the rarity!

Between the brutal ferocity of excessive male energy struggling in the market-place as in a battlefield and the unnatural greed generated by the perverted condition of female energy, it is not remarkable that the industrial evolution of humanity has shown peculiar symptoms. One of the minor effects of this last condition–this limiting of female industry to close personal necessities, and this tendency of her over-developed sex-nature to overestimate the so-called "duties of her position"–has been to produce an elaborate devotion to individuals and their personal needs,–not to the understanding and developing of their higher natures, but to the intensification of their bodily tastes and pleasure. The wife and mother, pouring the rising tide of racial power into the same old channels that were allowed her primitive ancestors, constantly ministers to the physical needs of her family with a ceaseless and concentrated intensity. They like it, of course. But it maintains in the individuals of the race an exaggerated sense of the importance of food and clothes and ornaments to themselves, without at all including a knowledge of their right use and value to us all. It developes personal selfishness.

Again, the consuming female, debarred from any free production, unable to estimate the labor involved in the making of what she so lightly destroys, and her consumption limited mainly to those things which minister to physical pleasure, creates a market for sensuous decoration and personal ornament, for all that is luxurious and enervating, and for a false and capricious variety in such supplies, which operates as a most deadly check to true industry and true art. As the priestess of the temple of consumption, as the limitless demander of things to use up, her economic influence is reactionary and injurious. Much, very much, of the current of useless production in which our economic energies run waste–man's strength poured out like water on the sand–depends on the creation and careful maintenance of this false market, this sink into which human labor vanishes with no return. Woman, in her false economic position, reacts injuriously upon industry, upon art, upon science, discovery, and progress. The sexuo-economic relation in its effect on the constitution of the individual keeps alive in us the instincts of savage individualism which we should otherwise have well outgrown. It sexualizes our industrial relation and commercializes our sex-relation. And, in the external effect upon the market, the oversexed woman, in her unintelligent and ceaseless demands, hinders and perverts the economic development of the world.

VII.

A CONDITION so long established, so widespread, so permanent as the sexuo-economic relation in the human species could not have been introduced and maintained in the course of social evolution without natural causes and uses. No wildest perversion of individual will could permanently maintain a condition wholly injurious to society. Church and State and social forms move and change with our growth, and we cannot hinder them long after the time has come for further progress. Once it was of advantage to society that the sexuo-economic relation should be established. Now that it is no longer of advantage to society, the "woman's movement" has set in; and the relation is changing under our eyes from year to year, from day to day, in spite of our traditional opposition. The change considered in these pages is not one merely to be prophesied and recommended: it is already taking place under the forces of social evolution; and only needs to be made clear to our conscious thought, that we may withdraw the futile but irritating resistance of our misguided will.

The original necessity for this distinctive human phenomenon lies very deep among the primal forces of social life. The relations required to develope individual organisms failed in the further development of the social organism of organization. Co-ordination requires first a common interest, and then the establishment of a common consciousness. It was for the common interest of the individual cells to obtain food easily, and this drew them into closer relation. That relation being established, their co-existence became a unit, an entity, a thing with a conscious life of its own. In the fullest development of the most elaborate organisms, this holds good. There must be a common interest to be served by all this co-ordinate activity; and there must be a common consciousness established, whereby to serve most easily the common interest. When the component cells in our tissues shrink and fail for lack of nutrition, when the several organs weary of inaction and fretfully demand their natural exercise, the man does not say, "My tissues need replenishment" or "My organs need exercise": he says, "I am hungry." And that "I," the personal consciousness directing the smooth interaction of all its parts, goes to work to get food. Social evolution rests on this common interest. Individual men are profited by social relation; and, therefore, they enter into social relation. Such relation requires a common consciousness, through which the co-ordinate action may take place; and the whole course of social development is marked by the constant extension of this social consciousness and its necessary vehicles. Language is our largest common medium, and leads on into literature, which is but preserved speech. The brain of man is the social organ, the organ of communication. Through it flows the current of thought, whereby we are enabled to work together. By so much as our brains hold in common, we can understand each other; and, therefore, some degree of common education is essential to free social development.

At the very beginning of this process, when the human animal was still but an animal,–but an individual,–came the imperative demand for the establishment of a common consciousness between these hitherto irreconcilable individuals. The first step in nature toward this end is found in the relation between mother and child. Where the young, after birth, are still dependent on the mother, the functions of the one separate living body needing the service of another separate living body, we have the overlapping of personality, the mutual need, which brings with it the essential instinct that holds together these interacting personalities. That instinct we call love. The child must have the mother's breast. The mother's breast must have the child. Therefore, between mother and child was born love, long before fatherhood was anything more than a momentary incident. But the common consciousness, the mutual attraction between mother and child, stopped there absolutely. It was limited in range to this closest relation; in duration, to the period of infancy.

The common interest of human beings must be served by racial faculties, not merely by the sex-functions of the female, or the duties of mother to child. As the male, acting through his natural instincts, steadily encroached upon the freedom of the female until she was reduced to the state of economic dependence, he thereby assumed the position of provider for this creature no longer able to provide for herself. He was not only compelled to serve her needs, but to fulfil in his own person the thwarted uses of maternity. He became, and has remained, a sort of man-mother, alone in creation in his remarkable position. By this common interest, existing now not only between mother and child, but between father, mother, and child, grew up a wider common consciousness. And, as the father served the child not through sex-function, but through race-function, this service was open to far wider development and longer duration than the mother's alone could ever have reached. Maternal energy is the force through which have come into the world both love and industry. It is through the tireless activity of this desire, the mother's wish to serve the young, that she began the first of the arts and crafts whereby we live. While the male savage was still a mere hunter and fighter, expressing masculine energy, the katabolic force, along its essential line, expanding, scattering, the female savage worked out in equally natural ways the conserving force of female energy. She gathered together and saved nutrition for the child, as the germ-cell gathers and saves nutrition in the unconscious silences of nature. She wrapped it in garments and built a shelter for its head as naturally as the same maternal function had loved, clothed, and sheltered the unborn. Maternal energy, working externally through our elaborate organism, is the source of productive industry, the main current of social life.

But not until this giant force could ally itself with others and work co-operatively, overcoming the destructive action of male energy in its blind competition, could our human life enter upon its full course of racial evolution. This is what was accomplished through the suppression of the free action of maternal energy in the female and its irresistible expression through the male. The two forces were combined, and he was the active factor in their manifestation. It was one of nature's calm, unsmiling miracles, no more wonderful than where she makes the guileless, greedy bee, who thinks he is merely getting his dinner, serve as an agent of reproduction to countless flowers. The bee might resent it if he knew what office he performed, and that his dinner was only there that he might fulfil that office. The subjection of woman has involved to an enormous degree the maternalizing of man. Under its bonds he has been forced into new functions, impossible to male energy alone. He has had to learn to love and care for some one besides himself. He has had to learn to work, to serve, to be human. Through the sex-passion, mightily overgrown, the human race has been led and driven up the long, steep path of progress, over all obstacles, through all dangers, carrying its accompanying conditions of disease and sin (and surmounting them), up and up in spite of all, until at last a degree of evolution is reached in which the extension of human service and human love makes possible a better way.

By the action of his own desires, through all its by-products of evil, man was made part mother; and so both man and woman were enabled to become human. It was an essential step in our racial progress, a means to an end. It should not be considered as an extreme maternal sacrifice, but as a novel and thorough system of paternal sacrifice,–the male of genus homo coerced by sex-necessity into the expression of maternal energy. The naturally destructive tendencies of the male have been gradually subverted to the conservative tendencies of the female, and this so palpably that the process is plainly to be observed throughout history. Into the male have been bred, by natural selection and unbroken training, the instincts and habits of the female, to his immense improvement. The female was dependent upon the male in individual economic relation. She was in a state of helpless slavery. She was treated with unspeakable injustice and cruelty. But nature's processes go on quite undisturbed among incidents like these. To blend the opposing sex-tendencies of two animals into the fruitful powers of a triumphant race was a painful process, but that does not matter. It was essential, and it has been fulfilled. There should be an end to the bitterness of feeling which has arisen between the sexes in this century. Right as is the change of attitude in the woman of to-day, she need feel no resentment as to the past, no shame, no sense of wrong. With a full knowledge of the initial superiority of her sex and the sociological necessity for its temporary subversion, she should feel only a deep and tender pride in the long patient ages during which she has waited and suffered, that man might slowly rise to full racial equality with her. She could afford to wait. She could afford to suffer.

It is high time that women began to understand their true position, primarily and eternally, and to see how little the long years of oppression have altered it. It was not well for the race to have the conservative processes of life so wholly confined to the female, the male being merely a temporary agent in reproduction and of no further use. His size, strength, and ferocity–admirable qualities in maintaining the life of an individual animal–were not the most desirable to develope the human race. We needed most the quality of co-ordination,–the facility in union, the power to make and to save rather than to spend and to destroy. These were female qualities. Acting from his own nature, man could not manifest traits that he did not possess. Throned as woman's master, chained as her servant, he has, through this strange combination of functions, acquired these traits under the heavy law of necessity. Originally, the two worked on divers lines, he spending and scattering, she saving and building. She was the deep, steady, main stream of life, and he the active variant, helping to widen and change that life, but rather as an adjunct than as an essential. Races there were and are which reproduce themselves without the masculine organism,–by hermaphroditism and parthenogenesis.

As the evolution of species progressed, we find a long series of practical experiments in males,–very tiny, transient, and inferior devices at first, but gradually developed into fuller and fuller equality with the female. In some of the lower forms, as in rotifers, insects, and crustaceans, are found the most inferior males, often none at all; and, where they do exist, they have no use save as an agent in reproduction. The most familiar instance of this is among the bees, where the drone, after fulfilling his functions, dies or is destroyed by the sturdy co-mothers of the hive. The common spider, too, has a tiny male, who tremblingly achieves his one brief purpose, and is then eaten up by his mate. She is the spider, a permanent flycatcher. He is merely a fertilizing agent. The little green aphis, so numerous on our rose-bushes, can reproduce parthenogenetically so long as conditions are good,–while it is warm and there is enough to eat; but, when conditions grow hard, males are developed, and the dual method of reproduction is introduced.

In the two great activities of life, self-preservation and race-preservation, the female in these lower species is better equipped than the male for the first, and carries almost the whole burden of the second. His short period of functional use is as nothing compared to her long period of gestation, and the services she performs, in many cases, in providing for her young after their birth. Race-preservation has been almost entirely a female function, sometimes absolutely so. But it has been proven better for the race to have two highly developed parents rather than to have one. Therefore, sexual equality has been slowly evolved, not only by increasing the importance of the male element in reproduction, but by developing race-qualities in the male, so long merely a reproductive agent. The last step of this process has been the elevation of the male of genus homo to full racial equality with the female, and this has involved her temporary subjection. Both her physical and psychical tendencies have been transplanted into the organism of the male. He has been made the working mother of the world. The sexuo-economic relation was necessary to raise and broaden, to deepen and sweeten, to make more feminine, and so more human, the male of the human race. If the female had remained in full personal freedom and activity, she would have remained superior to him, and both would have remained stationary. Since the female had not the tendency to vary which distinguished the male, it was essential that the expansive forces of masculine energy be combined with the preservative and constructive forces of feminine energy. The expansive and variable male energy, struggling under its new necessity for constructive labor, has caused that labor to vary and progress more than it would have done in feminine hands alone. Out of her wealth of power and patience, liking to work, to give, she toils on forever in the same primitive industries. He, impatient of obstacles, not liking to work, desirous to get rather than to give, splits his task into a thousand specialties, and invents countless ways to lighten his labors. Male energy made to expand itself in performing female functions is what has brought our industries to their present development. Without the economic dependence of the female, the male would still be merely the hunter and fighter, the killer, the destroyer; and she would continue to be the industrious mother, without change or progress.

> "What the children of Israel delighted in making
> The children of Egypt delighted in breaking,"

runs the old rhyme; but there is small gain in such a process. In her subordinate position, under every disadvantage, through the very walls of her prison, the constructive force of woman has made man its instrument, and worked for the upbuilding of the world. As his energy was purely individualistic, and only to be controlled by the power of sex-attraction, it needed precisely this form of union, with its peculiar exaggeration of sex-faculty, to hold him to his task. Woman's abnormal development of sex, restrained and imprisoned by every law, has acted like a coiled spring upon the only free agent in society,–man. Under its intense stimulus he has moved mountains. All the world has seen it; and we have always murmured admiringly, "Oh, 'tis love, 'tis love, 'tis love that makes the world go round." It has done so, indeed, or, at least, has driven man round the world in one long range of struggle and conquest, of work and war. And every man who loves, and says, "I am yours: do with me what you will," knows the power, and honors it.

Human development thus far has proceeded in the male line, under the force of male energy, spurred by sex-stimulus, and by the vast storage battery of female energy suppressed. Women can well afford their period of subjection for the sake of a conquered world, a civilized man. In spite of the agony of the process, the black, long ages of shame and pain and horror, women should remember that they are still here; and, thanks to the blessed power of heredity, they are not so far aborted that a few generations of freedom will not set them abreast of the age. When the centuries of slavery and dishonor, of torture and death, of biting injustice and slow, suffocating repression, seem long to women, let them remember the geologic ages, the millions and millions of years when puny, pygmy, parasitic males struggled for existence, and were used or not, as it happened, like a half-tried patent medicine. What train of wives and concubines was ever so ignominiously placed as the extra husbands carried among the scales of the careful female cirriped, lest she lose one or two! What neglect of faded wives can compare with the scorned, unnoticed death of the drone bee, starved, stung, shut out, walled up in wax, kept only for his momentary sex-function, and not absolutely necessary for that! What Bluebeard tragedy or cruelty of bride-murdering Eastern king can emulate the ruthless slaughter of the hapless little male spider, used by his ferocious mate "to coldly furnish forth a marriage breakfast"! Never once in the history of humanity has any outrage upon women compared with these sweeping sacrifices of helpless males in earlier species. The female has been dominant for the main duration of life on earth. She has been easily equal always up to our own race; and in our race she has been subjugated to the male during the earlier period of development for such enormous racial gain, such beautiful and noble uses, that the sacrifice should never be mentioned nor thought of by a womanhood that knows its power. For the upbuilding of human life on earth she could afford to have her own held back; and–closer, tenderer, lovelier service–for the raising of her fierce sex-mate to a free and gentle brotherhood, for the uplifting of the human soul in her dear son, she could have borne not only this, but more,–borne it smilingly, ungrudgingly, gladly, for his sake and the world's.

And now that the long strain is over, now that the time has come when neither he nor the world is any longer benefited by her subordination, now that she is coming steadily out into direct personal expression, into the joy of racial action in full freedom, of power upon the throne instead of behind it, it is unworthy of this supreme new birth to waste one regret upon the pain that had to be.

Thus it may be seen that, even allowing for the injury to the individual and to society through the check to race-development and the increase of sex-development in woman, with its transmitted effects; allowing, further, that our highly specialized motherhood cannot be shown to be an advantage to humanity,–still it remains true that our sexuo-economic relation, with its effect of carrying on human life through the male side only, in activities driven by intensified sex-energy, has reacted to the benefit of the individual and of the race in many ways, as already suggested: in the extension of female function through the male; in the blending of faculties which have resulted in the possibility of our civilization; in the superior fighting power developed in the male, and its effects in race-conquest, military and commercial; in the increased productivity developed by his assumption of maternal function; and by the sex-relation becoming mainly proportioned to his power to pay for it. Even motherhood has been indirectly the gainer in that, although the mother herself has been checked in direct maternal service, serving the race far more through her stimulation of male activities than through any activities of her own; yet the child has ultimately profited more by the materno-paternal services than he would have done by the maternal services alone.

All this may be granted as having been true in the past. And many, reassured by this frank admission, will ask, if it is so clear that the subjection of woman was useful, that this evil-working, monstrous sexuo-economic relation was after all of racial advantage, how we know that it is time to change. Principally, because we are changing. Social development is not caused by the promulgators of theories and by the writers of books. When Rousseau wrote of equality, free France was being born,–the spirit of the times thrilled through the human mind; and those who had ears to hear heard, those who had pens to write wrote. The condition of chattel slavery, working to its natural end, roused Garrison and Phillips and Harriet Beecher Stowe. They did not make the movement. The period of women's economic dependence is drawing to a close, because its racial usefulness is wearing out. We have already reached a stage of human relation where we feel the strength of social duty pull against the sex-ties that have been for so long the only ties that we have recognized. The common consciousness of humanity, the sense of social need and social duty, is making itself felt in both men and women. The time has come when we are open to deeper and wider impulses than the sex-instinct; the social instincts are strong enough to come into full use at last. This is shown by the twin struggle that convulses the world to-day,–in sex and economics,–the "woman's movement" and the "labor movement." Neither name is wholly correct. Both make a class issue of what is in truth a social issue, a question involving every human interest. But the women naturally feel most the growing healthful pain of their position. They personally revolt, and think it is they who are most to be benefited. Similarly, since the "laboring classes" feel most the growing healthful pain of their position, they as naturally revolt under the same conviction. Sociologically, these conditions, which some find so painful and alarming, mean but one thing,–the increase of social consciousness. The progress of social organization has produced a corresponding degree of individualization, which has reached at last even to women,–even to the lowest grade of unskilled labor. This higher degree of individualization means a sharp personal consciousness of the evils of a situation hitherto little felt. With this higher growth of individual consciousness, and forming a part of it, comes the commensurate growth of social consciousness. We have grown to care for one another.

The woman's movement rests not alone on her larger personality, with its tingling sense of revolt against injustice, but on the wide, deep sympathy of women for one another. It is a concerted movement, based on the recognition of a common evil and seeking a common good. So with the labor movement. It is not alone that the individual laborer is a better educated, more highly developed man than the stolid peasant of earlier days, but also that with this keener personal consciousness has come the wider social consciousness, without which no class can better its conditions. The traits incident to our sexuo-economic relation have developed till they forbid the continuance of that relation. In the economic world, excessive masculinity, in its fierce competition and primitive individualism; and excessive femininity, in its inordinate consumption and hindering conservatism; have reached a stage where they work more evil than good.

The increasing specialization of the modern woman, acquired by inheritance from the ceaselessly specializing male, makes her growing racial faculties strain against the primitive restrictions of a purely sexual relation. The desire to produce–the distinctive human quality–is no longer satisfied with a status that allows only reproduction. In our present stage of social evolution it is increasingly difficult and painful for women to endure their condition of economic dependence, and therefore they are leaving it. This does not mean that at a given day all women will stand forth free together, but that in slowly gathering numbers, now so great that all the world can see, women in the most advanced races are so standing free. Great advances along social lines come slowly, like the many-waved progress of the tide: they are not sudden jumps over yawning chasms.

But, besides this first plain perception that our strange relation is coming to an end, we may see how in its own working it developes forces which must end it or us. The method of action of our peculiar cat's-paw combination of the sexes–the mother-father doing the work of the helpless creature he carries on his back; the parasite mate devouring even when she should most feed–has been this, as repeatedly shown: because of sex-desire the male subjugates the female. Lest he lose her, he feeds her, and, perforce, her young. She, obtaining food through the sex-relation, becomes over-sexed, and acts with constantly increasing stimulus on his sex-activities; and, as these activities are made economic by their relation, she so stimulates industry and all progress. But,–and here is the natural end of an unnatural position, a position that serves its purpose for a time, but holds in itself the seeds of its own destruction,–through the unchecked sex-energy, accumulated under the abnormal pressure of the economic side of the relation, such excess is developed as tends to destroy both individual and race; and such psychic qualities are developed as tend also to our injury and extinction.

A relation that inevitably produces abnormal development cannot be permanently maintained. The intensification of sex-energy as a social force results in such limitless exaggeration of sex-instinct as finds expression sexually in the unnatural vices of advanced civilization, and, socially, in the strained economic relation between producer and consumer which breaks society in two. The sexuo-economic relation serves to bring social development to a certain level. After that level is reached, a higher relation must be adopted, or the lifting process comes to an end; and either the race succumbs to the morbid action of its own forces or some fresher race comes in, and begins the course of social evolution anew.

Under the stimulus of the sexuo-economic relation, one civilization after another has climbed up and fallen down in weary succession. It remains for us to develope a newer, better form of sex-relation and of economic relation therewith, and so to grasp the fruits of all previous civilizations, and grow on to the beautiful results of higher ones. The true and lasting social progress, beyond that which we have yet made, is based on a spirit of inter-human love, not merely the inter-sexual; and it requires an economic machinery organized and functioned for human needs, not sexual ones. The sexuo-economic relation drives man up to where he can become fully human. It deepens and developes the human soul until it is able to conceive and fulfil the larger social uses in which our further life must find expression. But, unless the human soul sees these new forces, feels them, gives way to them in loyal service, it fails to reach the level from which all further progress must proceed, and falls back. Again and again society has so risen, so failed to grasp new duties, so fallen back.

To-day it will not so fall again, because the social consciousness is at last so vital a force in both men and women that we feel clearly that our human life cannot be fully lived on sex-lines only. We are so far individualized, so far socialized, that men can work without the tearing spur of exaggerated sex-stimulus, work for some one besides mate and young; and women can love and serve without the slavery of economic dependence,–love better and serve more. Sex-stimulus begins and ends in individuals. The social spirit is a larger thing, a better thing, and brings with it a larger, nobler life than we could ever know on a sex-basis solely.

Moreover, it should be distinctly understood, as it is already widely and vaguely felt, that the higher development of social life following the economic independence of women makes possible a higher sex-life than has ever yet been known. As fast as the human individual rises in social progress to a certain degree of development, so fast this primitive form of sex-union chafes and drags: it is felt to be unsatisfying and injurious. This is a marked feature in modern life. The long, sure, upward trend of the human race toward monogamous marriage is no longer helped, but hindered by the economic side of the relation. The best marriage is between the best individuals; and the best individuals of both sexes to-day are increasingly injured by the economic basis of our marriage, which produces and maintains those qualities in men and women and their resultant industrial conditions which make marriage more difficult and precarious every day.

The women's movement, then, should be hailed by every right-thinking, far-seeing man and woman as the best birth of our century. The banner advanced proclaims "equality before the law," woman's share in political freedom; but the main line of progress is and has been toward economic equality and freedom. While life exists on earth, the economic conditions must underlie and dominate each existing form and its activities; and social life is no exception. A society whose economic unit is a sex-union can no more develope beyond a certain point industrially than a society like the patriarchal, whose political unit was a sex-union, could develope beyond a certain point politically.

The last freeing of the individual makes possible the last combination of individuals. While sons must bend to the will of a patriarchal father, no democracy is possible. Democracy means, requires, is, individual liberty. While the sexuo-economic relation makes the family the centre of industrial activity, no higher collectivity than we have to-day is possible. But, as women become free, economic, social factors, so becomes possible the full social combination of individuals in collective industry. With such freedom, such independence, such wider union, becomes possible also a union between man and woman such as the world has long dreamed of in vain.

VIII.

IN the face of so vital and radical a change in human life as this change of economic base in the position of women, it is well to call attention more at length to the illustrations of every-day facts in our common lives, which he who runs may read, if he knows how to read. We do not, as a rule, know how to read the most important messages to humanity,–the signs of the times. Historic crises, which have been slowly maturing, burst upon us in sudden birth before the majority of the people imagine that anything is going on. The first gun fired at Fort Sumter was an extreme surprise to most of the citizens of the Union. The Boston Tea Party was, no doubt, an unaccountable piece of insolence to many worthy Britons. When "the deluge" did pour over the noblesse of France, few had been really foreseeing enough to avoid it.

Fortunately, the laws of social evolution do not wait for our recognition or acceptance: they go straight on. And this greater and more important change than the world has ever seen, this slow emergence of the long-subverted human female to full racial equality, has been going on about us full long enough to be observed. It is seen more prominently in this country than in any other, for many reasons.

The Anglo-Saxon blood, that English mixture of which Tennyson sings,– "Saxon and Norman and Dane though we be,"–is the most powerful expression of the latest current of fresh racial life from the north,–from those sturdy races where the women were more like men, and the men no less manly because of it. The strong, fresh spirit of religious revolt in the new church that protested against and broke loose from the old, woke and stirred the soul of woman as well as the soul of man, and in the equality of martyrdom the sexes learned to stand side by side. Then, in the daring and exposure, the strenuous labor and bitter hardship of the pioneer life of the early settlers, woman's very presence was at a premium; and her labor had a high economic value. Sex-dependence was almost unfelt. She who moulded the bullets, and loaded the guns while the men fired them, was co-defender of the home and young. She who carded and dyed and wove and spun was co-provider for the family. Men and women prayed together, worked together, and fought together in comparative equality. More than all, the development of democracy has brought to us the fullest individualization that the world has ever seen. Although politically expressed by men alone, the character it has produced is inherited by their daughters. The Federal Democracy in its organic union, reacting upon individuals, has so strengthened, freed, emboldened, the human soul in America that we have thrown off slavery, and with the same impulse have set in motion the long struggle toward securing woman's fuller equality before the law.

This struggle has been carried on unflaggingly for fifty years, and fast nears its victorious end. It is not only in the four States where full suffrage is exercised by both sexes, nor in the twenty-four where partial suffrage is given to women, that we are to count progress; but in the changes legal and social, mental and physical, which mark the advance of the mother of the world toward her full place. Have we not all observed the change even in size of the modern woman, with its accompanying strength and agility? The Gibson Girl and the Duchess of Towers,–these are the new women; and they represent a noble type, indeed. The heroines of romance and drama to-day are of a different sort from the Evelinas and Arabellas of the last century. Not only do they look differently, they behave differently. The false sentimentality, the false delicacy, the false modesty, the utter falseness of elaborate compliment and servile gallantry which went with the other falsehoods,–all these are disappearing. Women are growing honester, braver, stronger, more healthful and skilful and able and free, more human in all ways.

The change in education is in large part a cause of this, and progressively a consequence. Day by day the bars go down. More and more the field lies open for the mind of woman to glean all it can, and it has responded most eagerly. Not only our pupils, but our teachers, are mainly women. And the clearness and strength of the brain of the woman prove continually the injustice of the clamorous contempt long poured upon what was scornfully called "the female mind." There is no female mind. The brain is not an organ of sex. As well speak of a female liver.

Woman's progress in the arts and sciences, the trades and professions, is steady; but it is most unwise to claim from these relative advances the superiority of women to men, or even their equality, in these fields. What is more to the purpose and easily to be shown is the superiority of the women of to-day to those of earlier times, the immense new development of racial qualities in the sex. No modern proverbs, if we expressed ourselves in proverbs now, would speak with such sweeping, unbroken contumely of the women of to-day as did those unerring exhibitors of popular feeling in former times.

The popular thought of our day is voiced in fiction, fluent verse, and an incessant play of humor. By what is freely written by most authors and freely read by most people is shown our change in circumstances and change in feeling. In old romances the woman was nothing save beautiful, high-born, virtuous, and perhaps "accomplished." She did nothing but love and hate, obey or disobey, and be handed here and there among villain, hero, and outraged parent, screaming, fainting, or bursting into floods of tears as seemed called for by the occasion.

In the fiction of to-day women are continually taking larger place in the action of the story. They are given personal characteristics beyond those of physical beauty. And they are no longer content simply to be: they do. They are showing qualities of bravery, endurance, strength, foresight, and power for the swift execution of well-conceived plans. They have ideas and purposes of their own; and even when, as in so many cases described by the more reactionary novelists, the efforts of the heroine are shown to be entirely futile, and she comes back with a rush to the self-effacement of marriage with economic dependence, still the efforts were there. Disapprove as he may, use his art to oppose and contemn as he may, the true novelist is forced to chronicle the distinctive features of his time; and no feature is more distinctive of this time than the increasing individualization of women. With lighter touch, but with equally unerring truth, the wit and humor of the day show the same development. The majority of our current jokes on women turn on their "newness," their advance.

No sociological change equal in importance to this clearly marked improvement of an entire sex has ever taken place in one century. Under it all, the crux of the whole matter, goes on the one great change, that of the economic relation. This follows perfectly natural lines. Just as the development of machinery constantly lowers the importance of mere brute strength of body and raises that of mental power and skill, so the pressure of industrial conditions demands an ever-higher specialization, and tends to break up that relic of the patriarchal age,–the family as an economic unit.

Women have been led under pressure of necessity into a most reluctant entrance upon fields of economic activity. The sluggish and greedy disposition bred of long ages of dependence has by no means welcomed the change. Most women still work only as they "have to," until they can marry and "be supported." Men, too, liking the power that goes with money, and the poor quality of gratitude and affection bought with it, resent and oppose the change; but all this disturbs very little the course of social progress.

A truer spirit is the increasing desire of young girls to be independent, to have a career of their own, at least for a while, and the growing objection of countless wives to the pitiful asking for money, to the beggary of their position. More and more do fathers give their daughters, and husbands their wives, a definite allowance,–a separate bank account,–something which they can play is all their own. The spirit of personal independence in the women of to-day is sure proof that a change has come.

For a while the introduction of machinery which took away from the home so many industries deprived woman of any importance as an economic factor; but presently she arose, and followed her lost wheel and loom to their new place, the mill. To-day there is hardly an industry in the land in which some women are not found. Everywhere throughout America are women workers outside the unpaid labor of the home, the last census giving three million of them. This is so patent a fact, and makes itself felt in so many ways by so many persons, that it is frequently and widely discussed. Without here going into its immediate advantages or disadvantages from an industrial point of view, it is merely instanced as an undeniable proof of the radical change in the economic position of women that is advancing upon us. She is assuming new relations from year to year before our eyes; but we, seeing all social facts from a personal point of view, have failed to appreciate the nature of the change.

Consider, too, the altered family relation which attends this movement. Entirely aside from the strained relation in marriage, the other branches of family life feel the strange new forces, and respond to them. "When I was a girl," sighs the gray-haired mother, "we sisters all sat and sewed while mother read to us. Now every one of my daughters has a different club!" She sighs, be it observed. We invariably object to changed conditions in those departments of life where we have established ethical values. For all the daughters to sew while the mother read aloud to them was esteemed right; and, therefore, the radiating diffusion of daughters among clubs is esteemed wrong,–a danger to home life. In the period of the common sewing and reading the women so assembled were closely allied in industrial and intellectual development as well as in family relationship. They all could do the same work, and liked to do it. They all could read the same book, and liked to read it. (And reading, half a century ago, was still considered half a virtue and the other half a fine art.) Hence the ease with which this group of women entered upon their common work and common pleasure.

The growing individualization of democratic life brings inevitable change to our daughters as well as to our sons. Girls do not all like to sew, many do not know how. Now to sit sewing together, instead of being a harmonizing process, would generate different degrees of restlessness, of distaste, and of nervous irritation. And, as to the reading aloud, it is not so easy now to choose a book that a well-educated family of modern girls and their mother would all enjoy together. As the race becomes more specialized, more differentiated, the simple lines of relation in family life draw with less force, and the more complex lines of relation in social life draw with more force; and this is a perfectly natural and desirable process for women as well as for men.

It may be suggested, in passing, that one of the causes of "Americanitis" is this increasing nervous strain in family relation, acting especially upon woman. As she becomes more individualized, she suffers more from the primitive and indifferentiated conditions of the family life of earlier times. What "a wife" and "a mother" was supposed to find perfectly suitable, this newly specialized wife and mother, who is also a personality, finds clumsy and ill-fitting,–a mitten where she wants a glove. The home cares and industries, still undeveloped, give no play for her increasing specialization. Where the embryonic combination of cook-nurse-laundress-chambermaid-housekeeper-waitress-governess was content to be "jack of all trades" and mistress of none; the woman who is able to be one of these things perfectly, and by so much less able to be all the others, suffers doubly from not being able to do what she wants to do, and from being forced to do what she does not want to do. To the delicately differentiated modern brain the jar and shock of changing from trade to trade a dozen times a day is a distinct injury, a waste of nervous force. With the larger socialization of the woman of to-day, the fitness for and accompanying desire for wider combinations, more general interest, more organized methods of work for larger ends, she feels more and more heavily the intensely personal limits of the more primitive home duties, interests, methods. And this pain and strain must increase with the advance of women until the new functional power makes to itself organic expression, and the belated home industries are elevated and organized, like the other necessary labors of modern life.

In the meantime, however, the very best and foremost women suffer most; and a heavy check is placed on social progress by this difficulty in enlarging old conditions to suit new powers. It should still be remembered it is not the essential relations of wife and mother which are thus injurious, but the industrial conditions born of the economic dependence of the wife and mother, and hitherto supposed to be part of her functions. The change we are making does not in any way militate against the true relations of the family, marriage, and parentage, but only against those sub-relations belonging to an earlier period and now in process of extinction.

The family as an entity, an economic and social unit, does not hold as it did. The ties between brother and sister, cousins and relatives generally, are gradually lessening their hold, and giving way under pressure of new forces which tend toward better things.

The change is more perceptible among women than among men, because of the longer survival of more primitive phases of family life in them. One of its most noticeable features is the demand in women not only for their own money, but for their own work for the sake of personal expression. Those who object to women's working on the ground that they should not compete with men or be forced to struggle for existence look only at work as a means of earning money. They should remember that human labor is an exercise of faculty, without which we should cease to be human; that to do and to make not only gives deep pleasure, but is indispensable to healthy growth. Few girls to-day fail to manifest some signs of this desire for individual expression. It is not only in the classes who are forced to it: even among the rich we find this same stirring of normal race-energy. To carve in wood, to hammer brass, to do "art dressmaking," to raise mushrooms in the cellar,–our girls are all wanting to do something individually. It is a most healthy state, and marks the development of race-distinction in women with a corresponding lowering of sex-distinction to its normal place.

In body and brain, wherever she touches life, woman is changing gloriously from the mere creature of sex, all her race-functions held in abeyance, to the fully developed human being, none the less true woman for being more truly human. What alarms and displeases us in seeing these things is our funny misconception that race-functions are masculine. Much effort is wasted in showing that women will become "unsexed" and "masculine" by assuming these human duties. We are told that a slight sex-distinction is characteristic of infancy and old age, and that the assumption of opposite traits by either sex shows either a decadent or an undeveloped condition. The young of any race are less marked by sex-distinction; and in old age the distinguishing traits are sometimes exchanged, as in the crowing of old hens and in the growing of the beard on old women. And we are therefore assured that the endeavor of women to perform these masculine economic functions marks a decadent civilization, and is greatly to be deprecated. There would be some reason in this objection if the common racial activities of humanity, into which women are now so eagerly entering, were masculine functions. But they are not. There is no more sublimated expression of our morbid ideas of sex-distinction than in this complacent claiming of all human life-processes as sex-functions of the male. "Masculine" and "feminine" are only to be predicated of reproductive functions,–processes of race-preservation. The processes of self-preservation are racial, peculiar to the species, but common to either sex.

If it could be shown that the women of to-day were growing beards, were changing as to pelvic bones, were developing bass voices, or that in their new activities they were manifesting the destructive energy, the brutal combative instinct, or the intense sex-vanity of the male, then there would be cause for alarm. But the one thing that has been shown in what study we have been able to make of women in industry is that they are women still, and this seems to be a surprise to many worthy souls. A female horse is no less female than a female starfish, but she has more functions. She can do more things, is a more highly specialized organism, has more intelligence, and, with it all, is even more feminine in her more elaborate and farther-reaching processes of reproduction. So the "new woman" will be no less female than the "old" woman, though she has more functions, can do more things, is a more highly specialized organism, has more intelligence. She will be, with it all, more feminine, in that she will develope far more efficient processes of caring for the young of the human race than our present wasteful and grievous method, by which we lose fifty per cent. of them, like a codfish. The average married pair, says the scientific dictator, in all sobriety, should have four children merely to preserve our present population, two to replace themselves and two to die,–a pleasant method this, and redounding greatly to the credit of our motherhood.

The rapid extension of function in the modern woman has nothing to do with any exchange of masculine and feminine traits: it is simply an advance in human development of traits common to both sexes, and is wholly good in its results. No one who looks at the life about us can fail to see the alteration going on. It is a pity that we so fail to estimate its value. On the other hand, the growth and kindling intensity of the social consciousness among us all is as conspicuous a feature of modern life as the change in woman's position, and closely allied therewith.

Never before have people cared so much about other people. From its first expression in greater kindliness and helpfulness toward individual human beings to its last expression in the vague, blind, groping movements toward international justice and law, the heart of the world is alive and stirring to-day. The whole social body is affected with sudden shudders of feeling over some world calamity or world rejoicing. When the message of "Uncle Tom's Cabin" ran from heart to heart around the world, kindling a streak of fire, the fire of human love and sympathy which is latent in us all and longing always for some avenue of common expression, it proved that in every civilized land of our time the people are of one mind on some subjects. Nothing could have so spread and so awakened a response in the Periclean, the Augustan, or even the Elizabethan age; for humanity was not then so far socialized and so far individualized as to be capable of such a general feeling.

Invention and the discoveries of science are steadily unifying the world to-day. The statement is frequently advanced that the minds of the men of Greece or of the great thinkers of the Middle Ages were stronger and larger than the minds of the men of to-day. Perhaps they were. So were the bodies of the megatherium and the ichthyosaurus stronger and larger than the bodies of the animals of to-day. Yet they were lower in the scale of organic evolution. The ability of the individual is not so much the criterion of social progress as that organic relation of individuals which makes the progress of each available to all. Emerson has done more for America than Plato could do for Greece. Indeed, Plato has done more for America than he could do for Greece, because the printing-press and the public school have made thought more freely and easily transmissible.

Human progress lies in the perfecting of the social organization, and it is here that the changes of our day are most marked. Whereas, in more primitive societies, injuries were only felt by the individual as they affected his own body or direct personal interests, and later his own nation or church, to-day there is a growing sensitiveness to social injuries, even to other nations. The civilized world has suffered in Armenia's agony, even though the machinery of social expression is yet unable fully to carry out the social feeling or the social will. Function comes before organ always; and the human heart and mind, which are the social heart and mind, must feel and think long before the social body can act in full expression.

Social sympathy and thought are growing more intense and active every day. In our cumbrous efforts at international arbitration, in the half-hearted alliances and agreements between great peoples, in the linking of humanity together across ocean and mountain and desert plain by steam and electricity, in the establishment of such world-functions as the international postal service,–in these, externally, our social unity has begun to act. In the more familiar field of personal life, who has not seen how unceasingly many of us are occupied in the interests of the community, even to the injury of our own? The rising manifestations of social interest among women were covered with ridicule at first, through such characters as Mrs. Jellyby or Mrs. Pardiggle, although a few women who were so great and so identified with religion and philanthropy as to command respect, women like the saintly Elizabeth Fry, Florence Nightingale, and Clara Barton, escaped. But both belong to the same age, are part of the same phenomena. To-day there is hardly a woman of intelligence in all America, to say nothing of other countries, who is not definitely and actively concerned in some social interest, who does not recognize some duty besides those incident to her own blood relationship.

The woman's club movement is one of the most important sociological phenomena of the century,–indeed, of all centuries,–marking as it does the first timid steps toward social organization of these so long unsocialized members of our race. Social life is absolutely conditioned upon organization. The military organizations which promote peace, the industrial organizations which maintain life, and all the educational, religious, and charitable organizations which serve our higher needs constitute the essential factors of that social activity in which, as individuals, we live and grow; and it is plain, therefore, that while women had no part in these organizations they had no part in social life. Their main relation to society was an individual one, an animal one, a sexual one. They produced the people of whom society was made, but they were not society. Of course, they were indispensable in this capacity; but one might as well call food a part of society because people could not exist without eating as to call women a social factor because people could not exist without being born. Women have made the people who made the world, and will always continue so to do. But they have heretofore had a most insignificant part in the world their sons have made.

The only form of organization possible to women was for long the celibate religious community. This has always been dear to them; and, as to-day many avoid undesired marriage for the sake of "independence," so in earlier times many fled from undesired marriage to the communal independence of the convent. The fondness of women for the church has been based, not only on religious feeling, but on the force of the human longing for co-ordinate interest and activities; and only here could this be gratified. In the church at least they could be together. They could feel in common and act in common,–the deepest human joy. As the church has widened its activities, it has found everywhere in women its most valuable and eager workers. To labor together, together to raise funds for a common end, for a new building or a new minister, for local charities or for foreign missions,–but to labor together, and for other needs than those of the family relation,–this has always met glad response from the struggling human soul in woman. When it became possible to work together for other than religious ends,–when large social service was made possible to women, as in our sanitary commission during the last war,–women everywhere rose to meet the need. The rise and spread of that greatest of women's organizations, the Woman's Christian Temperance Union, has shown anew how ready is the heart of woman to answer the demands of other than personal relations.

And now the whole country is budding into women's clubs. The clubs are uniting and federating by towns, States, nations: there are even world organizations. The sense of human unity is growing daily among women. Not to see it is impossible. Not to watch with pleasure and admiration this new growth in social life, this sudden and enormous re-enforcement of our best forces from the very springs of life, only shows how blind we are to true human advantage, how besotted in our fondness for sex-distinction in excess.

One of the most valuable features of this vast line of progress is the new heroism it is pouring into life. The crumbling and flattening of ambitions and ideals under pressure of our modern business life is a patent fact. We are growing to surrender taste and conscience and honor itself to the demands of business success, prostituting the noblest talents to the most ignoble uses with that last excuse of cowardice,–"A man must live." Into this phase of life comes a new spirit,–the spirit of such women as Elizabeth Cady Stanton and Susan B. Anthony; of Dr. Elizabeth Blackwell and her splendid sisterhood; of all the women who have battled and suffered for half a century, forcing their way, with sacrifices never to be told, into the field of freedom so long denied them,–not for themselves alone, but for one another. We have loudly cried out at the injury to the home and family which are supposed to follow such a course. We have unsparingly ridiculed the unattractive and unfeminine among these vanguard workers. But few have thought what manner of spirit it must take to leave the dear old easy paths so long trodden by so many feet, and go to hew out new ones alone. The nature of the effort involved and the nature of the opposition incurred conduced to lessen the soft charms and graces of the ultra-feminine state; but the women who follow and climb swiftly up the steps which these great leaders so laboriously built may do the new work in the new places, and still keep much of what these strenuous heroes had to lose.

It is not being a doctor that makes a woman unwomanly, but the treatment which the first women medical students and physicians received was such as to make even men unmanly. That time is largely past. The gates are nearly all open, at least in some places; and the racial activities of women are free to develope as rapidly as the nature of the case will allow. The main struggle now is with the distorted nature of the creature herself. Grand as are the women who embody at whatever cost the highest spirit of the age, there still remains to us the heavy legacy of the years behind,–the innumerable weak and little women, with the aspirations of an affectionate guinea pig. The soul of woman must speak through the long accumulations of her intensified sex-nature, through the uncertain impulses of a starved and thwarted class. She must recognize that she is handicapped. She must understand her difficulty, and meet it bravely and firmly.

But this is a matter for personal volition, for subjective consciousness. The thing to see and to rejoice in is that, with and without their conscious volition, with or without the approval and assistance of men, in spite of that crowning imbecility of history,–the banded opposition of some women to the advance of the others,–the female of our race is making sure and rapid progress in human development.

IX.

THE main justification for the subjection of women, which is commonly advanced, is the alleged advantage to motherhood resultant from her extreme specialization to the uses of maternity under this condition.

There are two weak points in this position. One is that the advantage to motherhood cannot be proved: the other, that it is not the uses of maternity to which she is specialized, but the uses of sex-indulgence. So far from the economic dependence of women working in the interests of motherhood, it is the steadily acting cause of a pathological maternity and a decreasing birth-rate.

In simple early times there was a period when women were economically profited by child-bearing; when, indeed, that was their sole use, and, failing it, they were entitled to no respect or profit whatever. Such a condition tended to increase the quantity of children, if not the quality. With industrial development and the increasing weight of economic cares upon the shoulders of the man, children come to be looked upon as a burden, and are dreaded instead of desired by the hard-worked father. They subtract from the family income; and the mother, absolutely dependent upon that income and also overworked in her position of unpaid house-servant, is not impelled to court maternity by any economic pressure. In the working classes–to which the great majority of people belong–the woman is by no means "segregated to the uses of maternity." Among the most intelligent and conscientious workingmen to-day there is a strong feeling against large families, and a consistent effort is made to prevent them.

Lest this be considered as not bearing directly upon the economic position of women, but rather on the general status of the working classes, let us examine the same condition among the wealthy. It is here that the economic dependence of women is carried to its extreme. The daughters and wives of the rich fail to perform even the domestic service expected of the women of poorer families. They are from birth to death absolutely non-productive in goods or labor of economic value, and consumers of such goods and labor to an extent limited only by the purchasing power of their male relatives. In this condition the economic advantage of the woman, married or unmarried, not merely in food and clothes, but in such social advantage as she desires, lies in her power to attract and hold the devotion of men; and this power is not the power of maternity. On the contrary, maternity, by lowering the personal charms and occupying the time of the mother, fails to bring her the pleasure and profit obtainable by the woman who is not a mother. It is through the sex-relation minus its natural consequence that she profits most; and, therefore, the force of economic advantage acts against maternity instead of toward it.

In the last extreme this is clear to all in the full flower of the sexuo-economic relation,–prostitution, than which nothing runs more absolutely counter to the improvement of the race through maternity. Specialization to uses of maternity, as in the queen bee, is one thing. Specialization to uses of sex without maternity is quite another. Yet this popular opinion, that we as a race are greatly benefited by having all our women saved from direct economic activity, and so allowed to concentrate all their energies on the beautiful work of motherhood, remains strong among us.

In The Forum for November, 1888, Lester F. Ward published a paper called "Our Better Halves," in which was clearly shown the biological supremacy of the female sex. This naturally aroused much discussion; and in an answering article, "Woman's Place in Nature" (The Forum, May, 1889), Mr. Grant Allen very thoroughly states the general view on this subject. He says of woman: "I believe it to be true that she is very much less the race than man; that she is, indeed, not even half the race at present, but rather a part of it told specially off for the continuance of the species, just as truly as drones or male spiders are parts of their species told off for the performance of male-functions, or as 'rotund' honey ants are individual insects told off to act as living honey jars to the community. She is the sex sacrificed to reproductive necessities."

Since biological facts point to the very gradual introduction and development of the male organism solely as a reproductive necessity, and since women are sacrificed not to reproductive necessities, but to a most unnecessary and injurious degree of sex-indulgence under economic necessity, such a statement as Mr. Grant Allen's has elements of humor. The opinion is held, however, not only by the special students of biology and sociology, but by the general public, and demands most careful attention. Those holding such a view may admit the over-development of sex consequent upon the economic relation between men and women, and the train of evils, individual and social, following that over-development. They may even admit, further, something of the alleged injury to economic evolution. But they will claim in answer that these morbid conditions are essential to human progress, and that the good to humanity through the segregation of the female to the uses of maternity overbalances the evil, great as this is; also, conversely, that the gain to the individual and to society to be obtained by the economic freedom of the female would be more than offset by the loss to the race caused by the removal of our highly specialized motherhood.

To meet this, it is necessary to show that our highly specialized motherhood is not so advantageous as believed; that it is below rather than above the efficacy of motherhood in other species; that its deficiency is due to the sexuo-economic relation; that the restoration of economic freedom to the female will improve motherhood; and, finally, to indicate in some sort the lines of social and individual development along which this improvement may be "practically" manifested.

In approaching this subject, we need something of special mental preparation. We need to realize that our ideas upon this theme are peculiarly colored by prejudice, that in no other field of thought are we so blinded by our emotions. We have felt more on this subject than on any other, and thought less. We have also felt much on the relation of the sexes; but it has been made a subject of study, of comparison, of speculation. There are differences of feeling on the sex question, but as to motherhood none. Here and there, to be sure, some isolated philosopher, a Plato, a Rousseau, dares advance some thought on this ground; but, on the whole, no theme of commensurate importance has been so little studied. More sacred than religion, more binding than the law, more habitual than methods of eating, we are each and all born into the accepted idea of motherhood and trained in it; and in maturity we hand it down unquestioningly. A man may question the purposes and methods of his God with less danger of outcry against him than if he dare to question the purposes and methods of his mother. This matriolatry is a sentiment so deep-seated, wide-spread, and long-established as to be dominant in every class of minds. It is so associated with our religious instincts, on the one hand, and our sex-instincts, on the other, both of which we have long been forbidden to discuss,–the one being too holy and the other too unholy,–that it is well-nigh impossible to think clearly and dispassionately on the subject. It is easy to understand why we are so triple-plated with prejudice in the case.

The instinct that draws the child to its mother is exactly as old as the instinct that draws the mother to her child; and that dates back to the period when the young first needed care,–among the later reptiles, perhaps. This tie has lasted unbroken through the whole line of progression, and is stronger with us than with any other creature, because in our social evolution the parent is of advantage to the child not only through its entire life, but even after death, by our laws of inheritance. So early, so radically important, so long accumulated an animal instinct, added to by social law, is a great force. Besides this, we must reckon with our long period of ancestor worship. This finally changed the hideous concepts of early idolaters into the idea of parental divinity; for, having first made a god of their father, they then made a father of God, and this deep religious feeling has added much to the heavy weight of instinct. Parental government, too, absolute in the patriarchal period, has added further to our devout, blind faith in parenthood until it is lèse-majesté to question its right fulfilment. Two most interesting developments are to be noted along this line. One is that the height of filial devotion was reached in the patriarchal age; when the father was the sole governor and feeder of the family, and could slay or sell his child at will; and that this relic of ancestor worship has steadily declined with the extension of government, until, in our democracy, with the fullest development of individual liberty and responsibility, is found the lowest degree of filial reverence and submission. Its place is taken, to our great gain, by such familiar, loving intercourse between parent and child as was utterly incompatible with the grovelling attitude of children in earlier times.

The other is the gradual swing from supreme devotion to the father, "the author of my being," as the child used to consider him, to our modern mother-worship. The dying soldier on the battlefield thinks of his mother, longs for her, not for his father. The traveller and exile dreams of his mother's care, his mother's doughnuts. The pathos of the popular tale to-day is in bringing the prodigal back to his mother, not to his father. If the original prodigal had a mother, she was probably busy in cooking the fatted calf. If to-day's prodigal has a father, he is merely engaged in paying for the veal. Our tenderest love, our deepest reverence, our fiercest resentment of insult, all centre about the mother to-day rather than about the father; and this is a strong proof that the recognition of woman's real power and place in life grow upon us just as our minds grow able to perceive it. Nothing can ever exceed the truth as to the value of the mother. Our instinct is a right one, as all deep-seated social instincts are; but about it has grown up a mass of falsehoods and absurdities such as always tend to confuse and impede the progress of great truths.

As the main agent in reproduction, the mother is most to be venerated on basic physiological grounds. As the main agent in developing love, the great human condition, she is the fountain of all our growth. As the beginner of industry, she is again a source of progress. As the first and final educator, she outwardly moulds what she has inwardly made; and, as she is the visible, tangible, lovable, living type of all this, the being in whose person is expressed the very sum of good to the individual, it is no wonder that our strongest, deepest, tenderest feelings cluster about the great word "mother."

Fully recognizing all this, it yet remains open to us to turn the light of science and the honest labor of thought upon this phase of human life as upon any other; to lay aside our feelings, and use our reason; to discover if even here we are justified in leaving the most important work of individual life to the methods of primitive instinct. Motherhood is but a process of life, and open to study as all processes of life are open. Among unconscious, early forms it fulfils its mission by a simple instinct. In the consciousness and complexity of human life it demands far more numerous and varied forces for its right fulfilment. It is with us a conscious process,–a process rife with consequences for good or evil. With this voluntary power come new responsibility and a need for new methods,–a need not merely to consider whether or not we will enter upon the duties of maternity, but how best we can fulfil them.

Motherhood, like every other natural process, is to be measured by its results. It is good or evil as it serves its purpose. Human motherhood must be judged as it serves its purpose to the human race. Primarily, its purpose is to reproduce the race by reproducing the individual; secondarily, to improve the race by improving the individual. The mere office of reproduction is as well performed by the laying of eggs to be posthumously hatched as by many years of exquisite devotion; but in the improvement of the species we come to other requirements. The functions of motherhood have been evolved as naturally as the functions of nutrition, and each stage of development has brought new duties to the mother. The mother bird must brood her young, the mother cow must suckle them, the mother cat must hunt for them; and, in every varied service which the mother gives, its value is to be measured by its effect upon the young. To perform that which is most good for the young of the species is the measure of right motherhood, and that which is most good for the young is what will help them to a better maturity than that of their parents. To leave in the world a creature better than its parent: this is the purpose of right motherhood.

In the human race this purpose is served by two processes: first, by the simple individual function of reproduction, of which all care and nursing are but an extension; and, second, by the complex social function of education. This was primarily a maternal process, and therefore individual; but it has long since become a racial rather than an individual function, and bears no relation to sex or other personal limitation. The young of the human race require for their best development not only the love and care of the mother, but the care and instruction of many besides their mother. So largely is this true that it may be said in extreme terms that it would be better for a child to-day to be left absolutely without mother or family of any sort, in the city of Boston, for instance, than to be supplied with a large and affectionate family and be planted with them in Darkest Africa.

Human functions are race-functions, social functions; and education is one of them. The duty of the human mother, and the measure of its right or wrong fulfilment, are to be judged along these two main lines, reproduction and education. As we have no species above us with which to compare our motherhood, we must measure by those below us. We must show improvement upon them in this function which we all hold in common.

Does the human mother succeed better than others of her order, mammalia, in the reproduction of the species? Does she bring forth and rear her young more perfectly than lower mothers? They, being less conscious, act simply under instinct, mating in their season, bringing forth young in their season, nursing, guarding, defending as best they may; and they leave in the world behind them creatures as good, or better, than their mothers. Of wild animals we have few reliable statistics, and of tame ones it is difficult to detach their natural processes from our interference therewith. But in both the simple maintenance of species shows that motherhood at least reproduces fairly well; and in those we breed for our advantage the wonderful possibilities of race-development through this process are made apparent. How do we, with the human brain and the human conscience, rich in the power and wisdom of our dominant race,–how do we, as mothers, compare with our forerunners?

Human motherhood is more pathological than any other, more morbid, defective, irregular, diseased. Human childhood is similarly pathological. We, as animals, are very inferior animals in this particular. When we take credit to ourselves for the sublime devotion with which we face "the perils of maternity," and boast of "going down to the gates of death" for our children, we should rather take shame to ourselves for bringing these perils upon both mother and child. The gates of death? They are the gates of life to the unborn; and there is no death there save what we, the mothers, by our unnatural lives, have brought upon our own children. Gates of death, indeed, to the thousands of babies late-born, prematurely born, misborn, and stillborn for lack of right motherhood. In the primal physical functions of maternity the human female cannot show that her supposed specialization to these uses has improved her fulfilment of them, rather the opposite. The more freely the human mother mingles in the natural industries of a human creature, as in the case of the savage woman, the peasant woman, the working-woman everywhere who is not overworked, the more rightly she fulfils these functions.

The more absolutely woman is segregated to sex-functions only, cut off from all economic use and made wholly dependent on the sex-relation as means of livelihood, the more pathological does her motherhood become. The over-development of sex caused by her economic dependence on the male reacts unfavorably upon her essential duties. She is too female for perfect motherhood! Her excessive specialization in the secondary sexual characteristics is a detrimental element in heredity. Small, weak, soft, ill-proportioned women do not tend to produce large, strong, sturdy, well-made men or women. When Frederic the Great wanted grenadiers of great size, he married big men to big women,–not to little ones. The female segregated to the uses of sex alone naturally deteriorates in racial development, and naturally transmits that deterioration to her offspring. The human mother, in the processes of reproduction, shows no gain in efficiency over the lower animals, but rather a loss, and so far presents no evidence to prove that her specialization to sex is of any advantage to her young. The mother of a dead baby or the baby of a dead mother; the sick baby, the crooked baby, the idiot baby; the exhausted, nervous, prematurely aged mother,–these are not uncommon among us; and they do not show much progress in our motherhood.

Since we cannot justify the human method of maternity in the physical processes of reproduction, can we prove its advantages in the other branch, education? Though the mother be sickly and the child the same, will not her loving care more than make up for it? Will not the tender devotion of the mother, and her unflagging attendance upon the child, render human motherhood sufficiently successful in comparison with that of other species to justify our peculiar method? We must now show that our motherhood, in its usually accepted sense, the "care" of the child (more accurately described as education), is of a superior nature.

Here, again, we lack the benefit of comparison. No other animal species is required to care for its young so long, to teach it so much. So far as they have it to do, they do it well. The hen with her brood is an accepted model of motherhood in this respect. She not only lays eggs and hatches them, but educates and protects her young so far as it is necessary. But beyond such simple uses as this we have no standard of comparison for educative motherhood. We can only study it among ourselves, comparing the child left motherless with the child mothered, the child with a mother and nothing else with the child whose mother is helped by servants and teachers, the child with what we recognize as a superior mother to the child with an inferior mother. This last distinction, a comparison between mothers, is of great value. We have tacitly formulated a certain vague standard of human motherhood, and loosely apply it, especially in the epithets "natural" and "unnatural" mother.

But these terms again show how prone we still are to consider the whole field of maternal action as one of instinct rather than of reason, as a function rather than a service. We do have a standard, however, loose and vague as it is; and even by that standard it is painful to see how many human mothers fail. Ask yourselves honestly how many of the mothers whose action toward their children confronts you in street and shop and car and boat, in hotel and boarding-house and neighboring yard,–how many call forth favorable comment compared with those you judge unfavorably? Consider not the rosy ideal of motherhood you have in your mind, but the coarse, hard facts of motherhood as you see them, and hear them, in daily life.

Motherhood in its fulfilment of educational duty can be measured only by its effects. If we take for a standard the noble men and women whose fine physique and character we so fondly attribute to "a devoted mother," what are we to say of the motherhood which has filled the world with the ignoble men and women, of depraved physique and character? If the good mother makes the good man, how about the bad ones? When we see great men and women, we give credit to their mothers. When we see inferior men and women,–and that is a common circumstance,–no one presumes to question the motherhood which has produced them. When it comes to congenital criminality, we are beginning to murmur something about "heredity"; and, to meet gross national ignorance, we do demand a better system of education. But no one presumes to suggest that the mothering of mankind could be improved upon; and yet there is where the responsibility really lies. If our human method of reproduction is defective, let the mother answer. She is the main factor in reproduction. If our human method of education is defective, let the mother answer. She is the main factor in education.

To this it is bitterly objected that such a claim omits the father and his responsibility. When the mother of the world is in her right place and doing her full duty, she will have no ground of complaint against the father. In the first place, she will make better men. In the second, she will hold herself socially responsible for the choice of a right father for her children. In the third place, as an economic free agent, she will do half duty in providing for the child. Men who are not equal to good fatherhood under such conditions will have no chance to become fathers, and will die with general pity instead of living with general condemnation. In his position, doing all the world's work, all the father's, and half the mother's, man has made better shift to achieve the impossible than woman has in hers. She has been supposed to have no work or care on earth save as mother. She has really had the work of the mother and that of the world's house service besides. But she has surely had as much time and strength to give to motherhood as man to fatherhood; and not until she can show that the children of the world are as well mothered as they are well fed can she cast on him the blame for our general deficiency.

There is no personal blame to be laid on either party. The sexuo-economic relation has its inevitable ill-effects on both motherhood and fatherhood. But it is to the mother that the appeal must be made to change this injurious relation. Having the deeper sense of duty to the young, the larger love, she must come to feel how her false position hurts her motherhood, and for her children's sake break away from it. Of man and his fatherhood she can make what she will.

The duty of the mother is first to produce children as good as or better than herself; to hand down the constitution and character of those behind her the better for her stewardship; to build up and improve the human race through her enormous power as mother; to make better people. This being done, it is then the duty of the mother, the human mother, so to educate her children as to complete what bearing and nursing have only begun. She carries the child nine months in her body, two years in her arms, and as long as she lives in her heart and mind. The education of the young is a tremendous factor in human reproduction. A right motherhood should be able to fulfil this great function perfectly. It should understand with an ever-growing power the best methods of developing, strengthening, and directing the child's faculties of body and mind, so that each generation, reaching maturity, would start clear of the last, and show a finer, fuller growth, both physically and mentally, than the preceding. That humanity does slowly improve is not here denied; but, granting our gradual improvement, is it all that we could make? And is the gain due to a commensurate improvement in motherhood?

To both we must say no. When we see how some families improve, while others deteriorate, and how uncertain and irregular is such improvement as appears, we know that we could make better progress if all children had the same rich endowment and wise care that some receive. And, when we see how much of our improvement is due to gains made in hygienic knowledge, in public provision for education and sanitary regulation, none of which has been accomplished by mothers, we are forced to see that whatever advance the race has made is not exclusively attributable to motherhood. The human mother does less for her young, both absolutely and proportionately, than any kind of mother on earth. She does not obtain food for them, nor covering, nor shelter, nor protection, nor defence. She does not educate them beyond the personal habits required in the family circle and in her limited range of social life. The necessary knowledge of the world, so indispensable to every human being, she cannot give, because she does not possess it. All this provision and education are given by other hands and brains than hers. Neither does the amount of physical care and labor bestowed on the child by its mother warrant her claims to superiority in motherhood: this is but a part of our idealism of the subject.

The poor man's wife has far too much of other work to do to spend all her time in waiting on her children. The rich man's wife could do it, but does not, partly because she hires some one to do it for her, and partly because she, too, has other duties to occupy her time. Only in isolated cases do we find a mother deputing all other service to others, and concentrating her energies on feeding, clothing, washing, dressing, and, as far as may be, educating her own child. When such cases are found, it remains to be shown that the child so reared is proportionately benefited by this unremittent devotion of its mother. On the contrary, the best service and education a child can receive involve the accumulated knowledge and exchanged activities of thousands upon thousands besides his mother,–the fathers of the race.

There does not appear, in the care and education of the child as given by the mother, any special superiority in human maternity. Measuring woman first in direct comparison of her reproductive processes with those of other animals, she does not fulfil this function so easily or so well as they. Measuring her educative processes by inter-personal comparison, the few admittedly able mothers with the many painfully unable ones, she seems more lacking, if possible, than in the other branch. The gain in human education thus far has not been acquired or distributed through the mother, but through men and single women; and there is nothing in the achievements of human motherhood to prove that it is for the advantage of the race to have women give all their time to it. Giving all their time to it does not improve it either in quantity or quality. The woman who works is usually a better reproducer than the woman who does not. And the woman who does not work is not proportionately a better educator.

An extra-terrestrial sociologist, studying human life and hearing for the first time of our so-called "maternal sacrifice" as a means of benefiting the species, might be touched and impressed by the idea. "How beautiful!" he would say. "How exquisitely pathetic and tender! One-half of humanity surrendering all other human interests and activities to concentrate its time, strength, and devotion upon the functions of maternity! To bear and rear the majestic race to which they can never fully belong! To live vicariously forever, through their sons, the daughters being only another vicarious link! What a supreme and magnificent martyrdom!" And he would direct his researches toward discovering what system was used to develope and perfect this sublime consecration of half the race to the perpetuation of the other half. He would view with intense and pathetic interest the endless procession of girls, born human as their brothers were, but marked down at once as "female–abortive type–only use to produce males." He would expect to see this "sex sacrificed to reproductive necessities," yet gifted with human consciousness and intelligence, rise grandly to the occasion, and strive to fit itself in every way for its high office. He would expect to find society commiserating the sacrifice, and honoring above all the glorious creature whose life was to be sunk utterly in the lives of others, and using every force properly to rear and fully to fit these functionaries for their noble office. Alas for the extra-terrestrial sociologist and his natural expectations! After exhaustive study, finding nothing of these things, he would return to Mars or Saturn or wherever he came from, marvelling within himself at the vastness of the human paradox.

If the position of woman is to be justified by the doctrine of maternal sacrifice, surely society, or the individual, or both, would make some preparation for it. No such preparation is made. Society recognizes no such function. Premiums have been sometimes paid for large numbers of children, but they were paid to the fathers of them. The elaborate social machinery which constitutes our universal marriage market has no department to assist or advance motherhood. On the contrary, it is directly inimical to it, so that in our society life motherhood means direct loss, and is avoided by the social devotee. And the individual? Surely here right provision will be made. Young women, glorying in their prospective duties, their sacred and inalienable office, their great sex-martyrdom to race-advantage, will be found solemnly preparing for this work. What do we find? We find our young women reared in an attitude which is absolutely unconscious of and often injurious to their coming motherhood,–an irresponsible, indifferent, ignorant class of beings, so far as motherhood is concerned. They are fitted to attract the other sex for economic uses or, at most, for mutual gratification, but not for motherhood. They are reared in unbroken ignorance of their supposed principal duties, knowing nothing of these duties till they enter upon them.

This is as though all men were to be soldiers with the fate of nations in their hands; and no man told or taught a word of war or military service until he entered the battle-field!

The education of young women has no department of maternity. It is considered indelicate to give this consecrated functionary any previous knowledge of her sacred duties. This most important and wonderful of human functions is left from age to age in the hands of absolutely untaught women. It is tacitly supposed to be fulfilled by the mysterious working of what we call "the divine instinct of maternity." Maternal instinct is a very respectable and useful instinct common to most animals. It is "divine" and "holy" only as all the laws of nature are divine and holy; and it is such only when it works to the right fulfilment of its use. If the race-preservative processes are to be held more sacred than the self-preservative processes, we must admit all the functions and faculties of reproduction to the same degree of reverence,–the passion of the male for the female as well as the passion of the mother for her young. And if, still further, we are to honor the race-preservative processes most in their highest and latest development, which is the only comparison to be made on a natural basis, we should place the great, disinterested, social function of education far above the second-selfishness of individual maternal functions. Maternal instinct, merely as an instinct, is unworthy of our superstitious reverence. It should be measured only as a means to an end, and valued in proportion to its efficacy.

Among animals, which have but a low degree of intelligence, instinct is at its height, and works well. Among savages, still incapable of much intellectual development, instinct holds large place. The mother beast can and does take all the care of her young by instinct; the mother savage, nearly all, supplemented by the tribal traditions, the educative influences of association, and some direct instruction. As humanity advances, growing more complex and varied, and as human intelligence advances to keep pace with new functions and new needs, instinct decreases in value. The human creature prospers and progresses not by virtue of his animal instinct, but by the wisdom and force of a cultivated intelligence and will, with which to guide his action and to control and modify the very instincts which used to govern him.

The human female, denied the enlarged activities which have developed intelligence in man, denied the education of the will which only comes by freedom and power, has maintained the rudimentary forces of instinct to the present day. With her extreme modification to sex, this faculty of instinct runs mainly along sex-lines, and finds fullest vent in the processes of maternity, where it has held unbroken sway. So the children of humanity are born into the arms of an endless succession of untrained mothers, who bring to the care and teaching of their children neither education for that wonderful work nor experience therein: they bring merely the intense accumulated force of a brute instinct,–the blind devoted passion of the mother for the child. Maternal love is an enormous force, but force needs direction. Simply to love the child does not serve him unless specific acts of service express this love. What these acts of service are and how they are performed make or mar his life forever.

Observe the futility of unaided maternal love and instinct in the simple act of feeding the child. Belonging to order mammalia, the human mother has an instinctive desire to suckle her young. (Some ultra-civilized have lost even that.) But this instinct has not taught her such habits of life as insure her ability to fulfil this natural function. Failing in the natural method, of what further use is instinct in the nourishment of the child? Can maternal instinct discriminate between Marrow's Food and Bridge's Food, Hayrick's Food and Pestle's Food, Pennywhistle's Sterilized Milk, and all the other infants' foods which are prepared and put upon the market by–men! These are not prepared by instinct, maternal or paternal, but by chemical analysis and physiological study; and their effect is observed and the diet varied by physicians, who do not do their work by instinct, either.

If the bottle-baby survive the loss of mother's milk, when he comes to the table, does maternal instinct suffice then to administer a proper diet for young children? Let the doctor and the undertaker answer. The wide and varied field of masculine activity in the interests of little children, from the peculiar human phenomenon of masculine assistance in parturition (there is one animal, the obstetric frog, where it also appears) to the manufacture of articles for feeding, clothing, protecting, amusing, and educating the baby, goes to show the utter inadequacy of maternal instinct in the human female. Another thing it shows also,–the criminal failure of that human female to supply by intelligent effort what instinct can no longer accomplish. For a reasoning, conscious being deliberately to undertake the responsibility of maintaining human life without making due preparation for the task is more than carelessness.

Before a man enters a trade, art, or profession, he studies it. He qualifies himself for the duties he is to undertake. He would be held a presuming impostor if he engaged in work he was not fitted to do, and his failure would mark him instantly with ridicule and reproach. In the more important professions, especially in those dealing with what we call "matters of life and death," the shipmaster or pilot, doctor or druggist, is required not only to study his business, but to pass an examination under those who have already become past masters, and obtain a certificate or a diploma or some credential to show that he is fit to be intrusted with the direct responsibility for human life.

Women enter a position which gives into their hands direct responsibility for the life or death of the whole human race with neither study nor experience, with no shadow of preparation or guarantee of capability. So far as they give it a thought, they fondly imagine that this mysterious "maternal instinct" will see them through. Instruction, if needed, they will pick up when the time comes: experience they will acquire as the children appear. "I guess I know how to bring up children!" cried the resentful old lady who was being advised: "I've buried seven!" The record of untrained instinct as a maternal faculty in the human race is to be read on the rows and rows of little gravestones which crowd our cemeteries. The experience gained by practising on the child is frequently buried with it.

No, the maternal sacrifice theory will not bear examination. As a sex specialized to reproduction, giving up all personal activity, all honest independence, all useful and progressive economic service for her glorious consecration to the uses of maternity, the human female has little to show in the way of results which can justify her position. Neither the enormous percentage of children lost by death nor the low average health of those who survive, neither physical nor mental progress, give any proof of race advantage from the maternal sacrifice.

X.

ALTHOUGH the superior maternity of the human female is so difficult to prove, so open to heavy charges of inadequacy, so erratic and pathological, there remain intact our devout belief in it, our reverence, our unshaken conviction that it is the one perfect thing. The facts as to our carelessness and ignorance in the fulfilment of this function are undeniable: the rate of infant mortality and children's diseases,–those classed by physicians as "preventable diseases," namely,–these mortal errors and failures confront us everywhere; but we ignore them all, or attribute them to any and every reason save deficient motherhood.

One of the most frequent excuses, among those who have gone far enough to admit that excuse is needed, is that the father is to blame for these conditions. His vices, it is alleged, weaken the constitution of the race. His failure to provide prevents the mother from giving the proper care. He is held responsible for what evil we see in our children; and still we worship the mother for the physical process of bearing a child,–now considered an act of heroism,–and for the "devotion" with which she clings to it afterward, irrespective of the wisdom or effectiveness of this devotion. A healthy and independent motherhood would no more think of taking credit to itself for the right fulfilment of its natural functions than would a cat for bringing forth her kittens or a sheep her lambs. The common fact that the women of the lower social grades bear more children and bear them more easily than the women of higher classes ought to give pause to this ridiculous assumption, but it does not. The more women weaken themselves and their offspring, and imperil their very lives by anti-maternal habits, the more difficulty, danger, and expense are associated with this natural process, the more do women solemnly take credit to themselves and receive it from others for the glorious self-sacrifice with which they risk their lives (and their babies' lives!) for the preservation of humanity. As to the father and his share in the evil results, nothing that he has ever done or can do removes from motherhood its primal responsibility.

Suppose the female of some other species, ignoring her racial duty of right selection, should mate with mangy, toothless cripples,–if there were such among her kind,–and so produce weak, malformed young, and help exterminate her race. Should she then blame him for the result? An entire sex, sacredly set apart for maternal functions so superior as to justify their lack of economic usefulness, should in the course of ages have learned how to select proper fathers. If the only way in which the human mother can feed and guard her children is through another person, a provider and protector on whom their lives and safety must depend, what natural, social, or moral excuse has she for not choosing a good one?

But how can a young girl know a good prospective father, we ask. That she is not so educated as to know proves her unfitness for her great task. That she does not think or care proves her dishonorable indifference to her great duty. She can in no way shirk the responsibility for criminal carelessness in choosing a father for her children, unless indeed there were no choice,–no good men left on earth. Moreover, we are not obliged to leave this crucial choice in the hands of young girls. Motherhood is the work of grown women, not of half-children; and, when we honestly care as much for motherhood as we pretend, we shall train the woman for her duty, not the girl for her guileless manoeuvres to secure a husband. We talk about the noble duties of the mother, but our maidens are educated for economically successful marriage.

Leaving this field of maternal duty through sex-selection, there remains the far larger ground to which the popular mind flees in triumph: that the later work of the mother proves the success of our racial division of labor on sex-lines, that in the care of the child, the education of the child, the beautiful life of the home and family, it is shown how well our system works. This is the last stronghold. Solidly intrenched herein sits popular thought, safe in the sacred precincts of the home. "Every man's home is his castle," is the common saying. The windows are shut to keep out the air. The curtains are down to keep out the light. The doors are barred to keep out the stranger. Within are the hearth fire and its gentle priestess, the initial combination of human life,–the family in the home.

Our thrones have been emptied, and turned into mere chairs for passing presidents. Our churches have been opened to the light of modern life, and the odor of sanctity has been freshened with sweet sunny air. We can see room for change in these old sanctuaries, but none in the sanctuary of the home. And this temple, with its rights, is so closely interwound with the services of subject woman, its altar so demands her ceaseless sacrifices, that we find it impossible to conceive of any other basis of human living. We are chilled to the heart's core by the fear of losing any of these ancient and hallowed associations. Without this blessed background of all our memories and foreground of all our hopes, life seems empty indeed. In homes we were all born. In homes we all die or hope to die. In homes we all live or want to live. For homes we all labor, in them or out of them. The home is the centre and circumference, the start and the finish, of most of our lives. We love it with a love older than the human race. We reverence it with the blind obeisance of those crouching centuries when its cult began. We cling to it with the tenacity of every inmost, oldest instinct of our animal natures, and with the enthusiasm of every latest word in the unbroken chant of adoration which we have sung to it since first we learned to praise.

And since we hold that our home life, just as we have it, is the best thing on earth, and that our home life plainly demands one whole woman at the least to each home, and usually more, it follows that anything which offers to change the position of woman threatens to "undermine the home," "strikes at the root of the family," and we will none of it. If, in honest endeavor to keep up to the modern standard of free thought and free speech, we do listen,–turning from our idol for a moment, and saying to the daring iconoclast, "Come, show us anything better!"–with what unlimited derision do we greet his proposed substitute! Yet everywhere about us to-day this inner tower, this castle keep of vanishing tradition, is becoming more difficult to defend or even to keep in repair. We buttress it anew with every generation; we love its very cracks and crumbling corners; we hang and drape it with endless decorations; we hide the looming dangers overhead with fresh clouds of incense; and we demand of the would-be repairers and rebuilders that they prove to us the desirability of their wild plans before they lift a hammer. But, when they show their plans, we laugh them to scorn.

It is a difficult case to meet. To call attention to existing conditions and to establish the relation between them and existing phenomena is one thing. To point out how a change of condition will produce new phenomena, and how these phenomena will benefit us, is quite another. Yet this is the task that is always involved in the conscious progress of the human race. While that progress was unconscious, it was enough that certain individuals and classes gradually entered into new relations in process of social evolution, and that they forced their conditions upon the reluctant conservatives who failed so to evolve.

In the quite recent passage from the feudal to the monarchical system, no time was wasted in the endeavor to persuade and convince the headstrong barons of their national duty. The growing power of the king struggled with and survived the lessening power of the barons,–that was all. Had a book been written then to urge the change, it could have proved clearly enough the evils of the feudal system; but, when it tried to portray the glories of national peace and power under a single monarch, it would have had small weight. National peace and power, which had been hitherto non-existent, would have failed to appeal to the sturdy lords of the soil, whose only idea of peace and power was to sit down and rest on their prostrate neighbors. Had their strength run in the line of argument, they would have scouted the "should be's" and "will be's" of the author, and defied him to prove that the new condition would be developed by the new processes; and, indeed, he would have found it hard.

So to-day, in questioning the economic status of woman and her position in the home and in the family, it is far easier to prove present evil than future good. Yet this is what is most exactingly demanded. It is required of the advocate of social reform not only that he convince the contented followers of the present system of its wrong, but that he prove to their satisfaction the superiority of some other system. This, in the nature of the case, is impossible. When people are contented, you cannot make them feel that what is is wrong, or that something else might be better. Even the discontented are far more willing to refer their troubles to some personal factor than to admit that their condition as a whole inevitably produces the general trouble in which they share. Even if convinced that a change of condition will remove the source of injury, they, like the fox with the swarm of flies, fear to be disturbed, lest their last state be worse than their first. In the face of this inevitable difficulty, however, the task must be undertaken.

Two things let us premise and agree upon before starting. First, that the duty of human life is progress, development; that we are here, not merely to live, but to grow,–not to be content with lean savagery or fat barbarism or sordid semi-civilization, but to toil on through the centuries, and build up the ever-nobler forms of life toward which social evolution tends. If this is not believed, if any hold that to keep alive and reproduce the species is the limit of our human duty, then they need look no farther here. That aim can be attained, and has been attained, for irrefutable centuries, through many forms of sex-relation and of economic relation. Human beings have lived and brought up children as good as their parents in free promiscuity and laziness, in forced polygamy and slavery, in willing polyandry and industry, and in monogamy plus prostitution and manufactures. Just to live and bear children does not prove the relative superiority of any system, either in sex or economics. But, when we believe that life means progress, then each succeeding form of sex-relation or economic relation is to be measured by its effect on that progress.

It may be necessary here to agree on a definition of human progress. According to the general law of organic evolution, it may be defined as follows: such progress in the individual and in his social relations as shall maintain him in health and happiness and increase the organic development of society.

If we accept such a definition of human progress, if we agree that progress is the duty of society, and that all social institutions are to be measured by it, we may proceed to our second premise. This is not to be ranked with the first in importance: it should be too commonly understood and accepted to be dragged into such a prominent position. But it is not commonly understood and accepted. In fact, it is misunderstood and denied to so general a degree that no apology is needed for insisting on it here.

The second premise is this: our enjoyment of a thing does not prove that it is right. Even our love, admiration, and reverence for a thing does not prove that it is right; and, even from an evolutionary point of view, our belief that a thing is "natural" does not prove that it is right. A thing may be right in one stage of evolution which becomes wrong in another. For instance, promiscuity is "natural"; the human animal, like many others, is quite easily inclined thereto. Monogamy is proven right by social evolution: it is the best way to carry on the human race in social relation; but it is not yet as "natural" as could be desired.

So, to return to our second premise, which is admittedly rather a large one, to show that any custom or status of ours is "natural" and enjoyable does not prove that it is right. It does not of course prevent its being right. Right things may be enjoyed, may be loved, admired, and reverenced, may even be "natural"; but so may wrong things. Even that subhuman faculty called instinct is only a true guide to conduct when the conditions are present which originally developed that instinct. The instinct that makes a modern house-dog turn around three times before he lies down is not worthy of much admiration to-day, though it served its purpose on the grassy plains and in the leafy hollows where it was formed. If these two premises are granted, that the duty of human life is progress, and that a given condition is not necessarily right because we like it, we may go on.

Is our present method of home life, based on the economic dependence of woman in the sex-relation, the best calculated to maintain the individual in health and happiness, and develope in him the higher social faculties? The individual is not maintained in health and happiness,–that is visible to all; and how little he is developed in social relation is shown in the jarring irregularity and wastefulness of our present economic system.

Economic independence for women necessarily involves a change in the home and family relation. But, if that change is for the advantage of individual and race, we need not fear it. It does not involve a change in the marriage relation except in withdrawing the element of economic dependence, nor in the relation of mother to child save to improve it. But it does involve the exercise of human faculty in women, in social service and exchange rather than in domestic service solely. This will of course require the introduction of some other form of living than that which now obtains. It will render impossible the present method of feeding the world by means of millions of private servants, and bringing up children by the same hand.

It is a melancholy fact that the vast majority of our children are reared and trained by domestic servants,–generally their mothers, to be sure, but domestic servants by trade. To become a producer, a factor in the economic activities of the world, must perforce interfere with woman's present status as a private servant. House mistress she may still be, in the sense of owning and ordering her home, but housekeeper or house-servant she may not be–and be anything else. Her position as mother will alter, too. Mother in the sense of bearer and rearer of noble children she will be, as the closest and dearest, the one most honored and best loved; but mother in the sense of exclusive individual nursery-maid and nursery-governess she may not be–and be anything else.

It is precisely here that the world calls a halt. Nothing, it says, can be better than our homes with their fair priestesses. Nothing can be better for children than the hourly care of their own mothers. It is the position of the feudal baron over again. We can perhaps be made to see the evils of existing conditions: we cannot be made to see any possibility of improving on them. Nevertheless, it may be tried.

Let us deliberately set ourselves to imagine, by sheer muscular effort as it were, a better kind of motherhood than that of the private nursery governess, a better way to feed and clean and clothe the world than by the private house-servant.

Here is felt the need of our second premise; for we enjoy things as they are (that is, some of us do, sometimes, and the rest of us think that we do). We love, admire, and reverence them; and it is "natural" to have them so. If it can be shown that human progress is better served by other methods, then other methods will be proven right; and we must grow to enjoy and honor them as fast as we can, and in due course of time we shall find them natural. If it can be shown that our babies would be better off if part of their time was passed in other care than their mothers', then such other care would be right; and it would be the duty of motherhood to provide it. If it can be shown that we could all be better provided for in our personal needs of nutrition, cleanliness, warmth, shelter, privacy, by some other method than that which requires the labor of one woman or more to each family, then it would be the duty of womanhood to find such method and to practise it.

Perhaps it is worth while to examine the nature of our feeling toward that social institution called "the family," and the probable effect upon it of the change in woman's economic status.

Marriage and "the family" are two institutions, not one, as is commonly supposed. We confuse the natural result of marriage in children, common to all forms of sex-union, with the family,–a purely social phenomenon. Marriage is a form of sex-union recognized and sanctioned by society. It is a relation between two or more persons, according to the custom of the country, and involves mutual obligations. Although made by us an economic relation, it is not essentially so, and will exist in much higher fulfilment after the economic phase is outgrown.

The family is a social group, an entity, a little state. It holds an important place in the evolution of society quite aside from its connection with marriage. There was a time when the family was the highest form of social relation,–indeed, the only form of social relation, when to the minds of pastoral, patriarchal tribes there was no conception so large as "my country," no State, no nation. There was only a great land spotted with families, each family its own little world, of which Grandpa was priest and king. The family was a social unit. Its interests were common to its members, and inimical to those of other families. It moved over the earth, following its food supply, and fighting occasionally with stranger families for the grass or water on which it depended. Indissoluble common interests are what make organic union, and those interests long rested on blood relationship.

While the human individual was best fed and guarded by the family, and so required the prompt, correlative action of all the members of that family, naturally the family must have a head; and that form of government known as the patriarchal was produced. The natural family relation, as seen in parents and young of other species, or in ourselves in later forms, involves no such governmental development: that is a feature of the family as a social entity alone.

One of the essentials of the patriarchal family life was polygamy, and not only polygamy, but open concubinage, and a woman slavery which was almost the same thing. The highest period of the family as a social institution was a very low period for marriage as a social institution,–a period, in fact, when marriage was but partially evolved from the early promiscuity of the primitive savage. The family seems indeed to be a gradually disappearing survival of the still looser unit of the horde, which again is more closely allied to the band or pack of gregarious carnivora than to an organic social relation. A loose, promiscuous group of animals is not a tribe; and the most primitive savage groups seem to have been no more than this.

The tribe in its true form follows the family,–is a natural extension of it, and derives its essential ties from the same relationship. These social forms, too, are closely related to economic conditions. The horde was the hunting unit; the family, and later the tribe, the pastoral unit. Agriculture and its resultant, commerce and manufacture, gradually weaken these crude blood ties, and establish the social relationship which constitutes the State. Before the pastoral era the family held no important position, and since that era it has gradually declined. With social progress we find human relations resting less and less on a personal and sex basis, and more and more on general economic independence. As individuals have become more highly specialized, they have made possible a higher form of marriage.

The family is a decreasing survival of the earliest grouping known to man. Marriage is an increasing development of high social life, not fully evolved. So far from being identical with the family, it improves and strengthens in inverse ratio to the family, as is easily seen by the broad contrast between the marriage relations of Jacob and the unquenchable demand for lifelong single mating that grows in our hearts to-day. There was no conception of marriage as a personal union for life of two well-matched individuals during the patriarchal era. Wives were valued merely for child-bearing. The family needed numbers of its own blood, especially males; and the man-child was the price of favor to women then. It was but a few degrees beyond the horde, not yet become a tribe in the full sense. Its bonds of union were of the loosest,–merely common paternity, with a miscellaneous maternity of inimical interests. Such a basis forever forbade any high individualization, and high individualization with its demands for a higher marriage forbids any numerical importance to the family. Marriage has risen and developed in social importance as the family has sunk and decreased.

It is most interesting to note that, under the comparatively similar conditions of the settlement of Utah, the numerical strength and easily handled common interests of many people under one head, which distinguish the polygamous family, were found useful factors in that great pioneering enterprise. In the further development of society a relation of individuals more fluent, subtle, and extensive was needed. The family as a social unit makes a ponderous body of somewhat irreconcilable constituents, requiring a sort of military rule to make it work at all; and it is only useful while the ends to be attained are of a simple nature, and allow of the slowest accomplishment. It is easy to see the family extending to the tribe by its own physical increase; and, similarly, the father hardening into the chief, under the necessities of larger growth. Then, as the steadily enlarging forces of national unity make the chief an outgrown name and the tribe an outgrown form, the family dwindles to a monogamic basis, as the higher needs of the sex-relation become differentiated from the more primitive economic necessities of the family.

And now, further, when our still developing social needs call for an ever-increasing delicacy and freedom in the inter-service and common service of individuals, we find that even what economic unity remains to the family is being rapidly eliminated. As the economic relation becomes rudimentary and disappears, the sex-relation asserts itself more purely; and the demand in the world to-day for a higher and nobler sex-union is as sharply defined as the growing objection to the existing economic union. Strange as it may seem to us, so long accustomed to confound the two, it is precisely the outgrown relics of a previously valuable family relation which so painfully retard the higher development of the monogamic marriage relation.

Each generation of young men and women comes to the formation of sex-union with higher and higher demands for a true marriage, with ever-growing needs for companionship. Each generation of men and women need and ask more of each other. A woman is no longer content and grateful to have "a kind husband": a man is no longer content with a patient Griselda; and, as all men and women, in marrying, revert to the economic status of the earlier family, they come under conditions which steadily tend to lower the standard of their mutual love, and make of the average marriage only a sort of compromise, borne with varying ease or difficulty according to the good breeding and loving-kindness of the parties concerned. This is not necessarily, to their conscious knowledge, an "unhappy marriage." It is as happy as those they see about them, as happy perhaps as we resignedly expect "on earth"; and in heaven we do not expect marriages. But it is not what they looked forward to when they were young.

When two young people love each other, in the long hours which are never long enough for them to be together in, do they dwell in ecstatic forecast on the duties of housekeeping? They do not. They dwell on the pleasure of having a home, in which they can be "at last alone"; on the opportunity of enjoying each other's society; and, always, on what they will do together. To act with those we love,–to walk together, work together, read together, paint, write, sing, anything you please, so that it be together,–that is what love looks forward to.

Human love, as it rises to an ever higher grade, looks more and more for such companionship. But the economic status of marriage rudely breaks in upon love's young dream. On the economic side, apart from all the sweetness and truth of the sex-relation, the woman in marrying becomes the house-servant, or at least the housekeeper, of the man. Of the world we may say that the intimate personal necessities of the human animal are ministered to by woman. Married lovers do not work together. They may, if they have time, rest together: they may, if they can, play together; but they do not make beds and sweep and cook together, and they do not go down town to the office together. They are economically on entirely different social planes, and these constitute a bar to any higher, truer union than such as we see about us. Marriage is not perfect unless it is between class equals. There is no equality in class between those who do their share in the world's work in the largest, newest, highest ways and those who do theirs in the smallest, oldest, lowest ways.

Granting squarely that it is the business of women to make the home life of the world true, healthful, and beautiful, the economically dependent woman does not do this, and never can. The economically independent woman can and will. As the family is by no means identical with marriage, so is the home by no means identical with either.

A home is a permanent dwelling-place, whether for one, two, forty, or a thousand, for a pair, a flock, or a swarm. The hive is the home of the bees as literally and absolutely as the nest is the home of mating birds in their season. Home and the love of it may dwindle to the one chamber of the bachelor or spread to the span of a continent, when the returning traveller sees land and calls it "home." There is no sweeter word, there is no dearer fact, no feeling closer to the human heart than this.

On close analysis, what are the bases of our feelings in the this connection? and what are their supporting facts? Far down below humanity, where "the foxes have holes, and the birds of the air have nests," there begins the deep home feeling. Maternal instinct seeks a place to shelter the defenceless young, while the mother goes abroad to search for food. The first sharp impressions of infancy are associated with the sheltering walls of home, be it the swinging cradle in the branches, the soft, dark hollow in the trunk of a tree, or the cave with its hidden lair. A place to be safe in; a place to be warm and dry in; a place to eat in peace and sleep in quiet; a place whose close, familiar limits rest the nerves from the continuous hail of impressions in the changing world outside; the same place over and over,–the restful repetition, rousing no keen response, but healing and soothing each weary sense,–that "feels like home." All this from our first consciousness. All this for millions and millions of years. No wonder we love it.

Then comes the gradual addition of tenderer associations, family ties of the earliest. Then, still primitive, but not yet outgrown, the groping religious sentiment of early ancestor-worship, adding sanctity to safety, and driving deep our sentiment for home. It was the place in which to pray, to keep alight the sacred fire, and pour libations to departed grandfathers. Following this, the slow-dying era of paternal government gave a new sense of honor to the place of comfort and the place of prayer. It became the seat of government also,–the palace and the throne. Upon this deep foundation we have built a towering superstructure of habit, custom, law; and in it dwell together every deepest, oldest, closest, and tenderest emotion of the human individual. No wonder we are blind and deaf to any suggested improvement in our lordly pleasure-house.

But look farther. Without contradicting any word of the above, it is equally true that the highest emotions of humanity arise and live outside the home and apart from it. While religion stayed at home, in dogma and ceremony, in spirit and expression, it was a low and narrow religion. It could never rise till it found a new spirit and a new expression in human life outside the home, until it found a common place of worship, a ceremonial and a morality on a human basis. Science, art, government, education, industry,–the home is the cradle of them all, and their grave, if they stay in it. Only as we live, think, feel, and work outside the home, do we become humanly developed, civilized, socialized.

The exquisite development of modern home life is made possible only as an accompaniment and result of modern social life. If the reverse were true, as is popularly supposed, all nations that have homes would continue to evolve a noble civilization. But they do not. On the contrary, those nations in which home and family worship most prevail, as in China, present a melancholy proof of the result of the domestic virtues without the social. A noble home life is the product of a noble social life. The home does not produce the virtues needed in society. But society does produce the virtues needed in such homes as we desire to-day. The members of the freest, most highly civilized and individualized nations, make the most delightful members of the home and family. The members of the closest and most highly venerated homes do not necessarily make the most delightful members of society.

In social evolution as in all evolution the tendency is from "indefinite, incoherent homogeneity to definite, coherent heterogeneity"; and the home, in its rigid maintenance of a permanent homogeneity, constitutes a definite limit to social progress. What we need is not less home, but more; not a lessening of the love of human beings for a home, but its extension through new and more effective expression. And, above all, we need the complete disentanglement in our thoughts of the varied and often radically opposed interests and industries so long supposed to be component parts of the home and family.

The change in the economic position of woman from dependence to independence must bring with it a rearrangement of these home interests and industries, to our great gain.

XI.

AS a natural consequence of our division of labor on sex-lines, giving to woman the home and to man the world in which to work, we have come to have a dense prejudice in favor of the essential womanliness of the home duties, as opposed to the essential manliness of every other kind of work. We have assumed that the preparation and serving of food and the removal of dirt, the nutritive and excretive processes of the family, are feminine functions; and we have also assumed that these processes must go on in what we call the home, which is the external expression of the family. In the home the human individual is fed, cleaned, warmed, and generally cared for, while not engaged in working in the world.

Human nutrition is a long process. There's many a ship 'twixt the cup and the lip, to paraphrase an old proverb. Food is produced by the human race collectively,–not by individuals for their own consumption, but by interrelated groups of individuals, all over the world, for the world's consumption. This collectively produced food circulates over the earth's surface through elaborate processes of transportation, exchange, and preparation, before it reaches the mouths of the consumers; and the final processes of selection and preparation are in the hands of woman. She is the final purchaser: she is the final handler in that process of human nutrition known as cooking, which is a sort of extra-organic digestion proven advantageous to our species. This department of human digestion has become a sex-function, supposed to pertain to women by nature.

If it is to the advantage of the human race that its food supply should be thus handled by a special sex, this advantage should be shown in superior health and purity of habit. But no such advantage is visible. In spite of all our power and skill in the production and preparation of food we remain "the sickest beast alive" in the matter of eating. Our impotent outcries against adulteration prove that part of the trouble is in the food products as offered for purchase, the pathetic reiteration of our numerous cook-books proves that part of the trouble is in the preparation of those products, and the futile exhortations of physicians and mothers prove that part of the trouble is in our morbid tastes and appetites. It would really seem as if the human race after all its long centuries had not learned how to prepare good food, nor how to cook it, nor how to eat it,–which is painfully true.

This great function of human nutrition is confounded with the sex-relation, and is considered a sex-function: it is in the helpless hands of that amiable but abortive agent, the economically dependent woman; and the essential incapacity of such an agent is not hard to show. In her position as private house-steward she is the last purchaser of the food of the world, and here we reach the governing factor in our incredible adulteration of food products.

All kinds of deceit and imposition in human service are due to that desire to get without giving, which, as has been shown in previous chapters, is largely due to the training of women as non-productive consumers. But the particular form of deceit and imposition practised by a given dealer is governed by the intelligence and power of the buyer. The dilution and adulteration of food products is a particularly easy path to profit, because the ultimate purchaser has almost no power and very little intelligence. The individual housewife must buy at short intervals and in small quantities. This operates to her pecuniary disadvantage, as is well known; but its effect on the quality of her purchases is not so commonly observed. Not unless she becomes the head of a wealthy household, and so purchases in quantity for family, servants, and guests, is her trade of sufficient value to have force in the market. The dealer who sells to a hundred poor women can and does sell a much lower quality of food than he who sells an equal amount to one purchaser. Therefore, the home, as a food agency, holds as essentially and permanently unfavorable position as a purchaser; and it is thereby the principal factor in maintaining the low standard of food products against which we struggle with the cumbrous machinery of legislation.

Most housekeepers will innocently prove their ignorance of these matters by denying that the standard of food products is so low. Let such offended ladies but examine the statutes and ordinances of their own cities,–of any civilized city,–and see how the bread, the milk, the meat, the fruit, are under a steady legislative inspection which endeavors to protect the ignorance and helplessness of the individual purchaser. If the private housekeeper had the technical intelligence as purchaser which is needed to discriminate in the selection of foods, if she were prepared to test her milk, to detect the foreign substance in her coffee and spices, rightly to estimate the quality of her meat and the age of her fruit and vegetables, she would then be able at least to protest against her supply, and to seek, as far as time, distance, and funds allowed, a better market. This technical intelligence, however, is only to be obtained by special study and experience; and its attainment only involves added misery and difficulty to the private purchaser, unless accompanied by the power to enforce what the intelligence demands.

As it is, woman brings to her selection from the world's food only the empirical experience gained by practising upon her helpless family, and this during the very time when her growing children need the wise care which she is only able to give them in later years. This experience, with its pitiful limitation and its practical check by the personal taste and pecuniary standing of the family, is lost where it was found. Each mother slowly acquires some knowledge of her business by practising it upon the lives and health of her family and by observing its effect on the survivors; and each daughter begins again as ignorant as her mother was before her. This "rule of thumb" is not transmissible. It is not a genuine education such as all important work demands, but a slow animal process of soaking up experience,–hopelessly ineffectual in protecting the health of society. As the ultimate selecting agent in feeding humanity, the private housewife fails, and this not by reason of any lack of effort on her part, but by the essential defect of her position as individual purchaser. Only organization can oppose such evils as the wholesale adulteration of food; and woman, the house-servant, belongs to the lowest grade of unorganized labor.

Leaving the selection of food, and examining its preparation, one would naturally suppose that the segregation of an entire sex to the fulfilment of this function would insure most remarkable results. It has, but they are not so favorable as might be expected. The art and science of cooking involve a large and thorough knowledge of nutritive value and of the laws of physiology and hygiene. As a science, it verges on preventive medicine. As an art, it is capable of noble expression within its natural bounds. As it stands among us to-day, it is so far from being a science and akin to preventive medicine, that it is the lowest of amateur handicrafts and a prolific source of disease; and, as an art, it has developed under the peculiar stimulus of its position as a sex-function into a voluptuous profusion as false as it is evil. Our innocent proverb, "The way to a man's heart is through his stomach," is a painfully plain comment on the way in which we have come to deprave our bodies and degrade our souls at the table.

On the side of knowledge it is permanently impossible that half the world, acting as amateur cooks for the other half, can attain any high degree of scientific accuracy or technical skill. The development of any human labor requires specialization, and specialization is forbidden to our cook-by-nature system. What progress we have made in the science of cooking has been made through the study and experience of professional men cooks and chemists, not through the Sisyphean labors of our endless generations of isolated women, each beginning again where her mother began before her.

Here, of course, will arise a pained outcry along the "mother's doughnuts" line, in answer to which we refer to our second premise in the last chapter. The fact that we like a thing does not prove it to be right. A Missouri child may regard his mother's saleratus biscuit with fond desire, but that does not alter their effect upon his spirits or his complexion. Cooking is a matter of law, not the harmless play of fancy. Architecture might be more sportive and varied if every man built his own house, but it would not be the art and science that we have made it; and, while every woman prepares food for her own family, cooking can never rise beyond the level of the amateur's work.

But, low as is the status of cooking as a science, as an art it is lower. Since the wife-cook's main industry is to please,–that being her chief means of getting what she wants or of expressing affection,–she early learned to cater to the palate instead of faithfully studying and meeting the needs of the stomach. For uncounted generations the grown man and the growing child have been subject to the constant efforts of her who cooked from affection, not from knowledge,–who cooked to please. This is one of the widest pathways of evil that has ever been opened. In every field of life it is an evil to put the incident before the object, the means before the end; and here it has produced that familiar result whereby we live to eat instead of eating to live.

This attitude of the woman has developed the rambling excess called "fancy cookery,"–a thing as far removed from true artistic development as a swinging ice-pitcher from a Greek vase. Through this has come the limitless unhealthy folly of high living, in which human labor and time and skill are wasted in producing what is neither pure food nor pure pleasure, but an artificial performance, to be appreciated only by the virtuoso. Lower living could hardly be imagined than that which results from this unnatural race between artifice and appetite, in which body and soul are both corrupted.

In the man, the subject of all this dining-room devotion, has been developed and maintained that cultivated interest in his personal tastes and their gratification,– that demand for things which he likes rather than for things which he knows to be good, wherein lies one of the most dangerous elements in character known to the psychologist. The sequences of this affectionate catering to physical appetites may be traced far afield to its last result in the unchecked indulgence in personal tastes and desires, in drug habits and all intemperance. The temperament which is unable to resist these temptations is constantly being bred at home.

As the concentration of woman's physical energies on the sex-functions, enforced by her economic dependence, has tended to produce and maintain man's excess in sex-indulgence, to the injury of the race; so the concentration of woman's industrial energies on the close and constant service of personal tastes and appetites has tended to produce and maintain an excess in table indulgence, both in eating and drinking, which is also injurious to the race. It is not here alleged that this is the only cause of our habits of this nature; but it is one of primal importance, and of ceaseless action.

We can perhaps see its working better by a light-minded analogy than by a bold statement. Suppose two large, healthy, nimble apes. Suppose that the male ape did not allow the female ape to skip about and pluck her own cocoanuts, but brought to her what she was to have. Suppose that she was then required to break the shell, pick out the meat, prepare for the male what he wished to consume; and suppose, further, that her share in the dinner, to say nothing of her chance of a little pleasure excursion in the treetops afterward, was dependent on his satisfaction with the food she prepared for him. She, as an ape of intelligence, would seek, by all devices known to her, to add stimulus and variety to the meals she arranged, to select the bits he especially preferred to please his taste and to meet his appetite; and he, developing under this agreeable pressure, would gradually acquire a fine discrimination in foods, and would look forward to his elaborate feasts with increasing complacency. He would have a new force to make him eat,–not only his need of food, with its natural and healthy demands, but her need of–everything, acting through his need of food.

This sounds somewhat absurd in a family of apes, but it is precisely what has occurred in the human family. To gratify her husband has been the woman's way of obtaining her own ends, and she has of necessity learned how to do it; and, as she has been in general an uneducated and unskilled worker, she could only seek to please him through what powers she had,–mainly those of house service. She has been set to serve two appetites, and to profit accordingly. She has served them well, but the profit to either party is questionable.

On lines of social development we are progressing from the gross gorging of the savage on whatever food he could seize, toward the discriminating selection of proper foods, and an increasing delicacy and accuracy in their use. Against this social tendency runs the cross-current of our sexuo-economic relation, making the preparation of food a sex function, and confusing all its processes with the ardor of personal affection and the dragging weight of self-interest. This method is applied, not only to the husband, but, in a certain degree, to the children; for, where maternal love and maternal energy are forced to express themselves mainly in the preparation of food, the desire properly to feed the child becomes confounded with an unwise desire to please, and the mother degrades her high estate by catering steadily to the lower tastes of humanity instead of to the higher.

Our general notion is that we have lifted and ennobled our eating and drinking by combining them with love. On the contrary, we have lowered and degraded our love by combining it with eating and drinking; and, what is more, we have lowered these habits also. Some progress has been made, socially; but this unhappy mingling of sex-interest and self-interest with normal appetites, this Cupid-in-the-kitchen arrangement, has gravely impeded that progress. Professional cooking has taught us much. Commerce and manufacture have added to our range of supplies. Science has shown us what we need, and how and when we need it. But the affectionate labor of wife and mother is little touched by these advances. If she goes to the cooking school, it is to learn how to make the rich delicacies that will please rather than to study the nutritive value of food in order to guard the health of the household. From the constantly enlarging stores opened to her through man's activities she chooses widely, to make "a variety" that shall kindle appetite, knowing nothing of the combination best for physical needs. As to science, chemistry, hygiene,–they are but names to her. "John likes it so." "Willie won't eat it so." "Your father never could bear cabbage." She must consider what he likes, not only because she loves to please him or because she profits by pleasing him, but because he pays for the dinner, and she is a private servant.

Is it not time that the way to a man's heart through his stomach should be relinquished for some higher avenue? The stomach should be left to its natural uses, not made a thoroughfare for stranger passions and purposes; and the heart should be approached through higher channels. We need a new picture of our overworked blind god,–fat, greasy, pampered with sweetmeats by the poor worshippers long forced to pay their devotion through such degraded means.

No, the human race is not well nourished by making the process of feeding it a sex function. The selection and preparation of food should be in the hands of trained experts. And woman should stand beside man as the comrade of his soul, not the servant of his body.

This will require large changes in our method of living. To feed the world by expert service, bringing to that great function the skill and experience of the trained specialist, the power of science, and the beauty of art, is impossible in the sexuo-economic relation. While we treat cooking as a sex-function common to all women and eating as a family function not otherwise rightly accomplished, we can develope no farther. We are spending much earnest study and hard labor to-day on the problem of teaching and training women in the art of cooking, both the wife and the servant; for, with our usual habit of considering voluntary individual conduct as the cause of conditions, we seek to modify conditions by changing individual conduct.

What we must recognize is that, while the conditions remain, the conduct cannot be altered. Any trade or profession, the development of which depended upon the labor of isolated individuals, assisted only by hired servants more ignorant than themselves, would remain at a similarly low level.

So far as health can be promoted by public means, we are steadily improving by sanitary regulations and medical inspection, by professionally prepared "health foods" and by the literature of hygiene, by special legislation as to contagious diseases and dangerous trades; but the health that lies in the hands of the house-wife is not reached by these measures. The nine-tenths of our women who do their own work cannot be turned into proficient purchasers and cooks any more than nine-tenths of our men could be turned into proficient tailors with no better training or opportunity than would be furnished by clothing their own families. The alternative remaining to the women who comprise the other tenth is that peculiar survival of earlier labor methods know as "domestic service."

As a method of feeding humanity, hired domestic service is inferior even to the service of the wife and mother, and brings to the art of cooking an even lower degree of training and a narrower experience. The majority of domestic servants are young girls who leave this form of service for marriage as soon as they are able; and we thus intrust the physical health of human beings, so far as cooking affects it, to the hands of untrained, immature women, of the lowest social grade, who are actuated by no higher impulse than that of pecuniary necessity. The love of the wife and mother stimulates at least her desire to feed her family well. The servant has no such motive. The only cases in which domestic cooking reaches anything like proficiency are those in which the wife and mother is "a natural-born cook," and regales her family with the products of genius, or those in which the households of the rich are able to command the service of professionals.

There was a time when kings and lords retained their private poets to praise and entertain them; but the poet is not truly great until he sings for the world. So the art of cooking can never be lifted to its true place as a human need and a social function by private service. Such an arrangement of our lives and of our houses as will allow cooking to become a profession is the only way in which to free this great art from its present limitations. It should be a reputable, well-paid profession, wherein those women or those men who were adapted to this form of labor could become cooks, as they would become composers or carpenters. Natural distinctions would be developed between the mere craftsman and the artist; and we should have large, new avenues of lucrative and honorable industry, and a new basis for human health and happiness.

This does not involve what is known as "co-operation." Co-operation, in the usual sense, is the union of families for the better performance of their supposed functions. The process fails because the principle is wrong. Cooking and cleaning are not family functions. We do not have a family mouth, a family stomach, a family face to be washed. Individuals require to be fed and cleaned from birth to death, quite irrespective of their family relations. The orphan, the bachelor, the childless widower, have as much need of these nutritive and excretive processes as any patriarchal parent. Eating is an individual function. Cooking is a social function. Neither is in the faintest degree a family function. That we have found it convenient in early stages of civilization to do our cooking at home proves no more than the allied fact that we have also found it convenient in such stages to do our weaving and spinning at home, our soap and candle making, our butchering and pickling, our baking and washing.

As society developes, its functions specialize; and the reasons why this great race-function of cooking has been so retarded in its natural growth is that the economic dependence of women has kept them back from their share in human progress. When women stand free as economic agents, they will lift and free their arrested functions, to the much better fulfilment of their duties as wives and mothers and to the vast improvement in health and happiness of the human race.

Co-operation is not what is required for this, but trained professional service and such arrangement of our methods of living as shall allow us to benefit by such service. When numbers of people patronize the same tailor or baker or confectioner, they do not co-operate. Neither would they co-operate in patronizing the same cook. The change must come from the side of the cook, not from the side of the family. It must come through natural functional development in society, and it is so coming. Woman, recognizing that her duty as feeder and cleaner is a social duty, not a sexual one, must face the requirements of the situation, and prepare herself to meet them. A hundred years ago this could not have been done. Now it is being done, because the time is ripe for it.

If there should be built and opened in any of our large cities to-day a commodious and well-served apartment house for professional women with families, it would be filled at once. The apartments would be without kitchens; but there would be a kitchen belonging to the house from which meals could be served to the families in their rooms or in a common dining-room, as preferred. It would be a home where the cleaning was done by efficient workers, not hired separately by the families, but engaged by the manager of the establishment; and a roof-garden, day nursery, and kindergarten, under well-trained professional nurses and teachers, would insure proper care of the children. The demand for such provision is increasing daily, and must soon be met, not by a boarding-house or a lodging-house, a hotel, a restaurant, or any makeshift patching together of these; but by a permanent provision for the needs of women and children, of family privacy with collective advantage. This must be offered on a business basis to prove a substantial business success; and it will so prove, for it is a growing social need.

There are hundreds of thousands of women in New York City alone who are wage-earners, and who also have families; and the number increases. This is true not only among the poor and unskilled, but more and more among business women, professional women, scientific, artistic, literary women. Our school-teachers, who form a numerous class, are not entirely without relatives. To board does not satisfy the needs of a human soul. These women want homes, but they do not want the clumsy tangle of rudimentary industries that are supposed to accompany the home. The strain under which such women labor is no longer necessary. The privacy of the home could be as well maintained in such a building as described as in any house in a block, any room, flat, or apartment, under present methods. The food would be better, and would cost less; and this would be true of the service and of all common necessities.

In suburban homes this purpose could be accomplished much better by a grouping of adjacent houses, each distinct and having its own yard, but all kitchenless, and connected by covered ways with the eating-house. No detailed prophecy can be made of the precise forms which would ultimately prove most useful and pleasant; but the growing social need is for the specializing of the industries practised in the home and for the proper mechanical provision for them.

The cleaning required in each house would be much reduced by the removal of the two chief elements of household dirt,–grease and ashes.

Meals could of course be served in the house as long as desired; but, when people become accustomed to pure, clean homes, where no steaming industry is carried on, they will gradually prefer to go to their food instead of having it brought to them. It is a perfectly natural process, and a healthful one, to go to one's food. And, after all, the changes between living in one room, and so having the cooking most absolutely convenient; going as far as the limits of a large house permit, to one's own dining-room; and going a little further to a dining-room not in one's own house, but near by,–these differ but in degree. Families could go to eat together, just as they can go to bathe together or to listen to music together; but, if it fell out that different individuals presumed to develope an appetite at different hours, they could meet it without interfering with other people's comfort or sacrificing their own. Any housewife knows the difficulty of always getting a family together at meals. Why try? Then arises sentiment, and asserts that family affection, family unity, the very existence of the family, depend on their being together at meals. A family unity which is only bound together with a table-cloth is of questionable value.

There are several professions involved in our clumsy method of housekeeping. A good cook is not necessarily a good manager, nor a good manager an accurate and thorough cleaner, nor a good cleaner a wise purchaser. Under the free development of these branches a woman could choose her position, train for it, and become a most valuable functionary in her special branch, all the while living in her home; that is, she would live in it as a man lives in his home, spending certain hours of the day at work and others at home.

The division of labor of housekeeping would require the service of fewer women for fewer hours a day. Where now twenty women in twenty homes work all the time, and insufficiently accomplish their varied duties, the same work in the hands of specialists could be done in less time by fewer people; and the others would be left free to do other work for which they were better fitted, thus increasing the productive power of the world. Attempts at co-operation so far have endeavored to lessen the existing labors of women without recognizing their need for other occupation, and this is one reason for their repeated failure.

It seems almost unnecessary to suggest that women as economic producers will naturally choose those professions which are compatible with motherhood, and there are many professions much more in harmony with that function than the household service. Motherhood is not a remote contingency, but the common duty and the common glory of womanhood. If women did choose professions unsuitable to maternity, Nature would quietly extinguish them by her unvarying process. Those mothers who persisted in being acrobats, horse-breakers, or sailors before the mast, would probably not produce vigorous and numerous children. If they did, it would simply prove that such work did not hurt them. There is no fear to be wasted on the danger of women's choosing wrong professions, when they are free to choose. Many women would continue to prefer the very kinds of work which they are doing now, in the new and higher methods of execution. Even cleaning, rightly understood and practised, is a useful, and therefore honorable, profession. It has been amusing heretofore to see how this least desirable of labors has been so innocently held to be woman's natural duty. It is woman, the dainty, the beautiful, the beloved wife and revered mother, who has by common consent been expected to do the chamber-work and scullery work of the world. All that is basest and foulest she in the last instance must handle and remove. Grease, ashes, dust, foul linen, and sooty ironware,–among these her days must pass. As we socialize our functions, this passes from her hands into those of man. The city's cleaning is his work. And even in our houses the professional cleaner is more and more frequently a man.

The organization of household industries will simplify and centralize its cleaning processes, allowing of many mechanical conveniences and the application of scientific skill and thoroughness. We shall be cleaner than we ever were before. There will be less work to do, and far better means of doing it. The daily needs of a well-plumbed house could be met easily by each individual in his or her own room or by one who liked to do such work; and the labor less frequently required would be furnished by an expert, who would clean one home after another with the swift skill of training and experience. The home would cease to be to us a workshop or a museum, and would become far more the personal expression of its occupants–the place of peace and rest, of love and privacy–than it can be in its present condition of arrested industrial development. And woman will fill her place in those industries with far better results than are now provided by her ceaseless struggles, her conscientious devotion, her pathetic ignorance and inefficiency.

XII.

AS self-conscious creatures, to whom is always open the easy error of mistaking feeling for fact, to whose consciousness indeed the feeling is the fact,–a further process of reasoning being required to infer the fact from the feeling,–we are not greatly to be blamed for laying such stress on sentiment and emotion. We may perhaps admit, in the light of cold reasoning, that the home is not the best place in which to do so much work in, nor the wife and mother the best person to do it. But this intellectual conviction by no means alters our feeling on the subject. Feeling, deep, long established, and over-stimulated, lies thick over the whole field of home life. Not what we think about it (for we never have thought about it very much), but what we feel about it, constitutes the sum of our opinion. Many of our feelings are true, right , legitimate. Some are fatuous absurdities, mere dangling relics of outgrown tradition, slowly moulting from us as we grow.

Consider, for instance, that long-standing popular myth known as "the privacy of the home." There is something repugnant in the idea of food cooked outside the home, even though served within it; still more in the going out of the family to eat, and more yet in the going out of separate individuals to eat. The limitless personal taste developed by "home cooking" fears that it will lose its own particular shade of brown on the bacon, its own hottest of hot cakes, its own corner biscuit.

This objection must be honestly faced, and admitted in some degree. A menu, however liberally planned by professional cooks, would not allow so much play for personal idiosyncrasy as do those prepared by the numerous individual cooks now serving us. There would be a far larger range of choice in materials, but not so much in methods of preparation and service. The difference would be like that between every man's making his own coat or having his women servants make it for him, on the one hand, and his selecting one from many ready made or ordering it of his tailor, on the other.

In the regular professional service of food there would be a good general standard, and the work of specialists for special occasions. We have long seen this process going on in the steady increase of professionally prepared food, from the cheap eating-house to the fashionable caterer, from the common "cracker" to the delicate "wafer." "Home cooking," robbed of its professional adjuncts, would fall a long way. We do not realize how far we have already progressed in this line, nor how fast we are going.

One of the most important effects of a steady general standard of good food will be the elevation of the popular taste. We should acquire a cultivated appreciation of what is good food, far removed from the erratic and whimsical self-indulgence of the private table. Our only standard of taste in cooking is personal appetite and caprice. That we "like" a dish is enough to warrant full approval. But liking is only adaptation. Nature is forever seeking to modify the organism to the environment; and, when it becomes so modified, so adapted, the organism "likes" the environment. In the earlier form, "it likes me," this derivation is plainer.

Each nation, each locality, each family, each individual, "likes," in large measure, those things to which it has been accustomed. What else it might have liked, if it had had it, can never be known; but the slow penetration of new tastes and habits, the reluctant adoption of the potato, the tomato, maize, and other new vegetables by old countries, show that it is quite possible to change a liking.

In the narrow range of family capacity to supply and of family ability to prepare our food, and in our exaggerated intensity of personal preference, we have grown very rigid in our little field of choice. We insist on the superiority of our own methods, and despise the methods of our neighbors, with a sublime ignorance of any higher standard of criticism than our own uneducated tastes. When we become accustomed from childhood to scientifically and artistically prepared foods, we shall grow to know what is good and to enjoy it, as we learn to know good music by hearing it.

As we learn to appreciate a wider and higher range of cooking, we shall also learn to care for simplicity in this art. Neither is attainable under our present system by the average person. As cooking becomes disassociated from the home, we shall gradually cease to attach emotions to it; and we shall learn to judge it impersonally upon a scientific and artistic basis. This will not, of course, prevent some persons' having peculiar tastes; but these will know that they are peculiar, and so will their neighbors. It will not prevent, either, the woman who has a dilettante fondness for some branch of cookery, wherewith she loves to delight herself and her friends, from keeping a small cooking plant within reach, as she might a sewing-machine or a turning-lathe.

In regard to the eating of food we are still more opposed by the "privacy of the home" idea, and a marked–indeed, a pained–disinclination to dissociate that function from family life. To eat together does, of course, form a temporary bond. To establish a medium of communication between dissimilar persons, some common ground must be found,–some rite, some game, some entertainment,–something that they can do together. And, if the persons desiring to associate have no other common ground than this physical function,–which is so common, indeed, that it includes not only all humanity, but all the animal kingdom,–then by all means let them seek that. On occasions of general social rejoicing to celebrate some event of universal importance, the feast will always be a natural and satisfying institution.

To the primitive husband with fighting for his industry, the primitive wife with domestic service for hers, the primitive children with no relation to their parents but the physical,–to such a common table was the only common tie; and the simplicity of their food furnished a medium that hurt no one. But in the higher individualization of modern life the process of eating is by no means the only common interest among members of a family, and by no means the best. The sweetest, tenderest, holiest memories of family life are not connected with the table, though many jovial and pleasant ones may be so associated. And on many an occasion of deep feeling, whether of joy or of pain, the ruthless averaging of the whole group three times a day at table becomes an unbearable strain. If good food suited to a wide range of needs were always attainable, a family could go and feast together when it chose or simply eat together when it chose; and each individual could go alone when he chose. This is not to be forced or hurried; but, with a steady supply of food, easy of access to all, the stomach need no longer be compelled to serve as a family tie.

We have so far held that the lower animals ate alone in their brutality, and that man has made eating a social function, and so elevated it. The elevation is the difficult part to prove, when we look at humanity's gross habits, morbid tastes, and deadly diseases, its artifice, and its unutterable depravity of gluttony and intemperance. The animals may be lower than we in their simple habit of eating what is good for them when they are hungry, but it serves their purpose well.

One result of our making eating a social function is that, the more elaborately we socialize it, the more we require at our feasts the service of a number of strangers absolutely shut out from social intercourse,–functionaries who do not eat with us, who do not talk with us, who must not by the twinkling of an eyelash show any interest in this performance, save to minister to the grosser needs of the occasion on a strictly commercial basis. Such extraneous presence must and does keep the conversation at one level. In the family without a servant both mother and father are too hard worked to make the meal a social success; and, as soon as servants are introduced, a limit is set to the range of conversation. The effect of our social eating, either in families or in larger groups, is not wholly good. It is well open to question whether we cannot, in this particular, improve our system of living.

When the cooking of the world is open to full development by those whose natural talent and patient study lead them to learn how better and better to meet the needs of the body by delicate and delicious combinations of the elements of nutrition, we shall begin to understand what food means to us, and how to build up the human body in sweet health and full vigor. A world of pure, strong, beautiful men and women, knowing what they ought to eat and drink, and taking it when they need it, will be capable of much higher and subtler forms of association than this much-prized common table furnishes. The contented grossness of to-day, the persistent self-indulgence of otherwise intelligent adults, the fatness and leanness and feebleness, the whole train of food-made disorders, together with all drug habits,– these morbid phenomena are largely traceable to the abnormal attention given to both eating and cooking, which must accompany them as family functions. When we detach them from this false position by untangling the knot of our sexuo-economic relation, we shall give natural forces a chance to work their own pure way in us, and make us better.

Our domestic privacy is held to be further threatened by the invasion of professional cleaners. We should see that a kitchenless home will require far less cleaning than is now needed, and that the daily ordering of one's own room could be easily accomplished by the individual, when desired. Many would so desire, keeping their own rooms, their personal inner chambers, inviolate from other presence than that of their nearest and dearest. Such an ideal of privacy may seem ridiculous to those who accept contentedly the gross publicity of our present method. Of all popular paradoxes, none is more nakedly absurd than to hear us prate of privacy in a place where we cheerfully admit to our table-talk and to our door service–yes, and to the making of our beds and the handling of our clothing–a complete stranger, a stranger not only by reason of new acquaintance and of the false view inevitable to new eyes let in upon our secrets, but a stranger by birth, almost always an alien in race, and, more hopeless still, a stranger by breeding, one who can never truly understand.

This stranger all of us who can afford it summon to our homes,–one or more at once, and many in succession. If, like barbaric kings of old or bloody pirates, of the main, we cut their tongues out that they might not tell, it would still remain an irreconcilable intrusion. But, as it is, with eyes to see, ears to hear, and tongues to speak, with no other interests to occupy their minds, and with the retaliatory fling that follows the enforced silence of those who must not "answer back,"–with this observing and repeating army lodged in the very bosom of the family, may we not smile a little bitterly at our fond ideal of "the privacy of the home'? The swift progress of professional sweepers, dusters, and scrubbers, through rooms where they were wanted, and when they were wanted, would be at least no more injurious to privacy than the present method. Indeed, the exclusion of the domestic servant, and the entrance of woman on a plane of interest at once more social and more personal, would bring into the world a new conception of the sacredness of privacy, a feeling for the rights of the individual as yet unknown.

Closely connected with the question of cleaning is that of household decoration and furnishing. The economically dependent woman, spending the accumulating energies of the race in her small cage, has thrown out a tangled mass of expression, as a large plant throws out roots in a small pot. She has crowded her limited habitat with unlimited things,–things useful and unuseful, ornamental and unornamental, comfortable and uncomfortable; and the labor of her life is to wait upon these things, and keep them clean.

The free woman, having room for full individual expression in her economic activities and in her social relation, will not be forced so to pour out her soul in tidies and photograph holders. The home will be her place of rest, not of uneasy activity; and she will learn to love simplicity at last. This will mean better sanitary conditions in the home, more beauty and less work. And the trend of the new conditions, enhancing the value of real privacy and developing the sense of beauty, will be towards a delicate loveliness in the interiors of our houses, which the owners can keep in order without undue exertion.

Besides these comparatively external conditions, there are psychic effects produced upon the family by the sexuo-economic relation not altogether favorable to our best growth. One is the levelling effect of the group upon its members, under pressure of this relation. Such privacy as we do have in our homes is family privacy, an aggregate privacy; and this does not insure–indeed it prevents–individual privacy. This is another of the lingering rudiments of methods of living belonging to ages long since outgrown, and maintained among us by the careful preservation or primitive customs in the unchanged position of women. In very early times a crude and undifferentiated people could flock in family groups in one small tent without serious inconvenience or injury. The effects of such grouping on modern people is known in the tenement districts of large cities, where families live in single rooms; and these effects are of a distinctly degrading nature.

The progressive individuation of human beings requires a personal home, one room at least for each person. This need forces some recognition for itself in family life, and is met so far as private purses in private houses can meet it; but for the vast majority of the population no such provision is possible. To women, especially, a private room is the luxury of the rich alone. Even where a partial provision for personal needs is made under pressure of social development, the other pressure of undeveloped family life is constantly against it. The home is the one place on earth where no one of the component individuals can have any privacy. A family is a crude aggregate of persons of different ages, sizes, sexes, and temperaments, held together by sex-ties and economic necessity; and the affection which should exist between the members of a family is not increased in the least by the economic pressure, rather it is lessened. Such affection as is maintained by economic forces is not the kind which humanity most needs.

At present any tendency to withdraw and live one's own life on any plane of separate interest or industry is naturally resented, or at least regretted, by the other members of the family. This affects women more than men, because men live very little in the family and very much in the world. The man has his individual life, his personal expression and its rights, his office, studio, shop: the women and children live in the home–because they must. For a woman to wish to spend much time elsewhere is considered wrong, and the children have no choice. The historic tendency of women to "gad abroad," of children to run away, to be forever teasing for permission to go and play somewhere else; the ceaseless, futile, well-meant efforts to "keep the boys at home,"–these facts, together with the definite absence of the man of the home for so much of the time, constitute a curious commentary upon our patient belief that we live at home, and like it. Yet the home ties bind us with a gentle dragging hold that few can resist. Those who do resist, and who insist upon living their individual lives, find that this costs them loneliness and privation; and they lose so much in daily comfort and affection that others are deterred from following them.

There is no reason why this painful choice should be forced upon us, no reason why the home life of the human race should not be such as to allow–yes, to promote–the highest development of personality. We need the society of those dear to us, their love and their companionship. These will endure. But the common cook-shops of our industrially undeveloped homes, and all the allied evils, are not essential, and need not endure.

To our general thought the home just as it stands is held to be what is best for us. We imagine that it is at home that we learn the higher traits, the nobler emotions,–that the home teaches us how to live. The truth beneath this popular concept is this: the love of the mother for the child is at the base of all our higher love for one another. Indeed, even behind that lies the generous giving impulse of sex-love, the out-going force of sex-energy. The family relations ensuing do underlie our higher, wider social relations. The "home comforts" are essential to the preservation of individual life. And the bearing and forbearing of home life, with the dominant, ceaseless influence of conservative femininity, is a most useful check to the irregular flying impulses of masculine energy. While the world lasts, we shall need not only the individual home, but the family home, the common sheath for the budded leaflets of each new branch, held close to the parent stem before they finally diverge.

Granting all this, there remains the steadily increasing ill effect, not of home life per se, but of the kind of home life based on the sexuo-economic relation. A home in which the rightly dominant feminine force is held at a primitive plane of development, and denied free participation in the swift, wide, upward movement of the world, reacts upon those who hold it down by holding them down in turn. A home in which the inordinate love of receiving things, so long bred into one sex, and the fierce hunger of procuring things, so carefully trained into the other, continually act upon the child, keeps ever before his eyes the fact that life consists in getting dinner and in getting the money to pay for it, getting the food from the market, working forever and ever to cook and serve it. These are the prominent facts of the home as we have made it. The kind of care in which our lives are spent, the things that wear and worry us, are things that should have been outgrown long, long ago if the human race had advanced evenly. Man has advanced, but woman has been kept behind. By inheritance she advances, by experience she is retarded, being always forced back to the economic grade of many thousand years ago.

If a modern man, with all his intellect and energy and resource, were forced to spend all his days hunting with a bow and arrow, fishing with a bone-pointed spear, waiting hungrily on his traps and snares in hope of prey, he could not bring to his children or to his wife the uplifting influences of the true manhood of our time. Even if he started with a college education, even if he had large books to read (when he had time to read them) and improving conversation, still the economic efforts of his life, the steady daily pressure of what he had to do for his living, would check the growth of higher powers. If all men had to be hunters from day to day, the world would be savage still. While all women have to be house servants from day to day, we are still a servile world.

A home life with a dependent mother, a servant-wife, is not an ennobling influence. We all feel this at times. The man, spreading and growing with the world's great growth, comes home, and settles into the tiny talk and fret, or the alluring animal comfort of the place, with a distinct sense of coming down. It is pleasant, it is gratifying to every sense, it is kept warm and soft and pretty to suit the needs of the feebler and smaller creature who is forced to stay in it. It is even considered a virtue for the man to stay in it and to prize it, to value his slippers and his newspaper, his hearth fire and his supper table, his spring bed, and his clean clothes above any other interests.

The harm does not lie in loving home and in staying there as one can, but in the kind of a home and in the kind of womanhood that it fosters, in the grade of industrial development on which it rests. And here, without prophesying, it is easy to look along the line of present progress, and see whither our home life tends. From the cave and tent and hovel up to a graded, differentiated home, with as much room for the individual as the family can afford; from the surly dominance of the absolute patriarch, with his silent servile women and chattel children, to the comparative freedom, equality, and finely diversified lives of a well-bred family of to-day; from the bottom grade of industry in the savage camp, where all things are cooked together by the same person in the same pot,–without neatness, without delicacy, without specialization,–to the million widely separated hands that serve the home to-day in a thousand wide-spread industries,–the man and the mill have achieved it all; the woman has but gone shopping outside; and stayed at the base of the pyramid within.

And, more important and suggestive yet, mark this: whereas, in historic beginnings, nothing but the home of the family existed; slowly, as we have grown, has developed the home of the individual. The first wider movement of social life meant a freer flux of population,–trade, commerce, exchange, communication. Along river courses and sea margins, from canoe to steamship, along paths and roads as they made them, from "shank's mare to the iron horse," faster and freer, wider and oftener, the individual human beings have flowed and mingled in the life that is humanity. At first the traveller's only help was hospitality,–the right of the stranger; but his increasing functional use brought with it, of necessity, the organic structure which made it easy, the transitory individual home. From the most primitive caravansary up to the square miles of floor-space in our grand hotels, the public house has met the needs of social evolution as no private house could have done.

To man, so far the only fully human being of his age, the bachelor apartment of some sort has been a temporary home for that part of his life wherein he has escaped from one family and not yet entered another. To woman this possibility is opening to-day. More and more we see women presuming to live and have a home, even though they have not a family. The family home itself is more and more yielding to the influence of progress. Once it was stationary and permanent, occupied from generation to generation. Now we move, even in families,–move with reluctance and painful objection and with bitter sacrifice of household gods; but move we must under the increasing irritation of irreconcilable conditions. And so has sprung up and grown to vast proportions that startling portent of our times, the "family hotel."

Consider it. Here is the inn, once a mere makeshift stopping-place for weary travellers. Yet even so the weary traveller long since noted the difference between his individual freedom there and his home restrictions, and cheerfully remarked, "I take mine ease in mine inn." Here is this temporary stopping-place for single men become a permanent dwelling-place for families! Not from financial necessity. These are inhabited by people who could well afford to "keep house." But they do not want to keep house. They are tired of keeping house. It is so difficult to keep house, the servant problem is so trying. The health of their wives is not equal to keeping house. These are the things they say.

But under these vague perceptions and expressions is heaving and stirring a slow, uprising social tide. The primitive home, based on the economic dependence of woman, with its unorganized industries, its servile labors, its smothering drag on individual development, is becoming increasingly unsuitable to the men and women of to-day. Of course, they hark back to it, of necessity, so long as marriage and childbearing are supposed to require it, so long as our fondest sentiments and our earliest memories so closely cling to it. But in its practical results, as shown by the ever-rising draught upon the man's purse and woman's strength, it is fast wearing out.

We have watched the approach of this condition, and have laid it to every cause but the real one. We have blamed men for not staying at home as they once did. We have blamed women for not being as good housekeepers as they once were. We have blamed the children for their discontent, the servants for their inefficiency, the very brick and mortar for their poor construction. But we have never thought to blame the institution itself, and see whether it could not be improved upon.

On wide Western prairies, or anywhere in lonely farm houses, the women of today, confined absolutely to this strangling cradle of the race, go mad by scores and hundreds. Our asylums show a greater proportion of insane women among farmers' wives than in any other class. In the cities, where there is less "home life," people seem to stand it better. There are more distractions, the men say, and seek them. There is more excitement, amusement, variety, the women say, and seek them. What is really felt is the larger social interests and the pressure of forces newer than those of the home circle.

Many fear this movement, and vainly strive to check it. There is no cause for alarm. We are not going to lose our homes nor our families, nor any of the sweetness and happiness that go with them. But we are going to lose our kitchens, as we have lost our laundries and bakeries. The cook-stove will follow the loom and wheel, the wool-carder and shears. We shall have homes that are places to live in and love in, to rest in and play in, to be alone in and to be together in; and they will not be confused and declassed by admixture with any industry whatever.

In homes like these the family life will have all its finer, truer spirit well maintained; and the cares and labors that now mar its beauty will have passed out into fields of higher fulfilment. The relation of wife to husband and mother to child is changing for the better with this outward alteration. All the personal relations of the family will be open to a far purer and fuller growth.

Nothing in the exquisite pathos of woman's long subjection goes deeper to the heart than the degradation of motherhood by the very conditions we supposed were essential to it. To see the mother's heart and mind longing to go with the child, to help it all the way, and yet to see it year by year pass farther from her, learn things she never was allowed to know, do things she never was allowed to do, go out into "the world"–their world, not hers–alone and

"To bear, to nurse, to rear, to love, and then to lose!"

this not by the natural separation of growth and personal divergence, but by the unnatural separation of falsely divided classes,–rudimentary women and more highly developed men. It is the fissure that opens before the boy is ten years old, and it widens with each year.

A mother economically free, a world-servant instead of a house-servant; a mother knowing the world and living in it,–can be to her children far more than has ever been possible before. Motherhood in the world will make that world a different place for her child.

XIII.

IN reconstructing in our minds the position of woman under conditions of economic independence, it is most difficult to think of her as a mother.

We are so unbrokenly accustomed to the old methods of motherhood, so convinced that all its processes are inter-relative and indispensable, and that to alter one of them is to endanger the whole relation, that we cannot conceive of any desirable change.

When definite plans for such change are suggested,–ways in which babies might be better cared for than at present,–we either deny the advantages of the change proposed or insist that these advantages can be reached under our present system. Just as in cooking we seek to train the private cook and to exalt and purify the private taste, so in baby-culture we seek to train the individual mother, and to call for better conditions in the private home; in both cases ignoring the relation between our general system and its particular phenomena. Though it may be shown, with clearness, that in physical conditions the private house, as a place in which to raise children, may be improved upon, yet all the more stoutly do we protest that the mental life, the emotional life, of the home is the best possible environment for the young.

There was a time in human history when this was true. While progress derived its main impetus from the sex-passion, and the highest emotions were those that held us together in the family relation, such education and such surroundings as fostered and intensified these emotions were naturally the best. But in the stage into which we are now growing, when the family relation is only a part of life, and our highest duties lie between individuals in social relation, the child has new needs.

This does not mean, as the scared rush of the unreasoning mind to an immediate opposite would suggest, a disruption of the family circle or the destruction of the home. It does not mean the separation of mother and child,–that instant dread of the crude instinct of animal maternity. But it does mean a change of basis in the family relation by the removal of its previous economic foundation, and a change of method in our child-culture. We are no more bound to maintain forever our early methods in baby-raising than we are bound to maintain them in the education of older children, or in floriculture. All human life is in its very nature open to improvement, and motherhood is not excepted. The relation between men and women, between husband and wife, between parent and child, changes inevitably with social advance; but we are loath to admit it. We think a change here must be wrong, because we are so convinced that the present condition is right.

On examination, however, we find that the existing relation between parent and children in the home is by no means what we unquestioningly assume. We all hold certain ideals of home life, of family life. When we see around us, or read of, scores and hundreds of cases of family unhappiness and open revolt, we lay it to the individual misbehavior of the parties concerned, and go on implicitly believing in the intrinsic perfection of the institution. When, on the other hand, we find people living together in this relation, in peace and love and courtesy, we do not conversely attribute this to individual superiority and virtue; but we point to it as instancing the innate beauty of the relation.

To the careful sociological observer what really appears is this: when individual and racial progress was best served by the close associations of family life, people were very largely developed in capacity for family affection. They were insensitive to the essential limitations and incessant friction of the relation. They assented to the absolute authority of the head of the family and to the minor despotism of lower functionaries, manifesting none of those sharply defined individual characteristics which are so inimical to the family relation.

But we have reached a stage where individual and racial progress is best served by the higher specialization of individuals and by a far wider sense of love and duty. This change renders the psychic condition of home life increasingly disadvantageous. We constantly hear of the inferior manners of the children of to-day, of the restlessness of the young, of the flat treason of deserting parents. It is visibly not so easy to live at home as it used to be. Our children are not more perversely constituted than the children of earlier ages, but the conditions in which they are reared are not suited to develope the qualities now needed in human beings.

This increasing friction between members of families should not be viewed with condemnation from a moral point of view, but studied with scientific interest. If our families are so relatively uncomfortable under present conditions, are there not conditions wherein the same families could be far more comfortable? No: we are afraid not. We think it is right to have things as they are, wrong to wish to change them. We think that virtue lies largely in being uncomfortable, and that there is special virtue in the existing family relation.

Virtue is a relative term. Human virtues change from age to age with the change in conditions. Consider the great virtue of loyalty,–our highest name for duty. This is a quality that became valuable in human life the moment we began to do things which were not instantly and visibly profitable to ourselves. The permanent application of the individual to a task not directly attractive was an indispensable social quality, and therefore a virtue. Steadfastness, faithfulness, loyalty, duty, that conscious, voluntary attitude of the individual which holds him to a previously assumed relation, even to his extreme personal injury,–to death itself,–from this results the cohesion of the social body: it is a first principle of social existence.

To the personal conscience a social necessity must express itself in a recognized and accepted pressure,–a force to which we bow, a duty, a virtue. So the virtue of loyalty came into early and lasting esteem, whether in the form of loyalty to one's own spoken word or vow–"He that sweareth to his hurt, and doeth it"–to a friend or group of friends in temporary union for some common purpose, or to a larger and more permanent relation. The highest form is, of course, loyalty to the largest common interest; and here we can plainly trace the growth of this quality.

First, we see it in the vague, nebulous, coherence of the horde of savages, then in the tense devotion of families,–that absolute duty to the highest known social group. It was in this period that obedience to parents was writ so large in our scale of virtues. The family feud, the vendetta of the Corsicans, is an over-development of this force of family devotion. Next came loyalty to the chief, passing even that due the father. And with the king–that dramatic personification of a nation, "Lo! royal England comes!"–loyalty became a very passion. It took precedence of every virtue, with good reason; for it was not, as was supposed, the person of the king which was so revered: it was the embodied nation, the far-reaching, collective interests of every citizen, the common good, which called for the willing sacrifice of every individual. We still exhibit all these phases of loyalty, in differently diminishing degrees; but we show, also, a larger form of this great virtue peculiar to our age.

The lines of social relation to-day are mainly industrial. Our individual lives, our social peace and progress, depend more upon our economic relations, than upon any other. For a long time society was organized only on a sex-basis, a religious basis, or a military basis, each of such organizations being comparatively transient; and its component individuals labored alone on an economic basis of helpless individualism.

Duty is a social sense, and developes only with social organization. As our civil organization has become national, we have developed the sense of duty to the State. As our industrial organization has grown to the world-encircling intricacies of to-day, as we have come to hold our place on earth by reason of our vast and elaborate economic relation with its throbbing and sensitive machinery of communication and universal interservice, the unerring response of the soul to social needs has given us a new kind of loyalty,–loyalty to our work. The engineer who sticks to his engine till he dies, that his trainload of passengers may live; the cashier who submits to torture rather than disclose the secret of the safe,–these are loyal exactly as was the servitor of feudal times, who followed his master to the death, or the subject who gave up all for his king. Professional honor, duty to one's employers, duty to the work itself, at any cost,–this is loyalty, faithfulness, the power to stay put in a relation necessary to the social good, though it may be directly against personal interest.

It is in the training of children for this stage of human life that the private home has ceased to be sufficient, or the isolated, primitive, dependent woman capable. Not that the mother does not have an intense and overpowering sense of loyalty and of duty; but it is duty to individuals, just as it was in the year one. What she is unable to follow, in her enforced industrial restriction, is the higher specialization of labor, and the honorable devotion of human lives to the development of their work. She is most slavishly bound to her daily duty, it is true; but it does not occur to her as a duty to raise the grade of her own labor for the sake of humanity, nor as a sin so to keep back the progress of the world by her contented immobility.

She cannot teach what she does not know. She cannot in any sincerity uphold as a duty what she does not practise. The child learns more of the virtues needed in modern life–of fairness, of justice, of comradeship, of collective interest and action–in a common school than can be taught in the most perfect family circle. We may preach to our children as we will of the great duty of loving and serving one's neighbor; but what the baby is born into, what the child grows up to see and feel, is the concentration of one entire life–his mother's–upon the personal aggrandizement of one's family, and the human service of another entire life–his father's–so warped and strained by the necessity of "supporting his family" that treason to society is the common price of comfort in the home. For a man to do any base, false work for which he is hired, work that injures producer and consumer alike; to prostitute what power and talent he possesses to whatever purchaser may use them,–this is justified among men by what they call duty to the family, and is unblamed by the moral sense of dependent women.

And this is the atmosphere in which the wholly home-bred, mother-taught child grows up. Why should not food and clothes and the comforts of his own people stand first in his young mind? Does he not see his mother, the all-loved, all-perfect one, peacefully spending her days in the arrangement of these things which his father's ceaseless labor has procured? Why should he not grow up to care for his own, to the neglect and willing injury of all the rest, when his earliest, deepest impressions are formed under such exclusive devotion?

It is not the home as a place of family life and love that injures the child, but as the centre of a tangled heap of industries, low in their ungraded condition, and lower still because they are wholly personal. Work the object of which is merely to serve one's self is the lowest. Work the object of which is merely to serve one's family is the next lowest. Work the object of which is to serve more and more people, in widening range, till it approximates the divine spirit that cares for all the world, is social service in the fullest sense, and the highest form of service that we can reach.

It is this personality in home industry that keeps it hopelessly down. The short range between effort and attainment, the constant attention given to personal needs, is bad for the man, worse for the woman, and worst for the child. It belittles his impressions of life at the start. It accustoms him to magnify the personal duties and minify the social ones, and it greatly retards his adjustment to larger life. This servant-motherhood, with all its unavoidable limitation and ill results, is the concomitant of the economic dependence of woman upon man, the direct and inevitable effect of the sexuo-economic relation.

The child is affected by it during his most impressionable years, and feels the effect throughout this life. The woman is permanently retarded by it; the man, less so, because of his normal social activities, wherein he is under more developing influence. But he is injured in great degree, and our whole civilization is checked and perverted.

We suffer also, our lives long, from an intense self-consciousness, from a sensitiveness beyond all need; we demand measureless personal attention and devotion, because we have been born and reared in a very hotbed of these qualities. A baby who spent certain hours of every day among other babies, being cared for because he was a baby, and not because he was "my baby," would grow to have a very different opinion of himself from that which is forced upon each new soul that comes among us by the ceaseless adoration of his own immediate family. What he needs to learn at once and for all, to learn softly and easily, but inexorably, is that he is one of many. We all dimly recognize this in our praise of larger families, and in our saying that "an only child is apt to be selfish." So is an only family. The earlier and more easily a child can learn that human life means many people, and their behavior to one another, the happier and stronger and more useful his life will be.

This could be taught him with no difficulty whatever, under certain conditions, just as he is taught his present sensitiveness and egotism by the present conditions. It is not only temperature and diet and rest and exercise which affect the baby. "He does love to be noticed," we say. "He is never so happy as when he has a dozen worshippers around him." But what is the young soul learning all the while? What does he gather, as he sees and hears and slowly absorbs impressions? With the inflexible, inferences of a clear, young brain, unsupplied with any counter-evidence until later in life; he learns that women are meant to wait on people, to get dinner, and sweep and pick up things; that men are made to bring home things, and are to be begged of according to circumstances; that babies are the object of concentrated admiration; that their hair, hands, feet, are specially attractive; that they are the heated focus of attention, to be passed from hand to hand, swung and danced and amused most violently, and also to be laid aside and have nothing done to them, with no regard to their preference in either case.

And then, in the midst of all this tingling self-consciousness and desire for loving praise, he learns that he is "naughty"! The grief, the shame, the anger at injustice, the hopeless bewilderment, the morbid sensitiveness of conscience or the stolid dulling of it, the gradual retirement of the baffled brain from all these premature sensations to a contentment with mere personal gratification and a growing ingenuity of obtaining it,–all these experiences are the common lot of the child among us, our common lot when we were children. Of course, we don't remember. Of course, we loved our mother, and thought her perfect. Comparisons among mothers are difficult for a baby. Of course, we loved our homes, and never dreamed of any other way of being "brought up." And, of course, when we have children of our own, we bring them up in the same way. What other way is there? What is there to be said on the subject? Children always were brought up at home. Isn't that enough?

And yet, insidiously, slowly, irresistibly, while we flatter ourselves that things remain the same, they are changing under our very eyes from year to year, from day to day. Education, hiding itself behind a wall of books, but consisting more and more fully in the grouping of children and in the training of faculties never mentioned in the curriculum,–education, which is our human motherhood, has crept nearer and nearer to its true place, its best work,–the care and training of the little child. Some women there are, and some men, whose highest service to humanity is the care of children. Such should not concentrate their powers upon their own children alone,–a most questionable advantage,–but should be so placed that their talent and skill, their knowledge and experience, would benefit the largest number of children. Many women there are, and many men, who, though able to bring forth fine children, are unable to educate them properly. Simply to bear children is a personal matter,–an animal function. Education is collective, human, a social function.

As we now arrange life, our children must take their chances while babies, and live or die, improve or deteriorate, according to the mother to whom they chance to be born. An inefficient mother does not prevent a child from having a good school education or a good college education; but the education of babyhood, the most important of all, is wholly in her hands. It is futile to say that mothers should be taught how to fulfil their duties. You cannot teach every mother to be a good school educator or a good college educator. Why should you expect every mother to be a good nursery educator? Whatever our expectations, she is not; and our mistrained babies, such of them as survive the maternal handling, grow to be such people as we see about us.

The growth and change in home and family life goes steadily on under and over and through our prejudices and convictions; and the education of the child has changed and become a social function, while we still imagine the mother to be doing it all.

In its earliest and most rudimentary manifestations, education was but part of the individual maternal function of the female animal. But no sooner did the human mind begin to show capacity for giving and receiving its impressions through language (thus attaining the power of acquiring information through sources other than its own experience) than the individual mother ceased to be the sole educator. The young savage receives not only guidance from his anxious mother, but from the chiefs and elders of his tribe. For a long time the aged were considered the only suitable teachers, because the major part of knowledge was still derived from personal experience; and, of course, the older the person, the greater his experience, other things being equal, and they were rather equal then. This primitive notion still holds among us. People still assume superior wisdom because of superior age, putting mere number of experiences against a more essential and better arranged variety, and quite forgetting that the needed wisdom of to-day is not the accumulation of facts, but the power to think about them to some purpose.

With our increased power to preserve and transmit individual experience through literature, and to disseminate such information through systematic education, we see younger and younger people, more rich in, say, chemical or electrical experience than "the oldest inhabitant" could have been in earlier times. Therefore, the teacher of to-day is not the graybeard and beldame, but the man and woman most newly filled with the gathered experience of the world. As this change from age to youth has taken place in the teacher, it has also shown itself in the taught. Grown men frequented the academic groves of Greece. Youths filled the universities of the Middle Ages. Boys and, later, girls were given the increasing school advantages of progressive centuries.

To-day the beautiful development of the kindergarten has brought education to the nursery door. Even our purblind motherhood is beginning to open that door; and we have at last entered upon the study of babyhood, its needs and powers, and are seeing that education begins with life itself. It is no new and daring heresy to suggest that babies need better education than the individual mother now gives them. It is simply a little further extension of the steadily expanding system of human education which is coming upon us, as civilization grows. And it no more infringes upon the mother's rights, the mother's duties, the mother's pleasures, than does the college or the school.

We think no harm of motherhood because our darlings go out each day to spend long hours in school. The mother is not held neglectful, nor the child bereft. It is not called a "separation of mother and child." There would be no further harm or risk or loss in a babyhood passed among such changed surroundings and skilled service as should meet its needs more perfectly than it is possible for the mother to meet them alone at home.

Better surroundings and care for babies, better education, do not mean, as some mothers may imagine, that the tiny monthling is to be taught to read, or even that it is to be exposed to cabalistical arrangements of color and form and sound which shall mysteriously force the young intelligence to flower. It would mean, mainly, a far quieter and more peaceful life than is possible for the heavily loved and violently cared for baby in the busy household; and the impressions which it did meet would be planned and maintained with an intelligent appreciation of its mental powers. The mother would not be excluded, but supplemented, as she is now, by the teacher and the school.

Try and imagine for yourself, if you like, a new kind of coming alive,–the mother breast and mother arms there, of course, fulfilling the service which no other, however tender, could supervene; but there would be other service also. The long, bright hours of the still widening days would find one in sunny, soft-colored rooms, or among the grass and flowers, or by the warm sand and waters. There would be about one more of one's self, others of the same size and age, in restful, helpful companionship. A year means an enormous difference in the ages of babies. Think what a passion little children have for playmates of exactly their own age, because in them alone is perfect equality, and then think that the home-kept baby never has such companionship, unless, indeed, there are twins!

In this larger grouping, in full companionship, the child would unconsciously absorb the knowledge that "we" were humanity, that "we" were creatures to be so fed, so watched, so laid to sleep, so kissed and cuddled and set free to roll and play. The mother-hours would be sweetest of all, perhaps. Here would be something wholly one's own, and the better appreciated for the contrast. But the long, steady days would bring their peaceful lessons of equality and common interest instead of the feverish personality of the isolated one-baby household, or the innumerable tyrannies and exactions, the forced submissions and exclusions, of the nursery full of brothers and sisters of widely differing ages and powers. Mothers accustomed to consider many babies besides their own would begin, on the one hand, to learn something of mere general babyness, and so understand that stage of life far better, and, on the other, to outgrow the pathetic idolatry of the fabled crow,–to recognize a difference in babies, and so to learn a new ideal in their great work of motherhood.

This alone is reason good for a wider maternity. As long as each mother dotes and gloats upon her own children, knowing no others, so long this animal passion overestimates or underestimates real human qualities in the child. So long as this endures, we must grow up with the false, unbalanced opinion of ourselves forced upon us in our infancy. We may think too well of ourselves or we may think too ill of ourselves; but we think always too much of ourselves, because of this untrained and unmodified concentration of maternal feeling. Our whole attitude toward the child is too intensely personal. Through all our aching later life we labor to outgrow the false perspective taught by primitive motherhood.

A baby, brought up with other babies, would never have that labor or that pain. However much his mother might love him, and he might enjoy her love, he would still find that for most of the time he was treated precisely like other people of the same age. Such a change would not involve any greater loss to home and family life than does the school or kindergarten. It would not rob the baby of his mother nor the mother of her baby. And such a change would give the mother certain free hours as a human being, as a member of a civilized community, as an economic producer, as a growing, self-realizing individual. This freedom, growth, and power will make her a wiser, stronger, and nobler mother.

After all is said of loving gratitude to our unfailing mother-nurse, we must have a most exalted sense of our own personal importance so to canonize the service of ourselves. The mother as a social servant instead of a home servant will not lack in true mother duty. She will love her child as well, perhaps better, when she is not in hourly contact with it, when she goes from its life to her own life, and back from her own life to its life, with ever new delight and power. She can keep the deep, thrilling joy of motherhood far fresher in her heart, far more vivid and open in voice and eyes and tender hands, when the hours of individual work give her mind another channel for her own part of the day. From her work, loved and honored though it is, she will return to the home life, the child life, with an eager, ceaseless pleasure, cleansed of all the fret and friction and weariness that so mar it now.

The child, also, will feel this beneficent effect. It is a mistake to suppose that the baby, more than the older child, needs the direct care and presence of the mother. Careful experiment has shown that a new-born baby does not know its own mother, and that a new-made mother does not know her own baby. They have been changed without the faintest recognition on either side.

The services of a foster-mother, a nurse, a grandma, are often liked by a baby as well as, and perhaps better than, those of its own mother. The mere bodily care of a young infant is as well given by one wise, loving hand as another. It is that trained hand that the baby needs, not mere blood-relationship. While the mother keeps her beautiful prerogative of nursing, she need never fear that any other will be dearer to the little heart than she who is the blessed provider of his highest known good. A healthy, happy, rightly occupied motherhood should be able to keep up this function longer than is now customary,–to the child's great gain. Aside from this special relationship, however, the baby would grow easily into the sense of other and wider relationship.

In the freedom and peace of his baby bedroom and baby parlor, in his easy association with others of his own age, he would absorb a sense of right human relation with his mother's milk, as it were,–a sense of others' rights and of his own. Instead of finding life a place in which all the fun was in being carried round and "done to" by others, and a place also in which these others were a tyranny and a weariness unutterable; he would find life a place in which to spread out, unhindered, getting acquainted with his own unfolding powers of body and mind in an atmosphere of physical warmth and ease and of quiet peace of mind.

Direct, concentrated, unvarying personal love is too hot an atmosphere for a young soul. Variations of loneliness, anger, and injustice, are not changes to be desired. A steady, diffused love, lighted with wisdom, based always on justice, and varied with rapturous draughts of our own mother's depth of devotion, would make us into a new people in a few generations. The bent and reach of our whole lives are largely modified by the surroundings of infancy; and those surroundings are capable of betterment, though not to be attained by the individual mother in the individual home.

There are three reasons why the individual mother can never be fit to take all the care of her children. The first two are so commonly true as to have much weight, the last so absolutely and finally true as to be sufficient in itself alone.

First, not every woman is born with the special qualities and powers needed to take right care of children: she has not the talent for it. Second, not every woman can have the instruction and training needed to fit her for the right care of children: she has not the education for it. Third, while each woman takes all the care of her own children herself, no woman can ever have the requisite experience for it. That is the final bar. That is what keeps back our human motherhood. No mother knows more than her mother knew: no mother has ever learned her business; and our children pass under the well-meaning experiments of an endless succession of amateurs.

We try to get "an experienced nurse." We insist on "an experienced physician." But our idea of an experienced mother is simply one who has borne many children, as if parturition was an educative process!

To experience the pangs of child-birth, or the further pangs of a baby's funeral, adds nothing whatever to the mother's knowledge of the proper care, clothing, feeding, and teaching of the child. The educative department of maternity is not a personal function: it is in its very nature a social function; and we fail grievously in its fulfilment.

The economically independent mother, widened and freed, strengthened and developed, by her social service, will do better service as mother than it has been possible to her before. No one thing could do more to advance the interests of humanity than the wiser care and wider love of organized human motherhood around our babies. This nobler mother, bearing nobler children, and rearing them in nobler ways, would go far toward making possible the world which we want to see. And this change is coming upon us overpoweringly in spite of our foolish fears.

XIV.

THE changes in our conception and expression of home life, so rapidly and steadily going on about us, involve many far-reaching effects, all helpful to human advancement. Not the least of these is the improvement in our machinery of social intercourse.

This necessity of civilization was unknown in those primitive ages when family intercourse was sufficient for all, and when any further contact between individuals meant war. Trade and its travel, the specialization of labor and the distribution of its products, with their ensuing development, have produced a wider, freer, and more frequent movement and interchange among the innumerable individuals whose interaction makes society. Only recently, and as yet but partially, have women as individuals come to their share of this fluent social intercourse which is the essential condition of civilization. It is not merely a pleasure or an indulgence: it is the human necessity.

For women as individuals to meet men and other women as individuals, with no regard whatever to the family relation, is a growing demand of our time. As a social necessity, it is perforce being met in some fashion; but its right development is greatly impeded by the clinging folds of domestic and social customs derived from the sexuo-ecoonomic relation. The demand for a wider and freer social intercourse between the sexes rests, primarily, on the needs of their respective natures, but is developed in modern life to a far subtler and higher range of emotion than existed in the primitive state, where they had but one need and but one way of meeting it; and this demand, too, calls for a better arrangement of our machinery of living.

Always in social evolution, as in other evolution, the external form suited to earlier needs is but slowly outgrown; and the period of transition, while the new functions are fumbling through the old organs, and slowly forcing mechanical expression for themselves, is necessarily painful. So far in our development, acting on a deep-seated conviction that the world consisted only of families and the necessary business arrangements involved in providing for those families, we have conscientiously striven to build and plan for family advantage, and either unconsciously or grudgingly have been forced to make transient provision for individuals. Whatever did not tend to promote family life, and did tend to provide for the needs of individuals not at the time in family relation, we have deprecated in principle, though reluctantly forced to admit it in practice.

To this day articles are written, seriously and humorously, protesting against the increasing luxury and comfort of bachelor apartments for men, as well as against the pecuniary independence of women, on the ground that these conditions militate against marriage and family life. Most men, even now, pass through a period of perhaps ten years, when they are individuals, business calling them away from their parental family, and business not allowing them to start new families of their own. Women, also, more and more each year, are entering upon a similar period of individual life. And there is a certain permanent percentage of individuals, "odd numbers" and "broken sets," who fall short of family life or who are left over from it; and these need to live.

The residence hotel, the boarding-house, club, lodging-house, and restaurant are our present provision for this large and constantly increasing class. It is not a travelling class. These are people who want to live somewhere for years at a time, but who are not married or otherwise provided with a family. Home life being in our minds inextricably connected with married life, a home being held to imply a family, and a family implying a head, these detached persons are unable to achieve any home life, and are thereby subjected to the inconvenience, deprivation, and expense, the often inhygienic, and sometimes immoral influences, of our makeshift substitutes.

What the human race requires is permanent provision for the needs of individuals, disconnected from the sex-relation. Our assumption that only married people and their immediate relatives have any right to live in comfort and health is erroneous. Every human being needs a home,–bachelor, husband, or widower, girl, wife, or widow, young or old. They need it from the cradle to the grave, and without regard to sex-connections. We should so build and arrange for the shelter and comfort of humanity as not to interfere with marriage, and yet not to make that comfort dependent upon marriage. With the industries of home life managed professionally, with rooms and suites of rooms and houses obtainable by any person or persons desiring them, we could live singly without losing home comfort and general companionship, we could meet bereavement without being robbed of the common conveniences of living as well as of the heart's love, and we could marry in ease and freedom without involving any change in the economic base of either party concerned.

Married people will always prefer a home together, and can have it; but groups of women or groups of men can also have a home together if they like, or contiguous rooms. And individuals even could have a house to themselves, without having, also, the business of a home upon their shoulders.

Take the kitchens out of the houses, and you leave rooms which are open to any form of arrangement and extension; and the occupancy of them does not mean "housekeeping." In such living, personal character and taste would flower as never before; the home of each individual would be at last a true personal expression; and the union of individuals in marriage would not compel the jumbling together of all the external machinery of their lives,–a process in which much of the delicacy and freshness of love, to say nothing of the power of mutual rest and refreshment, is constantly lost. The sense of lifelong freedom and self-respect and of the peace and permanence of one's own home will do much to purify and uplift the personal relations of life, and more to strengthen and extend the social relations. The individual will learn to feel himself an integral part of the social structure, in close, direct, permanent connection with the needs and uses of society.

This is especially needed for women, who are generally considered, and who consider themselves, mere fractions of families, and incapable of any wholesome life of their own. The knowledge that peace and comfort may be theirs for life, even if they do not marry,–and may be still theirs for life, even if they do,–will develope a serenity and strength in women most beneficial to them and to the world. It is a glaring proof of the insufficient and irritating character of our existing form of marriage that women must be forced to it by the need of food and clothes, and men by the need of cooks and housekeepers. We are absurdly afraid that, if men or women can meet these needs of life by other means, they will cheerfully renounce the marriage relation. And yet we sing adoringly of the power of love!

In reality, we may hope that the most valuable effect of this change in the basis of living will be the cleansing of love and marriage from this base admixture of pecuniary interest and creature comfort, and that men and women , eternally drawn together by the deepest force in nature, will be able at last to meet on a plane of pure and perfect love. We shame our own ideals, our deepest instincts, our highest knowledge, by this gross assumption that the noblest race on earth will not mate, or, at least, not mate monogamously, unless bought and bribed through the common animal necessities of food and shelter, and chained by law and custom.

The depth and purity and permanence of the marriage relation rest on the necessity for the prolonged care of children by both parents,–a law of racial development which we can never escape. When parents are less occupied in getting food and cooking it, in getting furniture and dusting it, they may find time to give new thought and new effort to the care of their children. The necessities of the child are far deeper than for bread and bed; those are his mere racial needs, held in common with all his kind. What he needs far more and receives far less is the companionship, the association, the personal touch, of his father and mother. When the common labors of life are removed from the home, we shall have the time, and perhaps the inclination, to make the personal acquaintance of our children. They will seem to us not so much creatures to be waited on as people to be understood. As the civil and military protection of society has long since superseded the tooth-and-claw defence of the fierce parent, without in the least endangering the truth and intensity of the family relation, so the economic provision of society will in time supersede the bringing home of prey by the parent, without evil effects to the love or prosperity of the family. These primitive needs and primitive methods of meeting them are unquestionably at the base of the family relation; but we have long passed them by, and the ties between parent and child are not weakened, but strengthened, by the change.

The more we grow away from these basic conditions, the more fully we realize the deeper and higher forms of relation which are the strength and the delight of human life. Full and permanent provision for individual life and comfort will not cut off the forces that draw men and women together or hold children to their parents; but it will purify and intensify these relations to a degree which we can somewhat foretell by observing the effect of such changes as are already accomplished in this direction. And, in freeing the individual, old and young, from enforced association on family lines, and allowing this emergence into free association on social lines, we shall healthfully assist the development of true social intercourse.

The present economic basis of family life holds our friendly and familiar intercourse in narrow grooves. Such visiting and mingling as is possible to us is between families rather than between individuals; and the growing specialization of individuals renders it increasingly unlikely that all the members of a given family shall please a given visitor or he please them. This, on our present basis, either checks the intercourse or painfully strains the family relation. The change of economic relation in families from a sex-basis to a social basis will make possible wide individual intercourse without this accompanying strain on the family ties.

This outgoing impulse among members of families, their growing desire for general and personal social intercourse, has been considered as a mere thirst for amusement, and deprecated by the moralist. He has so far maintained that the highest form of association was association with one's own family, and that a desire for a wider and more fluent relationship was distinctly unworthy. "He is a good family man," we say admiringly of him who asks only for his newspaper and slippers in the evening; and for the woman who dares admit that she wishes further society than that of her husband we have but one name. With the children, too, our constant effort is to "keep the boys at home," to "make home attractive," so that our ancient ideal, the patriarchal ideal, of a world of families and nothing else, may be maintained.

But this is a world of persons as well as of families. We are persons as soon as we are born, though born into families. We are persons when we step out of families, and persons still, even when we step into new families of our own. As persons, we need more and more, in each generation, to associate with other persons. It is most interesting to watch this need making itself felt, and getting itself supplied, by fair means or foul, through all these stupid centuries. In our besotted exaggeration of the sex-relation, we have crudely supposed that a wish for wider human relationship was a wish for wider sex-relationship, and was therefore to be discouraged, as in Spain it was held unwise to teach women to write, lest they become better able to communicate with their lovers, and so shake the foundations of society.

But, when our sex-relation is made pure and orderly by the economic independence of women, when sex-attraction is no longer a consuming fever, forever convulsing the social surface, under all its bars and chains, we shall not be content to sit down forever with half a dozen blood relations for our whole social arena. We shall need each other more, not less, and shall recognize that social need of one another as the highest faculty of this the highest race on earth.

The force which draws friends together is a higher one than that which draws the sexes together,–higher in the sense of belonging to a later race-development. "Passing the love of women" is no unmeaning phrase. Children need one another: young people need one another. Middle-aged people need one another: old people need one another. We all need one another, much and often. Just as every human creature needs a place to be alone in, a sacred, private "home" of his own, so all human creatures need a place to be together in, from the two who can show each other their souls uninterruptedly, to the largest throng that can throb and stir in unison.

Humanity means being together, and our unutterably outgrown way of living keeps us apart. How many people, if they dare face the fact, have often hopelessly longed for some better way of seeing their friends, their own true friends, relatives by soul, if not by body!

Acting always under the heated misconceptions of our over-sexed minds, we have pictured mankind as a race of beasts whose only desire to be together was based on one great, overworked passion, and who were only kept from universal orgies of promiscuity by being confined in homes. This is not true. It is not true even now in our over-sexed condition. It will be still less true when we are released from the artificial pressure of the sexuo-economic relation and grow natural again.

Men, women, and children need freedom to mingle on a human basis; and that means to mingle in their daily lives and occupations, not to go laboriously to see each other, with no common purpose. We all know the pleasant acquaintance and deep friendship that springs up when people are thrown together naturally, at school, at college, on shipboard, in the cars, in a camping trip, in business. The social need of one another rests at bottom on a common, functional development; and the common, functional service is its natural opportunity.

The reason why friendship means more to men than to women, and why they associate so much more easily and freely, is that they are further developed in race-functions, and that they work together. In the natural association of common effort and common relaxation is the true opening for human companionship. Just to put a number of human beings in the same room, to relate their bodies as to cubic space, does not relate their souls. Our present methods of association, especially for women, are most unsatisfactory. They arise, and go to "call" on one another. They solemnly "return" these calls. They prepare much food, and invite many people to come and eat it; or some dance, music, or entertainment is made the temporary ground of union. But these people do not really meet one another. They pass whole lifetimes in going through the steps of these elaborate games, and never become acquainted. There is a constant thirst among us for fuller and truer social intercourse; but our social machinery provides no means for quenching it.

Men have satisfied this desire in large measure; but between women, or between men and women, it is yet far from accomplishment. Men meet one another freely in their work, while women work alone. But the difference is sharpest in their play. "Girls don't have any fun!" say boys, scornfully; and they don't have very much. What they do have must come, like their bread and butter, on lines of sex. Some man must give them what amusement they have, as he must give them everything else. Men have filled the world with games and sports, from the noble contests of the Olympic plain to the brain and body training sports of to-day, good, bad, and indifferent. Through all the ages the men have played; and the women have looked on, when they were asked. Even the amusing occupation of seeing other people do things was denied them, unless they were invited by the real participants. The "queen of the ball-room" is but a wall-flower, unless she is asked to dance by the real king.

Even to-day, when athletics are fast opening to women, when tennis and golf and all the rest are possible to them, the two sexes are far from even in chances to play. To want a good time is not the same thing as to want the society of the other sex, and to make a girl's desire for a good time hang so largely on her power of sex-attraction is another of the grievous strains we put upon that faculty. That people want to see each other is construed by us to mean that "he" wants to see "her," and "she" wants to see "him." The fun and pleasure of the world are so interwound with the sex-dependence of women upon men that women are forced to court "attentions," when not really desirous of anything but amusement; and, as we force the association of the sexes on this plane, so we restrict it on a more wholesome one.

Even our little children in their play are carefully trained to accentuate sex; and a line of conduct for boys, differing from that for girls, is constantly insisted upon long before either would think of a necessity for such difference. Girls and boys, as they associate, are so commented on and teased as to destroy all wholesome friendliness, and induce a premature sex-consciousness. Young men and women are allowed to associate more or less freely, but always on a strictly sex-basis, friendship between man and woman being a common laughing-stock. Every healthy boy and girl resents this, and tries to hold free, natural relation; but such social pressure is hard to resist. She may have as many "beaux" as she can compass, he may "pay attention" to as many girls as he pleases; but that is their only way to meet.

The general discontinuance of all friendly visiting, upon the engagement of either party, proves the nature of the bond. Having chosen the girl he is to marry, why care to call upon any others? having chosen the man she is to marry, why receive attention from any others? these "calls" and "attentions" being all in the nature of tentative preliminaries to possible matrimony. And, after marriage, the wife is never supposed to wish to see any other man than her husband, or the husband any other woman than his wife. In some countries, we vary this arrangement by increasing the social freedom of married people; but the custom is accompanied by a commensurate lack of freedom before marriage, which causes questionable results, both in married life and in social life. In the higher classes of society there is always more freedom of social intercourse between the sexes after marriage; but, speaking generally of America, there is very little natural and serious acquaintance between men and women after the period of pre-matrimonial visiting.

Even the friendship which may have existed between husband and wife before marriage is often destroyed by that relation and its economic complications. They have not time to talk about things as they used: they are too near together, and too deeply involved in the industrial and financial concern of their new business. This works steadily against the development of higher and purer relations between men and women, and tends to keep them forever to the one primitive bond of sex-union.

A young man goes to a city to live and work. He needs the society of women as well as of men. Formerly he had his mother, his sisters, and his sisters' friends, his schoolmates. Now he must face our constrained social conditions. He may visit two kinds of women,–those whom we call "good," and those whom we call "bad." (This classification rests on but one moral quality, and that a sexual one.) He naturally prefers the good. The good are divided, again, into two kinds,–married and single. If he visit a married woman frequently, it is remarked upon: it becomes unpleasant, he does not do it. If he visit an unmarried woman frequently, it is also remarked upon; and he is considered to have "intentions." His best alternative is to visit a number of unmarried women, and distribute his attentions so cautiously that no one can claim them as personal.

Here he enters on the first phase of our sexuo-economic relation: he cannot even visit girls freely without paying for it. Simply to see the girl by calling on her in the family circle is hardly what either wants of the other. One does not meet half a dozen people of various ages and of both sexes as one meets a friend alone. To seek to see her alone is an "attention." To "take her out" costs money, and he cheerfully pays it. But he cannot do this too often, or he will become involved in what is naturally considered a "serious" affair; and every step of the acquaintance is watched and commented upon from a sexual point of view.

There is no natural, simple medium of social intercourse between men and women. The young man can but learn that his popularity depends largely on his pocket-book. The money that he might be saving for marriage is wasted on these miscellaneous preliminaries. As he sees what women like and how much it costs to please them, his hope of marriage recedes farther and farther. The period during which he must live as an individual grows longer; and he becomes accustomed to superficial acquaintance with many women, on the shallowest side of life, with no opportunity for genuine association and true friendship. What wonder that the other kind of woman, who also costs money, it is true, but who does not involve permanent obligation, has come to be so steady a factor in our social life? The sexuo-economic relation promotes vice in more ways than one.

The economic independence of woman will change all these conditions as naturally and inevitably as her dependence has introduced them. In her specialization in industry, she will develope more personality and less sexuality; and this will lower the pressure on this one relation in both women and men. And, in our social intercourse, the new character and new method of living will allow of broad and beautiful developments in human association. As the private home becomes a private home indeed, and no longer the woman's social and industrial horizon; as the workshops of the world–woman's sphere as well as man's–become homelike and beautiful under her influence; and as men and woman move freely together in the exercise of common racial functions,–we shall have new channels for the flow of human life.

We shall not move from the isolated home to the sordid shop and back again, in a world torn and dissevered by the selfish production of one sex and the selfish consumption of the other; but we shall live in a world of men and women humanly related, as well as sexually related, working together, as they were meant to do, for the common good of all. The home will be no longer an economic entity, with its cumbrous industrial machinery huddled vulgarly behind it, but a peaceful and permanent expression of personal life as withdrawn from social contact; and that social contact will be provided for by the many common meeting-places necessitated by the organization of domestic industries.

The assembling-room is as deep a need of human life as the retiring-room,–not some ball-room or theatre, to which one must be invited of set purpose, but great common libraries and parlors, baths and gymnasia, work-rooms and play-rooms, to which both sexes have the same access for the same needs, and where they may mingle freely in common human expression. The kind of buildings essential to the carrying out of the organization of home industry will provide such places. There will be the separate rooms for individuals and the separate houses for families; but there will be, also, the common rooms for all. These must include a place for the children, planned and built for the happy occupancy of many children for many years,–a home such as no children have ever had. This, as well as rooms everywhere for young people and old people, in which they can be together as naturally as they can be alone, without effort, question, or remark.

Such an environment would allow of free association among us, on lines of common interest; and, in its natural, easy flow, we should develope far higher qualities than are brought out by the uneasy struggles of our present "society" to see each other without wanting to. It would make an enormous difference to woman's power of choosing the right man. Cut off from the purchasing power which is now his easiest way to compass his desires, freely seen and known in his daily work and amusements, a woman could know and judge a man as she is wholly unable to do now. Her personality developed by a free and useful life, clear-headed and open-eyed,–a woman still, but a personality as well as a woman,–the girl trained to economic independence, and associating freely with young men in their common work and play, would learn a new estimate of what constitutes noble manhood.

The young man, no longer able to cover all his shortcomings with a dress-coat, and to obtain absolution for every offense by the simple penance of paying for it, unable really to do much that was wrong for lack of the old opportunity and the old incentive, constantly helped and inspired by the friendly presence of honest and earnest womanhood, would have all the force of natural law to lift him up instead of pulling him heavily downward, as it does now.

With the pressure of our over-developed sex-instinct lifted off the world, born clean and strong, of noble-hearted, noble-minded, noble-bodied mothers, trained in the large wisdom of the new motherhood, and living freely in daily association with the best womanhood, a new kind of man can and will grow on earth. What this will mean to the race in power and peace and happiness no eye can foresee. But this much we can see:–that our once useful sexuo-economic relation is being outgrown, that it now produces many evil phenomena, and that its displacement by the economic freedom of woman will of itself set free new forces, to develope in us, by their natural working, the very virtues for which we have striven and agonized so long.

This change is not a thing to prophesy and plead for. It is a change already instituted, and gaining ground among us these many years with marvelous rapidity. Neither men nor women wish the change. Neither men nor women have sought it. But the same great force of social evolution which brought us into the old relation–to our great sorrow and pain–is bringing us out, with equal difficulty and distress. The time has come when it is better for the world that women be economically independent, and therefore they are becoming so.

It is worth while for us to consider the case fully and fairly, that we may see what it is that is happening to us, and welcome with open arms the happiest change in human condition that ever came into the world. To free an entire half of humanity from an artificial position; to release vast natural forces from a strained and clumsy combination, and set them free to work smoothly and easily as they were intended to work; to introduce conditions that will change humanity from within, making for better motherhood and fatherhood, better babyhood and childhood, better food, better homes, better society,–this is to work for human improvement along natural lines. It means enormous racial advance, and that with great swiftness; for this change does not wait to create new forces, but sets free those already potentially strong, so that humanity will fly up like a released spring. And it is already happening. All we need to do is understand and help.

XV.

AS WE learn to see how close is the connection of that which we call the soul with our external conditions, how the moral sense and the behavior of man are modified by the environment, we must of course look for marked results in psychic development arising from so important a condition as our sexuo-economic relation.

The relation of the sexes, in whatever form, has always been observed to affect strongly the moral nature of mankind; and this is one reason why we have placed such disproportionate stress upon the special virtues of that relation. The word "moral" in common use means "chaste"; and, in the case of women, the word "virtue" itself simply implies the one virtue of chastity. Large, popular conceptions are never baseless. They are rooted in deep truths, felt rather than seen, and, however false and silly in external interpretation, may be trusted in their general trend. It is not that the virtue of chastity is so much more important to the race than the virtue of honesty, the virtue of courage, the virtues of cheerfulness, of courtesy, of kindness, but that upon the sex-relation in which we live depends so much of the further development and arrangement of our whole moral nature.

What we call the moral sense is an intellectual recognition of the relative importance of certain acts and their consequences. This appears vaguely and weakly among early savages, and was for long mainly applied to a few clearly defined and arbitrary rites and ceremonies, set rules in a game of priest-and-people. But the habit of associating a sense of worthiness with certain acts by which came praise and profit grew in the childish soul, and the range of moral deeds widened. It has been widening ever since, growing deeper and higher and far more subtle, developing with the other social qualities.

No human distinction is more absolutely and exclusively social than the moral sense. Ethics is a social science. There is no ethics for the individual. Taken by himself, man is but an animal; and his conduct bears relation only to the needs of the animal,–self-preservation and race-preservation. Every virtue, and the power to see and strive for it, is a social quality. The highest virtues are those wherein we best serve the most people, and their development in us keeps pace with the development of society. It is the social relation which calls for our virtues, and which maintains them.

A simple instance of this is in the prompt lapse to barbarism of a man cut off from his kind, and forced to live in conditions of savagery. Even a brief and partial change in conditions changes conduct at once, as is shown by the behavior of the most pious New Englanders when in mining camps. It is shown, also, by the different scale of virtue in the different classes and industries.

Every social relation has its ethics; and the general needs of society, as a whole, are the basis of ethics. In every age and race this may be studied, and a clear connection established always between the virtues and vices of a given people and their local conditions. The principal governing condition in the development of ethics is the economic environment. This may seem strange to one accustomed to consider moral laws as not of this world, and to see how often virtue costs its possessor dear. The relative behavior of a given number of people depends, first, upon the existence of those people. Such conduct as should tend to exterminate them would exterminate their ethics. Such conduct as should tend to preserve and increase them is the only conduct of which ethical value can be predicated. Ethics is, therefore, absolutely conditioned upon life and the maintenance thereof. From the lowest and narrowest view which calls an act right or wrong, according to its immediate effects upon one's present life, to the clear vision of ultimate results which calls a course of conduct right or wrong, according to its final effects upon one's eternal life, our ethics, small and great, is the science of human conduct measured by its results.

It is inevitable, then, that in all races we should find those acts whereby men live considered right, and should see a high degree of approval awarded to him who best performs them. In the hunting and fighting period the best hunter and fighter was the best man, praised and honored by this tribe. The virtues cultivated were such as enabled the possessor to hunt and kill most successfully, to maintain himself and be a credit and a help to his friends. Savage virtues are the simple reflection of savage conditions. To be patient and self-controlled was an economic necessity to the hunter: to bear pain and arduous exertion easily was a necessity to the fighter. Therefore, the savage, by precept and example, cultivated these virtues.

In the long agricultural and military periods we see the same thing. In the peasant the virtues of industry and patience were extolled: it takes industry and patience to raise corn. In the soldier the virtues of courage and obedience were extolled, and in every one the virtue of faith was the prime requisite of the existing religion. It took a great deal of faith to accept the religions of those times. The importance of faith as a virtue declines as religion grows more intelligible and applicable to life. It requires no effort to believe what you can understand and do. Slowly the industrial era dawned and grew, from the weak, sporadic efforts of the cringing packman and craftsman, the common prey of the dominant fighting class, to our colossal industrial organization, in which the soldier is ruthlessly exploited to some financial interests. With this change in economic conditions has changed the scale of virtues.

Physical courage has sunk: obedience, patience, faith, and the rest do not stand as they did. We praise and value to-day, as always, the virtues whereby we live. Every animal developes the virtues of his conditions: our human distinction is that we add the power of conscious perception and personal volition to the action of natural force. Not only in our own race, but in others, do we call "good" and "bad" those qualities which profit us; and the beasts that we train and use develope, of necessity, the qualities that profit them,–as, for instance, in our well-known friend, the dog.

The dog is an animal long since cut off from his natural means of support, and depending absolutely on man for food. As a free, wild dog, he was profited by a daring initiative, courage, ferocity. As a tame, slave dog, he is profited by abject submission, by a crawling will-lessness that grovels at a blow, and licks the foot that kicks it. We have quite made over the original dog; and his moral nature, his spirit, shows the change even more than his body. The force which has accomplished this is economic,–a change of base in the source of supplies and the processes of obtaining them.

Let us briefly examine the distinctive virtues of humanity, their order of introduction and development, and see how this one peculiar relation has affected them.

The main distinction of human virtue is in what we roughly describe as altruism,–"otherness." To love and serve one another, to care for one another, to feel for and with one another,–our racial adjective, "humane," implies these qualities. The very existence of humanity implies these qualities in some degree, and the development of humanity is commensurate with their development.

Our one great blunder in studying these things lies in our failure to appreciate the organic necessity of such moral qualities in human life. We have assumed that the practice of these social virtues involved a personal effort and sacrifice, and that there is an irreconcilable contest between the cosmic process of development and the ethical process, as Huxley puts it. Social evolution brings with it the essential qualities of social relation, and these are our much boasted virtues. The natural processes of human intercourse and interrelation develope the qualities without which such intercourse would be impossible; and this development is as orderly, as natural, as "cosmic," as the processes of organic activity within the individual body. It is as natural for an industrial society to live in peace as for a hunting society to live in war; and this peace is not the result of heroic and self-sacrificing effort on the part of the industrial society; it is the necessity of their condition.

The course of evolution in human ethics is marked by a gradual extension of our perception of common good and evil as distinct from our initial perception of individual good and evil. This becomes very keen in the more socialized natures among us, as in the far-seeing devotion of statesmanship, patriotism, and philanthropy. Each of these words shows in its construction that the quality described is social,–the statesman, one who thinks and works for the State; the patriot, one who loves and labors for his country; the philanthropist, one who loves mankind. All these qualities, in their extreme and in their first beginnings, are a mere recognition of the equal right of the next man, common "fair play" and courtesy; they are but the natural product of social conditions acting on the individual through primal laws of economic necessity. The individual, in the absolute economic isolation of the beast, is profited by pure egoism, and developes it. The individual, in the increasing economic interdependence of social relation, is profited by altruism; and he developes it.

All our virtues can be traced and accounted for. The great main stem of them all, what we call "love," is merely the first condition of social existence. It is cohesion, working among us at the constituent particles of society. Without some attraction to hold us together, we should not be able to hold together; and this attraction, as perceived by our consciousness, we call love. The virtue of obedience consists in the surrender of the individual will, so often necessary to the common good; and it stands highest in military organization, wherein great numbers of men must act together against their personal interests, even to the sacrifice of life, in the service of the community.

As we have grown into fuller social life, we have slowly and experimentally, painfully and expensively, discovered what kind of man was the best social factor. The type of a satisfactory member of society to-day is a man self-controlled, kind, gentle, strong, wise, brave, courteous, cheerful, true. In the Middle Ages, strong, brave, and true would have satisfied the demands of the time. We now require for our common good a larger range of qualities, a more elaborate moral organization. All this is a simple, evolutionary process of social life, and should have involved no more confusion, effort, and pain than any other natural process.

But the moral development of humanity is a most tempestuous and contradictory field of study. Some virtues we have developed in orderly fashion, hardly recognizing that they were virtues, because they came so easily into use. Accuracy and punctuality are qualities which were unknown to the savage, because they were not needed in his business. They have been developed in us, because they were required, and so have been gradually assumed under pressure of economic necessity. Obedience, even in its extreme form of self-sacrifice, has been produced in the soldier; and no quality is more altruistic, more unnatural, or more difficult of adoption by the sturdy individual will. The common, law-abiding citizen does not consider himself a hero; yet he is manifesting a high degree of social virtue, often at great personal sacrifice.

But in other virtues we have not progressed so smoothly. In the ordinary economic relations of life, and in our sex-relations, we are distinguished by peculiar and injurious qualities. Our condition may be described as consisting of a tenacious survival of qualities which we ought, on every ground of social good, to have long since outgrown; and an incessant struggle between these rudimentary survivals and the normal growth. This it is which has so forcibly assailed our consciousness since its awakening, and which we call the contest between good and evil. We have felt within ourselves the pull of diverse tendencies,–the impulse to do what was immediately good for ourselves, but which our growing social sense knew was bad for the community, and therefore wrong; and the impulse to do what might be immediately bad for ourselves, but which the same social sense knew was good for the community, and therefore right. This we felt, and cast about in our minds for an explanation of the way we behaved: we knew it was peculiar. The human brain is an organ that must have an explanation, if it has to make one. We made one.

The belated impulses of the individual beast–good in him because he needed them, bad in us because we were becoming human and had other needs–we lumped together, and, with our facile, dramatic, personifying tendency, called them "the devil." And, as these evil promptings were usually along the lines of physical impulse, we considered our own bodies, and nature in general, as part and parcel of the wrong,–"the world, the flesh, and the devil." We felt, also, within us the mighty stirrings of new powers and strange tendencies, that led us out of ourselves and toward each other, new loves and hopes and wishes, new desires to give instead of to take, to serve instead of to fight; and, realizing, with true social instinct, that this impulse tended to help us most, was really good for us, we called it the will of God, the voice of God, the way to God. The tearing contest between these ill-adjusted impulses and tendencies, with our growing power of self-conscious decision and voluntary adoption of one or another course of action,–this process in psychic evolution has given us the greatest world-drama ever conceived, the struggle between good and evil.

And, fumbling vaguely at the sources of our pain so far as we could trace them, judging always by persons, and not by conditions,–as a child strikes the chair he bumps his head upon,–race after race has located the cause of the trouble in woman. Not that she primarily invented all the evil, and brought it upon us,–our vague devil was the remoter cause,–but that woman let the trouble in. Pandora did not make the mischief-box; but she perversely opened it, even against the wise man's advice. Eve did not plant that apple-tree; but she ate of it, and tempted the superior man. It seems a childish and clumsy guess, but there is something in it. Nothing of the unspeakable blame and shame with which man has blackened the face of his mother through all these centuries, but a sociological truth for all that.

Not woman, but the condition of woman, has always been a doorway of evil. The sexuo-economic relation has debarred her from the social activities in which, and in which alone, are developed the social virtues. She was not allowed to acquire the qualities needed in our racial advance; and, in her position of arrested development, she has maintained the virtues and the vices of the period of human evolution at which she was imprisoned. At a period of isolated economic activity,–mere animal individualism,–at a period when social ties ceased with the ties of blood, woman was cut off from personal activity in social economics, and confined to the functional activities of her sex.

In keeping her on this primitive basis of economic life, we have kept half humanity tied to the starting-post, while the other half ran. We have trained and bred one kind of qualities into one-half the species, and another kind into the other half. And then we wonder at the contradictions of human nature! For instance, we have done all we could, in addition to natural forces, to make men brave. We have done all we could, in addition to natural forces, to make women cowards. And, since every human creature is born of two parents, it is not surprising that we are a little mixed.

We have trained in men the large qualities of social usefulness which the pressure of their economic conditions was also developing; and we have done this by means of conscious praise and blame, reward and punishment, and with the aid of the law and custom. We have trained in women, by the same means, the small qualities of personal usefulness which the pressure of their economic conditions was also developing. We have made a creature who is not homogeneous, whose life is fed by two currents of inheritance as dissimilar and opposed as could be well imagined. We have bred a race of psychic hybrids, and the moral qualities of hybrids are well know.

Away back in that early beginning, by dividing the economic conditions of women and men, we have divided their psychic development, and built into the constitution of the race the irreconcilable elements of these diverse characters. The incongruous behavior of this cross-bred product is the riddle of human life. We ourselves, by maintaining this artificial diversity between the sexes, have constantly kept before us the enigma which we found so hard to solve, and have preserved in our own characters the confusion and contradiction which is our greatest difficulty in life.

The largest and most radical effect of restoring women to economic independence will be in its result in clarifying and harmonizing the human soul. With a homogeneous nature bred of two parents in the same degree of social development, we shall be able to feel simply, to see clearly, to agree with ourselves, to be one person and master of our own lives, instead of wrestling in such hopeless perplexity with what we have called "man's dual nature." Marry a civilized man to a primitive savage, and their child will naturally have a dual nature. Marry an Anglo-Saxon to an African or Oriental, and their child has a dual nature. Marry any man of a highly developed nation, full of the specialized activities of his race and their accompanying moral qualities, to the carefully preserved, rudimentary female creature he has so religiously maintained by his side, and you have as result what we all know so well,–the human soul in its pitiful, well-meaning efforts, its cross-eyed, purblind errors, its baby fits of passion, and its beautiful and ceaseless upward impulse through all this wavering.

We are quite familiar with this result, but we have not so far accurately located the cause. We have had our glimmering perception that woman had something to do with it; and she has been treated accordingly, by many simple races, to her further injury, and to that of the whole people. What we need to see is that it is not woman as a sex who is responsible for this mis-mothered world, but the economic position of woman which makes her what she is. If men were so placed, it would have the same effect. Not the sex-relation, but the economic relation of the sexes, has so tangled the skein of human life.

Besides the essential evils of an unbalanced nature, many harmful qualities have been developed in human characters by these conditions. For countless centuries we have sought to develope, by selection and education, a timid submission in woman. When there did appear "a curst shrew," she was left unmarried; and her temper perished with her, or she was "tamed" by some Petruchio. The dependence of women on the personal favor of men has produced an exceeding cleverness in the adaptation of the dependent one to the source of her supplies. Under the necessity of pleasing, whether she wished or no, of interceding for a child's pardon or of suing for new pleasures for herself, "the vices of the slave" have been forever maintained in this housemaid of the world.

Another discord introduced by the condition of servitude is that between will and action. A servant places his time and strength at the disposal of another will. He must hold himself in readiness to do what he is told; and the mere physical law of conservation of energy, to say nothing of his own conscious judgment, forbids wasting nerve-force in planning and undertaking what he may not be able to accomplish. This produces a condition of inactivity, save under compulsion, and, on the other side, perverse, capricious willfulness in little things,–the reaction from a forced submission.

A more insidious, disintegrating force to offset the evolution of human character could hardly be imagined than this steady training of the habits of servitude into half the human race,–the mother of all of it. These results have been modified, of course, by the different education and environment of men, developing in them opposite qualities, and transmitting the contradictory traits to the children indiscriminately.

Heredity has no Salic law. The boy inherits from his mother, as well as from his father; the girl from her father, as well as from her mother. This has prevented the full evil of the results that might have ensued, but has also added to the personal difficulties of each of us, and retarded the general progress of the race.

Worse than the check set upon the physical activities of women has been the restriction of their power to think and judge for themselves. The extended use of the human will and its decisions is conditioned upon free, voluntary action. In her rudimentary position, woman was denied the physical freedom which underlies all knowledge, she was denied the mental freedom which is the path to further wisdom, she was denied the moral freedom of being mistress of her own action and of learning by the merciful law of consequences what was right and what was wrong; and she has remained, perforce, undeveloped in the larger judgment of ethics.

Her moral sense is large enough, morbidly large, because in this tutelage she is always being praised or blamed for her conduct. She lives in a forcing-bed of sensitiveness to moral distinctions, but the broad judgment that alone can guide and govern this sensitiveness she has not. Her contribution to moral progress has added to the anguish of the world the fierce sense of sin and shame, the desperate desire to do right, the fear of wrong; without giving it the essential help of a practical wisdom and a regulated will. Inheriting with each generation the accumulating forces of our social nature, set back in each generation by the conditions of the primitive human female, women have become vividly self-conscious centers of moral impulse, but poor guides as to the conduct which alone can make that impulse useful and build the habit of morality into the constitution of the race.

Recognizing her intense feeling on moral lines, and seeing in her the rigidly preserved virtues of faith, submission, and self-sacrifice,–qualities which in the Dark Ages were held to be the first of virtues,–we have agreed of late years to call woman the moral superior of man. But the ceaseless growth of human life, social life, has developed in him new virtues, later, higher, more needful; and the moral nature of woman, as maintained in this rudimentary stage by her economic dependence, is a continual check to the progress of the human soul. The main feature of her life–the restriction of her range of duty to the love and service of her own immediate family–acts upon us continually as a retarding influence, hindering the expansion of the spirit of social love and service on which our very lives depend. It keeps the moral standard of the patriarchal era still before us, and blinds our eyes to the full duty of man.

An intense self-consciousness, born of the ceaseless contact of close personal relation; an inordinate self-interest, bred by the constant personal attention and service of this relation; a feverish, torturing, moral sensitiveness, without the width and clarity of vision of a full-grown moral sense; a thwarted will, used to meek surrender, cunning evasion, or futile rebellion; a childish, wavering, short-range judgment, handicapped by emotion; a measureless devotion to one's own sex relatives, and a maternal passion swollen with the full strength of the great social heart, but denied social expression,–such psychic qualities as these, born in us all, are the inevitable result of the sexuo-economic relation.

It is not alone upon woman, and, through her, upon the race, that the ill-effects may be observed. Man, as master, has suffered from his position also. The lust for power and conquest, natural to the male of any species, has been fostered in him to an enormous degree by this cheap and easy lordship. His dominance is not that of one chosen as best fitted to rule or of one ruling by successful competition with "foemen worthy of his steel"; but it is a sovereignty based on the accident of sex, and holding over such helpless and inferior dependents as could not question or oppose. The easy superiority that needs no striving to maintain it; the temptation to cruelty always begotten by irresponsible power; the pride and self-will which surely accompany it,–these qualities have been bred into the souls of men by their side of the relation. When man's place was maintained by brute force, it made him more brutal: when his place was maintained by purchase, by the power of economic necessity, then he grew into the merciless use of such power as distinguishes him to-day.

Another giant evil engendered by this relation is what we call selfishness. Social life tends to reduce this feeling, which is but a belated individualism; but the sexuo-economic relation fosters and developes it. To have a whole human creature consecrated to his direct personal service, to pleasing and satisfying him in every way possible,–this has kept man selfish beyond the degree incidental to our stage of social growth. Even in our artificial society life men are more forbearing and considerate, more polite and kind, than they are at home. Pride, cruelty, and selfishness are the vices of the master; and these have been kept strong in the bosom of the family through the false position of woman. And every human soul is born, an impressionable child, into the close presence of these conditions. Our men must live in the ethics of a civilized, free, industrial, democratic age; but they are born and trained in the moral atmosphere of a primitive patriarchate. No wonder that we are all somewhat slow to rise to the full powers and privileges of democracy, to feel full social honor and social duty, while every soul of us is reared in this stronghold of ancient and outgrown emotions,–the economically related family.

So we may trace from the sexuo-economic relation of our species not only definite evils in psychic development, bred severally in men and women, and transmitted indifferently to their offspring, but the innate perversion of character resultant from the moral miscegenation of two so diverse souls,–the unfailing shadow and distortion which has darkened and twisted the spirit of man from its beginnings. We have been injured in body and in mind by the too dissimilar traits inherited from our widely separated parents, but nowhere is the injury more apparent than in its ill effects upon the moral nature of the race.

Yet here, as in the other evil results of the sexuo-economic relation, we can see the accompanying good that made the condition necessary in its time; and we can follow the beautiful results of our present changes with comforting assurance. A healthy, normal moral sense will be ours, freed from its exaggerations and contradictions; and, with that clear perception, we shall no longer conceive of the ethical process as something outside of and against nature, but as the most natural thing in the world.

Where now we strive and agonize after impossible virtues, we shall then grow naturally and easily into those very qualities; and we shall not even think of them as especially commendable. Where our progress hitherto has been warped and hindered by the retarding influence of surviving rudimentary forces, it will flow on smoothly and rapidly when both men and women stand equal in economic relation. When the mother of the race is free, we shall have a better world, by the easy right of birth and by the calm, slow, friendly forces of social evolution.

HERLAND

CHAPTER 1. A NOT UNNATURAL ENTERPRISE

This is written from memory, unfortunately. If I could have brought with me the material I so carefully prepared, this would be a very different story. Whole books full of notes, carefully copied records, firsthand descriptions, and the pictures—that's the worst loss. We had some bird's-eyes of the cities and parks; a lot of lovely views of streets, of buildings, outside and in, and some of those gorgeous gardens, and, most important of all, of the women themselves.

Nobody will ever believe how they looked. Descriptions aren't any good when it comes to women, and I never was good at descriptions anyhow. But it's got to be done somehow; the rest of the world needs to know about that country.

I haven't said where it was for fear some self-appointed missionaries, or traders, or land-greedy expansionists, will take it upon themselves to push in. They will not be wanted, I can tell them that, and will fare worse than we did if they do find it.

It began this way. There were three of us, classmates and friends—Terry O. Nicholson (we used to call him the Old Nick, with good reason), Jeff Margrave, and I, Vandyck Jennings.

We had known each other years and years, and in spite of our differences we had a good deal in common. All of us were interested in science.

Terry was rich enough to do as he pleased. His great aim was exploration. He used to make all kinds of a row because there was nothing left to explore now, only patchwork and filling in, he said. He filled in well enough—he had a lot of talents—great on mechanics and electricity. Had all kinds of boats and motorcars, and was one of the best of our airmen.

We never could have done the thing at all without Terry.

Jeff Margrave was born to be a poet, a botanist—or both—but his folks persuaded him to be a doctor instead. He was a good one, for his age, but his real interest was in what he loved to call "the wonders of science."

As for me, sociology's my major. You have to back that up with a lot of other sciences, of course. I'm interested in them all.

Terry was strong on facts—geography and meteorology and those; Jeff could beat him any time on biology, and I didn't care what it was they talked about, so long as it connected with human life, somehow. There are few things that don't.

We three had a chance to join a big scientific expedition. They needed a doctor, and that gave Jeff an excuse for dropping his just opening practice; they needed Terry's experience, his machine, and his money; and as for me, I got in through Terry's influence.

The expedition was up among the thousand tributaries and enormous hinterland of a great river, up where the maps had to be made, savage dialects studied, and all manner of strange flora and fauna expected.

But this story is not about that expedition. That was only the merest starter for ours.

My interest was first roused by talk among our guides. I'm quick at languages, know a good many, and pick them up readily. What with that and a really good interpreter we took with us, I made out quite a few legends and folk myths of these scattered tribes.

And as we got farther and farther upstream, in a dark tangle of rivers, lakes, morasses, and dense forests, with here and there an unexpected long spur running out from the big mountains beyond, I noticed that more and more of these savages had a story about a strange and terrible Woman Land in the high distance.

"Up yonder," "Over there," "Way up"—was all the direction they could offer, but their legends all agreed on the main point—that there was this strange country where no men lived—only women and girl children.

None of them had ever seen it. It was dangerous, deadly, they said, for any man to go there. But there were tales of long ago, when some brave investigator had seen it—a Big Country, Big Houses, Plenty People—All Women.

Had no one else gone? Yes—a good many—but they never came back. It was no place for men—of that they seemed sure.

I told the boys about these stories, and they laughed at them. Naturally I did myself. I knew the stuff that savage dreams are made of.

But when we had reached our farthest point, just the day before we all had to turn around and start for home again, as the best of expeditions must in time, we three made a discovery.

The main encampment was on a spit of land running out into the main stream, or what we thought was the main stream. It had the same muddy color we had been seeing for weeks past, the same taste.

I happened to speak of that river to our last guide, a rather superior fellow with quick, bright eyes.

He told me that there was another river—"over there, short river, sweet water, red and blue."

I was interested in this and anxious to see if I had understood, so I showed him a red and blue pencil I carried, and asked again.

Yes, he pointed to the river, and then to the southwestward. "River—good water—red and blue."

Terry was close by and interested in the fellow's pointing.

"What does he say, Van?"

I told him.

Terry blazed up at once.

"Ask him how far it is."

The man indicated a short journey; I judged about two hours, maybe three.

"Let's go," urged Terry. "Just us three. Maybe we can really find something. May be cinnabar in it."

"May be indigo," Jeff suggested, with his lazy smile.

It was early yet; we had just breakfasted; and leaving word that we'd be back before night, we got away quietly, not wishing to be thought too gullible if we failed, and secretly hoping to have some nice little discovery all to ourselves.

It was a long two hours, nearer three. I fancy the savage could have done it alone much quicker. There was a desperate tangle of wood and water and a swampy patch we never should have found our way across alone. But there was one, and I could see Terry, with compass and notebook, marking directions and trying to place landmarks.

We came after a while to a sort of marshy lake, very big, so that the circling forest looked quite low and dim across it. Our guide told us that boats could go from there to our camp—but "long way—all day."

This water was somewhat clearer than that we had left, but we could not judge well from the margin. We skirted it for another half hour or so, the ground growing firmer as we advanced, and presently we turned the corner of a wooded promontory and saw a quite different country—a sudden view of mountains, steep and bare.

"One of those long easterly spurs," Terry said appraisingly. "May be hundreds of miles from the range. They crop out like that."

Suddenly we left the lake and struck directly toward the cliffs. We heard running water before we reached it, and the guide pointed proudly to his river.

It was short. We could see where it poured down a narrow vertical cataract from an opening in the face of the cliff. It was sweet water. The guide drank eagerly and so did we.

"That's snow water," Terry announced. "Must come from way back in the hills."

But as to being red and blue—it was greenish in tint. The guide seemed not at all surprised. He hunted about a little and showed us a quiet marginal pool where there were smears of red along the border; yes, and of blue.

Terry got out his magnifying glass and squatted down to investigate.

"Chemicals of some sort—I can't tell on the spot. Look to me like dyestuffs. Let's get nearer," he urged, "up there by the fall."

We scrambled along the steep banks and got close to the pool that foamed and boiled beneath the falling water. Here we searched the border and found traces of color beyond dispute. More—Jeff suddenly held up an unlooked-for trophy.

It was only a rag, a long, raveled fragment of cloth. But it was a well-woven fabric, with a pattern, and of a clear scarlet that the water had not faded. No savage tribe that we had heard of made such fabrics.

The guide stood serenely on the bank, well pleased with our excitement.

"One day blue—one day red—one day green," he told us, and pulled from his pouch another strip of bright-hued cloth.

"Come down," he said, pointing to the cataract. "Woman Country—up there."

Then we were interested. We had our rest and lunch right there and pumped the man for further information. He could tell us only what the others had—a land of women—no men—babies, but all girls. No place for men—dangerous. Some had gone to see—none had come back.

I could see Terry's jaw set at that. No place for men? Dangerous? He looked as if he might shin up the waterfall on the spot. But the guide would not hear of going up, even if there had been any possible method of scaling that sheer cliff, and we had to get back to our party before night.

"They might stay if we told them," I suggested.

But Terry stopped in his tracks. "Look here, fellows," he said. "This is our find. Let's not tell those cocky old professors. Let's go on home with 'em, and then come back—just us—have a little expedition of our own."

We looked at him, much impressed. There was something attractive to a bunch of unattached young men in finding an undiscovered country of a strictly Amazonian nature.

Of course we didn't believe the story—but yet!

"There is no such cloth made by any of these local tribes," I announced, examining those rags with great care. "Somewhere up yonder they spin and weave and dye—as well as we do."

"That would mean a considerable civilization, Van. There couldn't be such a place—and not known about."

"Oh, well, I don't know. What's that old republic up in the Pyrenees somewhere—Andorra? Precious few people know anything about that, and it's been minding its own business for a thousand years. Then there's Montenegro—splendid little state—you could lose a dozen Montenegroes up and down these great ranges."

We discussed it hotly all the way back to camp. We discussed it with care and privacy on the voyage home. We discussed it after that, still only among ourselves, while Terry was making his arrangements.

He was hot about it. Lucky he had so much money—we might have had to beg and advertise for years to start the thing, and then it would have been a matter of public amusement—just sport for the papers.

But T. O. Nicholson could fix up his big steam yacht, load his specially-made big motorboat aboard, and tuck in a "dissembled" biplane without any more notice than a snip in the society column.

We had provisions and preventives and all manner of supplies. His previous experience stood him in good stead there. It was a very complete little outfit.

We were to leave the yacht at the nearest safe port and go up that endless river in our motorboat, just the three of us and a pilot; then drop the pilot when we got to that last stopping place of the previous party, and hunt up that clear water stream ourselves.

The motorboat we were going to leave at anchor in that wide shallow lake. It had a special covering of fitted armor, thin but strong, shut up like a clamshell.

"Those natives can't get into it, or hurt it, or move it," Terry explained proudly. "We'll start our flier from the lake and leave the boat as a base to come back to."

"If we come back," I suggested cheerfully.

"'Fraid the ladies will eat you?" he scoffed.

"We're not so sure about those ladies, you know," drawled Jeff. "There may be a contingent of gentlemen with poisoned arrows or something."

"You don't need to go if you don't want to," Terry remarked drily.

"Go? You'll have to get an injunction to stop me!" Both Jeff and I were sure about that.

But we did have differences of opinion, all the long way.

An ocean voyage is an excellent time for discussion. Now we had no eavesdroppers, we could loll and loaf in our deck chairs and talk and talk—there was nothing else to do. Our absolute lack of facts only made the field of discussion wider.

"We'll leave papers with our consul where the yacht stays," Terry planned. "If we don't come back in—say a month—they can send a relief party after us."

"A punitive expedition," I urged. "If the ladies do eat us we must make reprisals."

"They can locate that last stopping place easy enough, and I've made a sort of chart of that lake and cliff and waterfall."

"Yes, but how will they get up?" asked Jeff.

"Same way we do, of course. If three valuable American citizens are lost up there, they will follow somehow—to say nothing of the glittering attractions of that fair land—let's call it 'Feminisia,'" he broke off.

"You're right, Terry. Once the story gets out, the river will crawl with expeditions and the airships rise like a swarm of mosquitoes." I laughed as I thought of it. "We've made a great mistake not to let Mr. Yellow Press in on this. Save us! What headlines!"

"Not much!" said Terry grimly. "This is our party. We're going to find that place alone."

"What are you going to do with it when you do find it—if you do?" Jeff asked mildly.

Jeff was a tender soul. I think he thought that country—if there was one—was just blossoming with roses and babies and canaries and tidies, and all that sort of thing.

And Terry, in his secret heart, had visions of a sort of sublimated summer resort—just Girls and Girls and Girls—and that he was going to be—well, Terry was popular among women even when there were other men around, and it's not to be wondered at that he had pleasant dreams of what might happen. I could see it in his eyes as he lay there, looking at the long blue rollers slipping by, and fingering that impressive mustache of his.

But I thought—then—that I could form a far clearer idea of what was before us than either of them.

"You're all off, boys," I insisted. "If there is such a place—and there does seem some foundation for believing it—you'll find it's built on a sort of matriarchal principle, that's all. The men have a separate cult of their own, less socially developed than the women, and make them an annual visit—a sort of wedding call. This is a condition known to have existed—here's just a survival. They've got some peculiarly isolated valley or tableland up there, and their primeval customs have survived. That's all there is to it."

"How about the boys?" Jeff asked.

"Oh, the men take them away as soon as they are five or six, you see."

"And how about this danger theory all our guides were so sure of?"

"Danger enough, Terry, and we'll have to be mighty careful. Women of that stage of culture are quite able to defend themselves and have no welcome for unseasonable visitors."

We talked and talked.

And with all my airs of sociological superiority I was no nearer than any of them.

It was funny though, in the light of what we did find, those extremely clear ideas of ours as to what a country of women would be like. It was no use to tell ourselves and one another that all this was idle speculation. We were idle and we did speculate, on the ocean voyage and the river voyage, too.

"Admitting the improbability," we'd begin solemnly, and then launch out again.

"They would fight among themselves," Terry insisted. "Women always do. We mustn't look to find any sort of order and organization."

"You're dead wrong," Jeff told him. "It will be like a nunnery under an abbess—a peaceful, harmonious sisterhood."

I snorted derision at this idea.

"Nuns, indeed! Your peaceful sisterhoods were all celibate, Jeff, and under vows of obedience. These are just women, and mothers, and where there's motherhood you don't find sisterhood—not much."

"No, sir—they'll scrap," agreed Terry. "Also we mustn't look for inventions and progress; it'll be awfully primitive."

"How about that cloth mill?" Jeff suggested.

"Oh, cloth! Women have always been spinsters. But there they stop—you'll see."

We joked Terry about his modest impression that he would be warmly received, but he held his ground.

"You'll see," he insisted. "I'll get solid with them all—and play one bunch against another. I'll get myself elected king in no time—whew! Solomon will have to take a back seat!"

"Where do we come in on that deal?" I demanded. "Aren't we Viziers or anything?"

"Couldn't risk it," he asserted solemnly. "You might start a revolution—probably would. No, you'll have to be beheaded, or bowstrung—or whatever the popular method of execution is."

"You'd have to do it yourself, remember," grinned Jeff. "No husky black slaves and mamelukes! And there'd be two of us and only one of you—eh, Van?"

Jeff's ideas and Terry's were so far apart that sometimes it was all I could do to keep the peace between them. Jeff idealized women in the best Southern style. He was full of chivalry and sentiment, and all that. And he was a good boy; he lived up to his ideals.

You might say Terry did, too, if you can call his views about women anything so polite as ideals. I always liked Terry. He was a man's man, very much so, generous and brave and clever; but I don't think any of us in college days was quite pleased to have him with our sisters. We weren't very stringent, heavens no! But Terry was "the limit." Later on—why, of course a man's life is his own, we held, and asked no questions.

But barring a possible exception in favor of a not impossible wife, or of his mother, or, of course, the fair relatives of his friends, Terry's idea seemed to be that pretty women were just so much game and homely ones not worth considering.

It was really unpleasant sometimes to see the notions he had.

But I got out of patience with Jeff, too. He had such rose-colored halos on his womenfolks. I held a middle ground, highly scientific, of course, and used to argue learnedly about the physiological limitations of the sex.

We were not in the least "advanced" on the woman question, any of us, then.

So we joked and disputed and speculated, and after an interminable journey, we got to our old camping place at last.

It was not hard to find the river, just poking along that side till we came to it, and it was navigable as far as the lake.

When we reached that and slid out on its broad glistening bosom, with that high gray promontory running out toward us, and the straight white fall clearly visible, it began to be really exciting.

There was some talk, even then, of skirting the rock wall and seeking a possible footway up, but the marshy jungle made that method look not only difficult but dangerous.

Terry dismissed the plan sharply.

"Nonsense, fellows! We've decided that. It might take months—we haven't got the provisions. No, sir—we've got to take our chances. If we get back safe—all right. If we don't, why, we're not the first explorers to get lost in the shuffle. There are plenty to come after us."

So we got the big biplane together and loaded it with our scientifically compressed baggage: the camera, of course; the glasses; a supply of concentrated food. Our pockets were magazines of small necessities, and we had our guns, of course—there was no knowing what might happen.

Up and up and up we sailed, way up at first, to get "the lay of the land" and make note of it.

Out of that dark green sea of crowding forest this high-standing spur rose steeply. It ran back on either side, apparently, to the far-off white-crowned peaks in the distance, themselves probably inaccessible.

"Let's make the first trip geographical," I suggested. "Spy out the land, and drop back here for more gasoline. With your tremendous speed we can reach that range and back all right. Then we can leave a sort of map on board—for that relief expedition."

"There's sense in that," Terry agreed. "I'll put off being king of Ladyland for one more day."

So we made a long skirting voyage, turned the point of the cape which was close by, ran up one side of the triangle at our best speed, crossed over the base where it left the higher mountains, and so back to our lake by moonlight.

"That's not a bad little kingdom," we agreed when it was roughly drawn and measured. We could tell the size fairly by our speed. And from what we could see of the sides—and that icy ridge at the back end—"It's a pretty enterprising savage who would manage to get into it," Jeff said.

Of course we had looked at the land itself—eagerly, but we were too high and going too fast to see much. It appeared to be well forested about the edges, but in the interior there were wide plains, and everywhere parklike meadows and open places.

There were cities, too; that I insisted. It looked—well, it looked like any other country—a civilized one, I mean.

We had to sleep after that long sweep through the air, but we turned out early enough next day, and again we rose softly up the height till we could top the crowning trees and see the broad fair land at our pleasure.

"Semitropical. Looks like a first-rate climate. It's wonderful what a little height will do for temperature." Terry was studying the forest growth.

"Little height! Is that what you call little?" I asked. Our instruments measured it clearly. We had not realized the long gentle rise from the coast perhaps.

"Mighty lucky piece of land, I call it," Terry pursued. "Now for the folks—I've had enough scenery."

So we sailed low, crossing back and forth, quartering the country as we went, and studying it. We saw—I can't remember now how much of this we noted then and how much was supplemented by our later knowledge, but we could not help seeing this much, even on that excited day—a land in a state of perfect cultivation, where even the forests looked as if they were cared for; a land that looked like an enormous park, only it was even more evidently an enormous garden.

"I don't see any cattle," I suggested, but Terry was silent. We were approaching a village.

I confess that we paid small attention to the clean, well-built roads, to the attractive architecture, to the ordered beauty of the little town. We had our glasses out; even Terry, setting his machine for a spiral glide, clapped the binoculars to his eyes.

They heard our whirring screw. They ran out of the houses—they gathered in from the fields, swift-running light figures, crowds of them. We stared and stared until it was almost too late to catch the levers, sweep off and rise again; and then we held our peace for a long run upward.

"Gosh!" said Terry, after a while.

"Only women there—and children," Jeff urged excitedly.

"But they look—why, this is a CIVILIZED country!" I protested. "There must be men."

"Of course there are men," said Terry. "Come on, let's find 'em."

He refused to listen to Jeff's suggestion that we examine the country further before we risked leaving our machine.

"There's a fine landing place right there where we came over," he insisted, and it was an excellent one—a wide, flat-topped rock, overlooking the lake, and quite out of sight from the interior.

"They won't find this in a hurry," he asserted, as we scrambled with the utmost difficulty down to safer footing. "Come on, boys—there were some good lookers in that bunch."

Of course it was unwise of us.

It was quite easy to see afterward that our best plan was to have studied the country more fully before we left our swooping airship and trusted ourselves to mere foot service. But we were three young men. We had been talking about this country for over a year, hardly believing that there was such a place, and now—we were in it.

It looked safe and civilized enough, and among those upturned, crowding faces, though some were terrified enough, there was great beauty—on that we all agreed.

"Come on!" cried Terry, pushing forward. "Oh, come on! Here goes for Herland!"

CHAPTER 2. RASH ADVANCES

Not more than ten or fifteen miles we judged it from our landing rock to that last village. For all our eagerness we thought it wise to keep to the woods and go carefully.

Even Terry's ardor was held in check by his firm conviction that there were men to be met, and we saw to it that each of us had a good stock of cartridges.

"They may be scarce, and they may be hidden away somewhere—some kind of a matriarchate, as Jeff tells us; for that matter, they may live up in the mountains yonder and keep the women in this part of the country—sort of a national harem! But there are men somewhere—didn't you see the babies?"

We had all seen babies, children big and little, everywhere that we had come near enough to distinguish the people. And though by dress we could not be sure of all the grown persons, still there had not been one man that we were certain of.

"I always liked that Arab saying, 'First tie your camel and then trust in the Lord,'" Jeff murmured; so we all had our weapons in hand, and stole cautiously through the forest. Terry studied it as we progressed.

"Talk of civilization," he cried softly in restrained enthusiasm. "I never saw a forest so petted, even in Germany. Look, there's not a dead bough—the vines are trained—actually! And see here"—he stopped and looked about him, calling Jeff's attention to the kinds of trees.

They left me for a landmark and made a limited excursion on either side.

"Food-bearing, practically all of them," they announced returning. "The rest, splendid hardwood. Call this a forest? It's a truck farm!"

"Good thing to have a botanist on hand," I agreed. "Sure there are no medicinal ones? Or any for pure ornament?"

As a matter of fact they were quite right. These towering trees were under as careful cultivation as so many cabbages. In other conditions we should have found those woods full of fair foresters and fruit gatherers; but an airship is a conspicuous object, and by no means quiet—and women are cautious.

All we found moving in those woods, as we started through them, were birds, some gorgeous, some musical, all so tame that it seemed almost to contradict our theory of cultivation—at least until we came upon occasional little glades, where carved stone seats and tables stood in the shade beside clear fountains, with shallow bird baths always added.

"They don't kill birds, and apparently they do kill cats," Terry declared. "MUST be men here. Hark!"

We had heard something: something not in the least like a birdsong, and very much like a suppressed whisper of laughter—a little happy sound, instantly smothered. We stood like so many pointers, and then used our glasses, swiftly, carefully.

"It couldn't have been far off," said Terry excitedly. "How about this big tree?"

There was a very large and beautiful tree in the glade we had just entered, with thick wide-spreading branches that sloped out in lapping fans like a beech or pine. It was trimmed underneath some twenty feet up, and stood there like a huge umbrella, with circling seats beneath.

"Look," he pursued. "There are short stumps of branches left to climb on. There's someone up that tree, I believe."

We stole near, cautiously.

"Look out for a poisoned arrow in your eye," I suggested, but Terry pressed forward, sprang up on the seat-back, and grasped the trunk. "In my heart, more likely," he answered. "Gee! Look, boys!"

We rushed close in and looked up. There among the boughs overhead was something—more than one something—that clung motionless, close to the great trunk at first, and then, as one and all we started up the tree, separated into three swift-moving figures and fled upward. As we climbed we could catch glimpses of them scattering above us. By the time we had reached about as far as three men together dared push, they had left the main trunk and moved outward, each one balanced on a long branch that dipped and swayed beneath the weight.

We paused uncertain. If we pursued further, the boughs would break under the double burden. We might shake them off, perhaps, but none of us was so inclined. In the soft dappled light of these high regions, breathless with our rapid climb, we rested awhile, eagerly studying our objects of pursuit; while they in turn, with no more terror than a set of frolicsome children in a game of tag, sat as lightly as so many big bright birds on their precarious perches and frankly, curiously, stared at us.

"Girls!" whispered Jeff, under his breath, as if they might fly if he spoke aloud.

"Peaches!" added Terry, scarcely louder. "Peacherinos—apricot-nectarines! Whew!"

They were girls, of course, no boys could ever have shown that sparkling beauty, and yet none of us was certain at first.

We saw short hair, hatless, loose, and shining; a suit of some light firm stuff, the closest of tunics and kneebreeches, met by trim gaiters. As bright and smooth as parrots and as unaware of danger, they swung there before us, wholly at ease, staring as we stared, till first one, and then all of them burst into peals of delighted laughter.

Then there was a torrent of soft talk tossed back and forth; no savage sing-song, but clear musical fluent speech.

We met their laughter cordially, and doffed our hats to them, at which they laughed again, delightedly.

Then Terry, wholly in his element, made a polite speech, with explanatory gestures, and proceeded to introduce us, with pointing finger. "Mr. Jeff Margrave," he said clearly; Jeff bowed as gracefully as a man could in the fork of a great limb. "Mr. Vandyck Jennings"—I also tried to make an effective salute and nearly lost my balance.

Then Terry laid his hand upon his chest—a fine chest he had, too, and introduced himself; he was braced carefully for the occasion and achieved an excellent obeisance.

Again they laughed delightedly, and the one nearest me followed his tactics.

"Celis," she said distinctly, pointing to the one in blue; "Alima"—the one in rose; then, with a vivid imitation of Terry's impressive manner, she laid a firm delicate hand on her gold-green jerkin—"Ellador." This was pleasant, but we got no nearer.

"We can't sit here and learn the language," Terry protested. He beckoned to them to come nearer, most winningly—but they gaily shook their heads. He suggested, by signs, that we all go down together; but again they shook their heads, still merrily. Then Ellador clearly indicated that we should go down, pointing to each and all of us, with unmistakable firmness; and further seeming to imply by the sweep of a lithe arm that we not only go downward, but go away altogether—at which we shook our heads in turn.

"Have to use bait," grinned Terry. "I don't know about you fellows, but I came prepared." He produced from an inner pocket a little box of purple velvet, that opened with a snap—and out of it he drew a long sparkling thing, a necklace of big varicolored stones that would have been worth a million if real ones. He held it up, swung it, glittering in the sun, offered it first to one, then to another, holding it out as far as he could reach toward the girl nearest him. He stood braced in the fork, held firmly by one hand—the other, swinging his bright temptation, reached far out along the bough, but not quite to his full stretch.

She was visibly moved, I noted, hesitated, spoke to her companions. They chattered softly together, one evidently warning her, the other encouraging. Then, softly and slowly, she drew nearer. This was Alima, a tall long-limbed lass, well-knit and evidently both strong and agile. Her eyes were splendid, wide, fearless, as free from suspicion as a child's who has never been rebuked. Her interest was more that of an intent boy playing a fascinating game than of a girl lured by an ornament.

The others moved a bit farther out, holding firmly, watching. Terry's smile was irreproachable, but I did not like the look in his eyes—it was like a creature about to spring. I could already see it happen—the dropped necklace, the sudden clutching hand, the girl's sharp cry as he seized her and drew her in. But it didn't happen. She made a timid reach with her right hand for the gay swinging thing—he held it a little nearer—then, swift as light, she seized it from him with her left, and dropped on the instant to the bough below.

He made his snatch, quite vainly, almost losing his position as his hand clutched only air; and then, with inconceivable rapidity, the three bright creatures were gone.

They dropped from the ends of the big boughs to those below, fairly pouring themselves off the tree, while we climbed downward as swiftly as we could. We heard their vanishing gay laughter, we saw them fleeting away in the wide open reaches of the forest, and gave chase, but we might as well have chased wild antelopes; so we stopped at length somewhat breathless.

"No use," gasped Terry. "They got away with it. My word! The men of this country must be good sprinters!"

"Inhabitants evidently arboreal," I grimly suggested. "Civilized and still arboreal—peculiar people."

"You shouldn't have tried that way," Jeff protested. "They were perfectly friendly; now we've scared them."

But it was no use grumbling, and Terry refused to admit any mistake. "Nonsense," he said. "They expected it. Women like to be run after. Come on, let's get to that town; maybe we'll find them there. Let's see, it was in this direction and not far from the woods, as I remember."

When we reached the edge of the open country we reconnoitered with our field glasses. There it was, about four miles off, the same town, we concluded, unless, as Jeff ventured, they all had pink houses. The broad green fields and closely cultivated gardens sloped away at our feet, a long easy slant, with good roads winding pleasantly here and there, and narrower paths besides.

"Look at that!" cried Jeff suddenly. "There they go!"

Sure enough, close to the town, across a wide meadow, three bright-hued figures were running swiftly.

"How could they have got that far in this time? It can't be the same ones," I urged. But through the glasses we could identify our pretty tree-climbers quite plainly, at least by costume.

Terry watched them, we all did for that matter, till they disappeared among the houses. Then he put down his glass and turned to us, drawing a long breath. "Mother of Mike, boys—what Gorgeous Girls! To climb like that! to run like that! and afraid of nothing. This country suits me all right. Let's get ahead."

"Nothing venture, nothing have," I suggested, but Terry preferred "Faint heart ne'er won fair lady."

We set forth in the open, walking briskly. "If there are any men, we'd better keep an eye out," I suggested, but Jeff seemed lost in heavenly dreams, and Terry in highly practical plans.

"What a perfect road! What a heavenly country! See the flowers, will you?"

This was Jeff, always an enthusiast; but we could agree with him fully.

The road was some sort of hard manufactured stuff, sloped slightly to shed rain, with every curve and grade and gutter as perfect as if it were Europe's best. "No men, eh?" sneered Terry. On either side a double row of trees shaded the footpaths; between the trees bushes or vines, all fruit-bearing, now and then seats and little wayside fountains; everywhere flowers.

"We'd better import some of these ladies and set 'em to parking the United States," I suggested. "Mighty nice place they've got here." We rested a few moments by one of the fountains, tested the fruit that looked ripe, and went on, impressed, for all our gay bravado by the sense of quiet potency which lay about us.

Here was evidently a people highly skilled, efficient, caring for their country as a florist cares for his costliest orchids. Under the soft brilliant blue of that clear sky, in the pleasant shade of those endless rows of trees, we walked unharmed, the placid silence broken only by the birds.

Presently there lay before us at the foot of a long hill the town or village we were aiming for. We stopped and studied it.

Jeff drew a long breath. "I wouldn't have believed a collection of houses could look so lovely," he said.

"They've got architects and landscape gardeners in plenty, that's sure," agreed Terry.

I was astonished myself. You see, I come from California, and there's no country lovelier, but when it comes to towns—! I have often groaned at home to see the offensive mess man made in the face of nature, even though I'm no art sharp, like Jeff. But this place! It was built mostly of a sort of dull rose-colored stone, with here and there some clear white houses; and it lay abroad among the green groves and gardens like a broken rosary of pink coral.

"Those big white ones are public buildings evidently," Terry declared. "This is no savage country, my friend. But no men? Boys, it behooves us to go forward most politely."

The place had an odd look, more impressive as we approached. "It's like an exposition." "It's too pretty to be true." "Plenty of palaces, but where are the homes?" "Oh there are little ones enough—but—." It certainly was different from any towns we had ever seen.

"There's no dirt," said Jeff suddenly. "There's no smoke," he added after a little.

"There's no noise," I offered; but Terry snubbed me—"That's because they are laying low for us; we'd better be careful how we go in there."

Nothing could induce him to stay out, however, so we walked on.

Everything was beauty, order, perfect cleanness, and the pleasantest sense of home over it all. As we neared the center of the town the houses stood thicker, ran together as it were, grew into rambling palaces grouped among parks and open squares, something as college buildings stand in their quiet greens.

And then, turning a corner, we came into a broad paved space and saw before us a band of women standing close together in even order, evidently waiting for us.

We stopped a moment and looked back. The street behind was closed by another band, marching steadily, shoulder to shoulder. We went on—there seemed no other way to go—and presently found ourselves quite surrounded by this close-massed multitude, women, all of them, but—

They were not young. They were not old. They were not, in the girl sense, beautiful. They were not in the least ferocious. And yet, as I looked from face to face, calm, grave, wise, wholly unafraid, evidently assured and determined, I had the funniest feeling—a very early feeling—a feeling that I traced back and back in memory until I caught up with it at last. It was that sense of being hopelessly in the wrong that I had so often felt in early youth when my short legs' utmost effort failed to overcome the fact that I was late to school.

Jeff felt it too; I could see he did. We felt like small boys, very small boys, caught doing mischief in some gracious lady's house. But Terry showed no such consciousness. I saw his quick eyes darting here and there, estimating numbers, measuring distances, judging chances of escape. He examined the close ranks about us, reaching back far on every side, and murmured softly to me, "Every one of 'em over forty as I'm a sinner."

Yet they were not old women. Each was in the full bloom of rosy health, erect, serene, standing sure-footed and light as any pugilist. They had no weapons, and we had, but we had no wish to shoot.

"I'd as soon shoot my aunts," muttered Terry again. "What do they want with us anyhow? They seem to mean business." But in spite of that businesslike aspect, he determined to try his favorite tactics. Terry had come armed with a theory.

He stepped forward, with his brilliant ingratiating smile, and made low obeisance to the women before him. Then he produced another tribute, a broad soft scarf of filmy texture, rich in color and pattern, a lovely thing, even to my eye, and offered it with a deep bow to the tall unsmiling woman who seemed to head the ranks before him. She took it with a gracious nod of acknowledgment, and passed it on to those behind her.

He tried again, this time bringing out a circlet of rhinestones, a glittering crown that should have pleased any woman on earth. He made a brief address, including Jeff and me as partners in his enterprise, and with another bow presented this. Again his gift was accepted and, as before, passed out of sight.

"If they were only younger," he muttered between his teeth. "What on earth is a fellow to say to a regiment of old Colonels like this?"

In all our discussions and speculations we had always unconsciously assumed that the women, whatever else they might be, would be young. Most men do think that way, I fancy.

"Woman" in the abstract is young, and, we assume, charming. As they get older they pass off the stage, somehow, into private ownership mostly, or out of it altogether. But these good ladies were very much on the stage, and yet any one of them might have been a grandmother.

We looked for nervousness—there was none.

For terror, perhaps—there was none.

For uneasiness, for curiosity, for excitement—and all we saw was what might have been a vigilance committee of women doctors, as cool as cucumbers, and evidently meaning to take us to task for being there.

Six of them stepped forward now, one on either side of each of us, and indicated that we were to go with them. We thought it best to accede, at first anyway, and marched along, one of these close at each elbow, and the others in close masses before, behind, on both sides.

A large building opened before us, a very heavy thick-walled impressive place, big, and old-looking; of gray stone, not like the rest of the town.

"This won't do!" said Terry to us, quickly. "We mustn't let them get us in this, boys. All together, now—"

We stopped in our tracks. We began to explain, to make signs pointing away toward the big forest—indicating that we would go back to it—at once.

It makes me laugh, knowing all I do now, to think of us three boys—nothing else; three audacious impertinent boys—butting into an unknown country without any sort of a guard or defense. We seemed to think that if there were men we could fight them, and if there were only women—why, they would be no obstacles at all.

Jeff, with his gentle romantic old-fashioned notions of women as clinging vines. Terry, with his clear decided practical theories that there were two kinds of women—those he wanted and those he didn't; Desirable and Undesirable was his demarcation. The latter as a large class, but negligible—he had never thought about them at all.

And now here they were, in great numbers, evidently indifferent to what he might think, evidently determined on some purpose of their own regarding him, and apparently well able to enforce their purpose.

We all thought hard just then. It had not seemed wise to object to going with them, even if we could have; our one chance was friendliness—a civilized attitude on both sides.

But once inside that building, there was no knowing what these determined ladies might do to us. Even a peaceful detention was not to our minds, and when we named it imprisonment it looked even worse.

So we made a stand, trying to make clear that we preferred the open country. One of them came forward with a sketch of our flier, asking by signs if we were the aerial visitors they had seen.

This we admitted.

They pointed to it again, and to the outlying country, in different directions—but we pretended we did not know where it was, and in truth we were not quite sure and gave a rather wild indication of its whereabouts.

Again they motioned us to advance, standing so packed about the door that there remained but the one straight path open. All around us and behind they were massed solidly—there was simply nothing to do but go forward—or fight.

We held a consultation.

"I never fought with women in my life," said Terry, greatly perturbed, "but I'm not going in there. I'm not going to be—herded in—as if we were in a cattle chute."

"We can't fight them, of course," Jeff urged. "They're all women, in spite of their nondescript clothes; nice women, too; good strong sensible faces. I guess we'll have to go in."

"We may never get out, if we do," I told them. "Strong and sensible, yes; but I'm not so sure about the good. Look at those faces!"

They had stood at ease, waiting while we conferred together, but never relaxing their close attention.

Their attitude was not the rigid discipline of soldiers; there was no sense of compulsion about them. Terry's term of a "vigilance committee" was highly descriptive. They had just the aspect of sturdy burghers, gathered hastily to meet some common need or peril, all moved by precisely the same feelings, to the same end.

Never, anywhere before, had I seen women of precisely this quality. Fishwives and market women might show similar strength, but it was coarse and heavy. These were merely athletic—light and powerful. College professors, teachers, writers—many women showed similar intelligence but often wore a strained nervous look, while these were as calm as cows, for all their evident intellect.

We observed pretty closely just then, for all of us felt that it was a crucial moment.

The leader gave some word of command and beckoned us on, and the surrounding mass moved a step nearer.

"We've got to decide quick," said Terry.

"I vote to go in," Jeff urged. But we were two to one against him and he loyally stood by us. We made one more effort to be let go, urgent, but not imploring. In vain.

"Now for a rush, boys!" Terry said. "And if we can't break 'em, I'll shoot in the air."

Then we found ourselves much in the position of the suffragette trying to get to the Parliament buildings through a triple cordon of London police.

The solidity of those women was something amazing. Terry soon found that it was useless, tore himself loose for a moment, pulled his revolver, and fired upward. As they caught at it, he fired again—we heard a cry—.

Instantly each of us was seized by five women, each holding arm or leg or head; we were lifted like children, straddling helpless children, and borne onward, wriggling indeed, but most ineffectually.

We were borne inside, struggling manfully, but held secure most womanfully, in spite of our best endeavors.

So carried and so held, we came into a high inner hall, gray and bare, and were brought before a majestic gray-haired woman who seemed to hold a judicial position.

There was some talk, not much, among them, and then suddenly there fell upon each of us at once a firm hand holding a wetted cloth before mouth and nose—an order of swimming sweetness—anesthesia.

CHAPTER 3. A PECULIAR IMPRISONMENT

From a slumber as deep as death, as refreshing as that of a healthy child, I slowly awakened.

It was like rising up, up, up through a deep warm ocean, nearer and nearer to full light and stirring air. Or like the return to consciousness after concussion of the brain. I was once thrown from a horse while on a visit to a wild mountainous country quite new to me, and I can clearly remember the mental experience of coming back to life, through lifting veils of dream. When I first dimly heard the voices of those about me, and saw the shining snowpeaks of that mighty range, I assumed that this too would pass, and I should presently find myself in my own home.

That was precisely the experience of this awakening: receding waves of half-caught swirling vision, memories of home, the steamer, the boat, the airship, the forest—at last all sinking away one after another, till my eyes were wide open, my brain clear, and I realized what had happened.

The most prominent sensation was of absolute physical comfort. I was lying in a perfect bed: long, broad, smooth; firmly soft and level; with the finest linen, some warm light quilt of blanket, and a counterpane that was a joy to the eye. The sheet turned down some fifteen inches, yet I could stretch my feet at the foot of the bed free but warmly covered.

I felt as light and clean as a white feather. It took me some time to conscientiously locate my arms and legs, to feel the vivid sense of life radiate from the wakening center to the extremities.

A big room, high and wide, with many lofty windows whose closed blinds let through soft green-lit air; a beautiful room, in proportion, in color, in smooth simplicity; a scent of blossoming gardens outside.

I lay perfectly still, quite happy, quite conscious, and yet not actively realizing what had happened till I heard Terry.

"Gosh!" was what he said.

I turned my head. There were three beds in this chamber, and plenty of room for them.

Terry was sitting up, looking about him, alert as ever. His remark, though not loud, roused Jeff also. We all sat up.

Terry swung his legs out of bed, stood up, stretched himself mightily. He was in a long nightrobe, a sort of seamless garment, undoubtedly comfortable—we all found ourselves so covered. Shoes were beside each bed, also quite comfortable and goodlooking though by no means like our own.

We looked for our clothes—they were not there, nor anything of all the varied contents of our pockets.

A door stood somewhat ajar; it opened into a most attractive bathroom, copiously provided with towels, soap, mirrors, and all such convenient comforts, with indeed our toothbrushes and combs, our notebooks, and thank goodness, our watches—but no clothes.

Then we made a search of the big room again and found a large airy closet, holding plenty of clothing, but not ours.

"A council of war!" demanded Terry. "Come on back to bed—the bed's all right anyhow. Now then, my scientific friend, let us consider our case dispassionately."

He meant me, but Jeff seemed most impressed.

"They haven't hurt us in the least!" he said. "They could have killed us—or—or anything—and I never felt better in my life."

"That argues that they are all women," I suggested, "and highly civilized. You know you hit one in the last scrimmage—I heard her sing out—and we kicked awfully."

Terry was grinning at us. "So you realize what these ladies have done to us?" he pleasantly inquired. "They have taken away all our possessions, all our clothes—every stitch. We have been stripped and washed and put to bed like so many yearling babies—by these highly civilized women."

Jeff actually blushed. He had a poetic imagination. Terry had imagination enough, of a different kind. So had I, also different. I always flattered myself I had the scientific imagination, which, incidentally, I considered the highest sort. One has a right to a certain amount of egotism if founded on fact—and kept to one's self—I think.

"No use kicking, boys," I said. "They've got us, and apparently they're perfectly harmless. It remains for us to cook up some plan of escape like any other bottled heroes. Meanwhile we've got to put on these clothes—Hobson's choice."

The garments were simple in the extreme, and absolutely comfortable, physically, though of course we all felt like supes in the theater. There was a one-piece cotton undergarment, thin and soft, that reached over the knees and shoulders, something like the one-piece pajamas some fellows wear, and a kind of half-hose, that came up to just under the knee and stayed there—had elastic tops of their own, and covered the edges of the first.

Then there was a thicker variety of union suit, a lot of them in the closet, of varying weights and somewhat sturdier material—evidently they would do at a pinch with nothing further. Then there were tunics, knee-length, and some long robes. Needless to say, we took tunics.

We bathed and dressed quite cheerfully.

"Not half bad," said Terry, surveying himself in a long mirror. His hair was somewhat longer than when we left the last barber, and the hats provided were much like those seen on the prince in the fairy tale, lacking the plume.

The costume was similar to that which we had seen on all the women, though some of them, those working in the fields, glimpsed by our glasses when we first flew over, wore only the first two.

I settled my shoulders and stretched my arms, remarking: "They have worked out a mighty sensible dress, I'll say that for them." With which we all agreed.

"Now then," Terry proclaimed, "we've had a fine long sleep—we've had a good bath—we're clothed and in our right minds, though feeling like a lot of neuters. Do you think these highly civilized ladies are going to give us any breakfast?"

"Of course they will," Jeff asserted confidently. "If they had meant to kill us, they would have done it before. I believe we are going to be treated as guests."

"Hailed as deliverers, I think," said Terry.

"Studied as curiosities," I told them. "But anyhow, we want food. So now for a sortie!"

A sortie was not so easy.

The bathroom only opened into our chamber, and that had but one outlet, a big heavy door, which was fastened.

We listened.

"There's someone outside," Jeff suggested. "Let's knock."

So we knocked, whereupon the door opened.

Outside was another large room, furnished with a great table at one end, long benches or couches against the wall, some smaller tables and chairs. All these were solid, strong, simple in structure, and comfortable in use—also, incidentally, beautiful.

This room was occupied by a number of women, eighteen to be exact, some of whom we distinctly recalled.

Terry heaved a disappointed sigh. "The Colonels!" I heard him whisper to Jeff.

Jeff, however, advanced and bowed in his best manner; so did we all, and we were saluted civilly by the tall-standing women.

We had no need to make pathetic pantomime of hunger; the smaller tables were already laid with food, and we were gravely invited to be seated. The tables were set for two; each of us found ourselves placed vis-a-vis with one of our hosts, and each table had five other stalwarts nearby, unobtrusively watching. We had plenty of time to get tired of those women!

The breakfast was not profuse, but sufficient in amount and excellent in quality. We were all too good travelers to object to novelty, and this repast with its new but delicious fruit, its dish of large rich-flavored nuts, and its highly satisfactory little cakes was most agreeable. There was water to drink, and a hot beverage of a most pleasing quality, some preparation like cocoa.

And then and there, willy-nilly, before we had satisfied our appetites, our education began.

By each of our plates lay a little book, a real printed book, though different from ours both in paper and binding, as well, of course, as in type. We examined them curiously.

"Shades of Sauveur!" muttered Terry. "We're to learn the language!"

We were indeed to learn the language, and not only that, but to teach our own. There were blank books with parallel columns, neatly ruled, evidently prepared for the occasion, and in these, as fast as we learned and wrote down the name of anything, we were urged to write our own name for it by its side.

The book we had to study was evidently a schoolbook, one in which children learned to read, and we judged from this, and from their frequent consultation as to methods, that they had had no previous experience in the art of teaching foreigners their language, or of learning any other.

On the other hand, what they lacked in experience, they made up for in genius. Such subtle understanding, such instant recognition of our difficulties, and readiness to meet them, were a constant surprise to us.

Of course, we were willing to meet them halfway. It was wholly to our advantage to be able to understand and speak with them, and as to refusing to teach them—why should we? Later on we did try open rebellion, but only once.

That first meal was pleasant enough, each of us quietly studying his companion, Jeff with sincere admiration, Terry with that highly technical look of his, as of a past master—like a lion tamer, a serpent charmer, or some such professional. I myself was intensely interested.

It was evident that those sets of five were there to check any outbreak on our part. We had no weapons, and if we did try to do any damage, with a chair, say, why five to one was too many for us, even if they were women; that we had found out to our sorrow. It was not pleasant, having them always around, but we soon got used to it.

"It's better than being physically restrained ourselves," Jeff philosophically suggested when we were alone. "They've given us a room—with no great possibility of escape—and personal liberty—heavily chaperoned. It's better than we'd have been likely to get in a man-country."

"Man-Country! Do you really believe there are no men here, you innocent? Don't you know there must be?" demanded Terry.

"Ye—es," Jeff agreed. "Of course—and yet—"

"And yet—what! Come, you obdurate sentimentalist—what are you thinking about?"

"They may have some peculiar division of labor we've never heard of," I suggested. "The men may live in separate towns, or they may have subdued them—somehow—and keep them shut up. But there must be some."

"That last suggestion of yours is a nice one, Van," Terry protested. "Same as they've got us subdued and shut up! you make me shiver."

"Well, figure it out for yourself, anyway you please. We saw plenty of kids, the first day, and we've seen those girls—"

"Real girls!" Terry agreed, in immense relief. "Glad you mentioned 'em. I declare, if I thought there was nothing in the country but those grenadiers I'd jump out the window."

"Speaking of windows," I suggested, "let's examine ours."

We looked out of all the windows. The blinds opened easily enough, and there were no bars, but the prospect was not reassuring.

This was not the pink-walled town we had so rashly entered the day before. Our chamber was high up, in a projecting wing of a sort of castle, built out on a steep spur of rock. Immediately below us were gardens, fruitful and fragrant, but their high walls followed the edge of the cliff which dropped sheer down, we could not see how far. The distant sound of water suggested a river at the foot.

We could look out east, west, and south. To the southeastward stretched the open country, lying bright and fair in the morning light, but on either side, and evidently behind, rose great mountains.

"This thing is a regular fortress—and no women built it, I can tell you that," said Terry. We nodded agreeingly. "It's right up among the hills—they must have brought us a long way."

"We saw some kind of swift-moving vehicles the first day," Jeff reminded us. "If they've got motors, they ARE civilized."

"Civilized or not, we've got our work cut out for us to get away from here. I don't propose to make a rope of bedclothes and try those walls till I'm sure there is no better way."

We all concurred on this point, and returned to our discussion as to the women.

Jeff continued thoughtful. "All the same, there's something funny about it," he urged. "It isn't just that we don't see any men—but we don't see any signs of them. The—the—reaction of these women is different from any that I've ever met."

"There is something in what you say, Jeff," I agreed. "There is a different—atmosphere."

"They don't seem to notice our being men," he went on. "They treat us—well—just as they do one another. It's as if our being men was a minor incident."

I nodded. I'd noticed it myself. But Terry broke in rudely.

"Fiddlesticks!" he said. "It's because of their advanced age. They're all grandmas, I tell you—or ought to be. Great aunts, anyhow. Those girls were girls all right, weren't they?"

"Yes—" Jeff agreed, still slowly. "But they weren't afraid—they flew up that tree and hid, like schoolboys caught out of bounds—not like shy girls."

"And they ran like marathon winners—you'll admit that, Terry," he added.

Terry was moody as the days passed. He seemed to mind our confinement more than Jeff or I did; and he harped on Alima, and how near he'd come to catching her. "If I had—" he would say, rather savagely, "we'd have had a hostage and could have made terms."

But Jeff was getting on excellent terms with his tutor, and even his guards, and so was I. It interested me profoundly to note and study the subtle difference between these women and other women, and try to account for them. In the matter of personal appearance, there was a great difference. They all wore short hair, some few inches at most; some curly, some not; all light and clean and fresh-looking.

"If their hair was only long," Jeff would complain, "they would look so much more feminine."

I rather liked it myself, after I got used to it. Why we should so admire "a woman's crown of hair" and not admire a Chinaman's queue is hard to explain, except that we are so convinced that the long hair "belongs" to a woman. Whereas the "mane" in horses is on both, and in lions, buffalos, and such creatures only on the male. But I did miss it—at first.

Our time was quite pleasantly filled. We were free of the garden below our windows, quite long in its irregular rambling shape, bordering the cliff. The walls were perfectly smooth and high, ending in the masonry of the building; and as I studied the great stones I became convinced that the whole structure was extremely old. It was built like the pre-Incan architecture in Peru, of enormous monoliths, fitted as closely as mosaics.

"These folks have a history, that's sure," I told the others. "And SOME time they were fighters—else why a fortress?"

I said we were free of the garden, but not wholly alone in it. There was always a string of those uncomfortably strong women sitting about, always one of them watching us even if the others were reading, playing games, or busy at some kind of handiwork.

"When I see them knit," Terry said, "I can almost call them feminine."

"That doesn't prove anything," Jeff promptly replied. "Scotch shepherds knit—always knitting."

"When we get out—" Terry stretched himself and looked at the far peaks, "when we get out of this and get to where the real women are—the mothers, and the girls—"

"Well, what'll we do then?" I asked, rather gloomily. "How do you know we'll ever get out?"

This was an unpleasant idea, which we unanimously considered, returning with earnestness to our studies.

"If we are good boys and learn our lessons well," I suggested. "If we are quiet and respectful and polite and they are not afraid of us—then perhaps they will let us out. And anyway—when we do escape, it is of immense importance that we know the language."

Personally, I was tremendously interested in that language, and seeing they had books, was eager to get at them, to dig into their history, if they had one.

It was not hard to speak, smooth and pleasant to the ear, and so easy to read and write that I marveled at it. They had an absolutely phonetic system, the whole thing was as scientific as Esparanto yet bore all the marks of an old and rich civilization.

We were free to study as much as we wished, and were not left merely to wander in the garden for recreation but introduced to a great gymnasium, partly on the roof and partly in the story below. Here we learned real respect for our tall guards. No change of costume was needed for this work, save to lay off outer clothing. The first one was as perfect a garment for exercise as need be devised, absolutely free to move in, and, I had to admit, much better-looking than our usual one.

"Forty—over forty—some of 'em fifty, I bet—and look at 'em!" grumbled Terry in reluctant admiration.

There were no spectacular acrobatics, such as only the young can perform, but for all-around development they had a most excellent system. A good deal of music went with it, with posture dancing and, sometimes, gravely beautiful processional performances.

Jeff was much impressed by it. We did not know then how small a part of their physical culture methods this really was, but found it agreeable to watch, and to take part in.

Oh yes, we took part all right! It wasn't absolutely compulsory, but we thought it better to please.

Terry was the strongest of us, though I was wiry and had good staying power, and Jeff was a great sprinter and hurdler, but I can tell you those old ladies gave us cards and spades. They ran like deer, by which I mean that they ran not as if it was a performance, but as if it was their natural gait. We remembered those fleeting girls of our first bright adventure, and concluded that it was.

They leaped like deer, too, with a quick folding motion of the legs, drawn up and turned to one side with a sidelong twist of the body. I remembered the sprawling spread-eagle way in which some of the fellows used to come over the line—and tried to learn the trick. We did not easily catch up with these experts, however.

"Never thought I'd live to be bossed by a lot of elderly lady acrobats," Terry protested.

They had games, too, a good many of them, but we found them rather uninteresting at first. It was like two people playing solitaire to see who would get it first; more like a race or a—a competitive examination, than a real game with some fight in it.

I philosophized a bit over this and told Terry it argued against their having any men about. "There isn't a man-size game in the lot," I said.

"But they are interesting—I like them," Jeff objected, "and I'm sure they are educational."

"I'm sick and tired of being educated," Terry protested. "Fancy going to a dame school—at our age. I want to Get Out!"

But we could not get out, and we were being educated swiftly. Our special tutors rose rapidly in our esteem. They seemed of rather finer quality than the guards, though all were on terms of easy friendliness. Mine was named Somel, Jeff's Zava, and Terry's Moadine. We tried to generalize from the names, those of the guards, and of our three girls, but got nowhere.

"They sound well enough, and they're mostly short, but there's no similarity of termination—and no two alike. However, our acquaintance is limited as yet."

There were many things we meant to ask—as soon as we could talk well enough. Better teaching I never saw. From morning to night there was Somel, always on call except between two and four; always pleasant with a steady friendly kindness that I grew to enjoy very much. Jeff said Miss Zava—he would put on a title, though they apparently had none—was a darling, that she reminded him of his Aunt Esther at home; but Terry refused to be won, and rather jeered at his own companion, when we were alone.

"I'm sick of it!" he protested. "Sick of the whole thing. Here we are cooped up as helpless as a bunch of three-year-old orphans, and being taught what they think is necessary—whether we like it or not. Confound their old-maid impudence!"

Nevertheless we were taught. They brought in a raised map of their country, beautifully made, and increased our knowledge of geographical terms; but when we inquired for information as to the country outside, they smilingly shook their heads.

They brought pictures, not only the engravings in the books but colored studies of plants and trees and flowers and birds. They brought tools and various small objects—we had plenty of "material" in our school.

If it had not been for Terry we would have been much more contented, but as the weeks ran into months he grew more and more irritable.

"Don't act like a bear with a sore head," I begged him. "We're getting on finely. Every day we can understand them better, and pretty soon we can make a reasonable plea to be let out—"

"LET out!" he stormed. "LET out—like children kept after school. I want to Get Out, and I'm going to. I want to find the men of this place and fight!—or the girls—"

"Guess it's the girls you're most interested in," Jeff commented. "What are you going to fight WITH—your fists?"

"Yes—or sticks and stones—I'd just like to!" And Terry squared off and tapped Jeff softly on the jaw. "Just for instance," he said.

"Anyhow," he went on, "we could get back to our machine and clear out."

"If it's there," I cautiously suggested.

"Oh, don't croak, Van! If it isn't there, we'll find our way down somehow—the boat's there, I guess."

It was hard on Terry, so hard that he finally persuaded us to consider a plan of escape. It was difficult, it was highly dangerous, but he declared that he'd go alone if we wouldn't go with him, and of course we couldn't think of that.

It appeared he had made a pretty careful study of the environment. From our end window that faced the point of the promontory we could get a fair idea of the stretch of wall, and the drop below. Also from the roof we could make out more, and even, in one place, glimpse a sort of path below the wall.

"It's a question of three things," he said. "Ropes, agility, and not being seen."

"That's the hardest part," I urged, still hoping to dissuade him. "One or another pair of eyes is on us every minute except at night."

"Therefore we must do it at night," he answered. "That's easy."

"We've got to think that if they catch us we may not be so well treated afterward," said Jeff.

"That's the business risk we must take. I'm going—if I break my neck." There was no changing him.

The rope problem was not easy. Something strong enough to hold a man and long enough to let us down into the garden, and then down over the wall. There were plenty of strong ropes in the gymnasium—they seemed to love to swing and climb on them—but we were never there by ourselves.

We should have to piece it out from our bedding, rugs, and garments, and moreover, we should have to do it after we were shut in for the night, for every day the place was cleaned to perfection by two of our guardians.

We had no shears, no knives, but Terry was resourceful. "These Jennies have glass and china, you see. We'll break a glass from the bathroom and use that. 'Love will find out a way,'" he hummed. "When we're all out of the window, we'll stand three-man high and cut the rope as far up as we can reach, so as to have more for the wall. I know just where I saw that bit of path below, and there's a big tree there, too, or a vine or something—I saw the leaves."

It seemed a crazy risk to take, but this was, in a way, Terry's expedition, and we were all tired of our imprisonment.

So we waited for full moon, retired early, and spent an anxious hour or two in the unskilled manufacture of man-strong ropes.

To retire into the depths of the closet, muffle a glass in thick cloth, and break it without noise was not difficult, and broken glass will cut, though not as deftly as a pair of scissors.

The broad moonlight streamed in through four of our windows—we had not dared leave our lights on too long—and we worked hard and fast at our task of destruction.

Hangings, rugs, robes, towels, as well as bed-furniture—even the mattress covers—we left not one stitch upon another, as Jeff put it.

Then at an end window, as less liable to observation, we fastened one end of our cable, strongly, to the firm-set hinge of the inner blind, and dropped our coiled bundle of rope softly over.

"This part's easy enough—I'll come last, so as to cut the rope," said Terry.

So I slipped down first, and stood, well braced against the wall; then Jeff on my shoulders, then Terry, who shook us a little as he sawed through the cord above his head. Then I slowly dropped to the ground, Jeff following, and at last we all three stood safe in the garden, with most of our rope with us.

"Good-bye, Grandma!" whispered Terry, under his breath, and we crept softly toward the wall, taking advantage of the shadow of every bush and tree. He had been foresighted enough to mark the very spot, only a scratch of stone on stone, but we could see to read in that light. For anchorage there was a tough, fair-sized shrub close to the wall.

"Now I'll climb up on you two again and go over first," said Terry. "That'll hold the rope firm till you both get up on top. Then I'll go down to the end. If I can get off safely, you can see me and follow—or, say, I'll twitch it three times. If I find there's absolutely no footing—why I'll climb up again, that's all. I don't think they'll kill us."

From the top he reconnoitered carefully, waved his hand, and whispered, "OK," then slipped over. Jeff climbed up and I followed, and we rather shivered to see how far down that swaying, wavering figure dropped, hand under hand, till it disappeared in a mass of foliage far below.

Then there were three quick pulls, and Jeff and I, not without a joyous sense of recovered freedom, successfully followed our leader.

CHAPTER 4. OUR VENTURE

We were standing on a narrow, irregular, all too slanting little ledge, and should doubtless have ignominiously slipped off and broken our rash necks but for the vine. This was a thick-leaved, wide-spreading thing, a little like Amphelopsis.

"It's not QUITE vertical here, you see," said Terry, full of pride and enthusiasm. "This thing never would hold our direct weight, but I think if we sort of slide down on it, one at a time, sticking in with hands and feet, we'll reach that next ledge alive."

"As we do not wish to get up our rope again—and can't comfortably stay here—I approve," said Jeff solemnly.

Terry slid down first—said he'd show us how a Christian meets his death. Luck was with us. We had put on the thickest of those intermediate suits, leaving our tunics behind, and made this scramble quite successfully, though I got a pretty heavy fall just at the end, and was only kept on the second ledge by main force. The next stage was down a sort of "chimney"—a long irregular fissure; and so with scratches many and painful and bruises not a few, we finally reached the stream.

It was darker there, but we felt it highly necessary to put as much distance as possible behind us; so we waded, jumped, and clambered down that rocky riverbed, in the flickering black and white moonlight and leaf shadow, till growing daylight forced a halt.

We found a friendly nut-tree, those large, satisfying, soft-shelled nuts we already knew so well, and filled our pockets.

I see that I have not remarked that these women had pockets in surprising number and variety. They were in all their garments, and the middle one in particular was shingled with them. So we stocked up with nuts till we bulged like Prussian privates in marching order, drank all we could hold, and retired for the day.

It was not a very comfortable place, not at all easy to get at, just a sort of crevice high up along the steep bank, but it was well veiled with foliage and dry. After our exhaustive three- or four-hour scramble and the good breakfast food, we all lay down along that crack—heads and tails, as it were—and slept till the afternoon sun almost toasted our faces.

Terry poked a tentative foot against my head.

"How are you, Van? Alive yet?"

"Very much so," I told him. And Jeff was equally cheerful.

We had room to stretch, if not to turn around; but we could very carefully roll over, one at a time, behind the sheltering foliage.

It was no use to leave there by daylight. We could not see much of the country, but enough to know that we were now at the beginning of the cultivated area, and no doubt there would be an alarm sent out far and wide.

Terry chuckled softly to himself, lying there on that hot narrow little rim of rock. He dilated on the discomfiture of our guards and tutors, making many discourteous remarks.

I reminded him that we had still a long way to go before getting to the place where we'd left our machine, and no probability of finding it there; but he only kicked me, mildly, for a croaker.

"If you can't boost, don't knock," he protested. "I never said 'twould be a picnic. But I'd run away in the Antarctic ice fields rather than be a prisoner."

We soon dozed off again.

The long rest and penetrating dry heat were good for us, and that night we covered a considerable distance, keeping always in the rough forested belt of land which we knew bordered the whole country. Sometimes we were near the outer edge, and caught sudden glimpses of the tremendous depths beyond.

"This piece of geography stands up like a basalt column," Jeff said. "Nice time we'll have getting down if they have confiscated our machine!" For which suggestion he received summary chastisement.

What we could see inland was peaceable enough, but only moonlit glimpses; by daylight we lay very close. As Terry said, we did not wish to kill the old ladies—even if we could; and short of that they were perfectly competent to pick us up bodily and carry us back, if discovered. There was nothing for it but to lie low, and sneak out unseen if we could do it.

There wasn't much talking done. At night we had our marathon-obstacle race; we "stayed not for brake and we stopped not for stone," and swam whatever water was too deep to wade and could not be got around; but that was only necessary twice. By day, sleep, sound and sweet. Mighty lucky it was that we could live off the country as we did. Even that margin of forest seemed rich in foodstuffs.

But Jeff thoughtfully suggested that that very thing showed how careful we should have to be, as we might run into some stalwart group of gardeners or foresters or nut-gatherers at any minute. Careful we were, feeling pretty sure that if we did not make good this time we were not likely to have another opportunity; and at last we reached a point from which we could see, far below, the broad stretch of that still lake from which we had made our ascent.

"That looks pretty good to me!" said Terry, gazing down at it. "Now, if we can't find the 'plane, we know where to aim if we have to drop over this wall some other way."

The wall at that point was singularly uninviting. It rose so straight that we had to put our heads over to see the base, and the country below seemed to be a far-off marshy tangle of rank vegetation. We did not have to risk our necks to that extent, however, for at last, stealing along among the rocks and trees like so many creeping savages, we came to that flat space where we had landed; and there, in unbelievable good fortune, we found our machine.

"Covered, too, by jingo! Would you think they had that much sense?" cried Terry.

"If they had that much, they're likely to have more," I warned him, softly. "Bet you the thing's watched."

We reconnoitered as widely as we could in the failing moonlight—moons are of a painfully unreliable nature; but the growing dawn showed us the familiar shape, shrouded in some heavy cloth like canvas, and no slightest sign of any watchman near. We decided to make a quick dash as soon as the light was strong enough for accurate work.

"I don't care if the old thing'll go or not," Terry declared. "We can run her to the edge, get aboard, and just plane down—plop!—beside our boat there. Look there—see the boat!"

Sure enough—there was our motor, lying like a gray cocoon on the flat pale sheet of water.

Quietly but swiftly we rushed forward and began to tug at the fastenings of that cover.

"Confound the thing!" Terry cried in desperate impatience. "They've got it sewed up in a bag! And we've not a knife among us!"

Then, as we tugged and pulled at that tough cloth we heard a sound that made Terry lift his head like a war horse—the sound of an unmistakable giggle, yes—three giggles.

There they were—Celis, Alima, Ellador—looking just as they had when we first saw them, standing a little way off from us, as interested, as mischievous as three schoolboys.

"Hold on, Terry—hold on!" I warned. "That's too easy. Look out for a trap."

"Let us appeal to their kind hearts," Jeff urged. "I think they will help us. Perhaps they've got knives."

"It's no use rushing them, anyhow," I was absolutely holding on to Terry. "We know they can out-run and out-climb us."

He reluctantly admitted this; and after a brief parley among ourselves, we all advanced slowly toward them, holding out our hands in token of friendliness.

They stood their ground till we had come fairly near, and then indicated that we should stop. To make sure, we advanced a step or two and they promptly and swiftly withdrew. So we stopped at the distance specified. Then we used their language, as far as we were able, to explain our plight, telling how we were imprisoned, how we had escaped—a good deal of pantomime here and vivid interest on their part—how we had traveled by night and hidden by day, living on nuts—and here Terry pretended great hunger.

I know he could not have been hungry; we had found plenty to eat and had not been sparing in helping ourselves. But they seemed somewhat impressed; and after a murmured consultation they produced from their pockets certain little packages, and with the utmost ease and accuracy tossed them into our hands.

Jeff was most appreciative of this; and Terry made extravagant gestures of admiration, which seemed to set them off, boy-fashion, to show their skill. While we ate the excellent biscuits they had thrown us, and while Ellador kept a watchful eye on our movements, Celis ran off to some distance, and set up a sort of "duck-on-a-rock" arrangement, a big yellow nut on top of three balanced sticks; Alima, meanwhile, gathering stones.

They urged us to throw at it, and we did, but the thing was a long way off, and it was only after a number of failures, at which those elvish damsels laughed delightedly, that Jeff succeeded in bringing the whole structure to the ground. It took me still longer, and Terry, to his intense annoyance, came third.

Then Celis set up the little tripod again, and looked back at us, knocking it down, pointing at it, and shaking her short curls severely. "No," she said. "Bad—wrong!" We were quite able to follow her.

Then she set it up once more, put the fat nut on top, and returned to the others; and there those aggravating girls sat and took turns throwing little stones at that thing, while one stayed by as a setter-up; and they just popped that nut off, two times out of three, without upsetting the sticks. Pleased as Punch they were, too, and we pretended to be, but weren't.

We got very friendly over this game, but I told Terry we'd be sorry if we didn't get off while we could, and then we begged for knives. It was easy to show what we wanted to do, and they each proudly produced a sort of strong clasp-knife from their pockets.

"Yes," we said eagerly, "that's it! Please—" We had learned quite a bit of their language, you see. And we just begged for those knives, but they would not give them to us. If we came a step too near they backed off, standing light and eager for flight.

"It's no sort of use," I said. "Come on—let's get a sharp stone or something—we must get this thing off."

So we hunted about and found what edged fragments we could, and hacked away, but it was like trying to cut sailcloth with a clamshell.

Terry hacked and dug, but said to us under his breath. "Boys, we're in pretty good condition—let's make a life and death dash and get hold of those girls—we've got to."

They had drawn rather nearer to watch our efforts, and we did take them rather by surprise; also, as Terry said, our recent training had strengthened us in wind and limb, and for a few desperate moments those girls were scared and we almost triumphant.

But just as we stretched out our hands, the distance between us widened; they had got their pace apparently, and then, though we ran at our utmost speed, and much farther than I thought wise, they kept just out of reach all the time.

We stopped breathless, at last, at my repeated admonitions.

"This is stark foolishness," I urged. "They are doing it on purpose—come back or you'll be sorry."

We went back, much slower than we came, and in truth we were sorry.

As we reached our swaddled machine, and sought again to tear loose its covering, there rose up from all around the sturdy forms, the quiet determined faces we knew so well.

"Oh Lord!" groaned Terry. "The Colonels! It's all up—they're forty to one."

It was no use to fight. These women evidently relied on numbers, not so much as a drilled force but as a multitude actuated by a common impulse. They showed no sign of fear, and since we had no weapons whatever and there were at least a hundred of them, standing ten deep about us, we gave in as gracefully as we might.

Of course we looked for punishment—a closer imprisonment, solitary confinement maybe—but nothing of the kind happened. They treated us as truants only, and as if they quite understood our truancy.

Back we went, not under an anesthetic this time but skimming along in electric motors enough like ours to be quite recognizable, each of us in a separate vehicle with one able-bodied lady on either side and three facing him.

They were all pleasant enough, and talked to us as much as was possible with our limited powers. And though Terry was keenly mortified, and at first we all rather dreaded harsh treatment, I for one soon began to feel a sort of pleasant confidence and to enjoy the trip.

Here were my five familiar companions, all good-natured as could be, seeming to have no worse feeling than a mild triumph as of winning some simple game; and even that they politely suppressed.

This was a good opportunity to see the country, too, and the more I saw of it, the better I liked it. We went too swiftly for close observation, but I could appreciate perfect roads, as dustless as a swept floor; the shade of endless lines of trees; the ribbon of flowers that unrolled beneath them; and the rich comfortable country that stretched off and away, full of varied charm.

We rolled through many villages and towns, and I soon saw that the parklike beauty of our first-seen city was no exception. Our swift high-sweeping view from the 'plane had been most attractive, but lacked detail; and in that first day of struggle and capture, we noticed little. But now we were swept along at an easy rate of some thirty miles an hour and covered quite a good deal of ground.

We stopped for lunch in quite a sizable town, and here, rolling slowly through the streets, we saw more of the population. They had come out to look at us everywhere we had passed, but here were more; and when we went in to eat, in a big garden place with little shaded tables among the trees and flowers, many eyes were upon us. And everywhere, open country, village, or city—only women. Old women and young women and a great majority who seemed neither young nor old, but just women; young girls, also, though these, and the children, seeming to be in groups by themselves generally, were less in evidence. We caught many glimpses of girls and children in what seemed to be schools or in playgrounds, and so far as we could judge there were no boys. We all looked, carefully. Everyone gazed at us politely, kindly, and with eager interest. No one was impertinent. We could catch quite a bit of the talk now, and all they said seemed pleasant enough.

Well—before nightfall we were all safely back in our big room. The damage we had done was quite ignored; the beds as smooth and comfortable as before, new clothing and towels supplied. The only thing those women did was to illuminate the gardens at night, and to set an extra watch. But they called us to account next day. Our three tutors, who had not joined in the recapturing expedition, had been quite busy in preparing for us, and now made explanation.

They knew well we would make for our machine, and also that there was no other way of getting down—alive. So our flight had troubled no one; all they did was to call the inhabitants to keep an eye on our movements all along the edge of the forest between the two points. It appeared that many of those nights we had been seen, by careful ladies sitting snugly in big trees by the riverbed, or up among the rocks.

Terry looked immensely disgusted, but it struck me as extremely funny. Here we had been risking our lives, hiding and prowling like outlaws, living on nuts and fruit, getting wet and cold at night, and dry and hot by day, and all the while these estimable women had just been waiting for us to come out.

Now they began to explain, carefully using such words as we could understand. It appeared that we were considered as guests of the country—sort of public wards. Our first violence had made it necessary to keep us safeguarded for a while, but as soon as we learned the language—and would agree to do no harm—they would show us all about the land.

Jeff was eager to reassure them. Of course he did not tell on Terry, but he made it clear that he was ashamed of himself, and that he would now conform. As to the language—we all fell upon it with redoubled energy. They brought us books, in greater numbers, and I began to study them seriously.

"Pretty punk literature," Terry burst forth one day, when we were in the privacy of our own room. "Of course one expects to begin on child-stories, but I would like something more interesting now."

"Can't expect stirring romance and wild adventure without men, can you?" I asked. Nothing irritated Terry more than to have us assume that there were no men; but there were no signs of them in the books they gave us, or the pictures.

"Shut up!" he growled. "What infernal nonsense you talk! I'm going to ask 'em outright—we know enough now."

In truth we had been using our best efforts to master the language, and were able to read fluently and to discuss what we read with considerable ease.

That afternoon we were all sitting together on the roof—we three and the tutors gathered about a table, no guards about. We had been made to understand some time earlier that if we would agree to do no violence they would withdraw their constant attendance, and we promised most willingly.

So there we sat, at ease; all in similar dress; our hair, by now, as long as theirs, only our beards to distinguish us. We did not want those beards, but had so far been unable to induce them to give us any cutting instruments.

"Ladies," Terry began, out of a clear sky, as it were, "are there no men in this country?"

"Men?" Somel answered. "Like you?"

"Yes, men," Terry indicated his beard, and threw back his broad shoulders. "Men, real men."

"No," she answered quietly. "There are no men in this country. There has not been a man among us for two thousand years."

Her look was clear and truthful and she did not advance this astonishing statement as if it was astonishing, but quite as a matter of fact.

"But—the people—the children," he protested, not believing her in the least, but not wishing to say so.

"Oh yes," she smiled. "I do not wonder you are puzzled. We are mothers—all of us—but there are no fathers. We thought you would ask about that long ago—why have you not?" Her look was as frankly kind as always, her tone quite simple.

Terry explained that we had not felt sufficiently used to the language, making rather a mess of it, I thought, but Jeff was franker.

"Will you excuse us all," he said, "if we admit that we find it hard to believe? There is no such—possibility—in the rest of the world."

"Have you no kind of life where it is possible?" asked Zava.

"Why, yes—some low forms, of course."

"How low—or how high, rather?"

"Well—there are some rather high forms of insect life in which it occurs. Parthenogenesis, we call it—that means virgin birth."

She could not follow him.

"BIRTH, we know, of course; but what is VIRGIN?"

Terry looked uncomfortable, but Jeff met the question quite calmly. "Among mating animals, the term VIRGIN is applied to the female who has not mated," he answered.

"Oh, I see. And does it apply to the male also? Or is there a different term for him?"

He passed this over rather hurriedly, saying that the same term would apply, but was seldom used.

"No?" she said. "But one cannot mate without the other surely. Is not each then—virgin—before mating? And, tell me, have you any forms of life in which there is birth from a father only?"

"I know of none," he answered, and I inquired seriously.

"You ask us to believe that for two thousand years there have been only women here, and only girl babies born?"

"Exactly," answered Somel, nodding gravely. "Of course we know that among other animals it is not so, that there are fathers as well as mothers; and we see that you are fathers, that you come from a people who are of both kinds. We have been waiting, you see, for you to be able to speak freely with us, and teach us about your country and the rest of the world. You know so much, you see, and we know only our own land."

In the course of our previous studies we had been at some pains to tell them about the big world outside, to draw sketches, maps, to make a globe, even, out of a spherical fruit, and show the size and relation of the countries, and to tell of the numbers of their people. All this had been scant and in outlinc, but they quite understood.

I find I succeed very poorly in conveying the impression I would like to of these women. So far from being ignorant, they were deeply wise—that we realized more and more; and for clear reasoning, for real brain scope and power they were A No. 1, but there were a lot of things they did not know.

They had the evenest tempers, the most perfect patience and good nature—one of the things most impressive about them all was the absence of irritability. So far we had only this group to study, but afterward I found it a common trait.

We had gradually come to feel that we were in the hands of friends, and very capable ones at that—but we couldn't form any opinion yet of the general level of these women.

"We want you to teach us all you can," Somel went on, her firm shapely hands clasped on the table before her, her clear quiet eyes meeting ours frankly. "And we want to teach you what we have that is novel and useful. You can well imagine that it is a wonderful event to us, to have men among us—after two thousand years. And we want to know about your women."

What she said about our importance gave instant pleasure to Terry. I could see by the way he lifted his head that it pleased him. But when she spoke of our women—someway I had a queer little indescribable feeling, not like any feeling I ever had before when "women" were mentioned.

"Will you tell us how it came about?" Jeff pursued. "You said 'for two thousand years'—did you have men here before that?"

"Yes," answered Zava.

They were all quiet for a little.

"You should have our full history to read—do not be alarmed—it has been made clear and short. It took us a long time to learn how to write history. Oh, how I should love to read yours!"

She turned with flashing eager eyes, looking from one to the other of us.

"It would be so wonderful—would it not? To compare the history of two thousand years, to see what the differences are—between us, who are only mothers, and you, who are mothers and fathers, too. Of course we see, with our birds, that the father is as useful as the mother, almost. But among insects we find him of less importance, sometimes very little. Is it not so with you?"

"Oh, yes, birds and bugs," Terry said, "but not among animals—have you NO animals?"

"We have cats," she said. "The father is not very useful."

"Have you no cattle—sheep—horses?" I drew some rough outlines of these beasts and showed them to her.

"We had, in the very old days, these," said Somel, and sketched with swift sure touches a sort of sheep or llama, "and these"—dogs, of two or three kinds, "that that"—pointing to my absurd but recognizable horse.

"What became of them?" asked Jeff.

"We do not want them anymore. They took up too much room—we need all our land to feed our people. It is such a little country, you know."

"Whatever do you do without milk?" Terry demanded incredulously.

"MILK? We have milk in abundance—our own."

"But—but—I mean for cooking—for grown people," Terry blundered, while they looked amazed and a shade displeased.

Jeff came to the rescue. "We keep cattle for their milk, as well as for their meat," he explained. "Cow's milk is a staple article of diet. There is a great milk industry—to collect and distribute it."

Still they looked puzzled. I pointed to my outline of a cow. "The farmer milks the cow," I said, and sketched a milk pail, the stool, and in pantomime showed the man milking. "Then it is carried to the city and distributed by milkmen—everybody has it at the door in the morning."

"Has the cow no child?" asked Somel earnestly.

"Oh, yes, of course, a calf, that is."

"Is there milk for the calf and you, too?"

It took some time to make clear to those three sweet-faced women the process which robs the cow of her calf, and the calf of its true food; and the talk led us into a further discussion of the meat business. They heard it out, looking very white, and presently begged to be excused.

CHAPTER 5. A UNIQUE HISTORY

It is no use for me to try to piece out this account with adventures. If the people who read it are not interested in these amazing women and their history, they will not be interested at all.

As for us—three young men to a whole landful of women—what could we do? We did get away, as described, and were peacefully brought back again without, as Terry complained, even the satisfaction of hitting anybody.

There were no adventures because there was nothing to fight. There were no wild beasts in the country and very few tame ones. Of these I might as well stop to describe the one common pet of the country. Cats, of course. But such cats!

What do you suppose these Lady Burbanks had done with their cats? By the most prolonged and careful selection and exclusion they had developed a race of cats that did not sing! That's a fact. The most those poor dumb brutes could do was to make a kind of squeak when they were hungry or wanted the door open, and, of course, to purr, and make the various mother-noises to their kittens.

Moreover, they had ceased to kill birds. They were rigorously bred to destroy mice and moles and all such enemies of the food supply; but the birds were numerous and safe.

While we were discussing birds, Terry asked them if they used feathers for their hats, and they seemed amused at the idea. He made a few sketches of our women's hats, with plumes and quills and those various tickling things that stick out so far; and they were eagerly interested, as at everything about our women.

As for them, they said they only wore hats for shade when working in the sun; and those were big light straw hats, something like those used in China and Japan. In cold weather they wore caps or hoods.

"But for decorative purposes—don't you think they would be becoming?" pursued Terry, making as pretty a picture as he could of a lady with a plumed hat.

They by no means agreed to that, asking quite simply if the men wore the same kind. We hastened to assure her that they did not—drew for them our kind of headgear.

"And do no men wear feathers in their hats?"

"Only Indians," Jeff explained. "Savages, you know." And he sketched a war bonnet to show them.

"And soldiers," I added, drawing a military hat with plumes.

They never expressed horror or disapproval, nor indeed much surprise—just a keen interest. And the notes they made!—miles of them!

But to return to our pussycats. We were a good deal impressed by this achievement in breeding, and when they questioned us—I can tell you we were well pumped for information—we told of what had been done for dogs and horses and cattle, but that there was no effort applied to cats, except for show purposes.

I wish I could represent the kind, quiet, steady, ingenious way they questioned us. It was not just curiosity—they weren't a bit more curious about us than we were about them, if as much. But they were bent on understanding our kind of civilization, and their lines of interrogation would gradually surround us and drive us in till we found ourselves up against some admissions we did not want to make.

"Are all these breeds of dogs you have made useful?" they asked.

"Oh—useful! Why, the hunting dogs and watchdogs and sheepdogs are useful—and sleddogs of course!—and ratters, I suppose, but we don't keep dogs for their USEFULNESS. The dog is 'the friend of man,' we say—we love them."

That they understood. "We love our cats that way. They surely are our friends, and helpers, too. You can see how intelligent and affectionate they are."

It was a fact. I'd never seen such cats, except in a few rare instances. Big, handsome silky things, friendly with everyone and devotedly attached to their special owners.

"You must have a heartbreaking time drowning kittens," we suggested. But they said, "Oh, no! You see we care for them as you do for your valuable cattle. The fathers are few compared to the mothers, just a few very fine ones in each town; they live quite happily in walled gardens and the houses of their friends. But they only have a mating season once a year."

"Rather hard on Thomas, isn't it?" suggested Terry.

"Oh, no—truly! You see, it is many centuries that we have been breeding the kind of cats we wanted. They are healthy and happy and friendly, as you see. How do you manage with your dogs? Do you keep them in pairs, or segregate the fathers, or what?"

Then we explained that—well, that it wasn't a question of fathers exactly; that nobody wanted a—a mother dog; that, well, that practically all our dogs were males—there was only a very small percentage of females allowed to live.

Then Zava, observing Terry with her grave sweet smile, quoted back at him: "Rather hard on Thomas, isn't it? Do they enjoy it—living without mates? Are your dogs as uniformly healthy and sweet-tempered as our cats?"

Jeff laughed, eyeing Terry mischievously. As a matter of fact we began to feel Jeff something of a traitor—he so often flopped over and took their side of things; also his medical knowledge gave him a different point of view somehow.

"I'm sorry to admit," he told them, "that the dog, with us, is the most diseased of any animal—next to man. And as to temper—there are always some dogs who bite people—especially children."

That was pure malice. You see, children were the—the RAISON D'ETRE in this country. All our interlocutors sat up straight at once. They were still gentle, still restrained, but there was a note of deep amazement in their voices.

"Do we understand that you keep an animal—an unmated male animal—that bites children? About how many are there of them, please?"

"Thousands—in a large city," said Jeff, "and nearly every family has one in the country."

Terry broke in at this. "You must not imagine they are all dangerous—it's not one in a hundred that ever bites anybody. Why, they are the best friends of the children—a boy doesn't have half a chance that hasn't a dog to play with!"

"And the girls?" asked Somel.

"Oh—girls—why they like them too," he said, but his voice flatted a little. They always noticed little things like that, we found later.

Little by little they wrung from us the fact that the friend of man, in the city, was a prisoner; was taken out for his meager exercise on a leash; was liable not only to many diseases but to the one destroying horror of rabies; and, in many cases, for the safety of the citizens, had to go muzzled. Jeff maliciously added vivid instances he had known or read of injury and death from mad dogs.

They did not scold or fuss about it. Calm as judges, those women were. But they made notes; Moadine read them to us.

"Please tell me if I have the facts correct," she said. "In your country—and in others too?"

"Yes," we admitted, "in most civilized countries."

"In most civilized countries a kind of animal is kept which is no longer useful—"

"They are a protection," Terry insisted. "They bark if burglars try to get in."

Then she made notes of "burglars" and went on: "because of the love which people bear to this animal."

Zava interrupted here. "Is it the men or the women who love this animal so much?"

"Both!" insisted Terry.

"Equally?" she inquired.

And Jeff said, "Nonsense, Terry—you know men like dogs better than women do—as a whole."

"Because they love it so much—especially men. This animal is kept shut up, or chained."

"Why?" suddenly asked Somel. "We keep our father cats shut up because we do not want too much fathering; but they are not chained—they have large grounds to run in."

"A valuable dog would be stolen if he was let loose," I said. "We put collars on them, with the owner's name, in case they do stray. Besides, they get into fights—a valuable dog might easily be killed by a bigger one."

"I see," she said. "They fight when they meet—is that common?" We admitted that it was.

"They are kept shut up, or chained." She paused again, and asked, "Is not a dog fond of running? Are they not built for speed?" That we admitted, too, and Jeff, still malicious, enlightened them further.

"I've always thought it was a pathetic sight, both ways—to see a man or a woman taking a dog to walk—at the end of a string."

"Have you bred them to be as neat in their habits as cats are?" was the next question. And when Jeff told them of the effect of dogs on sidewalk merchandise and the streets generally, they found it hard to believe.

You see, their country was as neat as a Dutch kitchen, and as to sanitation—but I might as well start in now with as much as I can remember of the history of this amazing country before further description.

And I'll summarize here a bit as to our opportunities for learning it. I will not try to repeat the careful, detailed account I lost; I'll just say that we were kept in that fortress a good six months all told, and after that, three in a pleasant enough city where—to Terry's infinite disgust—there were only "Colonels" and little children—no young women whatever. Then we were under surveillance for three more—always with a tutor or a guard or both. But those months were pleasant because we were really getting acquainted with the girls. That was a chapter!—or will be—I will try to do justice to it.

We learned their language pretty thoroughly—had to; and they learned ours much more quickly and used it to hasten our own studies.

Jeff, who was never without reading matter of some sort, had two little books with him, a novel and a little anthology of verse; and I had one of those pocket encyclopedias—a fat little thing, bursting with facts. These were used in our education—and theirs. Then as soon as we were up to it, they furnished us with plenty of their own books, and I went in for the history part—I wanted to understand the genesis of this miracle of theirs.

And this is what happened, according to their records.

As to geography—at about the time of the Christian era this land had a free passage to the sea. I'm not saying where, for good reasons. But there was a fairly easy pass through that wall of mountains behind us, and there is no doubt in my mind that these people were of Aryan stock, and were once in contact with the best civilization of the old world. They were "white," but somewhat darker than our northern races because of their constant exposure to sun and air.

The country was far larger then, including much land beyond the pass, and a strip of coast. They had ships, commerce, an army, a king—for at that time they were what they so calmly called us—a bi-sexual race.

What happened to them first was merely a succession of historic misfortunes such as have befallen other nations often enough. They were decimated by war, driven up from their coastline till finally the reduced population, with many of the men killed in battle, occupied this hinterland, and defended it for years, in the mountain passes. Where it was open to any possible attack from below they strengthened the natural defenses so that it became unscalably secure, as we found it.

They were a polygamous people, and a slave-holding people, like all of their time; and during the generation or two of this struggle to defend their mountain home they built the fortresses, such as the one we were held in, and other of their oldest buildings, some still in use. Nothing but earthquakes could destroy such architecture—huge solid blocks, holding by their own weight. They must have had efficient workmen and enough of them in those days.

They made a brave fight for their existence, but no nation can stand up against what the steamship companies call "an act of God." While the whole fighting force was doing its best to defend their mountain pathway, there occurred a volcanic outburst, with some local tremors, and the result was the complete filling up of the pass—their only outlet. Instead of a passage, a new ridge, sheer and high, stood between them and the sea; they were walled in, and beneath that wall lay their whole little army. Very few men were left alive, save the slaves; and these now seized their opportunity, rose in revolt, killed their remaining masters even to the youngest boy, killed the old women too, and the mothers, intending to take possession of the country with the remaining young women and girls.

But this succession of misfortunes was too much for those infuriated virgins. There were many of them, and but few of these would-be masters, so the young women, instead of submitting, rose in sheer desperation and slew their brutal conquerors.

This sounds like Titus Andronicus, I know, but that is their account. I suppose they were about crazy—can you blame them?

There was literally no one left on this beautiful high garden land but a bunch of hysterical girls and some older slave women.

That was about two thousand years ago.

At first there was a period of sheer despair. The mountains towered between them and their old enemies, but also between them and escape. There was no way up or down or out—they simply had to stay there. Some were for suicide, but not the majority. They must have been a plucky lot, as a whole, and they decided to live—as long as they did live. Of course they had hope, as youth must, that something would happen to change their fate.

So they set to work, to bury the dead, to plow and sow, to care for one another.

Speaking of burying the dead, I will set down while I think of it, that they had adopted cremation in about the thirteenth century, for the same reason that they had left off raising cattle—they could not spare the room. They were much surprised to learn that we were still burying—asked our reasons for it, and were much dissatisfied with what we gave. We told them of the belief in the resurrection of the body, and they asked if our God was not as well able to resurrect from ashes as from long corruption. We told them of how people thought it repugnant to have their loved ones burn, and they asked if it was less repugnant to have them decay. They were inconveniently reasonable, those women.

Well—that original bunch of girls set to work to clean up the place and make their living as best they could. Some of the remaining slave women rendered invaluable service, teaching such trades as they knew. They had such records as were then kept, all the tools and implements of the time, and a most fertile land to work in.

There were a handful of the younger matrons who had escaped slaughter, and a few babies were born after the cataclysm—but only two boys, and they both died.

For five or ten years they worked together, growing stronger and wiser and more and more mutually attached, and then the miracle happened—one of these young women bore a child. Of course they all thought there must be a man somewhere, but none was found. Then they decided it must be a direct gift from the gods, and placed the proud mother in the Temple of Maaia—their Goddess of Motherhood—under strict watch. And there, as years passed, this wonder-woman bore child after child, five of them—all girls.

I did my best, keenly interested as I have always been in sociology and social psychology, to reconstruct in my mind the real position of these ancient women. There were some five or six hundred of them, and they were harem-bred; yet for the few preceding generations they had been reared in the atmosphere of such heroic struggle that the stock must have been toughened somewhat. Left alone in that terrific orphanhood, they had clung together, supporting one another and their little sisters, and developing unknown powers in the stress of new necessity. To this pain-hardened and work-strengthened group, who had lost not only the love and care of parents, but the hope of ever having children of their own, there now dawned the new hope.

Here at last was Motherhood, and though it was not for all of them personally, it might—if the power was inherited—found here a new race.

It may be imagined how those five Daughters of Maaia, Children of the Temple, Mothers of the Future—they had all the titles that love and hope and reverence could give—were reared. The whole little nation of women surrounded them with loving service, and waited, between a boundless hope and an equally boundless despair, to see if they, too, would be mothers.

And they were! As fast as they reached the age of twenty-five they began bearing. Each of them, like her mother, bore five daughters. Presently there were twenty-five New Women, Mothers in their own right, and the whole spirit of the country changed from mourning and mere courageous resignation to proud joy. The older women, those who remembered men, died off; the youngest of all the first lot of course died too, after a while, and by that time there were left one hundred and fifty-five parthenogenetic women, founding a new race.

They inherited all that the devoted care of that declining band of original ones could leave them. Their little country was quite safe. Their farms and gardens were all in full production. Such industries as they had were in careful order. The records of their past were all preserved, and for years the older women had spent their time in the best teaching they were capable of, that they might leave to the little group of sisters and mothers all they possessed of skill and knowledge.

There you have the start of Herland! One family, all descended from one mother! She lived to a hundred years old; lived to see her hundred and twenty-five great-granddaughters born; lived as Queen-Priestess-Mother of them all; and died with a nobler pride and a fuller joy than perhaps any human soul has ever known—she alone had founded a new race!

The first five daughters had grown up in an atmosphere of holy calm, of awed watchful waiting, of breathless prayer. To them the longed-for motherhood was not only a personal joy, but a nation's hope. Their twenty-five daughters in turn, with a stronger hope, a richer, wider outlook, with the devoted love and care of all the surviving population, grew up as a holy sisterhood, their whole ardent youth looking forward to their great office. And at last they were left alone; the white-haired First Mother was gone, and this one family, five sisters, twenty-five first cousins, and a hundred and twenty-five second cousins, began a new race.

Here you have human beings, unquestionably, but what we were slow in understanding was how these ultra-women, inheriting only from women, had eliminated not only certain masculine characteristics, which of course we did not look for, but so much of what we had always thought essentially feminine.

The tradition of men as guardians and protectors had quite died out. These stalwart virgins had no men to fear and therefore no need of protection. As to wild beasts—there were none in their sheltered land.

The power of mother-love, that maternal instinct we so highly laud, was theirs of course, raised to its highest power; and a sister-love which, even while recognizing the actual relationship, we found it hard to credit.

Terry, incredulous, even contemptuous, when we were alone, refused to believe the story. "A lot of traditions as old as Herodotus—and about as trustworthy!" he said. "It's likely women—just a pack of women—would have hung together like that! We all know women can't organize—that they scrap like anything—are frightfully jealous."

"But these New Ladies didn't have anyone to be jealous of, remember," drawled Jeff.

"That's a likely story," Terry sneered.

"Why don't you invent a likelier one?" I asked him. "Here ARE the women—nothing but women, and you yourself admit there's no trace of a man in the country." This was after we had been about a good deal.

"I'll admit that," he growled. "And it's a big miss, too. There's not only no fun without 'em—no real sport—no competition; but these women aren't WOMANLY. You know they aren't."

That kind of talk always set Jeff going; and I gradually grew to side with him. "Then you don't call a breed of women whose one concern is motherhood—womanly?" he asked.

"Indeed I don't," snapped Terry. "What does a man care for motherhood—when he hasn't a ghost of a chance at fatherhood? And besides—what's the good of talking sentiment when we are just men together? What a man wants of women is a good deal more than all this 'motherhood'!"

We were as patient as possible with Terry. He had lived about nine months among the "Colonels" when he made that outburst; and with no chance at any more strenuous excitement than our gymnastics gave us—save for our escape fiasco. I don't suppose Terry had ever lived so long with neither Love, Combat, nor Danger to employ his superabundant energies, and he was irritable. Neither Jeff nor I found it so wearing. I was so much interested intellectually that our confinement did not wear on me; and as for Jeff, bless his heart!—he enjoyed the society of that tutor of his almost as much as if she had been a girl—I don't know but more.

As to Terry's criticism, it was true. These women, whose essential distinction of motherhood was the dominant note of their whole culture, were strikingly deficient in what we call "femininity." This led me very promptly to the conviction that those "feminine charms" we are so fond of are not feminine at all, but mere reflected masculinity—developed to please us because they had to please us, and in no way essential to the real fulfillment of their great process. But Terry came to no such conclusion.

"Just you wait till I get out!" he muttered.

Then we both cautioned him. "Look here, Terry, my boy! You be careful! They've been mighty good to us—but do you remember the anesthesia? If you do any mischief in this virgin land, beware of the vengeance of the Maiden Aunts! Come, be a man! It won't be forever."

To return to the history:

They began at once to plan and built for their children, all the strength and intelligence of the whole of them devoted to that one thing. Each girl, of course, was reared in full knowledge of her Crowning Office, and they had, even then, very high ideas of the molding powers of the mother, as well as those of education.

Such high ideals as they had! Beauty, Health, Strength, Intellect, Goodness—for those they prayed and worked.

They had no enemies; they themselves were all sisters and friends. The land was fair before them, and a great future began to form itself in their minds.

The religion they had to begin with was much like that of old Greece—a number of gods and goddesses; but they lost all interest in deities of war and plunder, and gradually centered on their Mother Goddess altogether. Then, as they grew more intelligent, this had turned into a sort of Maternal Pantheism.

Here was Mother Earth, bearing fruit. All that they ate was fruit of motherhood, from seed or egg or their product. By motherhood they were born and by motherhood they lived—life was, to them, just the long cycle of motherhood.

But very early they recognized the need of improvement as well as of mere repetition, and devoted their combined intelligence to that problem—how to make the best kind of people. First this was merely the hope of bearing better ones, and then they recognized that however the children differed at birth, the real growth lay later—through education.

Then things began to hum.

As I learned more and more to appreciate what these women had accomplished, the less proud I was of what we, with all our manhood, had done.

You see, they had had no wars. They had had no kings, and no priests, and no aristocracies. They were sisters, and as they grew, they grew together—not by competition, but by united action.

We tried to put in a good word for competition, and they were keenly interested. Indeed, we soon found from their earnest questions of us that they were prepared to believe our world must be better than theirs. They were not sure; they wanted to know; but there was no such arrogance about them as might have been expected.

We rather spread ourselves, telling of the advantages of competition: how it developed fine qualities; that without it there would be "no stimulus to industry." Terry was very strong on that point.

"No stimulus to industry," they repeated, with that puzzled look we had learned to know so well. "STIMULUS? TO INDUSTRY? But don't you LIKE to work?"

"No man would work unless he had to," Terry declared.

"Oh, no MAN! You mean that is one of your sex distinctions?"

"No, indeed!" he said hastily. "No one, I mean, man or woman, would work without incentive. Competition is the—the motor power, you see."

"It is not with us," they explained gently, "so it is hard for us to understand. Do you mean, for instance, that with you no mother would work for her children without the stimulus of competition?"

No, he admitted that he did not mean that. Mothers, he supposed, would of course work for their children in the home; but the world's work was different—that had to be done by men, and required the competitive element.

All our teachers were eagerly interested.

"We want so much to know—you have the whole world to tell us of, and we have only our little land! And there are two of you—the two sexes—to love and help one another. It must be a rich and wonderful world. Tell us—what is the work of the world, that men do—which we have not here?"

"Oh, everything," Terry said grandly. "The men do everything, with us." He squared his broad shoulders and lifted his chest. "We do not allow our women to work. Women are loved—idolized—honored—kept in the home to care for the children."

"What is 'the home'?" asked Somel a little wistfully.

But Zava begged: "Tell me first, do NO women work, really?"

"Why, yes," Terry admitted. "Some have to, of the poorer sort."

"About how many—in your country?"

"About seven or eight million," said Jeff, as mischievous as ever.

CHAPTER 6. COMPARISONS ARE ODIOUS

I had always been proud of my country, of course. Everyone is. Compared with the other lands and other races I knew, the United States of America had always seemed to me, speaking modestly, as good as the best of them.

But just as a clear-eyed, intelligent, perfectly honest, and well-meaning child will frequently jar one's self-esteem by innocent questions, so did these women, without the slightest appearance of malice or satire, continually bring up points of discussion which we spent our best efforts in evading.

Now that we were fairly proficient in their language, had read a lot about their history, and had given them the general outlines of ours, they were able to press their questions closer.

So when Jeff admitted the number of "women wage earners" we had, they instantly asked for the total population, for the proportion of adult women, and found that there were but twenty million or so at the outside.

"Then at least a third of your women are—what is it you call them—wage earners? And they are all POOR. What is POOR, exactly?"

"Ours is the best country in the world as to poverty," Terry told them. "We do not have the wretched paupers and beggars of the older countries, I assure you. Why, European visitors tell us, we don't know what poverty is."

"Neither do we," answered Zava. "Won't you tell us?"

Terry put it up to me, saying I was the sociologist, and I explained that the laws of nature require a struggle for existence, and that in the struggle the fittest survive, and the unfit perish. In our economic struggle, I continued, there was always plenty of opportunity for the fittest to reach the top, which they did, in great numbers, particularly in our country; that where there was severe economic pressure the lowest classes of course felt it the worst, and that among the poorest of all the women were driven into the labor market by necessity.

They listened closely, with the usual note-taking.

"About one-third, then, belong to the poorest class," observed Moadine gravely. "And two-thirds are the ones who are—how was it you so beautifully put it?—'loved, honored, kept in the home to care for the children.' This inferior one-third have no children, I suppose?"

Jeff—he was getting as bad as they were—solemnly replied that, on the contrary, the poorer they were, the more children they had. That too, he explained, was a law of nature: "Reproduction is in inverse proportion to individuation."

"These 'laws of nature,'" Zava gently asked, "are they all the laws you have?"

"I should say not!" protested Terry. "We have systems of law that go back thousands and thousands of years—just as you do, no doubt," he finished politely.

"Oh no," Moadine told him. "We have no laws over a hundred years old, and most of them are under twenty. In a few weeks more," she continued, "we are going to have the pleasure of showing you over our little land and explaining everything you care to know about. We want you to see our people."

"And I assure you," Somel added, "that our people want to see you."

Terry brightened up immensely at this news, and reconciled himself to the renewed demands upon our capacity as teachers. It was lucky that we knew so little, really, and had no books to refer to, else, I fancy we might all be there yet, teaching those eager-minded women about the rest of the world.

As to geography, they had the tradition of the Great Sea, beyond the mountains; and they could see for themselves the endless thick-forested plains below them—that was all. But from the few records of their ancient condition—not "before the flood" with them, but before that mighty quake which had cut them off so completely—they were aware that there were other peoples and other countries.

In geology they were quite ignorant.

As to anthropology, they had those same remnants of information about other peoples, and the knowledge of the savagery of the occupants of those dim forests below. Nevertheless, they had inferred (marvelously keen on inference and deduction their minds were!) the existence and development of civilization in other places, much as we infer it on other planets.

When our biplane came whirring over their heads in that first scouting flight of ours, they had instantly accepted it as proof of the high development of Some Where Else, and had prepared to receive us as cautiously and eagerly as we might prepare to welcome visitors who came "by meteor" from Mars.

Of history—outside their own—they knew nothing, of course, save for their ancient traditions.

Of astronomy they had a fair working knowledge—that is a very old science; and with it, a surprising range and facility in mathematics.

Physiology they were quite familiar with. Indeed, when it came to the simpler and more concrete sciences, wherein the subject matter was at hand and they had but to exercise their minds upon it, the results were surprising. They had worked out a chemistry, a botany, a physics, with all the blends where a science touches an art, or merges into an industry, to such fullness of knowledge as made us feel like schoolchildren.

Also we found this out—as soon as we were free of the country, and by further study and question—that what one knew, all knew, to a very considerable extent.

I talked later with little mountain girls from the fir-dark valleys away up at their highest part, and with sunburned plains-women and agile foresters, all over the country, as well as those in the towns, and everywhere there was the same high level of intelligence. Some knew far more than others about one thing—they were specialized, of course; but all of them knew more about everything—that is, about everything the country was acquainted with—than is the case with us.

We boast a good deal of our "high level of general intelligence" and our "compulsory public education," but in proportion to their opportunities they were far better educated than our people.

With what we told them, from what sketches and models we were able to prepare, they constructed a sort of working outline to fill in as they learned more.

A big globe was made, and our uncertain maps, helped out by those in that precious yearbook thing I had, were tentatively indicated upon it.

They sat in eager groups, masses of them who came for the purpose, and listened while Jeff roughly ran over the geologic history of the earth, and showed them their own land in relation to the others. Out of that same pocket reference book of mine came facts and figures which were seized upon and placed in right relation with unerring acumen.

Even Terry grew interested in this work. "If we can keep this up, they'll be having us lecture to all the girls' schools and colleges—how about that?" he suggested to us. "Don't know as I'd object to being an Authority to such audiences."

They did, in fact, urge us to give public lectures later, but not to the hearers or with the purpose we expected.

What they were doing with us was like—like—well, say like Napoleon extracting military information from a few illiterate peasants. They knew just what to ask, and just what use to make of it; they had mechanical appliances for disseminating information almost equal to ours at home; and by the time we were led forth to lecture, our audiences had thoroughly mastered a well-arranged digest of all we had previously given to our teachers, and were prepared with such notes and questions as might have intimidated a university professor.

They were not audiences of girls, either. It was some time before we were allowed to meet the young women.

"Do you mind telling what you intend to do with us?" Terry burst forth one day, facing the calm and friendly Moadine with that funny half-blustering air of his. At first he used to storm and flourish quite a good deal, but nothing seemed to amuse them more; they would gather around and watch him as if it was an exhibition, politely, but with evident interest. So he learned to check himself, and was almost reasonable in his bearing—but not quite.

She announced smoothly and evenly: "Not in the least. I thought it was quite plain. We are trying to learn of you all we can, and to teach you what you are willing to learn of our country."

"Is that all?" he insisted.

She smiled a quiet enigmatic smile. "That depends."

"Depends on what?"

"Mainly on yourselves," she replied.

"Why do you keep us shut up so closely?"

"Because we do not feel quite safe in allowing you at large where there are so many young women."

Terry was really pleased at that. He had thought as much, inwardly; but he pushed the question. "Why should you be afraid? We are gentlemen."

She smiled that little smile again, and asked: "Are 'gentlemen' always safe?"

"You surely do not think that any of us," he said it with a good deal of emphasis on the "us," "would hurt your young girls?"

"Oh no," she said quickly, in real surprise. "The danger is quite the other way. They might hurt you. If, by any accident, you did harm any one of us, you would have to face a million mothers."

He looked so amazed and outraged that Jeff and I laughed outright, but she went on gently.

"I do not think you quite understand yet. You are but men, three men, in a country where the whole population are mothers—or are going to be. Motherhood means to us something which I cannot yet discover in any of the countries of which you tell us. You have spoken"—she turned to Jeff, "of Human Brotherhood as a great idea among you, but even that I judge is far from a practical expression?"

Jeff nodded rather sadly. "Very far—" he said.

"Here we have Human Motherhood—in full working use," she went on. "Nothing else except the literal sisterhood of our origin, and the far higher and deeper union of our social growth.

"The children in this country are the one center and focus of all our thoughts. Every step of our advance is always considered in its effect on them—on the race. You see, we are MOTHERS," she repeated, as if in that she had said it all.

"I don't see how that fact—which is shared by all women—constitutes any risk to us," Terry persisted. "You mean they would defend their children from attack. Of course. Any mothers would. But we are not savages, my dear lady; we are not going to hurt any mother's child."

They looked at one another and shook their heads a little, but Zava turned to Jeff and urged him to make us see—said he seemed to understand more fully than we did. And he tried.

I can see it now, or at least much more of it, but it has taken me a long time, and a good deal of honest intellectual effort.

What they call Motherhood was like this:

They began with a really high degree of social development, something like that of Ancient Egypt or Greece. Then they suffered the loss of everything masculine, and supposed at first that all human power and safety had gone too. Then they developed this virgin birth capacity. Then, since the prosperity of their children depended on it, the fullest and subtlest coordination began to be practiced.

I remember how long Terry balked at the evident unanimity of these women—the most conspicuous feature of their whole culture. "It's impossible!" he would insist. "Women cannot cooperate—it's against nature."

When we urged the obvious facts he would say: "Fiddlesticks!" or "Hang your facts—I tell you it can't be done!" And we never succeeded in shutting him up till Jeff dragged in the hymenoptera.

"'Go to the ant, thou sluggard'—and learn something," he said triumphantly. "Don't they cooperate pretty well? You can't beat it. This place is just like an enormous anthill—you know an anthill is nothing but a nursery. And how about bees? Don't they manage to cooperate and love one another? as that precious Constable had it. Just show me a combination of male creatures, bird, bug, or beast, that works as well, will you? Or one of our masculine countries where the people work together as well as they do here! I tell you, women are the natural cooperators, not men!"

Terry had to learn a good many things he did not want to. To go back to my little analysis of what happened:

They developed all this close inter-service in the interests of their children. To do the best work they had to specialize, of course; the children needed spinners and weavers, farmers and gardeners, carpenters and masons, as well as mothers.

Then came the filling up of the place. When a population multiplies by five every thirty years it soon reaches the limits of a country, especially a small one like this. They very soon eliminated all the grazing cattle—sheep were the last to go, I believe. Also, they worked out a system of intensive agriculture surpassing anything I ever heard of, with the very forests all reset with fruit- or nut-bearing trees.

Do what they would, however, there soon came a time when they were confronted with the problem of "the pressure of population" in an acute form. There was really crowding, and with it, unavoidably, a decline in standards.

And how did those women meet it?

Not by a "struggle for existence" which would result in an everlasting writhing mass of underbred people trying to get ahead of one another—some few on top, temporarily, many constantly crushed out underneath, a hopeless substratum of paupers and degenerates, and no serenity or peace for anyone, no possibility for really noble qualities among the people at large.

Neither did they start off on predatory excursions to get more land from somebody else, or to get more food from somebody else, to maintain their struggling mass.

Not at all. They sat down in council together and thought it out. Very clear, strong thinkers they were. They said: "With our best endeavors this country will support about so many people, with the standard of peace, comfort, health, beauty, and progress we demand. Very well. That is all the people we will make."

There you have it. You see, they were Mothers, not in our sense of helpless involuntary fecundity, forced to fill and overfill the land, every land, and then see their children suffer, sin, and die, fighting horribly with one another; but in the sense of Conscious Makers of People. Mother-love with them was not a brute passion, a mere "instinct," a wholly personal feeling; it was—a religion.

It included that limitless feeling of sisterhood, that wide unity in service, which was so difficult for us to grasp. And it was National, Racial, Human—oh, I don't know how to say it.

We are used to seeing what we call "a mother" completely wrapped up in her own pink bundle of fascinating babyhood, and taking but the faintest theoretic interest in anybody else's bundle, to say nothing of the common needs of ALL the bundles. But these women were working all together at the grandest of tasks—they were Making People—and they made them well.

There followed a period of "negative eugenics" which must have been an appalling sacrifice. We are commonly willing to "lay down our lives" for our country, but they had to forego motherhood for their country—and it was precisely the hardest thing for them to do.

When I got this far in my reading I went to Somel for more light. We were as friendly by that time as I had ever been in my life with any woman. A mighty comfortable soul she was, giving one the nice smooth mother-feeling a man likes in a woman, and yet giving also the clear intelligence and dependableness I used to assume to be masculine qualities. We had talked volumes already.

"See here," said I. "Here was this dreadful period when they got far too thick, and decided to limit the population. We have a lot of talk about that among us, but your position is so different that I'd like to know a little more about it.

"I understand that you make Motherhood the highest social service—a sacrament, really; that it is only undertaken once, by the majority of the population; that those held unfit are not allowed even that; and that to be encouraged to bear more than one child is the very highest reward and honor in the power of the state."

(She interpolated here that the nearest approach to an aristocracy they had was to come of a line of "Over Mothers"—those who had been so honored.)

"But what I do not understand, naturally, is how you prevent it. I gathered that each woman had five. You have no tyrannical husbands to hold in check—and you surely do not destroy the unborn—"

The look of ghastly horror she gave me I shall never forget. She started from her chair, pale, her eyes blazing.

"Destroy the unborn—!" she said in a hard whisper. "Do men do that in your country?"

"Men!" I began to answer, rather hotly, and then saw the gulf before me. None of us wanted these women to think that OUR women, of whom we boasted so proudly, were in any way inferior to them. I am ashamed to say that I equivocated. I told her of certain criminal types of women—perverts, or crazy, who had been known to commit infanticide. I told her, truly enough, that there was much in our land which was open to criticism, but that I hated to dwell on our defects until they understood us and our conditions better.

And, making a wide detour, I scrambled back to my question of how they limited the population.

As for Somel, she seemed sorry, a little ashamed even, of her too clearly expressed amazement. As I look back now, knowing them better, I am more and more and more amazed as I appreciate the exquisite courtesy with which they had received over and over again statements and admissions on our part which must have revolted them to the soul.

She explained to me, with sweet seriousness, that as I had supposed, at first each woman bore five children; and that, in their eager desire to build up a nation, they had gone on in that way for a few centuries, till they were confronted with the absolute need of a limit. This fact was equally plain to all—all were equally interested.

They were now as anxious to check their wonderful power as they had been to develop it; and for some generations gave the matter their most earnest thought and study.

"We were living on rations before we worked it out," she said. "But we did work it out. You see, before a child comes to one of us there is a period of utter exaltation—the whole being is uplifted and filled with a concentrated desire for that child. We learned to look forward to that period with the greatest caution. Often our young women, those to whom motherhood had not yet come, would voluntarily defer it. When that deep inner demand for a child began to be felt she would deliberately engage in the most active work, physical and mental; and even more important, would solace her longing by the direct care and service of the babies we already had."

She paused. Her wise sweet face grew deeply, reverently tender.

"We soon grew to see that mother-love has more than one channel of expression. I think the reason our children are so—so fully loved, by all of us, is that we never—any of us—have enough of our own."

This seemed to me infinitely pathetic, and I said so. "We have much that is bitter and hard in our life at home," I told her, "but this seems to me piteous beyond words—a whole nation of starving mothers!"

But she smiled her deep contented smile, and said I quite misunderstood.

"We each go without a certain range of personal joy," she said, "but remember—we each have a million children to love and serve—OUR children."

It was beyond me. To hear a lot of women talk about "our children"! But I suppose that is the way the ants and bees would talk—do talk, maybe.

That was what they did, anyhow.

When a woman chose to be a mother, she allowed the child-longing to grow within her till it worked its natural miracle. When she did not so choose she put the whole thing out of her mind, and fed her heart with the other babies.

Let me see—with us, children—minors, that is—constitute about three-fifths of the population; with them only about one-third, or less. And precious—! No sole heir to an empire's throne, no solitary millionaire baby, no only child of middle-aged parents, could compare as an idol with these Herland children.

But before I start on that subject I must finish up that little analysis I was trying to make.

They did effectually and permanently limit the population in numbers, so that the country furnished plenty for the fullest, richest life for all of them: plenty of everything, including room, air, solitude even.

And then they set to work to improve that population in quality—since they were restricted in quantity. This they had been at work on, uninterruptedly, for some fifteen hundred years. Do you wonder they were nice people?

Physiology, hygiene, sanitation, physical culture—all that line of work had been perfected long since. Sickness was almost wholly unknown among them, so much so that a previously high development in what we call the "science of medicine" had become practically a lost art. They were a clean-bred, vigorous lot, having the best of care, the most perfect living conditions always.

When it came to psychology—there was no one thing which left us so dumbfounded, so really awed, as the everyday working knowledge—and practice—they had in this line. As we learned more and more of it, we learned to appreciate the exquisite mastery with which we ourselves, strangers of alien race, of unknown opposite sex, had been understood and provided for from the first.

With this wide, deep, thorough knowledge, they had met and solved the problems of education in ways some of which I hope to make clear later. Those nation-loved children of theirs compared with the average in our country as the most perfectly cultivated, richly developed roses compare with—tumbleweeds. Yet they did not SEEM "cultivated" at all—it had all become a natural condition.

And this people, steadily developing in mental capacity, in will power, in social devotion, had been playing with the arts and sciences—as far as they knew them—for a good many centuries now with inevitable success.

Into this quiet lovely land, among these wise, sweet, strong women, we, in our easy assumption of superiority, had suddenly arrived; and now, tamed and trained to a degree they considered safe, we were at last brought out to see the country, to know the people.

CHAPTER 7. OUR GROWING MODESTY

Being at last considered sufficiently tamed and trained to be trusted with scissors, we barbered ourselves as best we could. A close-trimmed beard is certainly more comfortable than a full one. Razors, naturally, they could not supply.

"With so many old women you'd think there'd be some razors," sneered Terry. Whereat Jeff pointed out that he never before had seen such complete absence of facial hair on women.

"Looks to me as if the absence of men made them more feminine in that regard, anyhow," he suggested.

"Well, it's the only one then," Terry reluctantly agreed. "A less feminine lot I never saw. A child apiece doesn't seem to be enough to develop what I call motherliness."

Terry's idea of motherliness was the usual one, involving a baby in arms, or "a little flock about her knees," and the complete absorption of the mother in said baby or flock. A motherliness which dominated society, which influenced every art and industry, which absolutely protected all childhood, and gave to it the most perfect care and training, did not seem motherly—to Terry.

We had become well used to the clothes. They were quite as comfortable as our own—in some ways more so—and undeniably better looking. As to pockets, they left nothing to be desired. That second garment was fairly quilted with pockets. They were most ingeniously arranged, so as to be convenient to the hand and not inconvenient to the body, and were so placed as at once to strengthen the garment and add decorative lines of stitching.

In this, as in so many other points we had now to observe, there was shown the action of a practical intelligence, coupled with fine artistic feeling, and, apparently, untrammeled by any injurious influences.

Our first step of comparative freedom was a personally conducted tour of the country. No pentagonal bodyguard now! Only our special tutors, and we got on famously with them. Jeff said he loved Zava like an aunt—"only jollier than any aunt I ever saw"; Somel and I were as chummy as could be—the best of friends; but it was funny to watch Terry and Moadine. She was patient with him, and courteous, but it was like the patience and courtesy of some great man, say a skilled, experienced diplomat, with a schoolgirl. Her grave acquiescence with his most preposterous expression of feeling; her genial laughter, not only with, but, I often felt, at him—though impeccably polite; her innocent questions, which almost invariably led him to say more than he intended—Jeff and I found it all amusing to watch.

He never seemed to recognize that quiet background of superiority. When she dropped an argument he always thought he had silenced her; when she laughed he thought it tribute to his wit.

I hated to admit to myself how much Terry had sunk in my esteem. Jeff felt it too, I am sure; but neither of us admitted it to the other. At home we had measured him with other men, and, though we knew his failings, he was by no means an unusual type. We knew his virtues too, and they had always seemed more prominent than the faults. Measured among women—our women at home, I mean—he had always stood high. He was visibly popular. Even where his habits were known, there was no discrimination against him; in some cases his reputation for what was felicitously termed "gaiety" seemed a special charm.

But here, against the calm wisdom and quiet restrained humor of these women, with only that blessed Jeff and my inconspicuous self to compare with, Terry did stand out rather strong.

As "a man among men," he didn't; as a man among—I shall have to say, "females," he didn't; his intense masculinity seemed only fit complement to their intense femininity. But here he was all out of drawing.

Moadine was a big woman, with a balanced strength that seldom showed. Her eye was as quietly watchful as a fencer's. She maintained a pleasant relation with her charge, but I doubt if many, even in that country, could have done as well.

He called her "Maud," amongst ourselves, and said she was "a good old soul, but a little slow"; wherein he was quite wrong. Needless to say, he called Jeff's teacher "Java," and sometimes "Mocha," or plain "Coffee"; when specially mischievous, "Chicory," and even "Postum." But Somel rather escaped this form of humor, save for a rather forced "Some 'ell."

"Don't you people have but one name?" he asked one day, after we had been introduced to a whole group of them, all with pleasant, few-syllabled strange names, like the ones we knew.

"Oh yes," Moadine told him. "A good many of us have another, as we get on in life—a descriptive one. That is the name we earn. Sometimes even that is changed, or added to, in an unusually rich life. Such as our present Land Mother—what you call president or king, I believe. She was called Mera, even as a child; that means 'thinker.' Later there was added Du—Du-Mera—the wise thinker, and now we all know her as O-du-mera—great and wise thinker. You shall meet her."

"No surnames at all then?" pursued Terry, with his somewhat patronizing air. "No family name?"

"Why no," she said. "Why should we? We are all descended from a common source—all one 'family' in reality. You see, our comparatively brief and limited history gives us that advantage at least."

"But does not each mother want her own child to bear her name?" I asked.

"No—why should she? The child has its own."

"Why for—for identification—so people will know whose child she is."

"We keep the most careful records," said Somel. "Each one of us has our exact line of descent all the way back to our dear First Mother. There are many reasons for doing that. But as to everyone knowing which child belongs to which mother—why should she?"

Here, as in so many other instances, we were led to feel the difference between the purely maternal and the paternal attitude of mind. The element of personal pride seemed strangely lacking.

"How about your other works?" asked Jeff. "Don't you sign your names to them—books and statues and so on?"

"Yes, surely, we are all glad and proud to. Not only books and statues, but all kinds of work. You will find little names on the houses, on the furniture, on the dishes sometimes. Because otherwise one is likely to forget, and we want to know to whom to be grateful."

"You speak as if it were done for the convenience of the consumer—not the pride of the producer," I suggested.

"It's both," said Somel. "We have pride enough in our work."

"Then why not in your children?" urged Jeff.

"But we have! We're magnificently proud of them," she insisted.

"Then why not sign 'em?" said Terry triumphantly.

Moadine turned to him with her slightly quizzical smile. "Because the finished product is not a private one. When they are babies, we do speak of them, at times, as 'Essa's Lato,' or 'Novine's Amel'; but that is merely descriptive and conversational. In the records, of course, the child stands in her own line of mothers; but in dealing with it personally it is Lato, or Amel, without dragging in its ancestors."

"But have you names enough to give a new one to each child?"

"Assuredly we have, for each living generation."

Then they asked about our methods, and found first that "we" did so and so, and then that other nations did differently. Upon which they wanted to know which method has been proved best—and we had to admit that so far as we knew there had been no attempt at comparison, each people pursuing its own custom in the fond conviction of superiority, and either despising or quite ignoring the others.

With these women the most salient quality in all their institutions was reasonableness. When I dug into the records to follow out any line of development, that was the most astonishing thing—the conscious effort to make it better.

They had early observed the value of certain improvements, had easily inferred that there was room for more, and took the greatest pains to develop two kinds of minds—the critic and inventor. Those who showed an early tendency to observe, to discriminate, to suggest, were given special training for that function; and some of their highest officials spent their time in the most careful study of one or another branch of work, with a view to its further improvement.

In each generation there was sure to arrive some new mind to detect faults and show need of alterations; and the whole corps of inventors was at hand to apply their special faculty at the point criticized, and offer suggestions.

We had learned by this time not to open a discussion on any of their characteristics without first priming ourselves to answer questions about our own methods; so I kept rather quiet on this matter of conscious improvement. We were not prepared to show our way was better.

There was growing in our minds, at least in Jeff's and mine, a keen appreciation of the advantages of this strange country and its management. Terry remained critical. We laid most of it to his nerves. He certainly was irritable.

The most conspicuous feature of the whole land was the perfection of its food supply. We had begun to notice from that very first walk in the forest, the first partial view from our 'plane. Now we were taken to see this mighty garden, and shown its methods of culture.

The country was about the size of Holland, some ten or twelve thousand square miles. One could lose a good many Hollands along the forest-smothered flanks of those mighty mountains. They had a population of about three million—not a large one, but quality is something. Three million is quite enough to allow for considerable variation, and these people varied more widely than we could at first account for.

Terry had insisted that if they were parthenogenetic they'd be as alike as so many ants or aphids; he urged their visible differences as proof that there must be men—somewhere.

But when we asked them, in our later, more intimate conversations, how they accounted for so much divergence without cross-fertilization, they attributed it partly to the careful education, which followed each slight tendency to differ, and partly to the law of mutation. This they had found in their work with plants, and fully proven in their own case.

Physically they were more alike than we, as they lacked all morbid or excessive types. They were tall, strong, healthy, and beautiful as a race, but differed individually in a wide range of feature, coloring, and expression.

"But surely the most important growth is in mind—and in the things we make," urged Somel. "Do you find your physical variation accompanied by a proportionate variation in ideas, feelings, and products? Or, among people who look more alike, do you find their internal life and their work as similar?"

We were rather doubtful on this point, and inclined to hold that there was more chance of improvement in greater physical variation.

"It certainly should be," Zava admitted. "We have always thought it a grave initial misfortune to have lost half our little world. Perhaps that is one reason why we have so striven for conscious improvement."

"But acquired traits are not transmissible," Terry declared. "Weissman has proved that."

They never disputed our absolute statements, only made notes of them.

"If that is so, then our improvement must be due either to mutation, or solely to education," she gravely pursued. "We certainly have improved. It may be that all these higher qualities were latent in the original mother, that careful education is bringing them out, and that our personal differences depend on slight variations in prenatal condition."

"I think it is more in your accumulated culture," Jeff suggested. "And in the amazing psychic growth you have made. We know very little about methods of real soul culture—and you seem to know a great deal."

Be that as it might, they certainly presented a higher level of active intelligence, and of behavior, than we had so far really grasped. Having known in our lives several people who showed the same delicate courtesy and were equally pleasant to live with, at least when they wore their "company manners," we had assumed that our companions were a carefully chosen few. Later we were more and more impressed that all this gentle breeding was breeding; that they were born to it, reared in it, that it was as natural and universal with them as the gentleness of doves or the alleged wisdom of serpents.

As for the intelligence, I confess that this was the most impressive and, to me, most mortifying, of any single feature of Herland. We soon ceased to comment on this or other matters which to them were such obvious commonplaces as to call forth embarrassing questions about our own conditions.

This was nowhere better shown than in that matter of food supply, which I will now attempt to describe.

Having improved their agriculture to the highest point, and carefully estimated the number of persons who could comfortably live on their square miles; having then limited their population to that number, one would think that was all there was to be done. But they had not thought so. To them the country was a unit—it was theirs. They themselves were a unit, a conscious group; they thought in terms of the community. As such, their time-sense was not limited to the hopes and ambitions of an individual life. Therefore, they habitually considered and carried out plans for improvement which might cover centuries.

I had never seen, had scarcely imagined, human beings undertaking such a work as the deliberate replanting of an entire forest area with different kinds of trees. Yet this seemed to them the simplest common sense, like a man's plowing up an inferior lawn and reseeding it. Now every tree bore fruit—edible fruit, that is. In the case of one tree, in which they took especial pride, it had originally no fruit at all—that is, none humanly edible—yet was so beautiful that they wished to keep it. For nine hundred years they had experimented, and now showed us this particularly lovely graceful tree, with a profuse crop of nutritious seeds.

They had early decided that trees were the best food plants, requiring far less labor in tilling the soil, and bearing a larger amount of food for the same ground space; also doing much to preserve and enrich the soil.

Due regard had been paid to seasonable crops, and their fruit and nuts, grains and berries, kept on almost the year through.

On the higher part of the country, near the backing wall of mountains, they had a real winter with snow. Toward the south-eastern point, where there was a large valley with a lake whose outlet was subterranean, the climate was like that of California, and citrus fruits, figs, and olives grew abundantly.

What impressed me particularly was their scheme of fertilization. Here was this little shut-in piece of land where one would have thought an ordinary people would have been starved out long ago or reduced to an annual struggle for life. These careful culturists had worked out a perfect scheme of refeeding the soil with all that came out of it. All the scraps and leavings of their food, plant waste from lumber work or textile industry, all the solid matter from the sewage, properly treated and combined—everything which came from the earth went back to it.

The practical result was like that in any healthy forest; an increasingly valuable soil was being built, instead of the progressive impoverishment so often seen in the rest of the world.

When this first burst upon us we made such approving comments that they were surprised that such obvious common sense should be praised; asked what our methods were; and we had some difficulty in—well, in diverting them, by referring to the extent of our own land, and the—admitted—carelessness with which we had skimmed the cream of it.

At least we thought we had diverted them. Later I found that besides keeping a careful and accurate account of all we told them, they had a sort of skeleton chart, on which the things we said and the things we palpably avoided saying were all set down and studied. It really was child's play for those profound educators to work out a painfully accurate estimate of our conditions—in some lines. When a given line of observation seemed to lead to some very dreadful inference they always gave us the benefit of the doubt, leaving it open to further knowledge. Some of the things we had grown to accept as perfectly natural, or as belonging to our human limitations, they literally could not have believed; and, as I have said, we had all of us joined in a tacit endeavor to conceal much of the social status at home.

"Confound their grandmotherly minds!" Terry said. "Of course they can't understand a Man's World! They aren't human—they're just a pack of Fe-Fe-Females!" This was after he had to admit their parthenogenesis.

"I wish our grandfatherly minds had managed as well," said Jeff. "Do you really think it's to our credit that we have muddled along with all our poverty and disease and the like? They have peace and plenty, wealth and beauty, goodness and intellect. Pretty good people, I think!"

"You'll find they have their faults too," Terry insisted; and partly in self-defense, we all three began to look for those faults of theirs. We had been very strong on this subject before we got there—in those baseless speculations of ours.

"Suppose there is a country of women only," Jeff had put it, over and over. "What'll they be like?"

And we had been cocksure as to the inevitable limitations, the faults and vices, of a lot of women. We had expected them to be given over to what we called "feminine vanity"—"frills and furbelows," and we found they had evolved a costume more perfect than the Chinese dress, richly beautiful when so desired, always useful, of unfailing dignity and good taste.

We had expected a dull submissive monotony, and found a daring social inventiveness far beyond our own, and a mechanical and scientific development fully equal to ours.

We had expected pettiness, and found a social consciousness besides which our nations looked like quarreling children—feebleminded ones at that.

We had expected jealousy, and found a broad sisterly affection, a fair-minded intelligence, to which we could produce no parallel.

We had expected hysteria, and found a standard of health and vigor, a calmness of temper, to which the habit of profanity, for instance, was impossible to explain—we tried it.

All these things even Terry had to admit, but he still insisted that we should find out the other side pretty soon.

"It stands to reason, doesn't it?" he argued. "The whole thing's deuced unnatural—I'd say impossible if we weren't in it. And an unnatural condition's sure to have unnatural results. You'll find some awful characteristics—see if you don't! For instance—we don't know yet what they do with their criminals—their defectives—their aged. You notice we haven't seen any! There's got to be something!"

I was inclined to believe that there had to be something, so I took the bull by the horns—the cow, I should say!—and asked Somel.

"I want to find some flaw in all this perfection," I told her flatly. "It simply isn't possible that three million people have no faults. We are trying our best to understand and learn—would you mind helping us by saying what, to your minds, are the worst qualities of this unique civilization of yours?"

We were sitting together in a shaded arbor, in one of those eating-gardens of theirs. The delicious food had been eaten, a plate of fruit still before us. We could look out on one side over a stretch of open country, quietly rich and lovely; on the other, the garden, with tables here and there, far apart enough for privacy. Let me say right here that with all their careful "balance of population" there was no crowding in this country. There was room, space, a sunny breezy freedom everywhere.

Somel set her chin upon her hand, her elbow on the low wall beside her, and looked off over the fair land.

"Of course we have faults—all of us," she said. "In one way you might say that we have more than we used to—that is, our standard of perfection seems to get farther and farther away. But we are not discouraged, because our records do show gain—considerable gain.

"When we began—even with the start of one particularly noble mother—we inherited the characteristics of a long race-record behind her. And they cropped out from time to time—alarmingly. But it is—yes, quite six hundred years since we have had what you call a 'criminal.'

"We have, of course, made it our first business to train out, to breed out, when possible, the lowest types."

"Breed out?" I asked. "How could you—with parthenogenesis?"

"If the girl showing the bad qualities had still the power to appreciate social duty, we appealed to her, by that, to renounce motherhood. Some of the few worst types were, fortunately, unable to reproduce. But if the fault was in a disproportionate egotism—then the girl was sure she had the right to have children, even that hers would be better than others."

"I can see that," I said. "And then she would be likely to rear them in the same spirit."

"That we never allowed," answered Somel quietly.

"Allowed?" I queried. "Allowed a mother to rear her own children?"

"Certainly not," said Somel, "unless she was fit for that supreme task."

This was rather a blow to my previous convictions.

"But I thought motherhood was for each of you—"

"Motherhood—yes, that is, maternity, to bear a child. But education is our highest art, only allowed to our highest artists."

"Education?" I was puzzled again. "I don't mean education. I mean by motherhood not only child-bearing, but the care of babies."

"The care of babies involves education, and is entrusted only to the most fit," she repeated.

"Then you separate mother and child!" I cried in cold horror, something of Terry's feeling creeping over me, that there must be something wrong among these many virtues.

"Not usually," she patiently explained. "You see, almost every woman values her maternity above everything else. Each girl holds it close and dear, an exquisite joy, a crowning honor, the most intimate, most personal, most precious thing. That is, the child-rearing has come to be with us a culture so profoundly studied, practiced with such subtlety and skill, that the more we love our children the less we are willing to trust that process to unskilled hands—even our own."

"But a mother's love—" I ventured.

She studied my face, trying to work out a means of clear explanation.

"You told us about your dentists," she said, at length, "those quaintly specialized persons who spend their lives filling little holes in other persons' teeth—even in children's teeth sometimes."

"Yes?" I said, not getting her drift.

"Does mother-love urge mothers—with you—to fill their own children's teeth? Or to wish to?"

"Why no—of course not," I protested. "But that is a highly specialized craft. Surely the care of babies is open to any woman—any mother!"

"We do not think so," she gently replied. "Those of us who are the most highly competent fulfill that office; and a majority of our girls eagerly try for it—I assure you we have the very best."

"But the poor mother—bereaved of her baby—"

"Oh no!" she earnestly assured me. "Not in the least bereaved. It is her baby still—it is with her—she has not lost it. But she is not the only one to care for it. There are others whom she knows to be wiser. She knows it because she has studied as they did, practiced as they did, and honors their real superiority. For the child's sake, she is glad to have for it this highest care."

I was unconvinced. Besides, this was only hearsay; I had yet to see the motherhood of Herland.

CHAPTER 8. THE GIRLS OF HERLAND

At last Terry's ambition was realized. We were invited, always courteously and with free choice on our part, to address general audiences and classes of girls.

I remember the first time—and how careful we were about our clothes, and our amateur barbering. Terry, in particular, was fussy to a degree about the cut of his beard, and so critical of our combined efforts, that we handed him the shears and told him to please himself. We began to rather prize those beards of ours; they were almost our sole distinction among those tall and sturdy women, with their cropped hair and sexless costume. Being offered a wide selection of garments, we had chosen according to our personal taste, and were surprised to find, on meeting large audiences, that we were the most highly decorated, especially Terry.

He was a very impressive figure, his strong features softened by the somewhat longer hair—though he made me trim it as closely as I knew how; and he wore his richly embroidered tunic with its broad, loose girdle with quite a Henry V air. Jeff looked more like—well, like a Huguenot Lover; and I don't know what I looked like, only that I felt very comfortable. When I got back to our own padded armor and its starched borders I realized with acute regret how comfortable were those Herland clothes.

We scanned that audience, looking for the three bright faces we knew; but they were not to be seen. Just a multitude of girls: quiet, eager, watchful, all eyes and ears to listen and learn.

We had been urged to give, as fully as we cared to, a sort of synopsis of world history, in brief, and to answer questions.

"We are so utterly ignorant, you see," Moadine had explained to us. "We know nothing but such science as we have worked out for ourselves, just the brain work of one small half-country; and you, we gather, have helped one another all over the globe, sharing your discoveries, pooling your progress. How wonderful, how supremely beautiful your civilization must be!"

Somel gave a further suggestion.

"You do not have to begin all over again, as you did with us. We have made a sort of digest of what we have learned from you, and it has been eagerly absorbed, all over the country. Perhaps you would like to see our outline?"

We were eager to see it, and deeply impressed. To us, at first, these women, unavoidably ignorant of what to us was the basic commonplace of knowledge, had seemed on the plane of children, or of savages. What we had been forced to admit, with growing acquaintance, was that they were ignorant as Plato and Aristotle were, but with a highly developed mentality quite comparable to that of Ancient Greece.

Far be it from me to lumber these pages with an account of what we so imperfectly strove to teach them. The memorable fact is what they taught us, or some faint glimpse of it. And at present, our major interest was not at all in the subject matter of our talk, but in the audience.

Girls—hundreds of them—eager, bright-eyed, attentive young faces; crowding questions, and, I regret to say, an increasing inability on our part to answer them effectively.

Our special guides, who were on the platform with us, and sometimes aided in clarifying a question or, oftener, an answer, noticed this effect, and closed the formal lecture part of the evening rather shortly.

"Our young women will be glad to meet you," Somel suggested, "to talk with you more personally, if you are willing?"

Willing! We were impatient and said as much, at which I saw a flickering little smile cross Moadine's face. Even then, with all those eager young things waiting to talk to us, a sudden question crossed my mind: "What was their point of view? What did they think of us?" We learned that later.

Terry plunged in among those young creatures with a sort of rapture, somewhat as a glad swimmer takes to the sea. Jeff, with a rapt look on his high-bred face, approached as to a sacrament. But I was a little chilled by that last thought of mine, and kept my eyes open. I found time to watch Jeff, even while I was surrounded by an eager group of questioners—as we all were—and saw how his worshipping eyes, his grave courtesy, pleased and drew some of them; while others, rather stronger spirits they looked to be, drew away from his group to Terry's or mine.

I watched Terry with special interest, knowing how he had longed for this time, and how irresistible he had always been at home. And I could see, just in snatches, of course, how his suave and masterful approach seemed to irritate them; his too-intimate glances were vaguely resented, his compliments puzzled and annoyed. Sometimes a girl would flush, not with drooped eyelids and inviting timidity, but with anger and a quick lift of the head. Girl after girl turned on her heel and left him, till he had but a small ring of questioners, and they, visibly, were the least "girlish" of the lot.

I saw him looking pleased at first, as if he thought he was making a strong impression; but, finally, casting a look at Jeff, or me, he seemed less pleased—and less.

As for me, I was most agreeably surprised. At home I never was "popular." I had my girl friends, good ones, but they were friends—nothing else. Also they were of somewhat the same clan, not popular in the sense of swarming admirers. But here, to my astonishment, I found my crowd was the largest.

I have to generalize, of course, rather telescoping many impressions; but the first evening was a good sample of the impression we made. Jeff had a following, if I may call it that, of the more sentimental—though that's not the word I want. The less practical, perhaps; the girls who were artists of some sort, ethicists, teachers—that kind.

Terry was reduced to a rather combative group: keen, logical, inquiring minds, not overly sensitive, the very kind he liked least; while, as for me—I became quite cocky over my general popularity.

Terry was furious about it. We could hardly blame him.

"Girls!" he burst forth, when that evening was over and we were by ourselves once more. "Call those GIRLS!"

"Most delightful girls, I call them," said Jeff, his blue eyes dreamily contented.

"What do YOU call them?" I mildly inquired.

"Boys! Nothing but boys, most of 'em. A standoffish, disagreeable lot at that. Critical, impertinent youngsters. No girls at all."

He was angry and severe, not a little jealous, too, I think. Afterward, when he found out just what it was they did not like, he changed his manner somewhat and got on better. He had to. For, in spite of his criticism, they were girls, and, furthermore, all the girls there were! Always excepting our three!—with whom we presently renewed our acquaintance.

When it came to courtship, which it soon did, I can of course best describe my own—and am least inclined to. But of Jeff I heard somewhat; he was inclined to dwell reverently and admiringly, at some length, on the exalted sentiment and measureless perfection of his Celis; and Terry—Terry made so many false starts and met so many rebuffs, that by the time he really settled down to win Alima, he was considerably wiser. At that, it was not smooth sailing. They broke and quarreled, over and over; he would rush off to console himself with some other fair one—the other fair one would have none of him—and he would drift back to Alima, becoming more and more devoted each time.

She never gave an inch. A big, handsome creature, rather exceptionally strong even in that race of strong women, with a proud head and sweeping level brows that lined across above her dark eager eyes like the wide wings of a soaring hawk.

I was good friends with all three of them but best of all with Ellador, long before that feeling changed, for both of us.

From her, and from Somel, who talked very freely with me, I learned at last something of the viewpoint of Herland toward its visitors.

Here they were, isolated, happy, contented, when the booming buzz of our biplane tore the air above them.

Everybody heard it—saw it—for miles and miles, word flashed all over the country, and a council was held in every town and village.

And this was their rapid determination:

"From another country. Probably men. Evidently highly civilized. Doubtless possessed of much valuable knowledge. May be dangerous. Catch them if possible; tame and train them if necessary This may be a chance to re-establish a bi-sexual state for our people."

They were not afraid of us—three million highly intelligent women—or two million, counting only grown-ups—were not likely to be afraid of three young men. We thought of them as "Women," and therefore timid; but it was two thousand years since they had had anything to be afraid of, and certainly more than one thousand since they had outgrown the feeling.

We thought—at least Terry did—that we could have our pick of them. They thought—very cautiously and farsightedly—of picking us, if it seemed wise.

All that time we were in training they studied us, analyzed us, prepared reports about us, and this information was widely disseminated all about the land.

Not a girl in that country had not been learning for months as much as could be gathered about our country, our culture, our personal characters. No wonder their questions were hard to answer. But I am sorry to say, when we were at last brought out and—exhibited (I hate to call it that, but that's what it was), there was no rush of takers. Here was poor old Terry fondly imagining that at last he was free to stray in "a rosebud garden of girls"—and behold! the rosebuds were all with keen appraising eye, studying us.

They were interested, profoundly interested, but it was not the kind of interest we were looking for.

To get an idea of their attitude you have to hold in mind their extremely high sense of solidarity. They were not each choosing a lover; they hadn't the faintest idea of love—sex-love, that is. These girls—to each of whom motherhood was a lodestar, and that motherhood exalted above a mere personal function, looked forward to as the highest social service, as the sacrament of a lifetime—were now confronted with an opportunity to make the great step of changing their whole status, of reverting to their earlier bi-sexual order of nature.

Beside this underlying consideration there was the limitless interest and curiosity in our civilization, purely impersonal, and held by an order of mind beside which we were like—schoolboys.

It was small wonder that our lectures were not a success; and none at all that our, or at least Terry's, advances were so ill received. The reason for my own comparative success was at first far from pleasing to my pride.

"We like you the best," Somel told me, "because you seem more like us."

"More like a lot of women!" I thought to myself disgustedly, and then remembered how little like "women," in our derogatory sense, they were. She was smiling at me, reading my thought.

"We can quite see that we do not seem like—women—to you. Of course, in a bi-sexual race the distinctive feature of each sex must be intensified. But surely there are characteristics enough which belong to People, aren't there? That's what I mean about you being more like us—more like People. We feel at ease with you."

Jeff's difficulty was his exalted gallantry. He idealized women, and was always looking for a chance to "protect" or to "serve" them. These needed neither protection nor service. They were living in peace and power and plenty; we were their guests, their prisoners, absolutely dependent.

Of course we could promise whatsoever we might of advantages, if they would come to our country; but the more we knew of theirs, the less we boasted.

Terry's jewels and trinkets they prized as curios; handed them about, asking questions as to workmanship, not in the least as to value; and discussed not ownership, but which museum to put them in.

When a man has nothing to give a woman, is dependent wholly on his personal attraction, his courtship is under limitations.

They were considering these two things: the advisability of making the Great Change; and the degree of personal adaptability which would best serve that end.

Here we had the advantage of our small personal experience with those three fleet forest girls; and that served to draw us together.

As for Ellador: Suppose you come to a strange land and find it pleasant enough—just a little more than ordinarily pleasant—and then you find rich farmland, and then gardens, gorgeous gardens, and then palaces full of rare and curious treasures—incalculable, inexhaustible, and then—mountains—like the Himalayas, and then the sea.

I liked her that day she balanced on the branch before me and named the trio. I thought of her most. Afterward I turned to her like a friend when we met for the third time, and continued the acquaintance. While Jeff's ultra-devotion rather puzzled Celis, really put off their day of happiness, while Terry and Alima quarreled and parted, re-met and re-parted, Ellador and I grew to be close friends.

We talked and talked. We took long walks together. She showed me things, explained them, interpreted much that I had not understood. Through her sympathetic intelligence I became more and more comprehending of the spirit of the people of Herland, more and more appreciative of its marvelous inner growth as well as outer perfection.

I ceased to feel a stranger, a prisoner. There was a sense of understanding, of identity, of purpose. We discussed—everything. And, as I traveled farther and farther, exploring the rich, sweet soul of her, my sense of pleasant friendship became but a broad foundation for such height, such breadth, such interlocked combination of feeling as left me fairly blinded with the wonder of it.

As I've said, I had never cared very much for women, nor they for me—not Terry-fashion. But this one—

At first I never even thought of her "in that way," as the girls have it. I had not come to the country with any Turkish-harem intentions, and I was no woman-worshipper like Jeff. I just liked that girl "as a friend," as we say. That friendship grew like a tree. She was SUCH a good sport! We did all kinds of things together. She taught me games and I taught her games, and we raced and rowed and had all manner of fun, as well as higher comradeship.

Then, as I got on farther, the palace and treasures and snowy mountain ranges opened up. I had never known there could be such a human being. So—great. I don't mean talented. She was a forester—one of the best—but it was not that gift I mean. When I say GREAT, I mean great—big, all through. If I had known more of those women, as intimately, I should not have found her so unique; but even among them she was noble. Her mother was an Over Mother—and her grandmother, too, I heard later.

So she told me more and more of her beautiful land; and I told her as much, yes, more than I wanted to, about mine; and we became inseparable. Then this deeper recognition came and grew. I felt my own soul rise and lift its wings, as it were. Life got bigger. It seemed as if I understood—as I never had before—as if I could Do things—as if I too could grow—if she would help me. And then It came—to both of us, all at once.

A still day—on the edge of the world, their world. The two of us, gazing out over the far dim forestland below, talking of heaven and earth and human life, and of my land and other lands and what they needed and what I hoped to do for them—

"If you will help me," I said.

She turned to me, with that high, sweet look of hers, and then, as her eyes rested in mine and her hands too—then suddenly there blazed out between us a farther glory, instant, overwhelming—quite beyond any words of mine to tell.

Celis was a blue-and-gold-and-rose person; Alma, black-and-white-and-red, a blazing beauty. Ellador was brown: hair dark and soft, like a seal coat; clear brown skin with a healthy red in it; brown eyes—all the way from topaz to black velvet they seemed to range—splendid girls, all of them.

They had seen us first of all, far down in the lake below, and flashed the tidings across the land even before our first exploring flight. They had watched our landing, flitted through the forest with us, hidden in that tree and—I shrewdly suspect—giggled on purpose.

They had kept watch over our hooded machine, taking turns at it; and when our escape was announced, had followed along-side for a day or two, and been there at the last, as described. They felt a special claim on us—called us "their men"—and when we were at liberty to study the land and people, and be studied by them, their claim was recognized by the wise leaders.

But I felt, we all did, that we should have chosen them among millions, unerringly.

And yet "the path of true love never did run smooth"; this period of courtship was full of the most unsuspected pitfalls.

Writing this as late as I do, after manifold experiences both in Herland and, later, in my own land, I can now understand and philosophize about what was then a continual astonishment and often a temporary tragedy.

The "long suit" in most courtships is sex attraction, of course. Then gradually develops such comradeship as the two temperaments allow. Then, after marriage, there is either the establishment of a slow-growing, widely based friendship, the deepest, tenderest, sweetest of relations, all lit and warmed by the recurrent flame of love; or else that process is reversed, love cools and fades, no friendship grows, the whole relation turns from beauty to ashes.

Here everything was different. There was no sex-feeling to appeal to, or practically none. Two thousand years' disuse had left very little of the instinct; also we must remember that those who had at times manifested it as atavistic exceptions were often, by that very fact, denied motherhood.

Yet while the mother process remains, the inherent ground for sex-distinction remains also; and who shall say what long-forgotten feeling, vague and nameless, was stirred in some of these mother hearts by our arrival?

What left us even more at sea in our approach was the lack of any sex-tradition. There was no accepted standard of what was "manly" and what was "womanly."

When Jeff said, taking the fruit basket from his adored one, "A woman should not carry anything," Celis said, "Why?" with the frankest amazement. He could not look that fleet-footed, deep-chested young forester in the face and say, "Because she is weaker." She wasn't. One does not call a race horse weak because it is visibly not a cart horse.

He said, rather lamely, that women were not built for heavy work.

She looked out across the fields to where some women were working, building a new bit of wall out of large stones; looked back at the nearest town with its woman-built houses; down at the smooth, hard road we were walking on; and then at the little basket he had taken from her.

"I don't understand," she said quite sweetly. "Are the women in your country so weak that they could not carry such a thing as that?"

"It is a convention," he said. "We assume that motherhood is a sufficient burden—that men should carry all the others."

"What a beautiful feeling!" she said, her blue eyes shining.

"Does it work?" asked Alima, in her keen, swift way. "Do all men in all countries carry everything? Or is it only in yours?"

"Don't be so literal," Terry begged lazily. "Why aren't you willing to be worshipped and waited on? We like to do it."

"You don't like to have us do it to you," she answered.

"That's different," he said, annoyed; and when she said, "Why is it?" he quite sulked, referring her to me, saying, "Van's the philosopher."

Ellador and I talked it all out together, so that we had an easier experience of it when the real miracle time came. Also, between us, we made things clearer to Jeff and Celis. But Terry would not listen to reason.

He was madly in love with Alima. He wanted to take her by storm, and nearly lost her forever.

You see, if a man loves a girl who is in the first place young and inexperienced; who in the second place is educated with a background of caveman tradition, a middle-ground of poetry and romance, and a foreground of unspoken hope and interest all centering upon the one Event; and who has, furthermore, absolutely no other hope or interest worthy of the name—why, it is a comparatively easy matter to sweep her off her feet with a dashing attack. Terry was a past master in this process. He tried it here, and Alima was so affronted, so repelled, that it was weeks before he got near enough to try again.

The more coldly she denied him, the hotter his determination; he was not used to real refusal. The approach of flattery she dismissed with laughter, gifts and such "attentions" we could not bring to bear, pathos and complaint of cruelty stirred only a reasoning inquiry. It took Terry a long time.

I doubt if she ever accepted her strange lover as fully as did Celis and Ellador theirs. He had hurt and offended her too often; there were reservations.

But I think Alima retained some faint vestige of long-descended feeling which made Terry more possible to her than to others; and that she had made up her mind to the experiment and hated to renounce it.

However it came about, we all three at length achieved full understanding, and solemnly faced what was to them a step of measureless importance, a grave question as well as a great happiness; to us a strange, new joy.

Of marriage as a ceremony they knew nothing. Jeff was for bringing them to our country for the religious and the civil ceremony, but neither Celis nor the others would consent.

"We can't expect them to want to go with us—yet," said Terry sagely. "Wait a bit, boys. We've got to take 'em on their own terms—if at all." This, in rueful reminiscence of his repeated failures.

"But our time's coming," he added cheerfully. "These women have never been mastered, you see—" This, as one who had made a discovery.

"You'd better not try to do any mastering if you value your chances," I told him seriously; but he only laughed, and said, "Every man to his trade!"

We couldn't do anything with him. He had to take his own medicine.

If the lack of tradition of courtship left us much at sea in our wooing, we found ourselves still more bewildered by lack of tradition of matrimony.

And here again, I have to draw on later experience, and as deep an acquaintance with their culture as I could achieve, to explain the gulfs of difference between us.

Two thousand years of one continuous culture with no men. Back of that, only traditions of the harem. They had no exact analogue for our word HOME, any more than they had for our Roman-based FAMILY.

They loved one another with a practically universal affection, rising to exquisite and unbroken friendships, and broadening to a devotion to their country and people for which our word PATRIOTISM is no definition at all.

Patriotism, red hot, is compatible with the existence of a neglect of national interests, a dishonesty, a cold indifference to the suffering of millions. Patriotism is largely pride, and very largely combativeness. Patriotism generally has a chip on its shoulder.

This country had no other country to measure itself by—save the few poor savages far below, with whom they had no contact.

They loved their country because it was their nursery, playground, and workshop—theirs and their children's. They were proud of it as a workshop, proud of their record of ever-increasing efficiency; they had made a pleasant garden of it, a very practical little heaven; but most of all they valued it—and here it is hard for us to understand them—as a cultural environment for their children.

That, of course, is the keynote of the whole distinction—their children.

From those first breathlessly guarded, half-adored race mothers, all up the ascending line, they had this dominant thought of building up a great race through the children.

All the surrendering devotion our women have put into their private families, these women put into their country and race. All the loyalty and service men expect of wives, they gave, not singly to men, but collectively to one another.

And the mother instinct, with us so painfully intense, so thwarted by conditions, so concentrated in personal devotion to a few, so bitterly hurt by death, disease, or barrenness, and even by the mere growth of the children, leaving the mother alone in her empty nest—all this feeling with them flowed out in a strong, wide current, unbroken through the generations, deepening and widening through the years, including every child in all the land.

With their united power and wisdom, they had studied and overcome the "diseases of childhood"—their children had none.

They had faced the problems of education and so solved them that their children grew up as naturally as young trees; learning through every sense; taught continuously but unconsciously—never knowing they were being educated.

In fact, they did not use the word as we do. Their idea of education was the special training they took, when half grown up, under experts. Then the eager young minds fairly flung themselves on their chosen subjects, and acquired with an ease, a breadth, a grasp, at which I never ceased to wonder.

But the babies and little children never felt the pressure of that "forcible feeding" of the mind that we call "education." Of this, more later.

CHAPTER 9. OUR RELATIONS AND THEIRS

What I'm trying to show here is that with these women the whole relationship of life counted in a glad, eager growing-up to join the ranks of workers in the line best loved; a deep, tender reverence for one's own mother—too deep for them to speak of freely—and beyond that, the whole, free, wide range of sisterhood, the splendid service of the country, and friendships.

To these women we came, filled with the ideas, convictions, traditions, of our culture, and undertook to rouse in them the emotions which—to us—seemed proper.

However much, or little, of true sex-feeling there was between us, it phrased itself in their minds in terms of friendship, the one purely personal love they knew, and of ultimate parentage. Visibly we were not mothers, nor children, nor compatriots; so, if they loved us, we must be friends.

That we should pair off together in our courting days was natural to them; that we three should remain much together, as they did themselves, was also natural. We had as yet no work, so we hung about them in their forest tasks; that was natural, too.

But when we began to talk about each couple having "homes" of our own, they could not understand it.

"Our work takes us all around the country," explained Celis. "We cannot live in one place all the time."

"We are together now," urged Alima, looking proudly at Terry's stalwart nearness. (This was one of the times when they were "on," though presently "off" again.)

"It's not the same thing at all," he insisted. "A man wants a home of his own, with his wife and family in it."

"Staying in it? All the time?" asked Ellador. "Not imprisoned, surely!"

"Of course not! Living there—naturally," he answered.

"What does she do there—all the time?" Alima demanded. "What is her work?"

Then Terry patiently explained again that our women did not work—with reservations.

"But what do they do—if they have no work?" she persisted.

"They take care of the home—and the children."

"At the same time?" asked Ellador.

"Why yes. The children play about, and the mother has charge of it all. There are servants, of course."

It seemed so obvious, so natural to Terry, that he always grew impatient; but the girls were honestly anxious to understand.

"How many children do your women have?" Alima had her notebook out now, and a rather firm set of lip. Terry began to dodge.

"There is no set number, my dear," he explained. "Some have more, some have less."

"Some have none at all," I put in mischievously.

They pounced on this admission and soon wrung from us the general fact that those women who had the most children had the least servants, and those who had the most servants had the least children.

"There!" triumphed Alima. "One or two or no children, and three or four servants. Now what do those women DO?"

We explained as best we might. We talked of "social duties," disingenuously banking on their not interpreting the words as we did; we talked of hospitality, entertainment, and various "interests." All the time we knew that to these large-minded women whose whole mental outlook was so collective, the limitations of a wholly personal life were inconceivable.

"We cannot really understand it," Ellador concluded. "We are only half a people. We have our woman-ways and they have their man-ways and their both-ways. We have worked out a system of living which is, of course, limited. They must have a broader, richer, better one. I should like to see it."

"You shall, dearest," I whispered.

"There's nothing to smoke," complained Terry. He was in the midst of a prolonged quarrel with Alima, and needed a sedative. "There's nothing to drink. These blessed women have no pleasant vices. I wish we could get out of here!"

This wish was vain. We were always under a certain degree of watchfulness. When Terry burst forth to tramp the streets at night he always found a "Colonel" here or there; and when, on an occasion of fierce though temporary despair, he had plunged to the cliff edge with some vague view to escape, he found several of them close by. We were free—but there was a string to it.

"They've no unpleasant ones, either," Jeff reminded him.

"Wish they had!" Terry persisted. "They've neither the vices of men, nor the virtues of women—they're neuters!"

"You know better than that. Don't talk nonsense," said I, severely.

I was thinking of Ellador's eyes when they gave me a certain look, a look she did not at all realize.

Jeff was equally incensed. "I don't know what 'virtues of women' you miss. Seems to me they have all of them."

"They've no modesty," snapped Terry. "No patience, no submissiveness, none of that natural yielding which is woman's greatest charm."

I shook my head pityingly. "Go and apologize and make friends again, Terry. You've got a grouch, that's all. These women have the virtue of humanity, with less of its faults than any folks I ever saw. As for patience—they'd have pitched us over the cliffs the first day we lit among 'em, if they hadn't that."

"There are no—distractions," he grumbled. "Nowhere a man can go and cut loose a bit. It's an everlasting parlor and nursery."

"And workshop," I added. "And school, and office, and laboratory, and studio, and theater, and—home."

"HOME!" he sneered. "There isn't a home in the whole pitiful place."

"There isn't anything else, and you know it," Jeff retorted hotly. "I never saw, I never dreamed of, such universal peace and good will and mutual affection."

"Oh, well, of course, if you like a perpetual Sunday school, it's all very well. But I like Something Doing. Here it's all done."

There was something to this criticism. The years of pioneering lay far behind them. Theirs was a civilization in which the initial difficulties had long since been overcome. The untroubled peace, the unmeasured plenty, the steady health, the large good will and smooth management which ordered everything, left nothing to overcome. It was like a pleasant family in an old established, perfectly run country place.

I liked it because of my eager and continued interest in the sociological achievements involved. Jeff liked it as he would have liked such a family and such a place anywhere.

Terry did not like it because he found nothing to oppose, to struggle with, to conquer.

"Life is a struggle, has to be," he insisted. "If there is no struggle, there is no life—that's all."

"You're talking nonsense—masculine nonsense," the peaceful Jeff replied. He was certainly a warm defender of Herland. "Ants don't raise their myriads by a struggle, do they? Or the bees?"

"Oh, if you go back to insects—and want to live in an anthill—! I tell you the higher grades of life are reached only through struggle—combat. There's no Drama here. Look at their plays! They make me sick."

He rather had us there. The drama of the country was—to our taste—rather flat. You see, they lacked the sex motive and, with it, jealousy. They had no interplay of warring nations, no aristocracy and its ambitions, no wealth and poverty opposition.

I see I have said little about the economics of the place; it should have come before, but I'll go on about the drama now.

They had their own kind. There was a most impressive array of pageantry, of processions, a sort of grand ritual, with their arts and their religion broadly blended. The very babies joined in it. To see one of their great annual festivals, with the massed and marching stateliness of those great mothers, the young women brave and noble, beautiful and strong; and then the children, taking part as naturally as ours would frolic round a Christmas tree—it was overpowering in the impression of joyous, triumphant life.

They had begun at a period when the drama, the dance, music, religion, and education were all very close together; and instead of developing them in detached lines, they had kept the connection. Let me try again to give, if I can, a faint sense of the difference in the life view—the background and basis on which their culture rested.

Ellador told me a lot about it. She took me to see the children, the growing girls, the special teachers. She picked out books for me to read. She always seemed to understand just what I wanted to know, and how to give it to me.

While Terry and Alima struck sparks and parted—he always madly drawn to her and she to him—she must have been, or she'd never have stood the way he behaved—Ellador and I had already a deep, restful feeling, as if we'd always had one another. Jeff and Celis were happy; there was no question of that; but it didn't seem to me as if they had the good times we did.

Well, here is the Herland child facing life—as Ellador tried to show it to me. From the first memory, they knew Peace, Beauty, Order, Safety, Love, Wisdom, Justice, Patience, and Plenty. By "plenty" I mean that the babies grew up in an environment which met their needs, just as young fawns might grow up in dewy forest glades and brook-fed meadows. And they enjoyed it as frankly and utterly as the fawns would.

They found themselves in a big bright lovely world, full of the most interesting and enchanting things to learn about and to do. The people everywhere were friendly and polite. No Herland child ever met the overbearing rudeness we so commonly show to children. They were People, too, from the first; the most precious part of the nation.

In each step of the rich experience of living, they found the instance they were studying widen out into contact with an endless range of common interests. The things they learned were RELATED, from the first; related to one another, and to the national prosperity.

"It was a butterfly that made me a forester," said Ellador. "I was about eleven years old, and I found a big purple-and-green butterfly on a low flower. I caught it, very carefully, by the closed wings, as I had been told to do, and carried it to the nearest insect teacher"—I made a note there to ask her what on earth an insect teacher was—"to ask her its name. She took it from me with a little cry of delight. 'Oh, you blessed child,' she said. 'Do you like obernuts?' Of course I liked obernuts, and said so. It is our best food-nut, you know. 'This is a female of the obernut moth,' she told me. 'They are almost gone. We have been trying to exterminate them for centuries. If you had not caught this one, it might have laid eggs enough to raise worms enough to destroy thousands of our nut trees—thousands of bushels of nuts—and make years and years of trouble for us.'

"Everybody congratulated me. The children all over the country were told to watch for that moth, if there were any more. I was shown the history of the creature, and an account of the damage it used to do and of how long and hard our foremothers had worked to save that tree for us. I grew a foot, it seemed to me, and determined then and there to be a forester."

This is but an instance; she showed me many. The big difference was that whereas our children grow up in private homes and families, with every effort made to protect and seclude them from a dangerous world, here they grew up in a wide, friendly world, and knew it for theirs, from the first.

Their child-literature was a wonderful thing. I could have spent years following the delicate subtleties, the smooth simplicities with which they had bent that great art to the service of the child mind.

We have two life cycles: the man's and the woman's. To the man there is growth, struggle, conquest, the establishment of his family, and as much further success in gain or ambition as he can achieve.

To the woman, growth, the securing of a husband, the subordinate activities of family life, and afterward such "social" or charitable interests as her position allows.

Here was but one cycle, and that a large one.

The child entered upon a broad open field of life, in which motherhood was the one great personal contribution to the national life, and all the rest the individual share in their common activities. Every girl I talked to, at any age above babyhood, had her cheerful determination as to what she was going to be when she grew up.

What Terry meant by saying they had no "modesty" was that this great life-view had no shady places; they had a high sense of personal decorum, but no shame—no knowledge of anything to be ashamed of.

Even their shortcomings and misdeeds in childhood never were presented to them as sins; merely as errors and misplays—as in a game. Some of them, who were palpably less agreeable than others or who had a real weakness or fault, were treated with cheerful allowance, as a friendly group at whist would treat a poor player.

Their religion, you see, was maternal; and their ethics, based on the full perception of evolution, showed the principle of growth and the beauty of wise culture. They had no theory of the essential opposition of good and evil; life to them was growth; their pleasure was in growing, and their duty also.

With this background, with their sublimated mother-love, expressed in terms of widest social activity, every phase of their work was modified by its effect on the national growth. The language itself they had deliberately clarified, simplified, made easy and beautiful, for the sake of the children.

This seemed to us a wholly incredible thing: first, that any nation should have the foresight, the strength, and the persistence to plan and fulfill such a task; and second, that women should have had so much initiative. We have assumed, as a matter of course, that women had none; that only the man, with his natural energy and impatience of restriction, would ever invent anything.

Here we found that the pressure of life upon the environment develops in the human mind its inventive reactions, regardless of sex; and further, that a fully awakened motherhood plans and works without limit, for the good of the child.

That the children might be most nobly born, and reared in an environment calculated to allow the richest, freest growth, they had deliberately remodeled and improved the whole state.

I do not mean in the least that they stopped at that, any more than a child stops at childhood. The most impressive part of their whole culture beyond this perfect system of child-rearing was the range of interests and associations open to them all, for life. But in the field of literature I was most struck, at first, by the child-motive.

They had the same gradation of simple repetitive verse and story that we are familiar with, and the most exquisite, imaginative tales; but where, with us, these are the dribbled remnants of ancient folk myths and primitive lullabies, theirs were the exquisite work of great artists; not only simple and unfailing in appeal to the child-mind, but TRUE, true to the living world about them.

To sit in one of their nurseries for a day was to change one's views forever as to babyhood. The youngest ones, rosy fatlings in their mothers' arms, or sleeping lightly in the flower-sweet air, seemed natural enough, save that they never cried. I never heard a child cry in Herland, save once or twice at a bad fall; and then people ran to help, as we would at a scream of agony from a grown person.

Each mother had her year of glory; the time to love and learn, living closely with her child, nursing it proudly, often for two years or more. This perhaps was one reason for their wonderful vigor.

But after the baby-year the mother was not so constantly in attendance, unless, indeed, her work was among the little ones. She was never far off, however, and her attitude toward the co-mothers, whose proud child-service was direct and continuous, was lovely to see.

As for the babies—a group of those naked darlings playing on short velvet grass, clean-swept; or rugs as soft; or in shallow pools of bright water; tumbling over with bubbling joyous baby laughter—it was a view of infant happiness such as I had never dreamed.

The babies were reared in the warmer part of the country, and gradually acclimated to the cooler heights as they grew older.

Sturdy children of ten and twelve played in the snow as joyfully as ours do; there were continuous excursions of them, from one part of the land to another, so that to each child the whole country might be home.

It was all theirs, waiting for them to learn, to love, to use, to serve; as our own little boys plan to be "a big soldier," or "a cowboy," or whatever pleases their fancy; and our little girls plan for the kind of home they mean to have, or how many children; these planned, freely and gaily with much happy chattering, of what they would do for the country when they were grown.

It was the eager happiness of the children and young people which first made me see the folly of that common notion of ours—that if life was smooth and happy, people would not enjoy it.

As I studied these youngsters, vigorous, joyous, eager little creatures, and their voracious appetite for life, it shook my previous ideas so thoroughly that they have never been re-established. The steady level of good health gave them all that natural stimulus we used to call "animal spirits"—an odd contradiction in terms. They found themselves in an immediate environment which was agreeable and interesting, and before them stretched the years of learning and discovery, the fascinating, endless process of education.

As I looked into these methods and compared them with our own, my strange uncomfortable sense of race-humility grew apace.

Ellador could not understand my astonishment. She explained things kindly and sweetly, but with some amazement that they needed explaining, and with sudden questions as to how we did it that left me meeker than ever.

I betook myself to Somel one day, carefully not taking Ellador. I did not mind seeming foolish to Somel—she was used to it.

"I want a chapter of explanation," I told her. "You know my stupidities by heart, and I do not want to show them to Ellador—she thinks me so wise!"

She smiled delightedly. "It is beautiful to see," she told me, "this new wonderful love between you. The whole country is interested, you know—how can we help it!"

I had not thought of that. We say: "All the world loves a lover," but to have a couple of million people watching one's courtship—and that a difficult one—was rather embarrassing.

"Tell me about your theory of education," I said. "Make it short and easy. And, to show you what puzzles me, I'll tell you that in our theory great stress is laid on the forced exertion of the child's mind; we think it is good for him to overcome obstacles."

"Of course it is," she unexpectedly agreed. "All our children do that—they love to."

That puzzled me again. If they loved to do it, how could it be educational?

"Our theory is this," she went on carefully. "Here is a young human being. The mind is as natural a thing as the body, a thing that grows, a thing to use and enjoy. We seek to nourish, to stimulate, to exercise the mind of a child as we do the body. There are the two main divisions in education—you have those of course?—the things it is necessary to know, and the things it is necessary to do."

"To do? Mental exercises, you mean?"

"Yes. Our general plan is this: In the matter of feeding the mind, of furnishing information, we use our best powers to meet the natural appetite of a healthy young brain; not to overfeed it, to provide such amount and variety of impressions as seem most welcome to each child. That is the easiest part. The other division is in arranging a properly graduated series of exercises which will best develop each mind; the common faculties we all have, and most carefully, the especial faculties some of us have. You do this also, do you not?"

"In a way," I said rather lamely. "We have not so subtle and highly developed a system as you, not approaching it; but tell me more. As to the information—how do you manage? It appears that all of you know pretty much everything—is that right?"

This she laughingly disclaimed. "By no means. We are, as you soon found out, extremely limited in knowledge. I wish you could realize what a ferment the country is in over the new things you have told us; the passionate eagerness among thousands of us to go to your country and learn—learn—learn! But what we do know is readily divisible into common knowledge and special knowledge. The common knowledge we have long since learned to feed into the minds of our little ones with no waste of time or strength; the special knowledge is open to all, as they desire it. Some of us specialize in one line only. But most take up several—some for their regular work, some to grow with."

"To grow with?"

"Yes. When one settles too close in one kind of work there is a tendency to atrophy in the disused portions of the brain. We like to keep on learning, always."

"What do you study?"

"As much as we know of the different sciences. We have, within our limits, a good deal of knowledge of anatomy, physiology, nutrition—all that pertains to a full and beautiful personal life. We have our botany and chemistry, and so on—very rudimentary, but interesting; our own history, with its accumulating psychology."

"You put psychology with history—not with personal life?"

"Of course. It is ours; it is among and between us, and it changes with the succeeding and improving generations. We are at work, slowly and carefully, developing our whole people along these lines. It is glorious work—splendid! To see the thousands of babies improving, showing stronger clearer minds, sweeter dispositions, higher capacities—don't you find it so in your country?"

This I evaded flatly. I remembered the cheerless claim that the human mind was no better than in its earliest period of savagery, only better informed—a statement I had never believed.

"We try most earnestly for two powers," Somel continued. "The two that seem to us basically necessary for all noble life: a clear, far-reaching judgment, and a strong well-used will. We spend our best efforts, all through childhood and youth, in developing these faculties, individual judgment and will."

"As part of your system of education, you mean?"

"Exactly. As the most valuable part. With the babies, as you may have noticed, we first provide an environment which feeds the mind without tiring it; all manner of simple and interesting things to do, as soon as they are old enough to do them; physical properties, of course, come first. But as early as possible, going very carefully, not to tax the mind, we provide choices, simple choices, with very obvious causes and consequences. You've noticed the games?"

I had. The children seemed always playing something; or else, sometimes, engaged in peaceful researches of their own. I had wondered at first when they went to school, but soon found that they never did—to their knowledge. It was all education but no schooling.

"We have been working for some sixteen hundred years, devising better and better games for children," continued Somel.

I sat aghast. "Devising games?" I protested. "Making up new ones, you mean?"

"Exactly," she answered. "Don't you?"

Then I remembered the kindergarten, and the "material" devised by Signora Montessori, and guardedly replied: "To some extent." But most of our games, I told her, were very old—came down from child to child, along the ages, from the remote past.

"And what is their effect?" she asked. "Do they develop the faculties you wish to encourage?"

Again I remembered the claims made by the advocates of "sports," and again replied guardedly that that was, in part, the theory.

"But do the children LIKE it?" I asked. "Having things made up and set before them that way? Don't they want the old games?"

"You can see the children," she answered. "Are yours more contented—more interested—happier?"

Then I thought, as in truth I never had thought before, of the dull, bored children I had seen, whining; "What can I do now?"; of the little groups and gangs hanging about; of the value of some one strong spirit who possessed initiative and would "start something"; of the children's parties and the onerous duties of the older people set to "amuse the children"; also of that troubled ocean of misdirected activity we call "mischief," the foolish, destructive, sometimes evil things done by unoccupied children.

"No," said I grimly. "I don't think they are."

The Herland child was born not only into a world carefully prepared, full of the most fascinating materials and opportunities to learn, but into the society of plentiful numbers of teachers, teachers born and trained, whose business it was to accompany the children along that, to us, impossible thing—the royal road to learning.

There was no mystery in their methods. Being adapted to children it was at least comprehensible to adults. I spent many days with the little ones, sometimes with Ellador, sometimes without, and began to feel a crushing pity for my own childhood, and for all others that I had known.

The houses and gardens planned for babies had in them nothing to hurt—no stairs, no corners, no small loose objects to swallow, no fire—just a babies' paradise. They were taught, as rapidly as feasible, to use and control their own bodies, and never did I see such sure-footed, steady-handed, clear-headed little things. It was a joy to watch a row of toddlers learning to walk, not only on a level floor, but, a little later, on a sort of rubber rail raised an inch or two above the soft turf or heavy rugs, and falling off with shrieks of infant joy, to rush back to the end of the line and try again. Surely we have noticed how children love to get up on something and walk along it! But we have never thought to provide that simple and inexhaustible form of amusement and physical education for the young.

Water they had, of course, and could swim even before they walked. If I feared at first the effects of a too intensive system of culture, that fear was dissipated by seeing the long sunny days of pure physical merriment and natural sleep in which these heavenly babies passed their first years. They never knew they were being educated. They did not dream that in this association of hilarious experiment and achievement they were laying the foundation for that close beautiful group feeling into which they grew so firmly with the years. This was education for citizenship.

CHAPTER 10. THEIR RELIGIONS AND OUR MARRIAGES

It took me a long time, as a man, a foreigner, and a species of Christian—I was that as much as anything—to get any clear understanding of the religion of Herland.

Its deification of motherhood was obvious enough; but there was far more to it than that; or, at least, than my first interpretation of that.

I think it was only as I grew to love Ellador more than I believed anyone could love anybody, as I grew faintly to appreciate her inner attitude and state of mind, that I began to get some glimpses of this faith of theirs.

When I asked her about it, she tried at first to tell me, and then, seeing me flounder, asked for more information about ours. She soon found that we had many, that they varied widely, but had some points in common. A clear methodical luminous mind had my Ellador, not only reasonable, but swiftly perceptive.

She made a sort of chart, superimposing the different religions as I described them, with a pin run through them all, as it were; their common basis being a Dominant Power or Powers, and some Special Behavior, mostly taboos, to please or placate. There were some common features in certain groups of religions, but the one always present was this Power, and the things which must be done or not done because of it. It was not hard to trace our human imagery of the Divine Force up through successive stages of bloodthirsty, sensual, proud, and cruel gods of early times to the conception of a Common Father with its corollary of a Common Brotherhood.

This pleased her very much, and when I expatiated on the Omniscience, Omnipotence, Omnipresence, and so on, of our God, and of the loving kindness taught by his Son, she was much impressed.

The story of the Virgin birth naturally did not astonish her, but she was greatly puzzled by the Sacrifice, and still more by the Devil, and the theory of Damnation.

When in an inadvertent moment I said that certain sects had believed in infant damnation—and explained it—she sat very still indeed.

"They believed that God was Love—and Wisdom—and Power?"

"Yes—all of that."

Her eyes grew large, her face ghastly pale.

"And yet that such a God could put little new babies to burn—for eternity?" She fell into a sudden shuddering and left me, running swiftly to the nearest temple.

Every smallest village had its temple, and in those gracious retreats sat wise and noble women, quietly busy at some work of their own until they were wanted, always ready to give comfort, light, or help, to any applicant.

Ellador told me afterward how easily this grief of hers was assuaged, and seemed ashamed of not having helped herself out of it.

"You see, we are not accustomed to horrible ideas," she said, coming back to me rather apologetically. "We haven't any. And when we get a thing like that into our minds it's like—oh, like red pepper in your eyes. So I just ran to her, blinded and almost screaming, and she took it out so quickly—so easily!"

"How?" I asked, very curious.

"'Why, you blessed child,' she said, 'you've got the wrong idea altogether. You do not have to think that there ever was such a God—for there wasn't. Or such a happening—for there wasn't. Nor even that this hideous false idea was believed by anybody. But only this—that people who are utterly ignorant will believe anything—which you certainly knew before.'"

"Anyhow," pursued Ellador, "she turned pale for a minute when I first said it."

This was a lesson to me. No wonder this whole nation of women was peaceful and sweet in expression—they had no horrible ideas.

"Surely you had some when you began," I suggested.

"Oh, yes, no doubt. But as soon as our religion grew to any height at all we left them out, of course."

From this, as from many other things, I grew to see what I finally put in words.

"Have you no respect for the past? For what was thought and believed by your foremothers?"

"Why, no," she said. "Why should we? They are all gone. They knew less than we do. If we are not beyond them, we are unworthy of them—and unworthy of the children who must go beyond us."

This set me thinking in good earnest. I had always imagined—simply from hearing it said, I suppose—that women were by nature conservative. Yet these women, quite unassisted by any masculine spirit of enterprise, had ignored their past and built daringly for the future.

Ellador watched me think. She seemed to know pretty much what was going on in my mind.

"It's because we began in a new way, I suppose. All our folks were swept away at once, and then, after that time of despair, came those wonder children—the first. And then the whole breathless hope of us was for THEIR children—if they should have them. And they did! Then there was the period of pride and triumph till we grew too numerous; and after that, when it all came down to one child apiece, we began to really work—to make better ones."

"But how does this account for such a radical difference in your religion?" I persisted.

She said she couldn't talk about the difference very intelligently, not being familiar with other religions, but that theirs seemed simple enough. Their great Mother Spirit was to them what their own motherhood was—only magnified beyond human limits. That meant that they felt beneath and behind them an upholding, unfailing, serviceable love—perhaps it was really the accumulated mother-love of the race they felt—but it was a Power.

"Just what is your theory of worship?" I asked her.

"Worship? What is that?"

I found it singularly difficult to explain. This Divine Love which they felt so strongly did not seem to ask anything of them—"any more than our mothers do," she said.

"But surely your mothers expect honor, reverence, obedience, from you. You have to do things for your mothers, surely?"

"Oh, no," she insisted, smiling, shaking her soft brown hair. "We do things FROM our mothers—not FOR them. We don't have to do things FOR them—they don't need it, you know. But we have to live on—splendidly—because of them; and that's the way we feel about God."

I meditated again. I thought of that God of Battles of ours, that Jealous God, that Vengeance-is-mine God. I thought of our world-nightmare—Hell.

"You have no theory of eternal punishment then, I take it?"

Ellador laughed. Her eyes were as bright as stars, and there were tears in them, too. She was so sorry for me.

"How could we?" she asked, fairly enough. "We have no punishments in life, you see, so we don't imagine them after death."

"Have you NO punishments? Neither for children nor criminals—such mild criminals as you have?" I urged.

"Do you punish a person for a broken leg or a fever? We have preventive measures, and cures; sometimes we have to 'send the patient to bed,' as it were; but that's not a punishment—it's only part of the treatment," she explained.

Then studying my point of view more closely, she added: "You see, we recognize, in our human motherhood, a great tender limitless uplifting force—patience and wisdom and all subtlety of delicate method. We credit God—our idea of God—with all that and more. Our mothers are not angry with us—why should God be?"

"Does God mean a person to you?"

This she thought over a little. "Why—in trying to get close to it in our minds we personify the idea, naturally; but we certainly do not assume a Big Woman somewhere, who is God. What we call God is a Pervading Power, you know, an Indwelling Spirit, something inside of us that we want more of. Is your God a Big Man?" she asked innocently.

"Why—yes, to most of us, I think. Of course we call it an Indwelling Spirit just as you do, but we insist that it is Him, a Person, and a Man—with whiskers."

"Whiskers? Oh yes—because you have them! Or do you wear them because He does?"

"On the contrary, we shave them off—because it seems cleaner and more comfortable."

"Does He wear clothes—in your idea, I mean?"

I was thinking over the pictures of God I had seen—rash advances of the devout mind of man, representing his Omnipotent Deity as an old man in a flowing robe, flowing hair, flowing beard, and in the light of her perfectly frank and innocent questions this concept seemed rather unsatisfying.

I explained that the God of the Christian world was really the ancient Hebrew God, and that we had simply taken over the patriarchal idea—that ancient one which quite inevitably clothed its thought of God with the attributes of the patriarchal ruler, the grandfather.

"I see," she said eagerly, after I had explained the genesis and development of our religious ideals. "They lived in separate groups, with a male head, and he was probably a little—domineering?"

"No doubt of that," I agreed.

"And we live together without any 'head,' in that sense—just our chosen leaders—that DOES make a difference."

"Your difference is deeper than that," I assured her. "It is in your common motherhood. Your children grow up in a world where everybody loves them. They find life made rich and happy for them by the diffused love and wisdom of all mothers. So it is easy for you to think of God in the terms of a similar diffused and competent love. I think you are far nearer right than we are."

"What I cannot understand," she pursued carefully, "is your preservation of such a very ancient state of mind. This patriarchal idea you tell me is thousands of years old?"

"Oh yes—four, five, six thousand—every so many."

"And you have made wonderful progress in those years—in other things?"

"We certainly have. But religion is different. You see, our religions come from behind us, and are initiated by some great teacher who is dead. He is supposed to have known the whole thing and taught it, finally. All we have to do is believe—and obey."

"Who was the great Hebrew teacher?"

"Oh—there it was different. The Hebrew religion is an accumulation of extremely ancient traditions, some far older than their people, and grew by accretion down the ages. We consider it inspired—'the Word of God.'"

"How do you know it is?"

"Because it says so."

"Does it say so in as many words? Who wrote that in?"

I began to try to recall some text that did say so, and could not bring it to mind.

"Apart from that," she pursued, "what I cannot understand is why you keep these early religious ideas so long. You have changed all your others, haven't you?"

"Pretty generally," I agreed. "But this we call 'revealed religion,' and think it is final. But tell me more about these little temples of yours," I urged. "And these Temple Mothers you run to."

Then she gave me an extended lesson in applied religion, which I will endeavor to concentrate.

They developed their central theory of a Loving Power, and assumed that its relation to them was motherly—that it desired their welfare and especially their development. Their relation to it, similarly, was filial, a loving appreciation and a glad fulfillment of its high purposes. Then, being nothing if not practical, they set their keen and active minds to discover the kind of conduct expected of them. This worked out in a most admirable system of ethics. The principle of Love was universally recognized—and used.

Patience, gentleness, courtesy, all that we call "good breeding," was part of their code of conduct. But where they went far beyond us was in the special application of religious feeling to every field of life. They had no ritual, no little set of performances called "divine service," save those religious pageants I have spoken of, and those were as much educational as religious, and as much social as either. But they had a clear established connection between everything they did—and God. Their cleanliness, their health, their exquisite order, the rich peaceful beauty of the whole land, the happiness of the children, and above all the constant progress they made—all this was their religion.

They applied their minds to the thought of God, and worked out the theory that such an inner power demanded outward expression. They lived as if God was real and at work within them.

As for those little temples everywhere—some of the women were more skilled, more temperamentally inclined, in this direction, than others. These, whatever their work might be, gave certain hours to the Temple Service, which meant being there with all their love and wisdom and trained thought, to smooth out rough places for anyone who needed it. Sometimes it was a real grief, very rarely a quarrel, most often a perplexity; even in Herland the human soul had its hours of darkness. But all through the country their best and wisest were ready to give help.

If the difficulty was unusually profound, the applicant was directed to someone more specially experienced in that line of thought.

Here was a religion which gave to the searching mind a rational basis in life, the concept of an immense Loving Power working steadily out through them, toward good. It gave to the "soul" that sense of contact with the inmost force, of perception of the uttermost purpose, which we always crave. It gave to the "heart" the blessed feeling of being loved, loved and UNDERSTOOD. It gave clear, simple, rational directions as to how we should live—and why. And for ritual it gave first those triumphant group demonstrations, when with a union of all the arts, the revivifying combination of great multitudes moved rhythmically with march and dance, song and music, among their own noblest products and the open beauty of their groves and hills. Second, it gave these numerous little centers of wisdom where the least wise could go to the most wise and be helped.

"It is beautiful!" I cried enthusiastically. "It is the most practical, comforting, progressive religion I ever heard of. You DO love one another—you DO bear one another's burdens—you DO realize that a little child is a type of the kingdom of heaven. You are more Christian than any people I ever saw. But—how about death? And the life everlasting? What does your religion teach about eternity?"

"Nothing," said Ellador. "What is eternity?"

What indeed? I tried, for the first time in my life, to get a real hold on the idea.

"It is—never stopping."

"Never stopping?" She looked puzzled.

"Yes, life, going on forever."

"Oh—we see that, of course. Life does go on forever, all about us."

"But eternal life goes on WITHOUT DYING."

"The same person?"

"Yes, the same person, unending, immortal." I was pleased to think that I had something to teach from our religion, which theirs had never promulgated.

"Here?" asked Ellador. "Never to die—here?" I could see her practical mind heaping up the people, and hurriedly reassured her.

"Oh no, indeed, not here—hereafter. We must die here, of course, but then we 'enter into eternal life.' The soul lives forever."

"How do you know?" she inquired.

"I won't attempt to prove it to you," I hastily continued. "Let us assume it to be so. How does this idea strike you?"

Again she smiled at me, that adorable, dimpling, tender, mischievous, motherly smile of hers. "Shall I be quite, quite honest?"

"You couldn't be anything else," I said, half gladly and half a little sorry. The transparent honesty of these women was a never-ending astonishment to me.

"It seems to me a singularly foolish idea," she said calmly. "And if true, most disagreeable."

Now I had always accepted the doctrine of personal immortality as a thing established. The efforts of inquiring spiritualists, always seeking to woo their beloved ghosts back again, never seemed to me necessary. I don't say I had ever seriously and courageously discussed the subject with myself even; I had simply assumed it to be a fact. And here was the girl I loved, this creature whose character constantly revealed new heights and ranges far beyond my own, this superwoman of a superland, saying she thought immortality foolish! She meant it, too.

"What do you WANT it for?" she asked.

"How can you NOT want it!" I protested. "Do you want to go out like a candle? Don't you want to go on and on—growing and—and—being happy, forever?"

"Why, no," she said. "I don't in the least. I want my child—and my child's child—to go on—and they will. Why should I want to?"

"But it means Heaven!" I insisted. "Peace and Beauty and Comfort and Love—with God." I had never been so eloquent on the subject of religion. She could be horrified at Damnation, and question the justice of Salvation, but Immortality—that was surely a noble faith.

"Why, Van," she said, holding out her hands to me. "Why Van—darling! How splendid of you to feel it so keenly. That's what we all want, of course—Peace and Beauty, and Comfort and Love—with God! And Progress too, remember; Growth, always and always. That is what our religion teaches us to want and to work for, and we do!"

"But that is HERE," I said, "only for this life on earth."

"Well? And do not you in your country, with your beautiful religion of love and service have it here, too—for this life—on earth?"

None of us were willing to tell the women of Herland about the evils of our own beloved land. It was all very well for us to assume them to be necessary and essential, and to criticize—strictly among ourselves—their all-too-perfect civilization, but when it came to telling them about the failures and wastes of our own, we never could bring ourselves to do it.

Moreover, we sought to avoid too much discussion, and to press the subject of our approaching marriages.

Jeff was the determined one on this score.

"Of course they haven't any marriage ceremony or service, but we can make it a sort of Quaker wedding, and have it in the temple—it is the least we can do for them."

It was. There was so little, after all, that we could do for them. Here we were, penniless guests and strangers, with no chance even to use our strength and courage—nothing to defend them from or protect them against.

"We can at least give them our names," Jeff insisted.

They were very sweet about it, quite willing to do whatever we asked, to please us. As to the names, Alima, frank soul that she was, asked what good it would do.

Terry, always irritating her, said it was a sign of possession. "You are going to be Mrs. Nicholson," he said. "Mrs. T. O. Nicholson. That shows everyone that you are my wife."

"What is a 'wife' exactly?" she demanded, a dangerous gleam in her eye.

"A wife is the woman who belongs to a man," he began.

But Jeff took it up eagerly: "And a husband is the man who belongs to a woman. It is because we are monogamous, you know. And marriage is the ceremony, civil and religious, that joins the two together—'until death do us part,'" he finished, looking at Celis with unutterable devotion.

"What makes us all feel foolish," I told the girls, "is that here we have nothing to give you—except, of course, our names."

"Do your women have no names before they are married?" Celis suddenly demanded.

"Why, yes," Jeff explained. "They have their maiden names—their father's names, that is."

"And what becomes of them?" asked Alima.

"They change them for their husbands', my dear," Terry answered her.

"Change them? Do the husbands then take the wives' 'maiden names'?"

"Oh, no," he laughed. "The man keeps his own and gives it to her, too."

"Then she just loses hers and takes a new one—how unpleasant! We won't do that!" Alima said decidedly.

Terry was good-humored about it. "I don't care what you do or don't do so long as we have that wedding pretty soon," he said, reaching a strong brown hand after Alima's, quite as brown and nearly as strong.

"As to giving us things—of course we can see that you'd like to, but we are glad you can't," Celis continued. "You see, we love you just for yourselves—we wouldn't want you to—to pay anything. Isn't it enough to know that you are loved personally—and just as men?"

Enough or not, that was the way we were married. We had a great triple wedding in the biggest temple of all, and it looked as if most of the nation was present. It was very solemn and very beautiful. Someone had written a new song for the occasion, nobly beautiful, about the New Hope for their people—the New Tie with other lands—Brotherhood as well as Sisterhood, and, with evident awe, Fatherhood.

Terry was always restive under their talk of fatherhood. "Anybody'd think we were High Priests of—of Philoprogenitiveness!" he protested. "These women think of NOTHING but children, seems to me! We'll teach 'em!"

He was so certain of what he was going to teach, and Alima so uncertain in her moods of reception, that Jeff and I feared the worst. We tried to caution him—much good that did. The big handsome fellow drew himself up to his full height, lifted that great chest of his, and laughed.

"There are three separate marriages," he said. "I won't interfere with yours—nor you with mine."

So the great day came, and the countless crowds of women, and we three bridegrooms without any supporting "best men," or any other men to back us up, felt strangely small as we came forward.

Somel and Zava and Moadine were on hand; we were thankful to have them, too—they seemed almost like relatives.

There was a splendid procession, wreathing dances, the new anthem I spoke of, and the whole great place pulsed with feeling—the deep awe, the sweet hope, the wondering expectation of a new miracle.

"There has been nothing like this in the country since our Motherhood began!" Somel said softly to me, while we watched the symbolic marches. "You see, it is the dawn of a new era. You don't know how much you mean to us. It is not only Fatherhood—that marvelous dual parentage to which we are strangers—the miracle of union in life-giving—but it is Brotherhood. You are the rest of the world. You join us to our kind—to all the strange lands and peoples we have never seen. We hope to know them—to love and help them—and to learn of them. Ah! You cannot know!"

Thousands of voices rose in the soaring climax of that great Hymn of The Coming Life. By the great Altar of Motherhood, with its crown of fruit and flowers, stood a new one, crowned as well. Before the Great Over Mother of the Land and her ring of High Temple Counsellors, before that vast multitude of calm-faced mothers and holy-eyed maidens, came forward our own three chosen ones, and we, three men alone in all that land, joined hands with them and made our marriage vows.

CHAPTER 11. OUR DIFFICULTIES

We say, "Marriage is a lottery"; also "Marriages are made in Heaven"—but this is not so widely accepted as the other.

We have a well-founded theory that it is best to marry "in one's class," and certain well-grounded suspicions of international marriages, which seem to persist in the interests of social progress, rather than in those of the contracting parties.

But no combination of alien races, of color, of caste, or creed, was ever so basically difficult to establish as that between us, three modern American men, and these three women of Herland.

It is all very well to say that we should have been frank about it beforehand. We had been frank. We had discussed—at least Ellador and I had—the conditions of The Great Adventure, and thought the path was clear before us. But there are some things one takes for granted, supposes are mutually understood, and to which both parties may repeatedly refer without ever meaning the same thing.

The differences in the education of the average man and woman are great enough, but the trouble they make is not mostly for the man; he generally carries out his own views of the case. The woman may have imagined the conditions of married life to be different; but what she imagined, was ignorant of, or might have preferred, did not seriously matter.

I can see clearly and speak calmly about this now, writing after a lapse of years, years full of growth and education, but at the time it was rather hard sledding for all of us—especially for Terry. Poor Terry! You see, in any other imaginable marriage among the peoples of the earth, whether the woman were black, red, yellow, brown, or white; whether she were ignorant or educated, submissive or rebellious, she would have behind her the marriage tradition of our general history. This tradition relates the woman to the man. He goes on with his business, and she adapts herself to him and to it. Even in citizenship, by some strange hocus-pocus, that fact of birth and geography was waved aside, and the woman automatically acquired the nationality of her husband.

Well—here were we, three aliens in this land of women. It was small in area, and the external differences were not so great as to astound us. We did not yet appreciate the differences between the race-mind of this people and ours.

In the first place, they were a "pure stock" of two thousand uninterrupted years. Where we have some long connected lines of thought and feeling, together with a wide range of differences, often irreconcilable, these people were smoothly and firmly agreed on most of the basic principles of their life; and not only agreed in principle, but accustomed for these sixty-odd generations to act on those principles.

This is one thing which we did not understand—had made no allowance for. When in our pre-marital discussions one of those dear girls had said: "We understand it thus and thus," or "We hold such and such to be true," we men, in our own deep-seated convictions of the power of love, and our easy views about beliefs and principles, fondly imagined that we could convince them otherwise. What we imagined, before marriage, did not matter any more than what an average innocent young girl imagines. We found the facts to be different.

It was not that they did not love us; they did, deeply and warmly. But there are you again—what they meant by "love" and what we meant by "love" were so different.

Perhaps it seems rather cold-blooded to say "we" and "they," as if we were not separate couples, with our separate joys and sorrows, but our positions as aliens drove us together constantly. The whole strange experience had made our friendship more close and intimate than it would ever have become in a free and easy lifetime among our own people. Also, as men, with our masculine tradition of far more than two thousand years, we were a unit, small but firm, against this far larger unit of feminine tradition.

I think I can make clear the points of difference without a too painful explicitness. The more external disagreement was in the matter of "the home," and the housekeeping duties and pleasures we, by instinct and long education, supposed to be inherently appropriate to women.

I will give two illustrations, one away up, and the other away down, to show how completely disappointed we were in this regard.

For the lower one, try to imagine a male ant, coming from some state of existence where ants live in pairs, endeavoring to set up housekeeping with a female ant from a highly developed anthill. This female ant might regard him with intense personal affection, but her ideas of parentage and economic management would be on a very different scale from his. Now, of course, if she was a stray female in a country of pairing ants, he might have had his way with her; but if he was a stray male in an anthill—!

For the higher one, try to imagine a devoted and impassioned man trying to set up housekeeping with a lady angel, a real wings-and-harp-and-halo angel, accustomed to fulfilling divine missions all over interstellar space. This angel might love the man with an affection quite beyond his power of return or even of appreciation, but her ideas of service and duty would be on a very different scale from his. Of course, if she was a stray angel in a country of men, he might have had his way with her; but if he was a stray man among angels—!

Terry, at his worst, in a black fury for which, as a man, I must have some sympathy, preferred the ant simile. More of Terry and his special troubles later. It was hard on Terry.

Jeff—well, Jeff always had a streak that was too good for this world! He's the kind that would have made a saintly priest in parentagearlier times. He accepted the angel theory, swallowed it whole, tried to force it on us—with varying effect. He so worshipped Celis, and not only Celis, but what she represented; he had become so deeply convinced of the almost supernatural advantages of this country and people, that he took his medicine like a—I cannot say "like a man," but more as if he wasn't one.

Don't misunderstand me for a moment. Dear old Jeff was no milksop or molly-coddle either. He was a strong, brave, efficient man, and an excellent fighter when fighting was necessary. But there was always this angel streak in him. It was rather a wonder, Terry being so different, that he really loved Jeff as he did; but it happens so sometimes, in spite of the difference—perhaps because of it.

As for me, I stood between. I was no such gay Lothario as Terry, and no such Galahad as Jeff. But for all my limitations I think I had the habit of using my brains in regard to behavior rather more frequently than either of them. I had to use brain-power now, I can tell you.

The big point at issue between us and our wives was, as may easily be imagined, in the very nature of the relation.

"Wives! Don't talk to me about wives!" stormed Terry. "They don't know what the word means."

Which is exactly the fact—they didn't. How could they? Back in their prehistoric records of polygamy and slavery there were no ideals of wifehood as we know it, and since then no possibility of forming such.

"The only thing they can think of about a man is FATHERHOOD!" said Terry in high scorn. "FATHERHOOD! As if a man was always wanting to be a FATHER!"

This also was correct. They had their long, wide, deep, rich experience of Motherhood, and their only perception of the value of a male creature as such was for Fatherhood.

Aside from that, of course, was the whole range of personal love, love which as Jeff earnestly phrased it "passeth the love of women!" It did, too. I can give no idea—either now, after long and happy experience of it, or as it seemed then, in the first measureless wonder—of the beauty and power of the love they gave us.

Even Alima—who had a more stormy temperament than either of the others, and who, heaven knows, had far more provocation—even Alima was patience and tenderness and wisdom personified to the man she loved, until he—but I haven't got to that yet.

These, as Terry put it, "alleged or so-called wives" of ours, went right on with their profession as foresters. We, having no special learnings, had long since qualified as assistants. We had to do something, if only to pass the time, and it had to be work—we couldn't be playing forever.

This kept us out of doors with those dear girls, and more or less together—too much together sometimes.

These people had, it now became clear to us, the highest, keenest, most delicate sense of personal privacy, but not the faintest idea of that SOLITUDE A DEUX we are so fond of. They had, every one of them, the "two rooms and a bath" theory realized. From earliest childhood each had a separate bedroom with toilet conveniences, and one of the marks of coming of age was the addition of an outer room in which to receive friends.

Long since we had been given our own two rooms apiece, and as being of a different sex and race, these were in a separate house. It seemed to be recognized that we should breathe easier if able to free our minds in real seclusion.

For food we either went to any convenient eating-house, ordered a meal brought in, or took it with us to the woods, always and equally good. All this we had become used to and enjoyed—in our courting days.

After marriage there arose in us a somewhat unexpected urge of feeling that called for a separate house; but this feeling found no response in the hearts of those fair ladies.

"We ARE alone, dear," Ellador explained to me with gentle patience. "We are alone in these great forests; we may go and eat in any little summer-house—just we two, or have a separate table anywhere—or even have a separate meal in our own rooms. How could we be aloner?"

This was all very true. We had our pleasant mutual solitude about our work, and our pleasant evening talks in their apartments or ours; we had, as it were, all the pleasures of courtship carried right on; but we had no sense of—perhaps it may be called possession.

"Might as well not be married at all," growled Terry. "They only got up that ceremony to please us—please Jeff, mostly. They've no real idea of being married."

I tried my best to get Ellador's point of view, and naturally I tried to give her mine. Of course, what we, as men, wanted to make them see was that there were other, and as we proudly said "higher," uses in this relation than what Terry called "mere parentage." In the highest terms I knew I tried to explain this to Ellador.

"Anything higher than for mutual love to hope to give life, as we did?" she said. "How is it higher?"

"It develops love," I explained. "All the power of beautiful permanent mated love comes through this higher development."

"Are you sure?" she asked gently. "How do you know that it was so developed? There are some birds who love each other so that they mope and pine if separated, and never pair again if one dies, but they never mate except in the mating season. Among your people do you find high and lasting affection appearing in proportion to this indulgence?"

It is a very awkward thing, sometimes, to have a logical mind.

Of course I knew about those monogamous birds and beasts too, that mate for life and show every sign of mutual affection, without ever having stretched the sex relationship beyond its original range. But what of it?

"Those are lower forms of life!" I protested. "They have no capacity for faithful and affectionate, and apparently happy—but oh, my dear! my dear!—what can they know of such a love as draws us together? Why, to touch you—to be near you—to come closer and closer—to lose myself in you—surely you feel it too, do you not?"

I came nearer. I seized her hands.

Her eyes were on mine, tender radiant, but steady and strong. There was something so powerful, so large and changeless, in those eyes that I could not sweep her off her feet by my own emotion as I had unconsciously assumed would be the case.

It made me feel as, one might imagine, a man might feel who loved a goddess—not a Venus, though! She did not resent my attitude, did not repel it, did not in the least fear it, evidently. There was not a shade of that timid withdrawal or pretty resistance which are so—provocative.

"You see, dearest," she said, "you have to be patient with us. We are not like the women of your country. We are Mothers, and we are People, but we have not specialized in this line."

"We" and "we" and "we"—it was so hard to get her to be personal. And, as I thought that, I suddenly remembered how we were always criticizing OUR women for BEING so personal.

Then I did my earnest best to picture to her the sweet intense joy of married lovers, and the result in higher stimulus to all creative work.

"Do you mean," she asked quite calmly, as if I was not holding her cool firm hands in my hot and rather quivering ones, "that with you, when people marry, they go right on doing this in season and out of season, with no thought of children at all?"

"They do," I said, with some bitterness. "They are not mere parents. They are men and women, and they love each other."

"How long?" asked Ellador, rather unexpectedly.

"How long?" I repeated, a little dashed. "Why as long as they live."

"There is something very beautiful in the idea," she admitted, still as if she were discussing life on Mars. "This climactic expression, which, in all the other life-forms, has but the one purpose, has with you become specialized to higher, purer, nobler uses. It has—I judge from what you tell me—the most ennobling effect on character. People marry, not only for parentage, but for this exquisite interchange—and, as a result, you have a world full of continuous lovers, ardent, happy, mutually devoted, always living on that high tide of supreme emotion which we had supposed to belong only to one season and one use. And you say it has other results, stimulating all high creative work. That must mean floods, oceans of such work, blossoming from this intense happiness of every married pair! It is a beautiful idea!"

She was silent, thinking.

So was I.

She slipped one hand free, and was stroking my hair with it in a gentle motherly way. I bowed my hot head on her shoulder and felt a dim sense of peace, a restfulness which was very pleasant.

"You must take me there someday, darling," she was saying. "It is not only that I love you so much, I want to see your country—your people—your mother—" she paused reverently. "Oh, how I shall love your mother!"

I had not been in love many times—my experience did not compare with Terry's. But such as I had was so different from this that I was perplexed, and full of mixed feelings: partly a growing sense of common ground between us, a pleasant rested calm feeling, which I had imagined could only be attained in one way; and partly a bewildered resentment because what I found was not what I had looked for.

It was their confounded psychology! Here they were with this profound highly developed system of education so bred into them that even if they were not teachers by profession they all had a general proficiency in it—it was second nature to them.

And no child, stormily demanding a cookie "between meals," was ever more subtly diverted into an interest in house-building than was I when I found an apparently imperative demand had disappeared without my noticing it.

And all the time those tender mother eyes, those keen scientific eyes, noting every condition and circumstance, and learning how to "take time by the forelock" and avoid discussion before occasion arose.

I was amazed at the results. I found that much, very much, of what I had honestly supposed to be a physiological necessity was a psychological necessity—or so believed. I found, after my ideas of what was essential had changed, that my feelings changed also. And more than all, I found this—a factor of enormous weight—these women were not provocative. That made an immense difference.

The thing that Terry had so complained of when we first came—that they weren't "feminine," they lacked "charm," now became a great comfort. Their vigorous beauty was an aesthetic pleasure, not an irritant. Their dress and ornaments had not a touch of the "come-and-find-me" element.

Even with my own Ellador, my wife, who had for a time unveiled a woman's heart and faced the strange new hope and joy of dual parentage, she afterward withdrew again into the same good comrade she had been at first. They were women, PLUS, and so much plus that when they did not choose to let the womanness appear, you could not find it anywhere.

I don't say it was easy for me; it wasn't. But when I made appeal to her sympathies I came up against another immovable wall. She was sorry, honestly sorry, for my distresses, and made all manner of thoughtful suggestions, often quite useful, as well as the wise foresight I have mentioned above, which often saved all difficulty before it arose; but her sympathy did not alter her convictions.

"If I thought it was really right and necessary, I could perhaps bring myself to it, for your sake, dear; but I do not want to—not at all. You would not have a mere submission, would you? That is not the kind of high romantic love you spoke of, surely? It is a pity, of course, that you should have to adjust your highly specialized faculties to our unspecialized ones."

Confound it! I hadn't married the nation, and I told her so. But she only smiled at her own limitations and explained that she had to "think in we's."

Confound it again! Here I'd have all my energies focused on one wish, and before I knew it she'd have them dissipated in one direction or another, some subject of discussion that began just at the point I was talking about and ended miles away.

It must not be imagined that I was just repelled, ignored, left to cherish a grievance. Not at all. My happiness was in the hands of a larger, sweeter womanhood than I had ever imagined. Before our marriage my own ardor had perhaps blinded me to much of this. I was madly in love with not so much what was there as with what I supposed to be there. Now I found an endlessly beautiful undiscovered country to explore, and in it the sweetest wisdom and understanding. It was as if I had come to some new place and people, with a desire to eat at all hours, and no other interests in particular; and as if my hosts, instead of merely saying, "You shall not eat," had presently aroused in me a lively desire for music, for pictures, for games, for exercise, for playing in the water, for running some ingenious machine; and, in the multitude of my satisfactions, I forgot the one point which was not satisfied, and got along very well until mealtime.

One of the cleverest and most ingenious of these tricks was only clear to me many years after, when we were so wholly at one on this subject that I could laugh at my own predicament then. It was this: You see, with us, women are kept as different as possible and as feminine as possible. We men have our own world, with only men in it; we get tired of our ultra-maleness and turn gladly to the ultra-femaleness. Also, in keeping our women as feminine as possible, we see to it that when we turn to them we find the thing we want always in evidence. Well, the atmosphere of this place was anything but seductive. The very numbers of these human women, always in human relation, made them anything but alluring. When, in spite of this, my hereditary instincts and race-traditions made me long for the feminine response in Ellador, instead of withdrawing so that I should want her more, she deliberately gave me a little too much of her society.—always de-feminized, as it were. It was awfully funny, really.

Here was I, with an Ideal in mind, for which I hotly longed, and here was she, deliberately obtruding in the foreground of my consciousness a Fact—a fact which I coolly enjoyed, but which actually interfered with what I wanted. I see now clearly enough why a certain kind of man, like Sir Almroth Wright, resents the professional development of women. It gets in the way of the sex ideal; it temporarily covers and excludes femininity.

Of course, in this case, I was so fond of Ellador my friend, of Ellador my professional companion, that I necessarily enjoyed her society on any terms. Only—when I had had her with me in her de-feminine capacity for a sixteen-hour day, I could go to my own room and sleep without dreaming about her.

The witch! If ever anybody worked to woo and win and hold a human soul, she did, great superwoman that she was. I couldn't then half comprehend the skill of it, the wonder. But this I soon began to find: that under all our cultivated attitude of mind toward women, there is an older, deeper, more "natural" feeling, the restful reverence which looks up to the Mother sex.

So we grew together in friendship and happiness, Ellador and I, and so did Jeff and Celis.

When it comes to Terry's part of it, and Alima's, I'm sorry—and I'm ashamed. Of course I blame her somewhat. She wasn't as fine a psychologist as Ellador, and what's more, I think she had a far-descended atavistic trace of more marked femaleness, never apparent till Terry called it out. But when all is said, it doesn't excuse him. I hadn't realized to the full Terry's character—I couldn't, being a man.

The position was the same as with us, of course, only with these distinctions. Alima, a shade more alluring, and several shades less able as a practical psychologist; Terry, a hundredfold more demanding—and proportionately less reasonable.

Things grew strained very soon between them. I fancy at first, when they were together, in her great hope of parentage and his keen joy of conquest—that Terry was inconsiderate. In fact, I know it, from things he said.

"You needn't talk to me," he snapped at Jeff one day, just before our weddings. "There never was a woman yet that did not enjoy being MASTERED. All your pretty talk doesn't amount to a hill o'beans—I KNOW." And Terry would hum:

I've taken my fun where I found it.
I've rogued and I've ranged in my time,

and

The things that I learned from the yellow and black,
They 'ave helped me a 'eap with the white.

Jeff turned sharply and left him at the time. I was a bit disquieted myself.

Poor old Terry! The things he'd learned didn't help him a heap in Herland. His idea was to take—he thought that was the way. He thought, he honestly believed, that women like it. Not the women of Herland! Not Alima!

I can see her now—one day in the very first week of their marriage, setting forth to her day's work with long determined strides and hard-set mouth, and sticking close to Ellador. She didn't wish to be alone with Terry—you could see that.

But the more she kept away from him, the more he wanted her—naturally.

He made a tremendous row about their separate establishments, tried to keep her in his rooms, tried to stay in hers. But there she drew the line sharply.

He came away one night, and stamped up and down the moonlit road, swearing under his breath. I was taking a walk that night too, but I wasn't in his state of mind. To hear him rage you'd not have believed that he loved Alima at all—you'd have thought that she was some quarry he was pursuing, something to catch and conquer.

I think that, owing to all those differences I spoke of, they soon lost the common ground they had at first, and were unable to meet sanely and dispassionately. I fancy too—this is pure conjecture—that he had succeeded in driving Alima beyond her best judgment, her real conscience, and that after that her own sense of shame, the reaction of the thing, made her bitter perhaps.

They quarreled, really quarreled, and after making it up once or twice, they seemed to come to a real break—she would not be alone with him at all. And perhaps she was a bit nervous, I don't know, but she got Moadine to come and stay next door to her. Also, she had a sturdy assistant detailed to accompany her in her work.

Terry had his own ideas, as I've tried to show. I daresay he thought he had a right to do as he did. Perhaps he even convinced himself that it would be better for her. Anyhow, he hid himself in her bedroom one night...

The women of Herland have no fear of men. Why should they have? They are not timid in any sense. They are not weak; and they all have strong trained athletic bodies. Othello could not have extinguished Alima with a pillow, as if she were a mouse.

Terry put in practice his pet conviction that a woman loves to be mastered, and by sheer brute force, in all the pride and passion of his intense masculinity, he tried to master this woman.

It did not work. I got a pretty clear account of it later from Ellador, but what we heard at the time was the noise of a tremendous struggle, and Alima calling to Moadine. Moadine was close by and came at once; one or two more strong grave women followed.

Terry dashed about like a madman; he would cheerfully have killed them—he told me that, himself—but he couldn't. When he swung a chair over his head one sprang in the air and caught it, two threw themselves bodily upon him and forced him to the floor; it was only the work of a few moments to have him tied hand and foot, and then, in sheer pity for his futile rage, to anesthetize him.

Alima was in a cold fury. She wanted him killed—actually.

There was a trial before the local Over Mother, and this woman, who did not enjoy being mastered, stated her case.

In a court in our country he would have been held quite "within his rights," of course. But this was not our country; it was theirs. They seemed to measure the enormity of the offense by its effect upon a possible fatherhood, and he scorned even to reply to this way of putting it.

He did let himself go once, and explained in definite terms that they were incapable of understanding a man's needs, a man's desires, a man's point of view. He called them neuters, epicenes, bloodless, sexless creatures. He said they could of course kill him—as so many insects could—but that he despised them nonetheless.

And all those stern grave mothers did not seem to mind his despising them, not in the least.

It was a long trial, and many interesting points were brought out as to their views of our habits, and after a while Terry had his sentence. He waited, grim and defiant. The sentence was: "You must go home!"

CHAPTER 12. EXPELLED

We had all meant to go home again. Indeed we had NOT meant—not by any means—to stay as long as we had. But when it came to being turned out, dismissed, sent away for bad conduct, we none of us really liked it.

Terry said he did. He professed great scorn of the penalty and the trial, as well as all the other characteristics of "this miserable half-country." But he knew, and we knew, that in any "whole" country we should never have been as forgivingly treated as we had been here.

"If the people had come after us according to the directions we left, there'd have been quite a different story!" said Terry. We found out later why no reserve party had arrived. All our careful directions had been destroyed in a fire. We might have all died there and no one at home have ever known our whereabouts.

Terry was under guard now, all the time, known as unsafe, convicted of what was to them an unpardonable sin.

He laughed at their chill horror. "Parcel of old maids!" he called them. "They're all old maids—children or not. They don't know the first thing about Sex."

When Terry said SEX, sex with a very large S, he meant the male sex, naturally; its special values, its profound conviction of being "the life force," its cheerful ignoring of the true life process, and its interpretation of the other sex solely from its own point of view.

I had learned to see these things very differently since living with Ellador; and as for Jeff, he was so thoroughly Herlandized that he wasn't fair to Terry, who fretted sharply in his new restraint.

Moadine, grave and strong, as sadly patient as a mother with a degenerate child, kept steady watch on him, with enough other women close at hand to prevent an outbreak. He had no weapons, and well knew that all his strength was of small avail against those grim, quiet women.

We were allowed to visit him freely, but he had only his room, and a small high-walled garden to walk in, while the preparations for our departure were under way.

Three of us were to go: Terry, because he must; I, because two were safer for our flyer, and the long boat trip to the coast; Ellador, because she would not let me go without her.

If Jeff had elected to return, Celis would have gone too—they were the most absorbed of lovers; but Jeff had no desire that way.

"Why should I want to go back to all our noise and dirt, our vice and crime, our disease and degeneracy?" he demanded of me privately. We never spoke like that before the women. "I wouldn't take Celis there for anything on earth!" he protested. "She'd die! She'd die of horror and shame to see our slums and hospitals. How can you risk it with Ellador? You'd better break it to her gently before she really makes up her mind."

Jeff was right. I ought to have told her more fully than I did, of all the things we had to be ashamed of. But it is very hard to bridge the gulf of as deep a difference as existed between our life and theirs. I tried to.

"Look here, my dear," I said to her. "If you are really going to my country with me, you've got to be prepared for a good many shocks. It's not as beautiful as this—the cities, I mean, the civilized parts—of course the wild country is."

"I shall enjoy it all," she said, her eyes starry with hope. "I understand it's not like ours. I can see how monotonous our quiet life must seem to you, how much more stirring yours must be. It must be like the biological change you told me about when the second sex was introduced—a far greater movement, constant change, with new possibilities of growth."

I had told her of the later biological theories of sex, and she was deeply convinced of the superior advantages of having two, the superiority of a world with men in it.

"We have done what we could alone; perhaps we have some things better in a quiet way, but you have the whole world—all the people of the different nations—all the long rich history behind you—all the wonderful new knowledge. Oh, I just can't wait to see it!"

What could I do? I told her in so many words that we had our unsolved problems, that we had dishonesty and corruption, vice and crime, disease and insanity, prisons and hospitals; and it made no more impression on her than it would to tell a South Sea Islander about the temperature of the Arctic Circle. She could intellectually see that it was bad to have those things; but she could not FEEL it.

We had quite easily come to accept the Herland life as normal, because it was normal—none of us make any outcry over mere health and peace and happy industry. And the abnormal, to which we are all so sadly well acclimated, she had never seen.

The two things she cared most to hear about, and wanted most to see, were these: the beautiful relation of marriage and the lovely women who were mothers and nothing else; beyond these her keen, active mind hungered eagerly for the world life.

"I'm almost as anxious to go as you are yourself," she insisted, "and you must be desperately homesick."

I assured her that no one could be homesick in such a paradise as theirs, but she would have none of it.

"Oh, yes—I know. It's like those little tropical islands you've told me about, shining like jewels in the big blue sea—I can't wait to see the sea! The little island may be as perfect as a garden, but you always want to get back to your own big country, don't you? Even if it is bad in some ways?"

Ellador was more than willing. But the nearer it came to our really going, and to my having to take her back to our "civilization," after the clean peace and beauty of theirs, the more I began to dread it, and the more I tried to explain.

Of course I had been homesick at first, while we were prisoners, before I had Ellador. And of course I had, at first, rather idealized my country and its ways, in describing it. Also, I had always accepted certain evils as integral parts of our civilization and never dwelt on them at all. Even when I tried to tell her the worst, I never remembered some things—which, when she came to see them, impressed her at once, as they had never impressed me. Now, in my efforts at explanation, I began to see both ways more keenly than I had before; to see the painful defects of my own land, the marvelous gains of this.

In missing men we three visitors had naturally missed the larger part of life, and had unconsciously assumed that they must miss it too. It took me a long time to realize—Terry never did realize—how little it meant to them. When we say MEN, MAN, MANLY, MANHOOD, and all the other masculine derivatives, we have in the background of our minds a huge vague crowded picture of the world and all its activities. To grow up and "be a man," to "act like a man"—the meaning and connotation is wide indeed. That vast background is full of marching columns of men, of changing lines of men, of long processions of men; of men steering their ships into new seas, exploring unknown mountains, breaking horses, herding cattle, ploughing and sowing and reaping, toiling at the forge and furnace, digging in the mine, building roads and bridges and high cathedrals, managing great businesses, teaching in all the colleges, preaching in all the churches; of men everywhere, doing everything—"the world."

And when we say WOMEN, we think FEMALE—the sex.

But to these women, in the unbroken sweep of this two-thousand-year-old feminine civilization, the word WOMAN called up all that big background, so far as they had gone in social development; and the word MAN meant to them only MALE—the sex.

Of course we could TELL them that in our world men did everything; but that did not alter the background of their minds. That man, "the male," did all these things was to them a statement, making no more change in the point of view than was made in ours when we first faced the astounding fact—to us—that in Herland women were "the world."

We had been living there more than a year. We had learned their limited history, with its straight, smooth, upreaching lines, reaching higher and going faster up to the smooth comfort of their present life. We had learned a little of their psychology, a much wider field than the history, but here we could not follow so readily. We were now well used to seeing women not as females but as people; people of all sorts, doing every kind of work.

This outbreak of Terry's, and the strong reaction against it, gave us a new light on their genuine femininity. This was given me with great clearness by both Ellador and Somel. The feeling was the same—sick revulsion and horror, such as would be felt at some climactic blasphemy.

They had no faintest approach to such a thing in their minds, knowing nothing of the custom of marital indulgence among us. To them the one high purpose of motherhood had been for so long the governing law of life, and the contribution of the father, though known to them, so distinctly another method to the same end, that they could not, with all their effort, get the point of view of the male creature whose desires quite ignore parentage and seek only for what we euphoniously term "the joys of love."

When I tried to tell Ellador that women too felt so, with us, she drew away from me, and tried hard to grasp intellectually what she could in no way sympathize with.

"You mean—that with you—love between man and woman expresses itself in that way—without regard to motherhood? To parentage, I mean," she added carefully.

"Yes, surely. It is love we think of—the deep sweet love between two. Of course we want children, and children come—but that is not what we think about."

"But—but—it seems so against nature!" she said. "None of the creatures we know do that. Do other animals—in your country?"

"We are not animals!" I replied with some sharpness. "At least we are something more—something higher. This is a far nobler and more beautiful relation, as I have explained before. Your view seems to us rather—shall I say, practical? Prosaic? Merely a means to an end! With us—oh, my dear girl—cannot you see? Cannot you feel? It is the last, sweetest, highest consummation of mutual love."

She was impressed visibly. She trembled in my arms, as I held her close, kissing her hungrily. But there rose in her eyes that look I knew so well, that remote clear look as if she had gone far away even though I held her beautiful body so close, and was now on some snowy mountain regarding me from a distance.

"I feel it quite clearly," she said to me. "It gives me a deep sympathy with what you feel, no doubt more strongly still. But what I feel, even what you feel, dearest, does not convince me that it is right. Until I am sure of that, of course I cannot do as you wish."

Ellador, at times like this, always reminded me of Epictetus. "I will put you in prison!" said his master. "My body, you mean," replied Epictetus calmly. "I will cut your head off," said his master. "Have I said that my head could not be cut off?" A difficult person, Epictetus.

What is this miracle by which a woman, even in your arms, may withdraw herself, utterly disappear till what you hold is as inaccessible as the face of a cliff?

"Be patient with me, dear," she urged sweetly. "I know it is hard for you. And I begin to see—a little—how Terry was so driven to crime."

"Oh, come, that's a pretty hard word for it. After all, Alima was his wife, you know," I urged, feeling at the moment a sudden burst of sympathy for poor Terry. For a man of his temperament—and habits—it must have been an unbearable situation.

But Ellador, for all her wide intellectual grasp, and the broad sympathy in which their religion trained them, could not make allowance for such—to her—sacrilegious brutality.

It was the more difficult to explain to her, because we three, in our constant talks and lectures about the rest of the world, had naturally avoided the seamy side; not so much from a desire to deceive, but from wishing to put the best foot foremost for our civilization, in the face of the beauty and comfort of theirs. Also, we really thought some things were right, or at least unavoidable, which we could readily see would be repugnant to them, and therefore did not discuss. Again there was much of our world's life which we, being used to it, had not noticed as anything worth describing. And still further, there was about these women a colossal innocence upon which many of the things we did say had made no impression whatever.

I am thus explicit about it because it shows how unexpectedly strong was the impression made upon Ellador when she at last entered our civilization.

She urged me to be patient, and I was patient. You see, I loved her so much that even the restrictions she so firmly established left me much happiness. We were lovers, and there is surely delight enough in that.

Do not imagine that these young women utterly refused "the Great New Hope," as they called it, that of dual parentage. For that they had agreed to marry us, though the marrying part of it was a concession to our prejudices rather than theirs. To them the process was the holy thing—and they meant to keep it holy.

But so far only Celis, her blue eyes swimming in happy tears, her heart lifted with that tide of race-motherhood which was their supreme passion, could with ineffable joy and pride announce that she was to be a mother. "The New Motherhood" they called it, and the whole country knew. There was no pleasure, no service, no honor in all the land that Celis might not have had. Almost like the breathless reverence with which, two thousand years ago, that dwindling band of women had watched the miracle of virgin birth, was the deep awe and warm expectancy with which they greeted this new miracle of union.

All mothers in that land were holy. To them, for long ages, the approach to motherhood has been by the most intense and exquisite love and longing, by the Supreme Desire, the overmastering demand for a child. Every thought they held in connection with the processes of maternity was open to the day, simple yet sacred. Every woman of them placed motherhood not only higher than other duties, but so far higher that there were no other duties, one might almost say. All their wide mutual love, all the subtle interplay of mutual friendship and service, the urge of progressive thought and invention, the deepest religious emotion, every feeling and every act was related to this great central Power, to the River of Life pouring through them, which made them the bearers of the very Spirit of God.

Of all this I learned more and more—from their books, from talk, especially from Ellador. She was at first, for a brief moment, envious of her friend—a thought she put away from her at once and forever.

"It is better," she said to me. "It is much better that it has not come to me yet—to us, that is. For if I am to go with you to your country, we may have 'adventures by sea and land,' as you say [and as in truth we did], and it might not be at all safe for a baby. So we won't try again, dear, till it is safe—will we?"

This was a hard saying for a very loving husband.

"Unless," she went on, "if one is coming, you will leave me behind. You can come back, you know—and I shall have the child."

Then that deep ancient chill of male jealousy of even his own progeny touched my heart.

"I'd rather have you, Ellador, than all the children in the world. I'd rather have you with me—on your own terms—than not to have you."

This was a very stupid saying. Of course I would! For if she wasn't there I should want all of her and have none of her. But if she went along as a sort of sublimated sister—only much closer and warmer than that, really—why I should have all of her but that one thing. And I was beginning to find that Ellador's friendship, Ellador's comradeship, Ellador's sisterly affection, Ellador's perfectly sincere love—none the less deep that she held it back on a definite line of reserve—were enough to live on very happily.

I find it quite beyond me to describe what this woman was to me. We talk fine things about women, but in our hearts we know that they are very limited beings—most of them. We honor them for their functional powers, even while we dishonor them by our use of it; we honor them for their carefully enforced virtue, even while we show by our own conduct how little we think of that virtue; we value them, sincerely, for the perverted maternal activities which make our wives the most comfortable of servants, bound to us for life with the wages wholly at our own decision, their whole business, outside of the temporary duties of such motherhood as they may achieve, to meet our needs in every way. Oh, we value them, all right, "in their place," which place is the home, where they perform that mixture of duties so ably described by Mrs. Josephine Dodge Daskam Bacon, in which the services of "a mistress" are carefully specified. She is a very clear writer, Mrs. J. D. D. Bacon, and understands her subject—from her own point of view. But—that combination of industries, while convenient, and in a way economical, does not arouse the kind of emotion commanded by the women of Herland. These were women one had to love "up," very high up, instead of down. They were not pets. They were not servants. They were not timid, inexperienced, weak.

After I got over the jar to my pride (which Jeff, I truly think, never felt—he was a born worshipper, and which Terry never got over—he was quite clear in his ideas of "the position of women"), I found that loving "up" was a very good sensation after all. It gave me a queer feeling, way down deep, as of the stirring of some ancient dim prehistoric consciousness, a feeling that they were right somehow—that this was the way to feel. It was like—coming home to mother. I don't mean the underflannels-and-doughnuts mother, the fussy person that waits on you and spoils you and doesn't really know you. I mean the feeling that a very little child would have, who had been lost—for ever so long. It was a sense of getting home; of being clean and rested; of safety and yet freedom; of love that was always there, warm like sunshine in May, not hot like a stove or a featherbed—a love that didn't irritate and didn't smother.

I looked at Ellador as if I hadn't seen her before. "If you won't go," I said, "I'll get Terry to the coast and come back alone. You can let me down a rope. And if you will go—why you blessed wonder-woman—I would rather live with you all my life—like this—than to have any other woman I ever saw, or any number of them, to do as I like with. Will you come?"

She was keen for coming. So the plans went on. She'd have liked to wait for that Marvel of Celis's, but Terry had no such desire. He was crazy to be out of it all. It made him sick, he said, SICK; this everlasting mother-mother-mothering. I don't think Terry had what the phrenologists call "the lump of philoprogenitiveness" at all well developed.

"Morbid one-sided cripples," he called them, even when from his window he could see their splendid vigor and beauty; even while Moadine, as patient and friendly as if she had never helped Alima to hold and bind him, sat there in the room, the picture of wisdom and serene strength. "Sexless, epicene, undeveloped neuters!" he went on bitterly. He sounded like Sir Almwroth Wright.

Well—it was hard. He was madly in love with Alima, really; more so than he had ever been before, and their tempestuous courtship, quarrels, and reconciliations had fanned the flame. And then when he sought by that supreme conquest which seems so natural a thing to that type of man, to force her to love him as her master—to have the sturdy athletic furious woman rise up and master him—she and her friends—it was no wonder he raged.

Come to think of it, I do not recall a similar case in all history or fiction. Women have killed themselves rather than submit to outrage; they have killed the outrager; they have escaped; or they have submitted—sometimes seeming to get on very well with the victor afterward. There was that adventure of "false Sextus," for instance, who "found Lucrese combing the fleece, under the midnight lamp." He threatened, as I remember, that if she did not submit he would slay her, slay a slave and place him beside her and say he found him there. A poor device, it always seemed to me. If Mr. Lucretius had asked him how he came to be in his wife's bedroom overlooking her morals, what could he have said? But the point is Lucrese submitted, and Alima didn't.

"She kicked me," confided the embittered prisoner—he had to talk to someone. "I was doubled up with the pain, of course, and she jumped on me and yelled for this old harpy [Moadine couldn't hear him] and they had me trussed up in no time. I believe Alima could have done it alone," he added with reluctant admiration. "She's as strong as a horse. And of course a man's helpless when you hit him like that. No woman with a shade of decency—"

I had to grin at that, and even Terry did, sourly. He wasn't given to reasoning, but it did strike him that an assault like his rather waived considerations of decency.

"I'd give a year of my life to have her alone again," he said slowly, his hands clenched till the knuckles were white.

But he never did. She left our end of the country entirely, went up into the fir-forest on the highest slopes, and stayed there. Before we left he quite desperately longed to see her, but she would not come and he could not go. They watched him like lynxes. (Do lynxes watch any better than mousing cats, I wonder!)

Well—we had to get the flyer in order, and be sure there was enough fuel left, though Terry said we could glide all right, down to that lake, once we got started. We'd have gone gladly in a week's time, of course, but there was a great to-do all over the country about Ellador's leaving them. She had interviews with some of the leading ethicists—wise women with still eyes, and with the best of the teachers. There was a stir, a thrill, a deep excitement everywhere.

Our teaching about the rest of the world has given them all a sense of isolation, of remoteness, of being a little outlying sample of a country, overlooked and forgotten among the family of nations. We had called it "the family of nations," and they liked the phrase immensely.

They were deeply aroused on the subject of evolution; indeed, the whole field of natural science drew them irresistibly. Any number of them would have risked everything to go to the strange unknown lands and study; but we could take only one, and it had to be Ellador, naturally.

We planned greatly about coming back, about establishing a connecting route by water; about penetrating those vast forests and civilizing—or exterminating—the dangerous savages. That is, we men talked of that last—not with the women. They had a definite aversion to killing things.

But meanwhile there was high council being held among the wisest of them all. The students and thinkers who had been gathering facts from us all this time, collating and relating them, and making inferences, laid the result of their labors before the council.

Little had we thought that our careful efforts at concealment had been so easily seen through, with never a word to show us that they saw. They had followed up words of ours on the science of optics, asked innocent questions about glasses and the like, and were aware of the defective eyesight so common among us.

With the lightest touch, different women asking different questions at different times, and putting all our answers together like a picture puzzle, they had figured out a sort of skeleton chart as to the prevalence of disease among us. Even more subtly with no show of horror or condemnation, they had gathered something—far from the truth, but something pretty clear—about poverty, vice, and crime. They even had a goodly number of our dangers all itemized, from asking us about insurance and innocent things like that.

They were well posted as to the different races, beginning with their poison-arrow natives down below and widening out to the broad racial divisions we had told them about. Never a shocked expression of the face or exclamation of revolt had warned us; they had been extracting the evidence without our knowing it all this time, and now were studying with the most devout earnestness the matter they had prepared.

The result was rather distressing to us. They first explained the matter fully to Ellador, as she was the one who purposed visiting the Rest of the World. To Celis they said nothing. She must not be in any way distressed, while the whole nation waited on her Great Work.

Finally Jeff and I were called in. Somel and Zava were there, and Ellador, with many others that we knew.

They had a great globe, quite fairly mapped out from the small section maps in that compendium of ours. They had the different peoples of the earth roughly outlined, and their status in civilization indicated. They had charts and figures and estimates, based on the facts in that traitorous little book and what they had learned from us.

Somel explained: "We find that in all your historic period, so much longer than ours, that with all the interplay of services, the exchange of inventions and discoveries, and the wonderful progress we so admire, that in this widespread Other World of yours, there is still much disease, often contagious."

We admitted this at once.

"Also there is still, in varying degree, ignorance, with prejudice and unbridled emotion."

This too was admitted.

"We find also that in spite of the advance of democracy and the increase of wealth, that there is still unrest and sometimes combat."

Yes, yes, we admitted it all. We were used to these things and saw no reason for so much seriousness.

"All things considered," they said, and they did not say a hundredth part of the things they were considering, "we are unwilling to expose our country to free communication with the rest of the world—as yet. If Ellador comes back, and we approve her report, it may be done later—but not yet.

"So we have this to ask of you gentlemen [they knew that word was held a title of honor with us], that you promise not in any way to betray the location of this country until permission—after Ellador's return."

Jeff was perfectly satisfied. He thought they were quite right. He always did. I never saw an alien become naturalized more quickly than that man in Herland.

I studied it awhile, thinking of the time they'd have if some of our contagions got loose there, and concluded they were right. So I agreed.

Terry was the obstacle. "Indeed I won't!" he protested. "The first thing I'll do is to get an expedition fixed up to force an entrance into Ma-land."

"Then," they said quite calmly, "he must remain an absolute prisoner, always."

"Anesthesia would be kinder," urged Moadine.

"And safer," added Zava.

"He will promise, I think," said Ellador.

And he did. With which agreement we at last left Herland.

SUFFRAGE SONGS and VERSES

NOTE:
The Poems marked * are from *In This Our World*, 1898;
those marked † are from *The Woman's Journal*;
and those marked [f] are from *The Forerunner.*

SHE WALKETH VEILED AND SLEEPING*

SHE WALKETH veiled and sleeping,
For she knoweth not her power;
She obeyeth but the pleading
Of her heart, and the high leading
Of her soul, unto this hour.
Slow advancing, halting, creeping,
Comes the Woman to the hour!–
She walketh veiled and sleeping,
For she knoweth not her power.

COMING[f]

Because the time is ripe, the age is ready,
Because the world her woman's help demands,
Out of the long subjection and seclusion
Come to our field of warfare and confusion
The mother's heart and hands.

Long has she stood aside, endured and waited,
While man swung forward, toiling on alone;
Now, for the weary man, so long ill-mated,
Now, for the world for which she was created,
Comes woman to her own.

Not for herself! though sweet the air of freedom;
Not for herself, though dear the new-born power;
But for the child, who needs a nobler mother,
For the whole people, needing one another,
Comes woman to her hour.

LOCKED INSIDE[f]

She beats upon her bolted door,
  With faint weak hands;
Drearily walks the narrow floor;
Sullenly sits, blank walls before;
  Despairing stands.

Life calls her, Duty, Pleasure, Gain–
  Her dreams respond;
But the blank daylights wax and wane,
Dull peace, sharp agony, slow pain–
  No hope beyond.

Till she comes a thought! She lifts her head,
  The world grows wide!
A voice–as if clear words were said–
"Your door, O long imprisonéd,
  Is locked inside!"

NOW[f]

With God Above–Beneath–Beside–
  Without–Within–and Everywhere;
Rising with the resistless tide
  Of life, and Sure of Getting There.

Patient with Nature's long delay,
  Proud of our conscious upward swing;
Not sorry for a single day,
  And Not Afraid of Anything!

With Motherhood at last awake–
  With Power to Do and Light to See–
Women may now begin to Make
  The People we are Meant to Be!

WOMEN OF TO-DAY*

You women of today who fear so much
The women of the future, showing how
The dangers of her course are such and such–
        What are you now?

Mothers and Wives and Housekeepers, forsooth!
Great names, you cry, full scope to rule and please,
Room for wise age and energetic youth!–
        But are you these?

Housekeepers? Do you then, like those of yore,
Keep house with power and pride, with grace and ease?
No, you keep servants only! What is more–
        You don't keep these!

Wives, say you? Wives! Blessed indeed are they
Who hold of love the everlasting keys,
Keeping your husbands' hearts! Alas the day!
        You don't keep these!

And mothers? Pitying Heaven! Mark the cry
From cradle death-beds! Mothers on their knees!
Why, half the children born, as children, die!
        You don't keep these!

And still the wailing babies come and go,
And homes are waste, and husband's hearts fly far;
There is no hope until you dare to know
        The thing you are!

BOYS WILL BE BOYS[f]

"Boys will be boys," and boys have had their day;
  Boy-mischief and boy-carelessness and noise
Extenuated all, allowed, excused and smoothed away,
  Each duty missed, each damaging wild act,
  By this meek statement of unquestioned fact–
        Boys will be boys!

Now, "women will be women." Mark the change;
  Calm motherhood in place of boisterous youth;
No warfare now; to manage and arrange,
  To nurture with wise care, is woman's way,
  In peace and fruitful industry her sway,
        In love and truth.

FOR FEAR[f]

For fear of prowling beasts at night
  They blocked the cave;
Women and children hid from sight,
  Men scarce more brave.

For fear of warrior's sword and spear
  They barred the gate;
Women and children lived in fear,
  Men lived in hate.

For fear of criminals today
  We lock the door;
Women and children still to stay
  Hid evermore.

Come out! Ye need no longer hide!
  What fear you now?
No wolf or lion waits outside–
  Only a cow.

Come out! The world approaches peace,
  War nears its end;
No warrior watches your release–
  Only a friend.

Come out! The night of crime has fled–
  Day is begun;
Here is no criminal to dread–
  Only your son.

The world, half yours, demands your care,
  Waken and come!
Make it a woman's world; safe, fair,
  Garden and home.

MOTHER TO CHILD*

How best can I serve thee, my child! My child!
Flesh of my flesh and dear heart of my heart!
Once thou wast within me–I held thee–I fed thee–
By the force of my loving and longing I led thee–
    Now we are apart!

I may blind thee with kisses and crush with embracing,
Thy warm mouth in my neck and our arms interlacing;
But here in my body my soul lives alone,
And thou answerest me from a house of thine own–
    The house which I builded!

Which we builded together, thy father and I;
In which thou must live, O my darling, and die!
Not one stone can I alter, one atom relay–
Not to save or defend thee or help thee to stay–
    That gift is completed!

How best can I serve thee? O child, if they knew
How my heart aches with loving! How deep and how true,
How brave and enduring, how patient, how strong,
How longing for good and how fearful of wrong,
    Is the love of thy mother!

Could I crown thee with riches! Surround, overflow thee
With fame and with power till the whole world should know thee;
With wisdom and genius to hold the world still,
To bring laughter and tears, joy and pain, at thy will,
    Still–thou mightst not be happy!

Such have lived–and in sorrow. The greater the mind
The wider and deeper the grief it can find.
The richer, the gladder, the more thou canst feel
The keen stings that a lifetime is sure to reveal.
    O my child! Must thou suffer?

Is there no way my life can save thine from a pain?
Is the love of a mother no possible gain?
No labor of Hercules–search for the Grail–
No way for this wonderful love to avail?
    God in Heaven–O teach me!

My prayer has been answered. The pain thou must bear
Is the pain of the world's life which thy life must share,
Thou art one with the world–though I love thee the best;
And to save thee from pain I must save all the rest–
    Well–with God's help I'll do it.

Thou art one with the rest. I must love thee in them.
Thou wilt sin with the rest; and thy mother must stem
The world's sin. Thou wilt weep, and thy mother must dry
The tears of the world lest her darling should cry.
    I will do it–God helping!

And I stand not alone. I will gather a band
Of all loving mothers from land unto land.
Our children are part of the world! Do ye hear?
They are one with the world–we must hold them all dear!
    Love all for the child's sake!

For the sake of my child I must hasten to save
All the children on earth from the jail and the grave.
For so, and so only, I lighten the share
Of the pain of the world that my darling must bear–
    Even so, and so only!

A QUESTION[f]

Why is it, God, that mother's hearts are made
  So very deep and wide?
How does it help the world that we should hold
Such swelling floods of pain till we are old,
Because when we were young one grave was laid–
One baby died?

THE HOUSEWIFE[f]

Here is the House to hold me–cradle of all the race;
Here is my lord and my love, here are my children dear–
Here is the House enclosing, the dear-loved dwelling place;
Why should I ever weary for aught that I find not here?

Here for the hours of the day and the hours of the night;
Bound with the bands of Duty, rivetted tight;
Duty older than Adam–Duty that saw
Acceptance utter and hopeless in the eyes of the serving squaw.

Food and the serving of food–that is my daylong care;
What and when we shall eat, what and how we shall wear;
Soiling and cleaning of things–that is my task in the main–
Soil them and clean them and soil them–soil them and clean them again.

To work at my trade by the dozen and never a trade to know;
To plan like a Chinese puzzle–fitting and changing so;
To think of a thousand details, each in a thousand ways;
For my own immediate people and a possible love and praise.

My mind is trodden in circles, tiresome, narrow and hard,
Useful, commonplace, private–simply a small backyard;
And I the Mother of Nations!–Blind their struggle and vain!
I cover the earth with my children–each with a housewife's brain.

WEDDED BLISS*

"O come and be my mate!" said the Eagle to the Hen,
"I love to soar, but then
I want my mate to rest
Forever in the nest!"
Said the Hen, "I cannot fly,
I have no wish to try,
But I joy to see my mate careening through the sky!"
They wed, and cried, "Ah, this is Love, my own!"
And the Hen sat, the Eagle soared, alone.

"O come and be my mate!" said the Lion to the Sheep;
"My love for you is deep!
I slay, a Lion should,
But you are mild and good!"
Said the sheep, "I do no ill–
Could not, had I the will–.
But I joy to see my mate pursue, devour and kill. "
They wed, and cried, "Ah, this is Love, my own!"
And the Sheep browsed, the Lion prowled, alone.

"O come and be my mate!" said the Salmon to the Clam;
"You are not wise, but I am.
I know sea and stream as well.
You know nothing but your shell."
Said the Clam, "I'm slow of motion,
But my love is all devotion,
And I joy to have my mate traverse lake and stream and ocean! "
They wed, and cried, "Ah, this is Love, my own!"
And the Clam sucked, the Salmon swam, alone.

FEMALES*

The female fox she is a fox;
The female whale a whale;
The female eagle holds her place
As representative of race
As truly as the male.

The mother hen doth scratch for her chicks,
And scratch for herself beside;
The mother cow doth nurse her calf,
Yet fares as well as her other half
In the pasture far and wide.

The female bird doth soar in air;
The female fish doth swim;
The fleet-foot mare upon the course
Doth hold her own with the flying horse–
Yea and she beateth him!

One female in the world we find
Telling a different tale.
It is the female of our race,
Who holds a parasitic place
Dependent on the male.

Not so, saith she, ye slander me!
No parasite am I.
I earn my living as a wife;
My children take my very life;
Why should I share in human strife,
To plant and build and buy?

The human race holds highest place
In all the world so wide,
Yet these inferior females wive,
And raise their little ones alive,
And feed themselves beside.

Thre race is higher than the sex,
Though sex be fair and good;
A Human Creature is your state,
And to be human is more great
Than even womanhood!

The female fox she is a fox;
The female whale a whale;
The female eagle holds her place
As representative of race
As truly as the male.

"WE AS WOMEN"*

There's a cry in the air about us–
We hear it, before, behind–
Of the way in which "We, as women,"
Are going to lift mankind!

With our white frocks starched and ruffled,
And our soft hair brushed and curled–
Hats off! for "We, as women,"
Are coming to save the world.

Fair sisters! listen one moment–
And perhaps you'll pause for ten:
The business of women as women
Is only with men as men!

What we do, "We, as women,"
We have done all through our life;
The work that is ours as women
Is the work of mother and wife.

But to elevate public opinion,
And to lift up erring man,
Is the work of the Human Being;
Let us do it–if we can.

But wait, warm-hearted sisters–
Not quite so fast, so far.
Tell me how we are going to lift a thing
Any higher than we are!

We are going to "purify politics,"
And to "elevate the press."
We enter the foul paths of the world
To sweeten and cleanse and bless.

To hear the high things we are going to do,
And the horrors of man we tell,
One would think, "We, as women," were angels,
And our brothers were fiends of hell.

We, that were born of one mother,
And reared in the self-same place,
In the school and the church together,
We of one blood, one race!

Now then, all forward together!
But remember, every one,
That 'tis not by feminine innocence
The work of the world is done.

The world needs strength and courage,
And wisdom to help and feed–
When, "We, as women" bring these to man,
We shall lift the world indeed.

GIRLS OF TO-DAY*

Girls of today! Give ear!
Never since time began
Has come to the race of man
A year, a day, an hour,
So full of promise and power
As the time that now is here!

Never in all the lands
Was there a power so great,
To move the wheels of state,
To lift up body and mind,
To waken the deaf and blind,
As the power that is in your hands!

Here at the gates of gold
You stand in the pride of youth,
Strong in courage and truth,
Stirred by a force kept back
Through centuries long and black,
Armed with a power threefold!

First: You are makers of men!
Then Be the things you preach!
Let your own greatness teach!
When Mothers like this you see
Men will be strong and free–
Then, and not till then!

Second: Since Adam fell,
Have you not heard it said
That men by women are led?
True is the saying–true!
See to it what you do!
See that you lead them well.

Third: You have work of your own!
Maid and mother and wife,
Look in the face of life!
There are duties you owe the race!
Outside your dwelling-place
There is work for you alone!

Maid and mother and wife,
See your own work be done!
Be worthy a noble son!
Help man in the upward way!
Truly, a girl today
Is the strongest thing in life!

WOMEN TO MEN†

Dear father, from my cradle I acknowledge
All your wise kindness, tender care, and love,
Through days of kindergarten, school, and college.
Now there is one gift lacking–one above
All other gifts of God, this highest trust is,
The one great gift, beyond all power and pelf–
Give me my freedom, father; give me justice,
That I may guard my children and myself.

My brother, you and I were reared together;
We played together, even-handed quite;
We went to school in every kind of weather,
Studied and ranked together as was right.
We work together now and earn our living,
You know how equal is the work we do;
Come, brother, with the love you're always giving,
Give justice! It's for me as well as you.

And you, my lover, kneeling here before me
With tender eyes that burn, warm lips that plead,
Protesting that you worship, aye, adore me;
Begging my love as life's supremest meed,
Vowing to make me happy. Ah, how dare you!
Freedom and happiness have both one key!
Lover and husband, by the love I bear you,
Give justice! I can love you better, free!

Son, my own son! Man-child that once was lying
All rosy, tender, helpless on my breast,
Your strength, all dimples, your stern voice but crying,
Looking to me for comfort, food and rest,
Asking your life of me, and not another–
And asking not in vain till life be done–
Oh, my boy-baby! Is it I, your mother,
Who comes to ask of justice from her son?

Now to the voter–tax-payer (or shirker)
Please lay your private feelings on the shelf;
O Man-at-large! Friend! Comrade! Fellow-worker;
I am a human being like yourself.
I'm not your wife and mother. Can't be, whether
I would or not: each to his own apart;
But in the world we're people altogether–
Suffrage is not a question of the heart.

Son–Father–Brother–Lover unsupplanted–
We'll talk at home. This thing concerns the nation;
A point of justice which is to be granted
By men to women who are no relation.
Perceive this fact, as salient as a steeple,
Please try to argue from it if you can;
Women have standing-room on earth as people
Outside of their relation to some man.

As wife and sweetheart, daughter, sister, mother,
Each woman privately her views explains;
As people of America–no other–
We claim the right our government maintains.
You who deny it stand in history's pages
Withholding justice! Pitiless and plain
Your record stands down all the brightening ages–
You fought with progress, but you fought in vain.

REASSURANCE*

Can you imagine nothing better, brother,
Than that which you have always had before?
Have you been so content with "wife and mother,"
    You dare hope nothing more?

Have you forever prized her, praised her, sung her,
The happy queen of a most happy reign?
Never dishonored her, despised her, flung her
    Derision and disdain?

Go ask the literature of all the ages!
Books that were written before women read!
Pagan and Christian, satirists and sages–
    Read what the world has said.

There was no power on earth to bid you slacken
The generous hand that painted her disgrace!
There was no shame on earth too black to blacken
    That much-praised woman-face.

Eve and Pandora!–always you begin it–
The ancients called her Sin and Shame and Death.
"There is no evil without woman in it,"
    The modern proverb saith.

She has been yours in uttermost possession–
Your slave, your mother, your well-chosen bride–
And you have owned in million-fold confession,
    You were not satisfied.

Peace then! Fear not the coming woman, brother.
Owning herself, she giveth all the more.
She shall be better woman, wife and mother,
    Than man hath known before.

THE SOCIALIST AND THE SUFFRAGIST[f]

Said the Socialist to the Suffragist:
"My cause is greater than yours!
You only work for a Special Class,
We work for the gain of the General Mass,
Which every good ensures!"

Said the Suffragist to the Socialist:
"You underrate my Cause!
While women remain a Subject Class,
You never can move the General Mass,
With your Economic Laws!"

Said the Socialist to the Suffragist:
"You misinterpret facts!
There is no room for doubt or schism
In Economic Determinism–
It governs all our acts!"

Said the Suffragist to the Socialist:
"You men will always find
That this old world will never move
More swiftly in its ancient groove
While women stay behind! "

"A lifted world lifts women up,"
The Socialist explained.
"You cannot lift the world at all
While half of it is kept so small,"
The Suffragist maintained.

The world awoke, and tartly spoke:
"Your work is all the same:
Work together or work apart,
Work, each of you, with all your heart–
Just get into the game!"

THE MALINGERER[f]

Exempt! She "does not have to work!"
    So might one talk
Defending long, bedridden ease,
Weak yielding ankles, flaccid knees,
    With "I don't have to walk!"

Not have to work. Why not? Who gave
    Free pass to you?
You're housed and fed and taught and dressed
By age-long labor of the rest–
    Work other people do!

What do you give in honest pay
    For clothes and food?–
Then as a shield, defence, excuse,
She offers her exclusive use–
    Her function–Motherhood!

Is motherhood a trade you make
    A living by?
And does the wealth you so may use,
Squander, accumulate, abuse,
    Show motherhood as high?

Or does the motherhood of those
    Whose toil endures,
The farmers' and mechanics' wives,
Hard working servants all their lives–
    Deserve less price than yours?

We're not exempt! Man's world runs on,
    Motherless, wild;
Our servitude and long duress,
Our shameless, harem idleness,
    Both fail to serve the child.

THE ANTI-SUFFRAGISTS*

Fashionable women in luxurious homes,
With men to feed them, clothe them, pay their bills,
Bow, doff the hat, and fetch the handkerchief;
Hostess or guest; and always so supplied
With graceful deference and courtesy;
Surrounded by their horses, servants, dogs–
These tell us they have all the rights they want.

Successful women who have won their way
Alone, with strength of their unaided arm,
Or helped by friends, or softly climbing up
By the sweet aid of "woman's influence";
Successful any way, and caring naught
For any other woman's unsuccess–
These tell us they have all the rights they want.

Religious women of the feebler sort–
Not the religion of a righteous world,
A free, enlightened, upward-reaching world,
But the religion that considers life
As something to back out of !– whose ideal
Is to renounce, submit, and sacrifice.
Counting on being patted on the head
And given a high chair when they get to heaven–
These tell us they have all the rights they want.

Ignorant women–college bred sometimes,
But ignorant of life's realities
And principles of righteous government,
And how the privileges they enjoy
Were won with blood and tears by those before–
Those they condemn, whose ways they now oppose;
Saying, "Why not let well enough alone?"
Our world is very pleasant as it is"–

These tell us they have all the rights they want.

And selfish women–pigs in petticoats–
Rich, poor, wise, unwise, top or bottom round,
But all sublimely innocent of thought,
And guiltless of ambition, save the one
Deep, voiceless aspiration–to be fed!
These have no use for rights or duties more.
Duties today are more than they can meet,
And law insures their right to clothes and food–
These tell us they have all the rights they want.

And, more's the pity, some good women too;
Good, conscientious women with ideas;
Who think–or think they think–that woman's cause
Is best advanced by letting it alone;
That she somehow is not a human thing,

And not to be helped on by human means,
Just added to humanity–an "L"–
A wing, a branch, an extra, not mankind–
These tell us they have all the rights they want.

And out of these has come a monstrous thing,
A strange, down-sucking whirlpool of disgrace,
Women uniting against womanhood,
And using that great name to hide their sin!
Vain are their words as that old king's command
Who set his will against the rising tide.
But who shall measure the historic shame
Of these poor traitors–traitors are they all–
To great Democracy and Womanhood!

THE "ANTI" AND THE FLY[f]

The fly upon the Cartwheel
  Thought she made all the Sound;
He thought he made the Cart go on–
  And made the wheels go round.

The Fly upon the Cartwheel
  Has won undying fame
For Conceit that was colossal,
  And Ignorance the same.

But today he has a Rival
  As we roll down History's Track–
For the "Anti" on the Cartwheel
  Thinks she makes the Wheels go back!

TO THE INDIFFERENT WOMEN*
A SESTINA

You who are happy in a thousand homes,
Or overworked therein, to a dumb peace;
Whose souls are wholly centered in the life
Of that small group you personally love–
Who told you that you need not know or care
About the sin and sorrow of the world?

Do you believe the sorrow of the world
Does not concern you in your little homes ?
That you are licensed to avoid the care
And toil for human progress, human peace,
And the enlargement of our power of love
Until it covers every field of life?

The one first duty of all human life
Is to promote the progress of the world
In righteousness, in wisdom, truth and love;
And you ignore it, hidden in your homes,
Content to keep them in uncertain peace,
Content to leave all else without your care.

Yet you are mothers! And a mother's care
Is the first step towards friendly human life.
Life where all nations in untroubled peace
Unite to raise the standard of the world
And make the happiness we seek in homes
Spread everywhere in strong and fruitful love.

You are content to keep that mighty love
In its first steps forever; the crude care
Of animals for mate and young and homes,
Instead of poring it abroad in life,
Its mighty current feeding all the world
Till every human child shall grow in peace.

You cannot keep your small domestic peace,
Your little pool of undeveloped love,
While the neglected, starved, unmothered world
Struggles and fights for lack of mother's care,
And its tempestuous, bitter, broken life
Beats in upon you in your selfish homes.

We all may have our homes in joy and peace
When woman's life, in its rich power of love
Is joined with man's to care for all the world!

WOMEN DO NOT WANT IT*

When the woman suffrage argument first stood upon its legs,
They answered it with cabbages, they answered it with eggs,
They answered it with ridicule, they answered it with scorn,
They thought it a monstrosity that should not have been born.

When the woman suffrage argument grew vigorous and wise,
And was not to be answered by these opposite replies,
They turned their opposition into reasoning severe
Upon the limitations of our God-appointed sphere.

We were told of disabilities–a long array of these,
Till one could think that womanhood was merely a disease;
And "the maternal sacrifice" was added to the plan
Of the various sacrifices we have always made–to man.

Religionists and scientists, in amity and bliss,
However else they disagreed, could all agree on this,
And the gist of all their discourse, when you got down in it,
Was–we could not have the ballot because we were not fit!

They would not hear the reason, they would not fairly yield,
They would not own their arguments were beaten in the field;
But time passed on, and someway, we need not ask them how,
Whatever ails those arguments–we do not hear them now!

You may talk of suffrage now with an educated man,
And he agrees with all you say, as sweetly as he can:
'T would be better for us all, of course, if womanhood was free;
But "the women do not want it"–and so it must not be!

'T is such a tender thoughtfulness! So exquisite a care!
Not to pile on our frail shoulders what we do not wish to bear!
But, oh, most generous brother! Let us look a little more–
Have we women always wanted what you gave to us before?

Did we ask for veils and harems in the Oriental races?
Did we beseech to be "unclean," shut out of sacred places?
Did we beg for scolding bridles and ducking stools to come?
And clamour for the beating stick no thicker than your thumb?

Did we ask to be forbidden from all the trades that pay?
Did we claim the lower wages for a man's full work today?
Have we petitioned for the laws wherein our shame is shown:
That not a woman's child–nor her own body–is her own?

What women want has never been a strongly acting cause,
When woman has been wronged by man in churches, customs, laws;
Why should he find this preference so largely in his way,
When he himself admits the right of what we ask today?

SONG FOR EQUAL SUFFRAGE†

Day of hope and day of glory! After slavery and woe,
Comes the dawn of woman's freedom, and the light shall grow and grow
Until every man and woman equal liberty shall know,
In Freedom marching on!

Woman's right is woman's duty! For our share in life we call!
Our will it is not weakened and our power it is not small.
We are half of every nation! We are mothers of them all!
In Wisdom marching on!

Not for self but larger service has our cry for freedom grown,
There is crime, disease and warfare in a world of men alone,
In the name of love we're rising now to serve and save our own,
As Peace comes marching on!

By every sweet and tender tie around our heartstrings curled,
In the cause of nobler motherhood is woman's flag unfurled,
Till every child shall know the joy and peace of mother's world–
As Love comes marching on!

We will help to make a pruning hook of every outgrown sword,
We will help to knit the nations in continuing accord,
In humanity made perfect is the glory of the Lord,
As His world goes marching on!

ANOTHER STAR[f]

(Suffrage Campaign Song for California)
TUNE: "Buy a Broom"

There are five a-light before us,
In the flag flying o'er us,
There'll be six on next election–
    We bring a new star!
We are coming like the others,
Free Sisters, Free Brothers,
In the pride of our affection
    For California.
CHORUS: A ballot for the Lady!
For the Home and for the Baby!
Come, vote ye for the Lady,
    The Baby, the Home!

Star of Hope and Star of Beauty!
Of Freedom! Of Duty!
Star of childhood's new protection,
    That rises so high!
We will work for it together
In the golden, gay weather,
And we'll have it next election,
    Or we will know why.
CHORUS: A ballot for the Lady!
For the Home and for the Baby!
Come, vote ye for the Lady,
    The Baby, the Home!

SHE WHO IS TO COME*

A woman–in so far as she beholdeth
Her one Beloved's face;
A mother–with a great heart that enfoldeth
The children of the Race;
A body, free and strong, with that high beauty
That comes of perfect use, is built thereof;
A mind where Reason ruleth over Duty,
And Justice reigns with Love;
A self-poised, royal soul, brave, wise and tender,
No longer blind and dumb;
A Human Being, of an unknown splendor,
Is she who is to come!

Also from Benediction Books ...
Wandering Between Two Worlds: Essays on Faith and Art
Anita Mathias
Benediction Books, 2007
152 pages
ISBN: 0955373700

Available from www.amazon.com, www.amazon.co.uk

In these wide-ranging lyrical essays, Anita Mathias writes, in lush, lovely prose, of her naughty Catholic childhood in Jamshedpur, India; her large, eccentric family in Mangalore, a sea-coast town converted by the Portuguese in the sixteenth century; her rebellion and atheism as a teenager in her Himalayan boarding school, run by German missionary nuns, St. Mary's Convent, Nainital; and her abrupt religious conversion after which she entered Mother Teresa's convent in Calcutta as a novice. Later rich, elegant essays explore the dualities of her life as a writer, mother, and Christian in the United States-- Domesticity and Art, Writing and Prayer, and the experience of being "an alien and stranger" as an immigrant in America, sensing the need for roots.

About the Author

Anita Mathias is the author of *Wandering Between Two Worlds: Essays on Faith and Art.* She has a B.A. and M.A. in English from Somerville College, Oxford University, and an M.A. in Creative Writing from the Ohio State University, USA. Anita won a National Endowment of the Arts fellowship in Creative Nonfiction in 1997. She lives in Oxford, England with her husband, Roy, and her daughters, Zoe and Irene.

Visit Anita at http://www.anitamathias.com.

The Church Thad Had Too Much
Anita Mathias
Benediction Books, 2010
52 pages
ISBN: 9781849026567

Available from www.amazon.com, www.amazon.co.uk

The Church That Had Too Much was very well-intentioned. She wanted to love God, she wanted to love people, but she was both hampered by her muchness and the abundance of her possessions, and beset by ambition, power struggles and snobbery. Read about the surprising way The Church That Had Too Much began to resolve her problems in this deceptively simple and enchanting fable.

About the Author

Anita Mathias is the author of *Wandering Between Two Worlds: Essays on Faith and Art.* She has a B.A. and M.A. in English from Somerville College, Oxford University, and an M.A. in Creative Writing from the Ohio State University, USA. Anita won a National Endowment of the Arts fellowship in Creative Nonfiction in 1997. She lives in Oxford, England with her husband, Roy, and her daughters, Zoe and Irene.

Visit Anita at http://www.anitamathias.com

Francesco, Artist of Florence: The Man Who Gave Too Much
Anita Mathias
Benediction Books, 2014
52 pages (full colour)
ISBN: 978-1781394175

In this lavishly illustrated book by Anita Mathias, Francesco, artist of Florence, creates magic in pietre dure, inlaying precious stones in marble in life-like "paintings." While he works, placing lapis lazuli birds on clocks, and jade dragonflies on vases, he is purely happy. However, he must sell his art to support his family. Francesco, who is incorrigibly soft-hearted, cannot stand up to his haggling customers. He ends up almost giving away an exquisite jewellery box to Signora Farnese's bambina, who stands, captivated, gazing at a jade parrot nibbling a cherry. Signora Stallardi uses her daughter's wedding to cajole him into discounting his rainbowed marriage chest. His old friend Girolamo bullies him into letting him have the opulent table he hoped to sell to the Medici almost at cost. Carrara is raising the price of marble; the price of gems keeps rising. His wife is in despair. Francesco fears ruin.

* * *

Sitting in the church of Santa Maria Novella at Mass, very worried, Francesco hears the words of Christ. The lilies of the field and the birds of the air do not worry, yet their Heavenly Father looks after them. As He will look after us. He resolves not to worry. And as he repeats the prayer the Saviour taught us, Francesco resolves to forgive the friends and neighbours who repeatedly put their own interests above his. But can he forgive himself for his own weakness, as he waits for the eternal city of gold whose walls are made of jasper, whose gates are made of pearls, and whose foundations are sapphire, emerald, ruby and amethyst? There time and money shall be no more, the lion shall live with the lamb, and we shall dwell trustfully together. Francesco leaves Santa Maria Novella, resolving to trust the One who told him to live like the lilies and the birds, deciding to forgive those who haggled him into bad bargains--while making a little resolution for the future

www.ingramcontent.com/pod-product-compliance
Lightning Source LLC
Chambersburg PA
CBHW081138300726
48982CB00006B/997
* 9 7 8 1 7 8 9 4 3 2 6 8 8 *